THE VAN NOSTRAND SERIES IN SOCIOLOGY

Edited by

WILBERT E. MOORE

Professor of Sociology, Princeton University

Additional titles will be listed and announced as published.

JUVENILE DELINQUENCY IN MODERN SOCIETY

MARTIN H. NEUMEYER

Professor of Sociology
University of Southern California

SECOND EDITION

D. VAN NOSTRAND COMPANY, INC.

PRINCETON, NEW JERSEY

TORONTO   LONDON

NEW YORK

D. VAN NOSTRAND COMPANY, INC.

120 Alexander St., Princeton, New Jersey *(Principal office)*
257 Fourth Avenue, New York 10, New York

D. VAN NOSTRAND COMPANY, LTD.

358, Kensington High Street, London, W.14, England

D. VAN NOSTRAND COMPANY (Canada), LTD.

25 Hollinger Road, Toronto 16, Canada

Library of Congress Catalogue Card No. 55-6257

First Published, January 1949
Four Reprintings

Second Edition, February 1955
Reprinted August 1956, March 1959

PRINTED IN THE UNITED STATES OF AMERICA

PREFACE

In this revision, the material has been brought up to date; the theoretical frame of reference has been stated more clearly, especially in the introductions to the parts of the volume; and recent reports of research in the field are described in greater detail. The point of view and the main outline are essentially the same as found in the earlier book, but in presenting this edition it is hoped that the analysis of the subject matter has been improved.

Most of the material used in this volume deals with juvenile delinquency in contemporary American society, chiefly from the viewpoint of modern social science, indicating the extent and trends of the problem, the basic factors and conditions that cause delinquency, and the most effective agencies and methods of its control. The data are subject to change, yet certain theories and findings of earlier studies are important for a full understanding of current trends and developments. No attempt is made to provide a "system" of juvenile delinquency and no particularistic approach is emphasized, but the analysis of the data in terms of a general conceptional frame of reference aids in the interpretation and understanding of the problem of delinquent behavior.

Considerable attention is given to delinquency trends in modern society, the broad outlines of which are indicated in Part One, followed by more detailed studies in subsequent chapters. Changes have occurred not only in the meaning, extent, distribution, and causation of juvenile delinquency, but progress has been made in the treatment of offenders and in methods of prevention.

The chief emphasis in this volume is on the understanding of the main causes of delinquent behavior. Although there is no agreement as to the specific causes of this problem, because the etiological factors are complex and difficult to ascertain, it is apparent that no "single cause" explanation suffices. In general, it can be said that delinquent and other forms of deviant behavior arise out of the matrix of environment factors, the conditions of personality, and the sequence of experiences and influences that play a part in the child's

v

development. It is the product of a dynamic social process, involving personal and social disorganization, the impact of delinquency traditions, and the failure of personal and social controls. The functional interrelationships of the variables connected with delinquency must be recognized and studied. It is not possible to describe all of the causes of delinquency, but the chapters in Part Two give a broad framework of analysis designed to assist students in more systematically orienting their thinking with reference to the chief aspects of the problem. The sequence of items indicates to some extent the historical development of research in the field.

The literature on the subject is so voluminous that it is impossible to mention all of the more important studies. The books, official documents, and magazine articles that show evidence of the use of scientific methods or that describe effective means of treatment and prevention are referred to most extensively. This accounts for repeated references to selected sources. Most of the references are to American authors, although selected European publications are used in some instances. The questions, research topics, and bibliographies are designed to aid students in extending the inquiries into special phases of the subject.

The author is grateful to writers and publishers for the use of data, especially the quoted passages. The footnote citations have assigned credit insofar as it is possible to do so. It is impossible to acknowledge adequately the indebtedness to all authors who have in one way or another contributed to this work. A considerable amount of the content of the book is the outgrowth of experience in teaching courses in juvenile delinquency. The staff and research committees of the Delinquency Control Institute of the University of Southern California were helpful in preparing the first edition of this book. Subsequent research reports have enriched considerably the present edition. A book of this type is possible only because of the wide field of research from which the main data are drawn.

MARTIN H. NEUMEYER

CONTENTS

vii

PART ONE

DELINQUENCY IN A CHANGING SOCIETY

This volume is divided into three parts, designed to cover the major aspects of the problem of juvenile delinquency in a changing society, the basic factors and conditions that tend to cause delinquent behavior, and the methods of delinquency control. Most of the material deals with juvenile misconduct and deviant forms of behavior. Adult crime is discussed briefly in places where such discussion adds to the understanding of the total problem of law violation. Differences in the methods of dealing with juvenile and adult offenders are likewise indicated. The concrete data are drawn chiefly from American sources, but some references are made to studies of delinquency in other countries. Delinquency is not peculiar to any one country. It is a world-wide problem.[1]

Part One is devoted to a consideration of delinquency in the United States, with special emphasis on delinquent behavior as a social problem, its extent and distribution, and the trend in the volume of law violation during recent decades. Particular attention is given to the background of social problems; the meaning of delinquency and crime, including a consideration of the changing conceptions of delinquency and of the delinquents; numerical material regarding the volume of delinquency and crime, including the sources of information, and the values and inadequacies of statistical

---

[1] Cf. *Comparative Survey on Juvenile Delinquency: Part I. North America*, prepared by Paul W. Tappan (New York: Division of Social Welfare, Department of Social Affairs, United Nations, 1952). The other four regional studies deal with Asia and the Far East, Europe, Latin America, and the Middle East. Compare *International Review of Criminal Policy* (New York: Department of Social Affairs, United Nations, No. 1, January, 1952; No. 2, July 1952; No. 3, January, 1953; No. 4, July, 1953; and subsequent issues). These volumes, published semiannually, contain topical bibliographies of current periodical literature on crime and delinquency.

data; the composition of the delinquent population and the types of offenses; ecological distributions; the trends of law violations as affected by economic conditions, the war, and postwar changes; and the difficulties of adequately measuring the volume and trends of delinquency in modern society.

I

JUVENILE DELINQUENCY AS A SOCIAL PROBLEM

Juvenile delinquency is an old problem, a problem that has been intensified and given new emphasis during recent years. Law viola-tion, whether by juveniles or by adults, has become a national con-cern. One of the most critical problems confronting the American people is the maladjustment of children and adolescent youth. Mod-ern society is passing through a period of extensive changes and social disorganization. Maladjustments seem to be the inevitable consequences of rapid and unequal changes in the social order. Juveniles, in particular, seem to be affected in an unusual way by these rapidly changing conditions.

So much publicity has been given to juvenile delinquency and to adult crime in recent years that some are inclined to believe that

3

a veritable epidemic of law violation has swept over the entire world. The best available statistics, if properly interpreted, do not justify extensive generalizations in regard to the changes in the volume of crime; but that law violation is a serious problem is apparent to anyone who has made studies of crime trends. True, the public knows more about criminal behavior now than was known a few decades ago, for increased publicity is given to crime, especially to the more serious offenses. The numerous reports of studies of the various aspects of delinquency and crime that have been published have provided a considerable amount of authentic information on the subject.

Delinquency is not an isolated problem and cannot be understood without consideration of the background of the current social problems. The basic conditions of delinquent behavior are an integral part of the fabric of the entire social order and involve the numerous social changes that have grown out of the past.

BACKGROUND OF SOCIAL PROBLEMS

The social problems of contemporary society have their roots in the past and their consequences in the present and in the future. A thorough knowledge of any complex problem necessitates an understanding of the historical and cultural backgrounds, the conditions that affect it, and the fundamental elements of the problem itself. No adequate solution is possible without an understanding of the basic factors involved in the situation.

The present volume is not designed as a treatise on the historical development of juvenile delinquency and its treatment. The focus of attention is chiefly upon the present extent and trends, the basic conditioning factors, and the methods of control. But the study of the etiology of any problem requires an exploration of the conditions that may be deeply embedded in the social order. Even the means of social control, whether they be a part of the treatment process or of preventive techniques, have their historical aspects.

Students of social problems must recognize both the continuity of culture and the continuous changes that take place in modern society. If the social order could go on with little change, or if the changes in the different parts of society were to progress at equal rates, there would be little social disorganization. Problems are chiefly the results of rapid or unequal changes, the failure to make adequate social adjustments to the changing conditions of the time, and the inability to control the underlying causes.

Modern society, especially in America, is dynamic, ever changing. Social changes are not peculiar to any one country, or to the present epoch in history; but the widespread character of current changes has significant consequences.

The twentieth century has witnessed great scientific achievements, catastrophic changes, and a cavalcade of history-laden events and problems. Since 1900, we have gone through two world wars and have experienced both economic depressions and prosperous eras. The Magic Wand of science has utterly transformed life, industrialization and urbanization have changed the structure and functions of society, and many events have occurred to change the course of history.

In a broad sense, social change includes many kinds of movements, transformations, modifications, and variations in social life. It involves changes in physical resources and in their uses, natural disasters, accomplishments in science and technology, the industrialization and urbanization processes, population movements and composition, the transformation of institutions and organizations, and consequently the alterations of various kinds of societal functions. It includes broad cultural changes, the social processes that operate in group life, and the results of these processes. Social disorganization is one of the most noticeable consequences of the changing social order.

Social Disorganization versus Social Stability. Living in groups is a universal phenomenon, and the social process is the central core of human life. Social interaction and cooperative living are necessary for human existence. They are essential for the development of personality and culture, the maintenance of the social order, and societal welfare.

A successful society achieves a relatively stable system of organization (structure) and functions with a reasonable degree of efficiency. There exist a consensus of attitudes and a unity of purpose. At any rate, general agreements in regard to basic issues and shared values tend to unify the group; otherwise, collective action would not be possible. This does not mean that all persons and subgroups in a society think alike and have uniformly shared values. Complete unity, even if it were possible, is not necessary for cooperative action. But there exists a balance, an equilibrium, of the different and somewhat diverse elements.

Preliterate societies and simple folk cultures have been cited as examples of stability and solidarity. In the more stable preliterate groups and in relatively isolated folk communities a certain degree of continuity prevails, which tends to stabilize social organization and control. Accordingly, few deviations occur and, as judged by the prevailing standards, social problems are at a minimum, even though conditions are not satisfactory from the point of view of the standards of living existing in more advanced countries. A highly integrated folk society may be stable but it may also be stagnant, allowing insufficient adjustments to changing conditions. Positive values do not necessarily accrue from stability alone, for changes are often of great value also.

The maintenance of the social order requires a certain degree of integration of the various elements, but not all groups have the same degree of integration. The larger and more complex societies do not possess the functional unity that can be found in smaller groups. Social usages may be functional in some groups and dysfunctional for others in the same society.

In a dynamic society, such as exists in the United States today, group life is frequently disrupted by the processes of social opposition and disorganization. Thus, social stability is offset by social disintegration. Social problems are likely to arise in a complex, changing, and highly differentiated society. It is, therefore, evident that social disorganization and problems imply a changing society.

Modern Society in Transition. Many factors have contributed to the rapid progress that has been made in the United States, but the abundance of natural resources and the scientific and technological advances are among the most significant ones. A comparison of the strategic situations of the great powers of the world indicates that the United States has a natural sufficiency in most types of raw materials and essential industrial products, in terms of comparative consumption demands, considerably in excess of other countries. Natural resources and physical creations of man have an important bearing on economic and social life. The great abundance and accessibility of various types of resources have saved us a number of times from economic stress, but these conditions have also encouraged waste and exploitation. While some resources have become relatively scarce, man's inventive genius in developing new methods of utilizing natural resources and in finding or making substitutes for scarce materials has in part offset the limitations imposed by diminishing supplies.

Natural occurrences and disasters, such as floods, droughts, storms, earthquakes, fires, insect pests, and various kinds of diseases, and other destructive forces have had disastrous consequences. A variety of methods have been developed to prevent certain forms of disasters or to provide financial and other forms of protection for the victims.

Possibly the most far-reaching changes have occurred in science and technology. New inventions and discoveries have revolutionized life, so much so that it is difficult for social institutions and agencies to keep pace with them. It is generally recognized that technology brings about social changes, but the exact impact of the various inventions has not been fully measured.[1]

Industrialization and urbanization have accompanied technological advances and have produced many fundamental changes in modern society. The factory system of production, modern business and commerce, occupations and the employment situation, and many other phases of the new economy have changed other aspects of life. The American economy itself has changed a great deal during recent decades. To be sure, private property, individual initiative, free competition, and the profit system still prevail, but the growth of corporations, the expansion of markets, the rise of labor organizations, price regulation and control, the expansion of government control of economic processes and operations are evidences of changes that have affected the very core of the American economy.

The growth of cities has provided new ways of living. The modern city is known for its size, heterogeneity of the population, great mobility and fluidity, occupational differentiation, cultural variations, overcrowded conditions of living, and the focal point of many problems. Urbanization has created new types of problems and has affected all phases of life, rural as well as urban.

Although institutional changes are likely to be slower than those in the technological and economic fields, they are nevertheless important. All institutions must be adjusted to the changing conditions of the time; otherwise disorganization is a natural consequence. According to the cultural lag concept,[2] technological and economic changes, if accompanied by slower institutional changes, produce fissures in the social structure and the relative functions of society. By cultural lag is meant the unequal progression of the different phases of culture. For instance, scientific discoveries and mechanical inventions tend to instigate changes in economic activities and organizations most closely associated with them. Slower changes occur in government agencies, social institutions, and community organi-

---

[1] Compare William F. Ogburn, *The Social Impact of Aviation* (New York: Houghton Mifflin Co., 1946).

[2] Cf. William F. Ogburn, *Social Change* (New York: The Viking Press, 1923 and 1950); and Report of the President's Committee on Social Trends, *Recent Social Trends* (New York: McGraw-Hill Book Co., Inc., 1933, 2 vols.).

zation. Changes in mores and social philosophy are likely to be slowest of all, although a new theory may precede changes in social organization.

Changes in the different parts of culture vary from time to time and in communities, and it is difficult to measure their relative importance; but it is generally believed that the condition of cultural lag exists in certain aspects of modern society. Proponents of the cultural lag hypothesis have called attention to the enormous discrepancy that exists between the scientific and mechanical achievements, on the one hand, and the social thinking and institutional structure, on the other, by means of which the mechanical era needs to be controlled. When the factory system was developed, the installation of safety devices lagged behind the production process. For all our high-speed production methods and business efficiency, periodic depressions and widespread unemployment have occurred. In the field of politics, many government organizations still operate according to old methods, and political corruption is found in certain government agencies. In education, vocational training has lagged behind occupational specialization. Many other applications of the theory have been made to show the striking inequalities in the rates of change and the lack of coordination of the various elements in the evolving society.

The cultural lag concept has not been without its critics. Obviously, whether the alleged lag is deplorable or admirable depends upon the value-frame within which we view the situation. Frequently the cultural lag idea is used to designate the disparity between a given condition and the observer's notion of what ought to be. It is obviously difficult to measure the differential rates of change. Not all phases of culture are of equal value. When culture is closely integrated, it changes as a whole. If it is not closely integrated, with subsystems, each with some degree of autonomy, then only strong changes in the most important parts lead to changes of the culture as a whole. Changes may occur in the subsystems of a culture without affecting other parts. The distinction between material and nonmaterial cultures is not clear, for the two types overlap considerably. Though the cultural lag concept has certain weaknesses, especially as applied to the study of social problems, if properly defined and carefully applied to social situations, and if value-judgment elements are recognized, it can be a useful tool to ascertain certain elements of social disorganization.

Processes of Social Disorganization. There is no universal agreement as to the exact nature of social disorganization; but when there is a breakdown of the consensus and unity of purpose of the group, the equilibrium of structure is upset, and the working relations of society are thrown out of balance, it is appropriate to consider these conditions as evidences of disorganization. In such a situation, individuals and groups tend to become maladjusted, and the patterns and mechanisms of human relations are seriously disturbed. The disruption of the functional relations among persons interfere with the performance of the accepted tasks of the group.[3] A certain amount of deterioration may accompany social disorganization; but the unbalanced conditions growing out of the inadequate adjustment of persons and groups, institutions and standards to the changing conditions of the time constitute the chief characteristics of social disorganization.

Social disorganization is not merely a maladjusted condition, for it is chiefly a process. As such, it represents a series of events and occurrences that tend to disrupt the normal functioning of persons and groups. As a process of characteristic recurrent changes, it is made up of a number of specific social processes, chiefly competition, conflict, social differentiation, and mobility. These processes involve elements that work against one another and upset the processes of integration and cooperation. The series of events often culminate in antisocial acts. Hence, such problems as juvenile delinquency and adult crime often are the direct outgrowth of the disruptive processes involved in social disorganization.

Another point to be kept in mind is that a maladjusted situation often constitutes a real crisis in the group. Any social situation may involve elements of a crisis, but social crises are usually conceived of as serious disturbances in the group.

Basic Aspects of Social Problems. A social problem is a condition of social disorganization that affects a substantial number of persons adversely, which condition is recognized by at least the competent observers in the group, and the solution calls for social action. Accordingly, there are at least three basic elements or aspects of a social problem: (1) the objective situation of social and personal disorganization; (2) the recognition of this condition, or at least an

---

[3] See the author's *Social Problems and the Changing Society* (New York: D. Van Nostrand Company, Inc., 1953), Chapter I. Compare Robert E. L. Faris, *Social Disorganization* (New York: The Ronald Press Co., 1948), 19 and 49; Mabel A. Elliott and Francis E. Merrill, *Social Disorganization* (New York: Harper & Brothers, 1950), Chapter II; John E. Nordskog, Edward C. McDonagh, and Melvin J. Vincent, *Analyzing Social Problems* (New York: The Dryden Press, Inc., 1950), Chapter I; and John F. Cuber and Robert A. Harper, *Problems of American Society: Values in Conflict* (New York: Henry Holt and Co., 1951), 438-451.

awareness of it by some persons, which means that a value-judgment is applied to the situation; and (3) the necessity for social action and control.

The objective social situation involves some kind of conflict, disturbance, or deviation from a norm. Natural disasters, chronic disorganization characterized by a more or less constant erosion of social norms through nonconformity and deviant behavior, extensive community dislocation, ideological conflicts, and various forms of group crises are evidences of social disorganization. If a condition affects only a few isolated individuals, it may be regarded as constituting a personal, and not a social, problem.

The subjective element is equally important, even though the connection between a value-judgment and an objective situation is not always clearly apparent. A condition may affect a substantial number of persons adversely, but if the group is not aware of it, in so far as the group is concerned the situation does not constitute a social problem. Outside observers may have a different conception of the situation.

In the final analysis, social problems turn out to be problems of social control. The basic conditions underlying problems are usually social in origin and in nature. Likewise, they are social in consequences, and hence their solution requires group action; no individual alone or even a number of isolated individuals can solve a complex problem.[4]

Law Violation in Modern Society. Law violation is an important problem in modern society and, as such, it must be interpreted in terms of its background. This problem increases when rapid social changes take place and when social disorganization becomes widespread.

---

4 Besides the books mentioned in footnote 3, the following references on social disorganization and problems may be consulted: Harry Elmer Barnes and Oreen M. Ruedi, *The American Way of Life* (New York: Prentice-Hall, Inc., 1942 and 1950); Herbert A. Block, *Disorganization: Personal and Social* (New York: Alfred A. Knopf, Inc., 1952); John L. Gillin, Clarence G. Dittmer, Roy J. Colbert, and Norman M. Kastler, *Social Problems* (New York: Appleton-Century-Crofts, Inc., 1952); Abbott P. Herman, *An Approach to Social Problems* (Boston: Ginn & Company, 1949); Paul H. Landis, *Social Policies in the Making: A Dynamic View of Social Problems* (New York: D. C. Heath & Company, 1947 and 1952); Alfred M. and Elizabeth B. Lee, *Social Problems in America: A Source Book* (New York: Henry Holt & Co., 1949); Edwin M. Leimert, *Social Pathology* (New York: McGraw-Hill Book Co., Inc., 1951); Howard W. Odum, *American Social Problems* (New York: Henry Holt & Co., 1945); Harold A. Phelps and David Henderson, *Contemporary Social Problems* (New York: Prentice-Hall, Inc., 1947 and 1952); James M. Reinhardt, Paul Meadows, and John M. Gillette, *Social Problems and Social Policy* (New York: American Book Company, 1952); Paul A. F. Walter, *The Social Sciences: A Problem Approach* (New York: D. Van Nostrand Co., Inc., 1949); and W. Wallace Weaver, *Social Problems* (New York: William Sloane Associates, 1951).

In appraising the current crime situation, in comparison with the volume of law violation at the beginning of the present century, it is not always recognized that conditions have changed a great deal during the past half century. To make valid comparisons of violations of law over a period of time, it is necessary to have comparable conditions. That crime has increased during the present century is evident and can be shown by an array of statistics of arrests, court cases, inmates in correctional and penal institutions, and those on probation or parole. But the statistics of crime at the beginning of the century were far less adequate than they are today.

The increase of the population, the multiplication of laws and the expansion of law enforcing machinery, the changed conditions of living, and the inadequacy of the older forms of control in the present era are some of the factors that must be noted in appraising the crime situation from one period to another. The population more than doubled from 1900 to 1950, which would seem to indicate that crime should have doubled also, provided the rate of crime remained constant during this period. Innumerable new laws—federal, state, and local—have been passed, which have increased the possibilities of law violation. For instance, traffic regulations, rent and price controls, compulsory school attendance and child labor laws, curfew laws, and a variety of other forms of legislation were practically unknown at the beginning of the century. The additions of legislative enactments and provisions have necessitated the expansion of law enforcement agencies and personnel, thereby multiplying the possibilities of crime detection. Hence, more people are arrested, apprehended, prosecuted, and handled by courts and penal institutions.

Society has become more complex and social change has proceeded at an accelerated tempo. New forms of social control have not kept pace with the changing situation, and no strong and consistent public opinion has been developed favorable to law enforcement and observance at all times. Sutherland,[5] who so ably described the historical background of present-day delinquency and crime in terms of social processes by which criminality has developed, summarizes the matter by stating that the industrial and democratic revolutions started social processes that produced criminality in at least three ways. First, the need for social control was increased because the area of social interaction was widened from the local community to the entire earth, people were driven by the pressure of competition and ambition for luxury and easy money,

---

[5] Edwin H. Sutherland, *Principles of Criminology* (New York: J. B. Lippincott Co., 1947), 74 ff.

and a competitive ideology of individual rights and privileges rather than duties and social welfare provided a background for the criminal. Second, the old agencies of control in the local community were weakened. Third, law as an agency of control in the wider area was kept relatively weak by certain groups who emphasized that the least government was the best, or who resorted to direct bribery. Sutherland proceeds to state further that nations of the Occident have not been equally criminalistic, for they have not become equally mobile, competitive, capitalistic, or individualistic.

In the older rural communities, in which the influences surrounding people were steady, uniform, and more or less consistent, few deviants were found. The immediate family and the larger groups of relatives, the local institutions, the folkways and the mores, and the community spirit exerted strong influence. Individuals found satisfaction and security in conforming to group standards, for conforming produced approval and even praise. Violators of law and nonconformists were severely reprimanded and censured, if not formally punished. Deviant behavior is still relatively uncommon in communities where such uniformity of influences and controls exists.

Today, in a changing society, especially in urban areas, no such uniformity exists. Young people in particular are confronted with a variety of cultural influences and conflicting controls. Even in the home, parental attitudes, beliefs, rules of conduct, and devices of control change from time to time; and often there is no agreement among parents as to the course of conduct that children should pursue. Sometimes parents are inconsistent in their efforts to supervise the conduct of their children. The processes of mobility, social differentiation, competition, and conflict tend to disrupt the normal functioning of the group. The extension of the range of social contacts, the development of individualism and of differentiated groups, the acceleration of social change, and the consequent breakdown of existing rules of conduct have opened the way for deviant behavior. When social interaction is on a personal basis, behavior is controlled in a direct manner; but when interaction is extended beyond the area of personal association, the problem of control becomes increasingly more complicated.

The problem of delinquency is closely associated with social disorganization. Certain specific antisocial acts of particular individuals may be due to incidental or special conditions, but the more serious offenses, certainly the more complex forms of delinquencies, involve personal and social conflicts and disorganization. In other words, like all complex problems, juvenile delinquency has numerous causal factors.

Although the mobile, changing, conflicting, and disorganized conditions of modern society account in a large measure for the increase in criminality, it must be recognized that certain reorganizing tendencies also are in operation. A wider uniformity and identification of self with others are secured by newspapers, radio and television, theaters, public education, and other modern media of communication and education. Certain constructive forces are in operation to reorganize society and to affect new social controls, but some of these in turn are neutralized in part by excessive mobility and change, underlying social conflicts, and disintegration tendencies.

CHANGING ATTITUDES TOWARD JUVENILE OFFENDERS AND TYPES OF APPROACHES TO DELINQUENCY

Although the conceptions of delinquency and the attitudes toward juvenile offenders have changed, traditional views and misconceptions are still held by certain groups. The prevailing views of crime tend to lag behind the findings in studies of criminal behavior. Unfavorable newspaper publicity sometimes creates false impressions of the nature and seriousness of certain offenses. Often people are viciously stigmatized because of their records or because of certain accusations levied against them. The ancient custom of branding people who do not conform to the mores and laws of the group is still practiced. Under the law a person is innocent until found guilty, but the public may prejudge an individual, whether juvenile or adult, without waiting for the court hearing of the case. Some of the recent theories of delinquency have been one-sided and particularistic and have accentuated certain popular misconceptions of offenders.

Traditional and Popular Misconceptions. Some of the traditional misconceptions of criminals root in fallacious views of human nature and of personality. Cesare Lombroso, on the basis of rather naïve and superficial evidence, concluded that criminals possessed certain inherited traits, that they were in essence primitive people at odds with civilization, and that they could be identified by marked asymmetry and ear deformation. Morphologically, they were midway between savages and lunatics. He assumed that criminals were more or less the same type the world over, irrespective of race, nationality, and culture. The born-criminal type idea has been advocated by various other writers. According to this view, juvenile delinquents constitute a special biological type, differing in physical and mental traits from law-abiding citizens. This approach or interpretation has been labeled the "positive school." [6]

Although the notion of inborn criminal traits is no longer regarded as scientifically valid, the stereotyped view that criminals are born with certain tendencies toward misconduct is still lodged in the minds of uninformed people. Some criminals, unfortunately, possess certain personality traits that lend credence to this view. Even though delinquents may not be regarded as born criminals, the notion that delinquency has its roots in heredity is still fairly prevalent. The relatively high rate of feeble-minded and dull normal individuals among offenders has furnished support for this view. Certain inherited traits, of course, may and sometimes do contribute to delinquent behavior, especially if they affect the status and activities of the individual in the group.

Delinquents have been labeled as "being possessed," as "degenerates," as "morons," or as having other specific personality traits that mark them as criminals. "He looks like a criminal," "He is just a natural-born thief," and "He is a degenerate," are statements typical of this view. Newspaper descriptions of certain delinquents have led to the belief that offenders are depraved and dangerous individuals. Reckless and Smith [7] cite the case of Gussie, a neighborhood terror, who was regarded as being possessed. A committee of citizens from a low-class industrial area of a city petitioned the juvenile court to remove the 12-year-old, cross-eyed, unkempt, malnourished, undersized girl, who was considered by them as a menace. She stole, begged, lied, swore, and threw stones at the neighborhood children. Gussie looked possessed and wild, and she had a ferocious temper. She had not been in school for several years, and she was refused participation in a local settlement house. The mother supported the family by working in a hosiery mill. The desertion of the father, the reputed immorality of the mother, the inability of the stepfather to provide a corrective influence, and the fierce temper of the girl added to the low status of the family in the neighborhood. Although it was true that Gussie was mentally retarded, the

---

6 Enrico Ferri, distinguished pupil and successor of Lombroso, explains the principles, methods, and objectives of the positive school of criminology in *The Positive School of Criminology*, originally printed in Italian in 1883. For excerpts from the writings of Lombroso and Ferri, and the opposite theories that crime is the result of imitation by Gabriel De Tarde and that the criminal is the product of the capitalistic system by William A. Bonger, see Clyde B. Vedder, Samuel Koenig, and Robert E. Clark, *Criminology: A Book of Readings* (New York: The Dryden Press, 1953), 132-165.

7 Walter C. Reckless and Mapheus Smith, *Juvenile Delinquency* (New York: McGraw-Hill Book Co., Inc., 1932), 1-3.

experts who studied the case regarded this retardation as the result of malnutrition, lack of home training, and inadequate schooling. Fortunately, the social agencies of the community could provide some correctives.

Although the older theory that criminal conduct was some kind of diabolical possession and instigation is no longer held, some groups still ascribe delinquency to a particular type of condition. They blame the families of delinquents or contend that delinquency is caused by certain movies, or dance halls, or radio and television programs, or crime comics, or lack of moral discipline. In fact, a wide range of particularistic explanations are still held, usually without any specific knowledge of the multifarious conditions that may cause delinquency. Others, with more scientific interest, but with specialties, emphasize special biological factors to the exclusion of environmental influences; whereas others overemphasize certain social pressures that may affect individuals. The controversy of "freedom of the will" versus "determinism" is still being waged.

Legalistic View: The Classical School. Until the present century, prior to the development of the juvenile court and new methods of dealing with juvenile offenders, juveniles who violated laws were treated approximately the same as adult offenders. Except for consideration given to the age factor in some courts, criminal court procedures were applied to all offenders. The idea of the juvenile court with more informal procedure and differential treatment had not yet emerged.

The legalistic view of crime and criminals stresses the rigid application of law to all offenders regardless of age. In spite of more than half a century of progress in developing the juvenile court to its present stage of efficiency, in some communities the older methods of trial and punishment are still applied to juveniles. The concern is chiefly with the guilt or innocence of the child and fitting punishment for the crime, if guilty.

The classical school, which emphasized that punishment must fit the crime, assumed that if exact and severe penalties were applied and offenders knew beforehand that they would be applied, crime could be reduced to a minimum. The punishment should be sufficiently severe to outweigh the profit or pleasure that might otherwise accrue from criminal careers. It was assumed that the surest way to stop crime was to enforce the law rigidly and swiftly.

It must be recognized that the line of demarcation between juveniles and adults is somewhat arbitrary, for it is difficult to determine exactly when the juvenile age period ends and adulthood begins. Individuals differ a great deal in psychological and social ages, even though chronologically they may be of the same age, but the difference may be chiefly a matter of degree rather than kind.

The steady progress of juvenile court and probation treatment of juvenile offenders, the studies of individual cases and of more general conditioning factors, and the changed attitude toward the treatment of children who are in difficulty have contributed much to produce a more scientific approach to the problem of delinquency.[8]

Individualistic Views. The individualistic and group approaches to the analysis of the causes of delinquency will be discussed in Part Two and need not be elaborated here, except to emphasize the underlying attitudes toward delinquents which are inherent in these approaches.

The individualistic or individual approaches emphasize that the causes of delinquency rest essentially within the individual, although the results may be directed outwardly against others. When William Healy published *The Individual Delinquent* in 1915, after five years of study of hundreds of cases in the Juvenile Psychopathic Institute in Chicago, he blazed a new trail in the diagnosis and prognosis of offenders. Even though several causative factors were recognized, his main approach was individualistic. The individual was regarded as the dynamic center of the problem and, in dealing with delinquents, psychological methods were used.

The case studies involved a consideration of hereditary factors, developmental and physical conditions (especially developmental physical abnormalities), stimulants and narcotics, mental habits, abnormal sexualism, mental abnormalities and defects or dullness, psychic constitutional inferiority, mental aberrations, and various other mental peculiarities. Environmental influences were considered as these impinged upon the individual factors.

Healy felt that immediately back of an action is an idea, a wish, or an impulse, existing as a mental content. Some actions have no representation in consciousness, either before or after performance, but nevertheless they are controlled by mental processes. He cautioned that in many cases sole dependence on the psychological standpoint would be a mistake, for it is sometimes difficult to determine which is the most investigatory vantage ground—social, medical, or psychological. Yet, he believed that both psychologists

---

[8] For a brief summary of the theories of causation, including the *classical school* and the *positive* or *positivistic school,* see C. S. Mihanovich, *Principles of Juvenile Delinquency* (Milwaukee: The Bruce Publishing Co., 1950), Chapter III.

and sociologists were beginning to recognize the value of the individual approach.

While Healy was making these early studies, he understood the importance of getting data regarding the family history, as well as the developmental history of the individual. In subsequent works, in collaboration with Augusta F. Bronner, especially the Judge Baker Foundation *Case Studies* (1922-1923) and *New Light on Delinquency and Its Control* (1936), he delved into the family background of cases and considered some of the other environmental conditions that affected the conduct of the cases studied.

Several recent studies have been made to determine the connection between biological characteristics of individuals and their criminal behavior. Among these, the works of Hooton and Sheldon are best known. Hooton [9] maintains that criminals as a group represent an aggregate of biologically (also sociologically) inferior individuals, with marked deficiency in gross bodily dimensions and in other physical traits. Since criminals are organically inferior, crime is the result of the impact of environment upon low-grade organisms. Sheldon [10] has presented the thesis that behavior is the result of bodily functions. The structure-behavior continuum thesis is used in analyzing 200 cases of young men. The quantification of the primary component determining the morphological structure of an individual is called "somatotype," of which there are several components or types. Sheldon maintains that there is no break, no discontinuation between the physical structure of the individual and his behavior. This has been designated as the "constitutional psychology" approach to the study of delinquency. These and related theories will be considered more fully in Chapter IV.

The individualistic views of delinquency have led to an overemphasis on personal factors, including the inherited constitution and the weaknesses of the physical organism. Consequently, environmental influences are minimized or omitted as factors of causation. This point of view has affected the process and method of treatment and the preventive programs. The correction of biological and psychological conditions supersedes the changing of environmental pressures.

It is recognized by most of the researchers in this field that a case study of the delinquent is important and that certain personality

---

[9] Earnest A. Hooton, *Crime and the Man* (Cambridge: Harvard University Press, 1939).

[10] William H. Sheldon, *Varieties of Delinquent Youth* (New York: Harper and Brothers, 1949).

traits are significant sources of misconduct. Considerable attention has been given to the analysis of personal disorganization. Maladjustments of children range all the way from minor difficulties to extreme upheavals and conflicts. Many studies have been made of problem and unadjusted children and youth.[11] Case studies of maladjusted children indicate the importance of personality factors, but they also reveal the influence of environmental pressures. One cannot isolate either personal or social factors. The more comprehensive approach includes a consideration of the total personal-social-situational complex.

Group Approaches. The various types of group emphases to delinquency causation have stressed environmental influences, such as those emanating from home life, gangs, and community conditions. The extremists have stressed environmental pressures as the chief causes of deviant behavior, omitting important personality factors.

Few phases of the etiology of delinquency, other than the emphasis on individual causation, have received as much attention as the relation of broken or maladjusted homes to deviant behavior. Consequently, the conditions of the families of delinquents have been studied in great detail. Case records of delinquents abound with data on their family life. The extent of family disorganization in the homes of delinquents has led some to believe that the real delinquents are the parents, not their children. Juveniles are simply the victims of circumstances. This being the case, they should be treated as such and the parents should be dealt with by law enforcement agencies. But blaming the parents for the misconduct of their children does not solve the problem. Family reorganization is an important phase of the treatment process and the prevention of future difficulties, but the family situation cannot be isolated from other elements that may play a vital part in the process.

Apart from the analysis of the family background of individual delinquents, the study of the relation of gangs and companionship to delinquency was given considerable impetus by the publication of

---

11 For some of the earlier studies of this type, see: Mary B. Sayles, *Three Problem Children* (New York: Commonwealth Fund: Division of Publication, 1924, prepared by the Joint Committee on Methods of Preventing Delinquency); Miriam Van Waters, *Youth in Conflict* (New York: New Republic, Inc., 1952); William I. Thomas, *The Unadjusted Girl* (Boston: Little, Brown & Co., 1924); and William I. Thomas and Dorothy S. Thomas, *The Child in America* (New York: Alfred A. Knopf, Inc., 1928). These writers should not be identified with the individualistic approach to the study of delinquency, for they recognize social as well as individual factors.

reports of the prevalence of gangs in urban areas.[12] Thrasher's study of 1,313 gangs in Chicago revealed, among other things, that boys seldom commit delinquencies alone, but usually get into trouble in association with others, and that gangs for the most part have demoralizing influences. Delinquency rates are high in the areas where gangs are prevalent. Ganglands are the geographically and socially interstitial areas in cities, the regions or spaces that intervene between normal residential areas. Ganging is especially prevalent in slums and blighted areas of cities.

In addition to the study of family background and peer group relationships, various other group approaches have been emphasized, such as the influence of community institutions and communicative systems, cultural contacts and conflicts, and ecological situations. Of these, the cultural and ecological approaches have received the emphasis by investigators of etiological factors in delinquency, and they have also received critical appraisals.

Cultural contacts and conflicts are the sources of much delinquency, especially in groups in which culture hybridism exists. A number of writers have stressed the importance of culture conflicts and hybridism as factors in delinquency.[13] When a succession of culture groups occurs and one system of culture comes in conflict with another system, the customary rules of behavior tend to break down. Cultural hybridism, in particular, tends to result in a confusion of behavior norms, excessive conflicts are likely to occur, and the subsequent breakdown of effective and unified social control produces the condition in which extensive law violation prevails.

The study of delinquency in urban areas includes the ecological approach to determine the distribution of cases in order to ascertain the regions of high rates. The most comprehensive ecological studies have been made in Chicago,[14] which will be discussed in Chapter X. In these studies it was found that delinquency is correlated with a

---

[12] Cf. Frederic M. Thrasher, *The Gang* (Chicago: University of Chicago Press, 1927); and William Foote Whyte, *Street Corner Society* (Chicago: University of Chicago Press, 1943).

[13] Cf. Thorsten Sellin, *Culture Conflict and Crime* (New York: Social Science Research Council, 1938); Pauline V. Young, *The Pilgrims of Russian-Town* (Chicago: University of Chicago Press, 1932); Edwin H. Sutherland, *Principles of Criminology* (New York: J. B. Lippincott Co., 1947), Chapter IX; and the studies of race and nationality factors in relation to delinquency and crime.

[14] Cf. Clifford R. Shaw and Henry D. McKay, *Juvenile Delinquency in Urban Areas: A Study of Rates of Delinquents in Relation to Differential Characteristics of Local Communities in American Cities* (Chicago: University of Chicago Press, 1942); also Clifford R. Shaw, Henry D. McKay, Frederick Zorbaugh, and Leonard S. Cottrell, *Delinquency Areas* (Chicago: University of Chicago Press, 1929); and, "Social Factors in Juvenile Delinquency," *Report on the Causes of Crime,* National Commission on Law Observance and Enforcement, No. 13, Vol. II, 1931.

number of presumably separate factors. The high delinquency areas are characterized by certain more or less clearly differentiated conditions.

These various approaches reveal the historical background of the development of theories of delinquency and the changed attitudes toward delinquents. The changed approaches and attitudes have affected the definition of delinquent behavior. Possibly the greatest effect of the changed conception of delinquency can be seen in the analysis of causation, the methods of treatment of cases, and the prevention of the occurrence of law violation, which will be discussed in Parts Two and Three of this text.

Reviewing the changing conception of delinquency may lead to the impression that the different and sometimes conflicting attitudes mean uncertainty and confusion. One should not draw the conclusion that the various types of explanations of social behavior, particularly deviant conduct, constitute a welter of conflicting hypotheses and theories. They represent stages in the development of the theoretical formulations. Progress has been made in scientific findings, which in turn is reflected in the explanations of crime and delinquency.

MEANING AND NATURE OF DELINQUENCY AND CRIME [15]

Criminal Law and Crime. Criminal law is a body of specific rules and regulations regarding human conduct that have been established by political authority through constitutions, legislative enactments, treaties, and systems of "common law," and in judicial decisions and administrative regulations. Crime is defined legally as a violation of criminal law, involving both an overt act or the omission of a duty required of citizens and a culpable intent. The criminal code not only defines the types of offenses but specifies the procedure of prosecution and trial and, if the person is found guilty, the penalty is prescribed.

Although the foregoing description suffices for a general statement of what crime is, offenders have been variously classified according to the kinds and degrees of crime. The types of crimes have been classified as: (1) offenses against the state's regulatory functions; (2) offenses against bodily security; (3) offenses against property; (4)

---

[15] For more complete definitions of terms pertaining to crime, delinquency, and criminology, consult Vernon C. Branham and Samuel B. Kutash, *Encyclopedia of Criminology* (New York: Philosophical Library, Inc., 1949); Henry Pratt Fairchild, Editor, *Dictionary of Sociology* (New York: Philosophical Library, Inc., 1944); and texts on criminology and delinquency.

offenses against religion and morality; (5) crimes relating to crimes themselves, such as fixing criminal acts and the enforcement of criminal law; and (6) possession of burglar's tools, firearms, and the like.[16]

Treason is an offense against the state. A felony is a more serious offense than a misdemeanor. Offenses against persons include murder, kidnapping, abduction, rape, and robbery, in which the state, as the protector of citizens, has a vital interest. A capital crime refers to an offense where the punishment may be death, regardless of whether or not the penalty is inflicted. Crimes against property include stealing, pilfering, cheating, fraud, and deprivation of personal belongings.

Broadly stated, a criminal is a person who has committed an offense, that is, has violated a law. Offenders may be classified according to the types of crimes committed, but the condition and background of the offender and the circumstances of the offense are recognized under certain conditions in order to determine the offender's responsibility. The first offense of an otherwise law-abiding citizen, especially if the offense is classified as a misdemeanor, may not be regarded as a serious matter; but when crime becomes a mode of life, as in the case of a criminal career, the person is classified as a chronic offender. A recidivist is dealt with more severely than a first offender, even for the same offense. If an offender is mentally abnormal or disorganized, he is often classified as criminally insane or simply as mentally disorganized or feeble-minded, whatever the main condition may be. The state of mind or attitude (motive) of the offender is likewise an important factor in many cases, regardless of whether or not the person is otherwise normal or abnormal. The intent, which is a concomitant of the physical act, is an element in crime. To be criminally liable, a person committing an offense must have done so of his own volition and must be capable of distinguishing between lawful and unlawful behavior. Ignorance of the law, however, is not regarded as a reason for dismissing a case. Certain circumstances may negate or minimize responsibility under the criminal law.

The concept "crime" has been extended, and people have be-

---

16 Cf. Nicholas Atlas, "Criminal Law and Procedure," *Encyclopedia of Criminology, op. cit.,* 87-96. For a discussion of the difficulties involved in the classification of criminals, consult Alfred R. Lindesmith and H. Warren Dunham, "Some Principles of Criminal Typology," *Social Forces,* Vol. 19, No. 3 (March, 1941), 307-314. The classification of law violators into a fixed number of mutually exclusive categories, such as felon and misdemeanant and their subgroups, is not satisfactory. Criminals vary widely from one another as to their motivation, social orientation, seriousness and frequency of offenses, and types or specialties of behavior.

come aware of offenses that were not common until recent decades, as indicated by white-collar crime, black-market operations, tax evasions, and "absence without leave" or desertion from military forces.[17] In general, white-collar crime refers to an offense committed by a person of respectability in the course of his occupation. Corporations may commit such offenses as the restraint of trade, unfair labor practices, misrepresentations, and certain practices of rebates. During the war, violations of rationing of certain commodities and rent controls were extensive. In the military forces "Absence without Leave" (AWOL) and desertion, as well as evasions of the draft act, became serious offenses. These forms of offenses apply chiefly to adults, but children and young people were affected by them and by the attitudes toward law observance expressed or implied in the actions of parents and other adults. Some children were directly involved in some of these offenses.

Criminal law applies to all ages, but the age factor is taken into consideration in the treatment procedure. A person under age is classed as a juvenile delinquent if he violates a law, and he is treated accordingly. Besides, certain laws apply only to juveniles, as will be indicated later.

Who Is a Juvenile? There is considerable variation by states as to the age range of juveniles who are under the jurisdiction of juvenile authorities, such as the juvenile court.

. . . Court jurisdiction over juvenile delinquency is defined in terms of upper age limits for the children covered as well as by substantive norms of conduct. In the United States these limits range from 16 to 21, but 18 is the most common age adopted in the several states. In five and in parts of five others, the age limit for boys is 16; in eleven it is 17; in five states, and for girls in one other, certain cases may be covered to the age of 21; in most of the remainder, including the Federal government and the District of Columbia the upper limit is 18. In most of the jurisdictions (about forty), however, there is overlapping or concurrence between the jurisdiction of the criminal and the juvenile courts, in several of these all the way down to the age of 7. Moreover, in about half of the states the criminal courts have exclusive jurisdiction over certain offenses, ordi-

---

17 Cf. Edwin H. Sutherland, *White Collar Crime* (New York: Dryden Press, Inc., 1949); Marshall B. Clinard, "Criminological Theories of Violations of Wartime Regulations," *American Sociological Review*, Vol. XI (June, 1946), 258-277; War Department Pamphlet No. 20-5, *Absence without Leave* (Washington, D. C.: United States Government Printing Office, 1944); Samuel A. Stouffer, *et al.*, *Studies in Social Psychology in World War II* (Princeton: Princeton University Press, 1949-1950), 4 vols.; and Arnold M. Rose, "The Social Psychology of Desertion from Combat," *American Sociological Review*, Vol. XVI (October, 1951) 614-629.

narily for the crime of murder or for capital and life-imprisonment cases, in some states for "infamous crimes" or for any crime at all.[18]

There is overlapping or concurrence between the jurisdiction of criminal and juvenile courts, but the common practice is to give the juvenile court exclusive jurisdiction over juveniles with no limitation placed upon it, unless the judge of the court desires to transfer cases to the criminal court. Once a juvenile court has obtained jurisdiction over a case, it may continue such jurisdiction until the child has attained majority. Thus, not only does the upper age limit of juvenile court jurisdiction vary by states, but the procedure is somewhat flexible.

Most of the juvenile court laws do not set a minimum age limit or floor regarding delinquency, but in several of the states the penal law provides that a child under a particular age, usually 7 years of age, may not be convicted of crime. In these states, however, children under the specified age may be classed as delinquents for acts that are prohibited by penal laws. The assumption underlying the differential treatment is that, under a certain age (but there is no agreement as to which age), a child is not regarded as mature enough to be responsible for certain acts. Small children may commit offenses without knowing the wrongfulness of the acts. If a criminal procedure is to be instituted against a child under a specified age, the state must prove affirmatively that such a child had sufficient capacity to entertain the criminal intent. In juvenile courts these presumptions regarding responsibility of children do not exist, for juvenile court laws do not retain such provisions.[19]

Although these are the age limits for juvenile and criminal court jurisdictions, it must be remembered that children and young adolescents differ greatly in their physical, mental, and social age levels, especially the last. Delinquency is more directly associated with social age than with either the physical or mental age levels, for social age involves emotional stability and maturity, attitudes and habits, and a degree of understanding and socialization.

---

[18] *Comparative Survey on Juvenile Delinquency.* Part I. North America, report prepared by Paul W. Tappan (New York: Department of Social Affairs of the Division of Social Welfare, United Nations, 1952). Used by permission of the United Nations, Division of Social Welfare. Compare Paul W. Tappan, "Children and Youth in the Criminal Court," *The Annals of the American Academy of Political and Social Science,* Vol. 261 (January, 1949), 128-136; Frederick B. Sussmann, *Law of Juvenile Delinquency: The Laws of the Forty-eight States* (New York: Oceana Publications, 1950); and examine the tables of court jurisdiction over juveniles in these sources and the state-by-state summary in the book by Sussmann.

[19] Cf. Sol Rubin, "The Legal Character of Juvenile Delinquency," *The Annals, ibid.,* 1-8.

What Is Delinquency? There is no agreement as to the exact meaning and nature of juvenile delinquency. In a legal sense, it is what the law says it is. This includes offenses committed by juveniles (whose ages conform to the age group specified by law as juveniles) that are in violation of federal, state, and local laws, which breaches of the law by adults would be punishable by fines or imprisonment; certain forms of behavior peculiar to youth, such as habitually running away from home without consent, excessive truancy from school, incorrigibility, and similar forms of deviant behavior; and being in places or living in surroundings that are regarded as harmful to youth and that lawfully may be interpreted as requiring official action. But, as already indicated, juvenile and criminal courts are given considerable discretion in the matter of handling cases.

Definitions of delinquency in juvenile court acts include violation of laws and ordinances by children, but the legal provisions do not stop there. Sussmann [20] presents a summary list of acts or conditions included in delinquency definitions or descriptions, tabulated in decreasing order of frequency, and he indicates the items included in the laws of the various states and territories. Stated briefly, these acts and conditions are:

(1) violates any law or ordinance; (2) habitually truant; (3) (knowingly) associates with thieves, vicious or immoral persons; (4) incorrigible; (5) beyond control of parent or guardian; (6) growing up in idleness or crime; (7) so deports self as to injure or endanger self or others; (8) absents self from home (without just cause and without consent); (9) immoral and indecent conduct; (10) (habitually) uses vile, obscene or vulgar language (in public place); (11) (knowingly) enters, visits house of ill repute; (12) patronizes, visits policy shop or gaming place; (13) (habitually) wanders about railroad yards and tracks; (14) jumps train or enters car or engine without authority; (15) patronizes saloon or dram house where intoxicating liquor is sold; (16) wanders streets at night, not on lawful business; (17) patronizes public poolroom or bucket shop; (18) immoral conduct around school (or in public place); (19) engages in illegal occupation; (20) in occupation or situation dangerous or injurious to self or others; (21) smokes cigarettes (or uses tobacco in any form); (22) frequents place whose existence violates law; (23) is found in place for permitting which adult may be punished; (24) addicted to drugs; (25) disorderly; (26) begging; (27) uses intoxicating liquor; (28) makes indecent proposals; (29) loiters, sleeps in alleys, vagrant; (30) runs away from state or charity institution; (31) found on premises occupied or used for illegal purposes; (32) operates motor vehicle dangerously while under the influence of liquor; (33) attempts to marry without consent, in violation of law; and (34) given to sexual irregularities.

20 Frederick B. Sussmann, *op. cit.*, 20-21. Used by permission of Oceana Publications. Compare Sol Rubin, *op. cit.*, 2.

To give a concrete example of a legal definition of delinquency, the New York State law may be cited, for New York has written its juvenile law rather broadly.

> . . . the words "delinquent child" shall mean a child over seven and under sixteen years of age: (a) who violates any law of the United States or of this state or ordinance of the City of New York, or who commits any act which if committed by an adult would be a crime, except any child fifteen years of age who commits any act which if committed by an adult would be a crime punishable by death or life imprisonment, unless an order removing the action to the children's court has been made and filed pursuant to section three hundred twelve-c, subdivision (c) and section three hundred twelve-f, subdivision (a) and (b) of the code of criminal procedure; (b) who is incorrigible, ungovernable or habitually disobedient and beyond the control of his parents, guardian, custodian or other lawful authority; (c) who is habitually truant; (d) who, without just cause and without the consent of his parent, guardian or other custodian, deserts his home or place of abode; (e) who engages in any occupation which is in violation of law; (f) who begs or who solicits alms or money in public places; (g) who associates with immoral or vicious persons; (h) who frequents any place the maintenance of which is in violation of law; (i) who habitually uses obscene or profane language; or (j) who so deports himself as wilfully to injure or endanger the morals or health of himself or others.[21]

It is evident that numerous items are included under the heading of delinquency, especially if the thirty-four items are examined, which represent a summary of the laws of the forty-eight states, three territories, and the federal law. Besides, the phraseology of several of the items indicates that some of the laws are outmoded. The Standard Juvenile Court Act, published by the National Probation and Parole Association, which is regarded as a model act, avoids most of these delinquency classes and brings the phraseology up to date. It simply describes the situations of children over which the juvenile court has jurisdiction. Even though most of the states have only eight or nine items in addition to violations of laws that apply to all ages, except the very young, the delinquency tag may be applied to individuals who should not be so classified. In fact, there is a growing tendency to avoid applying the delinquency tag to children, except possibly in cases of serious offenses or to recidivists.

Sheldon and Eleanor Glueck, in comparing 500 delinquents with 500 nondelinquents, state that, actually, any child who commits even a single minor act in violation of law is technically a delinquent, but

---

[21] Criminal Code, Domestic Relations Court Act of the City of New York, Section 2, (15), as amended 1948. Quoted from *Police and Children*, A Study of New York City's Juvenile Aid Bureau, Citizens' Committee on Children of New York City, Inc., 1951.

that this is not a valid definition to use in making comparisons between delinquents and nondelinquents. So, for the purpose of their study they define delinquency as

> . . . repeated acts of a kind which when committed by persons beyond the statutory juvenile court age of sixteen (referring to Massachusetts) are punishable as crimes (either felonies or misdemeanors)—except for a few instances of persistent stubbornness, truancy, running away, associating with immoral persons, and the like. Children who once or twice during the period of growing up in an excitingly attractive mileau steal a toy in a ten-cent store, sneak into a subway or motion picture theatre, play hooky, and the like and soon outgrow such peccadillos are not true delinquents even though they have violated the law.[22]

Edwin Powers and Helen Witmer [23] found in their study that, in order to define the real delinquents, it was necessary to take into consideration three concepts or criteria, namely: (a) the seriousness of the behavior, (b) its frequency, and (c) the attitude of the offender toward a lawfully constituted society. Applying these categories, they classified the delinquents into five groups—most, ordinary, occasional, seldom, and least delinquent.

Lowell J. Carr,[24] in trying to determine what delinquency statistics mean, raises the question— What is a delinquent? To illustrate the possible meanings, he presents a diagram of concentric circles, which he designates "A Target for Consistent Reference." The inner circle (7) includes only the adjudged delinquents, that is, all court antisocial deviants who have been found guilty; the next circle (6) includes the alleged delinquents—all apprehended antisocial deviants brought to court; (5) agency delinquents—all detected antisocial deviants reaching any agency; (4) detected delinquents—all antisocial deviants detected; (3) legal delinquents—all deviants committing antisocial acts as defined by law; (2) juvenile deviants—all children showing deviant behavior; and the outer circle (1) includes the total juvenile population in a given area, below a given age as specified by law. This graphic picture indicates how confusing our definitions of delinquency are and how difficult it is to determine who actually is a delinquent.

This picture is made even more confusing because the juvenile

---

22 *Unraveling Juvenile Delinquency* (New York: The Commonwealth Fund, 1950), 13. Used by permission of The Commonwealth Fund and Harvard University Press. Compare *Delinquents in the Making: Paths to Prevention,* by the Gluecks (New York: Harper & Brothers, 1952), 18.

23 *Prevention of Delinquency: The Cambridge-Somerville Youth Study* (New York: Columbia University Press, 1951), 180-186.

24 *Delinquency Control* (New York: Harper & Brothers, 1950), 89-92.

courts handle both delinquency and welfare or neglected cases. Referring to the New York Law (cf. Chapter 482 of the Laws of 1933),

. . . the words "neglected child" shall mean a child under sixteen years of age (a) who is without proper guardianship; (b) who has been abandoned or deserted by either or both of its parents, or by any other person or persons lawfully charged with its care and custody; (c) whose parent, guardian or person with whom the child lives, by reason of cruelty, mental incapacity, immorality or depravity is unfit properly to care for such child; (d) whose parent or guardian has been sentenced to imprisonment for crime; (e) who is under lawful or improper supervision, care, custody or restraint by any person; (f) who wanders about without lawful occupation or restraint, or who is unlawfully kept out of school; (g) whose parent, guardian or custodian neglects or refuses, when able to do so, to provide necessary medical, surgical, institutional or hospital care for such child; (h) who is found in any place the maintenance of which is in violation of law; (i) who is in such condition of want or suffering or is under such improper guardianship or control as to injure or endanger the morals or health of himself or others.

One can see from this summary, in comparison with the definition of a "delinquent child," that the two concepts overlap. This is precisely the condition in actual experience, for it is not always possible to distinguish between the "sinner" and the person who has been "sinned against."

Judging by the intent as well as by the letter of the law—federal, state or local—the law-enforcing agencies are given considerable latitude in dealing with cases of delinquency and/or neglect, and it is not always necessary to decide whether a child is a delinquent or a neglected person in order to proceed with a program of action.

The legal definition of delinquency is complicated further by the fact that it contains a mixture of moral judgments, somewhat tempered by middle-class ideology. The interpretations and applications of law vary by cultural groups. Thus, what is considered antisocial behavior in one group may be regarded as fairly normal behavior in another group. The legal concept of delinquency simply states the type of conduct forbidden by law, which does not include the larger connotation.

In the broader cultural or social sense, delinquency implies that the behavior is in contradiction with the value demands of the dominant culture within which a given child lives. That is, the behavior runs counter to the dominant value system within which the child's character formation takes place. Although some laws are not deeply rooted in the mores of society, numerous mores have not been translated into legal provisions. Thus, delinquency implies some form of antisocial behavior, involving personal and social disorganization, a value-judgment applied to the form of conduct in terms of the norms and laws of society, and the act tends to affect people adversely. The individual may be seriously affected by his own action, but behavior is usually regarded as antisocial when the group is affected adversely.

When delinquency is described as a form of antisocial behavior, in the sense of both antagonism toward and withdrawal from society, this does not apply to all group relations of the individual. Gang members may be antisocial in so far as their relations with the community is concerned, but in their own group they are highly integrated and follow the gang norms. They "play the game" in their own group, to which they give undivided allegiance, but they defy the mores and laws of society.

From a social psychological point of view, a juvenile is delinquent because he conceives of himself as being a delinquent person. Once labeled as a delinquent, either by official action or by the community, his attitudes and behavior are affected by the realization that he is regarded as a law violator or as being an antisocial person.

The juvenile offender is usually regarded as a problem child, but not all problem children are law violators. The distinction between a delinquent and a problem child is an arbitrary one. It is a matter of degree, of a gradual continuity, with the normal merging into the abnormal by almost imperceptible shades. The extreme cases merge into the borderline ones, and the borderline cases into the nondelinquent, with no sudden transition.

Juvenile delinquency is a social problem. In order to fully appraise the problem, it is necessary to analyze the complexity of the objective personal-social situation in which it arises, including the sequence of events and functional interrelationships of the various factors and variables, the value-judgment that is applied to the form of conduct in terms of an accepted standard of measurement, and the consequences of the behavior.

QUESTIONS AND PROJECTS

For Class Discussion and Research

1. What is a social problem? When does a condition in society become a social problem? Classify the major social problems of today.

2. How is a social problem related to social change and social or cultural disorganization?

3. In what sense is juvenile delinquency a social problem?

4. Trace the changing attitude toward delinquency and the delinquents. What factors have been chiefly responsible for this change of attitude?

5. By means of questionnaires or interviews, study the prevailing attitude of the people in your community toward delinquents.

6. What are the difficulties involved in defining concisely the concept "juvenile delinquency"? Formulate a broad and comprehensive definition.

7. Differentiate between delinquent and behavior problem cases. In what ways do these types of cases overlap?

8. What are the main types of conduct commonly classed as delinquent acts? Study the laws of a particular state regarding delinquency and welfare cases that are regarded as subject to official action.

9. What is the relationship of juvenile delinquency to adult crime? What is the relationship of earlier maladjustments to delinquency?

10. Trace the development of juvenile court legislation.

11. Discuss federal laws regarding delinquency.

SELECTED REFERENCES

Annals of the American Academy of Political and Social Science, Vol. 261 (January, 1949), entire issue.

BARNES, HARRY ELMER, AND NEGLEY K. TEETERS, *New Horizons in Criminology* (New York: Prentice-Hall, Inc., 1943 and 1949).

BRANHAM, VERNON C., AND SAMUEL B. KUTASH, *Encyclopedia of Criminology* (New York: Philosophical Library, 1949).

BURT, CYRIL, *The Young Delinquent* (New York: D. Appleton and Co., 1925 and 1938).

CABOT, P. S. DE Q., *Juvenile Delinquency: A Critical Annotated Bibliography* (New York: The H. W. Wilson Co., 1946).

CARR, LOWELL J., *Delinquency Control* (New York: Harper & Brothers, 1940 and 1950).

CARR-SAUNDERS, A. M., HERMANN MANNHEIM, AND E. C. RHODES, *Young Offenders: An Inquiry into Juvenile Delinquency* (New York: The Macmillan Co., 1944).

CAVAN, RUTH SHONLE, *Criminology* (New York: Thomas Y. Crowell Co., 1948).

Comparative Survey on Juvenile Delinquency, Part I. North America, prepared by Paul W. Tappan (New York: Division of Social Welfare, Department of Social Affairs, United Nations, 1952). Other volumes deal with Asia and the Far East, Europe, Latin America, and The Middle East.

ELLIOTT, MABEL A., *Crime in Modern Society* (New York: Harper & Brothers, 1952).

FAIRCHILD, HENRY PRATT, Editor, *Dictionary of Sociology* (New York: Philosophical Library, 1944).

GILLIN, JOHN L., *Criminology and Penology* (New York: D. Appleton-Century Co., 1945).

GOLDBERG, HARRIET L., *Child Offenders: A Study in Diagnosis and Treatment* (New York: Grune and Stratton, 1948).

HEALY, WILLIAM, AND AGUSTA F. BRONNER, *New Light on Delinquency and Its Treatment* (New Haven, Conn.: Yale University Press, 1936).

KURTZ, RUSSELL H., Editor, *Social Work Year Book, 1951* (New York: American Association of Social Workers, 1954).

MIHANOVICH, CLEMENT S., *Principles of Juvenile Delinquency* (Milwaukee, Wis.: The Bruce Publishing Co., 1950).

PORTERFIELD, AUSTIN L., *Youth in Trouble: Studies in Delinquency and Despair* (Fort Worth, Texas: The Leo Potishman Foundation, 1946).

RECKLESS, WALTER C., *The Crime Problem* (New York: Appleton-Century-Crofts, Inc., 1950).

RECKLESS, WALTER C., AND MAPHEUS SMITH, *Juvenile Delinquency* (New York: McGraw-Hill Book Co., Inc., 1932).

SELLIN, JOHAN T., *The Criminality of Youth* (Philadelphia: American Law Institute, 1940).

SHAW, CLIFFORD R., AND HENRY D. McKAY, *Juvenile Delinquency in Urban Areas* (Chicago: University of Chicago Press, 1942).

SUSSMANN, FREDERICK B., *Law of Juvenile Delinquency: The Laws of the Forty-eight States* (New York: Oceana Publications, Legal Almanac Series No. 2, 1951).

SUTHERLAND, EDWIN H., *Principles of Criminology* (New York: J. B. Lippincott Co., 1947).

TAFT, DONALD R., *Criminology: An Attempt at a Synthetic Interpretation with a Cultural Emphasis* (New York: The Macmillan Co., 1942 and 1950).

TAPPAN, PAUL W., *Juvenile Delinquency* (New York: McGraw-Hill Book Co., Inc., 1949).

TEETERS, NEGLEY K., AND JOHN O. REINEMANN, *The Challenge of Delinquency* (New York: Prentice-Hall, Inc., 1950).

THURSTON, HENRY W., *Concerning Juvenile Delinquency* (New York: Columbia University Press, 1942).

VEDDER, CLYDE B., *The Juvenile Offender* (Garden City, N. Y.: Doubleday and Co., Inc., 1954).

VEDDER, CLYDE B., SAMUEL KOENIG, AND ROBERT E. CLARK, *Criminology: A Book of Readings* (New York: The Dryden Press, 1953).

VON HENTIG, HANS, *Crime: Causes and Conditions* (New York: McGraw-Hill Book Co., 1947).

WOOD, ARTHUR E., AND JOHN B. WAITE, *Crime and Its Treatment* (New York: American Book Co., 1941).

YOUNG, PAULINE V., *Social Treatment in Probation and Delinquency: Treatise and Casebook* (New York: McGraw-Hill Book Co., 1937 and 1952).

Periodicals in which articles on juvenile delinquency, adult crime, and behavior problems have appeared in considerable quantity or periodically:

American Journal of Orthopsychiatry: A Journal of Human Behavior. Official publication of the American Orthopsychiatry Association.

American Journal of Psychiatry. Official organ of the American Psychiatric Association.

American Journal of Sociology. The University of Chicago Press.

American Sociological Review. Official organ of the American Sociological Society.

Annals of the American Academy of Political and Social Science.

British Journal of Delinquency. Official organ of the Institute for the Study and Treatment of Delinquency.

Children (formerly *The Child*). United States Children's Bureau.

Federal Probation: A Journal of Correctional Philosophy and Practice. Published by the Administrative Office of the United States Courts.

Focus (formerly *Probation*). Published by the National Probation and Parole Association.

Journal of Criminal Law, Criminology, and Police Science (formerly *Journal of Criminal Law and Criminology*). Northwestern University School of Law.

Journal of Social Hygiene. American Social Hygiene Association.

Journal of Criminal Psychopathology. Medical Journal, Monticello, New York.

Mental Hygiene. National Committee on Mental Hygiene.

Social Forces: A Scientific Medium of Social Study and Interpretation. The Williams and Wilkins Company.

Social Service Review. School of Social Service Administration. University of Chicago Press.

Sociology and Social Research: An International Journal. University of Southern California Press.

For extended topical bibliographies of periodical literature on crime and delinquency, with addresses of publishing headquarters, see: *International Review of Criminal Policy,* Department of Social Affairs, United Nations, New York. The first issue (No. 1) was published January, 1952

II

EXTENT AND DISTRIBUTION OF JUVENILE DELINQUENCY

It is the purpose of the present chapter to indicate the sources of numerical data, to point out some of the inadequacies of the present national data, and to present the best available statistics on delinquency in the United States. An analysis of the composition of the delinquency population throws light upon its distribution in so far as age, sex, race, and nationality factors are concerned. The ecological distribution reveals rural-urban and regional differences in rates, the patterns of distribution in cities, and the effects of community conditions on variations in rates. In Chapter III, the general trends of delinquency, particularly as these are affected by economic and wartime conditions, will be considered.

Delinquency is not a recent problem, but the problem has become more serious during the last fifteen years as evidenced by the increases in totals and rates since the depression years of the early 1930's. An unusual increase of delinquency occurred during World War II, and there has been an increase again since about 1948. The

sudden increase of delinquency during wartime has led to the conclusion that war conditions provide an unusual stimulus to law violation. This is not altogether a satisfactory explanation, for the rate
of delinquency was on the increase before war began, because of
entirely different conditions, and the rate is likely to stay fairly high
during the postwar period.

NUMERICAL DATA REGARDING JUVENILE OFFENDERS

The sources and types of numerical data need to be carefully
scrutinized before considering the extent of delinquency. The inadequacies of statistics of the total number of cases of delinquency
during a year or over a longer period of time must be recognized.
There is no over-all agency to compile comprehensive, nation-wide
statistics. Hence, complete data on the extent of delinquency are
not available; but several government bureaus collect data of certain types of cases that include a relatively large portion of the cases
handled by law enforcing agencies. The statisticians of these agencies are aware of the incompleteness of the data and state so in their
reports. It should be added that considerable progress has been
made during the past two or three decades in compiling information
on the subject. Some attempts have been made to integrate the
available data.

Sources of Statistical Data. The Federal Bureau of Investigation
(FBI), United States Department of Justice, publishes the *Uniform
Crime Reports,* annually and semiannually. They are chiefly summary reports of "offenses known to the police." Since the reporting
is on a voluntary basis, it is difficult to obtain universal coverage.
Besides, not all jurisdictions have reported fully on juvenile cases.
Statistical data indicating the age, sex, race of persons arrested for
the years up through 1951 were drawn from the only source available, the fingerprint arrest records received by the Identification
Division of the FBI. Beginning in 1952, however, these data were
made available from an entirely different and much more complete
source. The data now are obtained by means of the age, sex, and
race summary arrest reports forwarded by the police departments
throughout the country. Although it was the first year during which
the new type of reports were used, it was possible to prepare the
summary data presented in the Annual Bulletin of the *Uniform
Crime Reports* for 1952 (Vol. XXIII, No. 2, 1953. See pp. 110-112
for description of the new method of reporting.) The data were
derived from reports received from 232 cities with population in

excess of 25,000. The 1953 figures are for arrests in 1,174 cities, the reporting area covers about 42 per cent of the city population (Vol. XXIV, No. 2, 1954, pp. 108-114). Since the summary data were compiled from a new source of information, they cannot be compared with similar data drawn from fingerprint records as presented in prior issues of the *Uniform Crime Reports*.

The data regarding adult arrests have been more extensive and represent a more complete coverage than the statistics pertaining to juveniles. While great progress has been made in obtaining more complete data, it must be recognized that changes in police practices regarding fingerprinting and other variables affect the number of arrests reported. Furthermore, it is difficult to interpret the data against the background of changes in population.

The United States Children's Bureau has collected summary reports from juvenile courts since 1927. During recent years the reports have included both official and unofficial cases disposed of by the juvenile courts reporting, as submitted by state and local agencies interested in forwarding these statistics to the Bureau. For official cases, the reports have included information regarding age and sex composition, types of detention care, and disposition of cases. The Bureau has also collected data from state agencies on the number of children in detention and correction institutions. Both series of reports have been on the voluntary basis and not all states or all jurisdictions in the states have submitted reports. The data have been reported in *Statistical Series* (special issues dealing with juvenile court statistics), in issues of *Children* (formerly *The Child*), published six times annually, and in other publications. In 1952, the Advisory Committee on Juvenile Delinquency Statistics recommended that the Children's Bureau request annually from state agencies only the minimum amount of data needed to indicate national trends in the volumes of cases disposed of by the juvenile courts. Beginning with this first report, the annual report is to be limited to a count of the number of children's cases disposed of officially and unofficially by courts during the calendar year according to the types of cases (delinquency, dependency and neglect, and special proceedings). Official cases involve the filing of petitions for formal judicial hearing. The unofficial cases are handled without the filing of petitions for formal court hearing.

It is difficult to obtain juvenile court statistics that constitute a completely representative sample of all courts in terms of geographic areas and of the distribution of rural-urban population. Administrative practices of law enforcement agencies tend to influence the number of cases disposed of and reported. Variations by states in the

matter of legal definitions, detection, and apprehension, age jurisdiction of the courts, the facilities and personnel of the courts, and
the extent to which courts use other law enforcement or youth serving agencies in dealing with cases affect the statistics of the volume
of cases handled.

Prior to 1927, the only available data of significance were those
pertaining to commitments to penal and correctional institutions,
and occasional reports of the population in these institutions on
specific dates. The statistics of offenders were not clearly separated
from the general statistics of the total number of cases handled.
Since then, considerable progress has been made in gathering data.
From 1927 to 1945 the Children's Bureau reports increased the coverage from 15 to 37 per cent of the population. Beginning with
data for 1946, the Bureau has endeavored to obtain summary reports
from states, which include a tabulation of all children's cases (delinquency and dependency or neglect or special proceedings) disposed
of officially or unofficially, and an unduplicated count of the number
of children involved in the total volume of cases disposed of during
the year. Only those courts that have been reporting on both official
and unofficial cases are included in the tabulations.

Juvenile court cases include only the cases disposed of by the reporting courts, which is not a complete index of the total volume
of delinquency. Many cases are handled by police, sheriff and school
authorities, or by social agencies in the community, and are not referred to courts. Then, too, not all cases are apprehended. On the
other hand, cases dealt with may include not only the more serious
offenses but different kinds of alleged delinquents. Because of these
and other limitations, the statistics are only partially complete and
may be misleading.

Several other federal agencies give reports of special types of
cases. The Federal Bureau of Prisons obtains statistics on all juveniles charged with violations of federal statutes from arresting agencies, United States Probation officers, and United States marshals.
The data show by judicial district the child's age, sex, race, the offense, type of detention, length of sentence if committed or other
types of disposition. For juveniles committed to the custody of the
Attorney General and to federal institutions, the Bureau of Prisons
collects also from the receiving institutions detailed social data including the age, sex, race, intelligence quotient, previous delinquency record, religious background, and education. The statistics
on federal juvenile offenders are published in *Federal Prisons*, the
annual report of the Bureau of Prisons. The Administrative Office
of the United States Courts collects data from the United States

courts on all juveniles charged with violating federal statutes who
elect to be tried under the Federal Juvenile Delinquency Act and
whose cases have not been referred to state or local authorities. The
data are included in the *Annual Report of the Director of the Administrative Office of the United States Courts.* The Office of Education collects information on public and private residential schools
for delinquents. The data include the type of administrative control, the number of officers and teachers, the number of pupils enrolled, and the number in attendance by race. The reports are
published in *Statistics of Children in Special Schools and Classes
for Exceptional Children.*

It is apparent from these reports that each agency collects data
for a specific purpose, using the definitions and procedures most
appropriate for that purpose. Because of the different programs of
each agency, the definitions and procedures developed for each series
are not standardized for all series. Furthermore, no individual series
represents completely accurate statistics of the extent of delinquency.
An interagency committee has been at work for some time to integrate these statistics and strengthen and improve each individual
series. The Children's Bureau has established a Juvenile Delinquency Branch in its Division of Social Services, designed chiefly to
better facilities for the prevention and treatment of juvenile delinquency. These efforts point toward improved statistics of delinquency and more effective prevention programs.

The Volume of Delinquency. In view of the incompleteness of
the statistical data, it is desirable to be cautious in arriving at estimates of the extent, increases and decreases, and other numerical
changes in the volume of delinquency. Students should learn to
analyze all reports objectively, recognizing the limitations of the
sources of the data. Nevertheless, the available reports of adult
crime and juvenile delinquency may be used to indicate the approximate extent of the problem of law violation.

The Federal Bureau of Investigation reported [1] an estimated
total of 2,159,080 serious offenses during 1953. This was an increase
of 6.0 per cent over the 1952 figure, and the 1952 total of 2,036,510
crimes committed was 8.2 per cent over the 1951 figure. In 1953,

1 *Uniform Crime Reports,* Annual Bulletin, Vol. XXIV, No. 2, 1953 (Washington,
D. C.: United States Government Printing Office, 1954). In publishing the data sent
in by chiefs of police in different cities and by other law enforcement officers, the FBI
is cautious in stating that it does not vouch for their accuracy. They are given out
as current information, which may throw some light on problems of crime and criminal-
law enforcement.

urban crime rose 4.5 per cent and rural crime rose 9.6 per cent. A total of 5728 law enforcement agencies forwarded one or more crime reports in 1953 under the uniform crime reporting program.

On the basis of the state-local reports submitted to the Children's Bureau,[2] it is estimated that a total of 435,000 juvenile delinquency cases were handled by juvenile courts during 1953, representing an increase of from 45 to 50 per cent between 1948 and 1953, whereas the number of children, 10 to 17 years old, increased no more than 7 per cent during the five-year period. Approximately 2 per cent of all children in this age bracket are dealt with, officially or unofficially, by juvenile courts across the country during a given year.

The report for 1952 indicates that approximately 385,000 children were brought to the attention of juvenile courts for delinquency behavior during the year, representing an increase of 35,000 cases over 1951. The number of courts sending in complete reports is increasing: in 1951, 459 courts sent in complete reports; and in 1952, 586 courts reported. About 200 juvenile courts have sent in complete reports regularly for a number of years. In 1952, three fourths of all juvenile court cases were delinquency cases, and more than half of all juvenile court cases were handled unofficially.

A much larger number of cases, perhaps a million or so, come to the attention of police and other law enforcement agencies on account of misbehavior. In 1951, when the juvenile courts handled 350,000 cases of delinquents, about 250,000 of them were referred to the courts by the law enforcement agencies. The remaining 100,-000 who were referred to juvenile courts came from schools, social agencies, parents, and other sources. Of the children brought to juvenile courts, about a third are held overnight or longer in detention facilities, police houses, or jails. About half of the total cases are dismissed, adjusted, or held open without further action by the courts. Of the remaining juveniles, over 95,000 are placed on probation annually, about 40,000 are committed to training institutions designed primarily for the rehabilitation of delinquents, and the rest are referred to various types of agencies or handled in other ways.

The trends in the volume of delinquency will be discussed in the following chapter. The recent increases in the number of juvenile

2 Cf. *News Notes on Juvenile Delinquency* (Children's Bureau, United States Department of Health, Education, and Welfare, May 10, 1954. For more comprehensive detail statistics for the years 1950-1952, especially 1952, see: *Juvenile Court Statistics, 1950-1952,* Children's Bureau Statistical Series No. 18, 1954. Compare *News Notes on Juvenile Delinquency,* October 13, 1953; *Some Facts About Juvenile Delinquency* (pamphlet), Publication No. 340, 1953; and "A Few Facts about Juvenile Delinquency," *The Child,* Vol. 17, No. 4 (December, 1952), 63-64.

court cases indicate the seriousness of the problem.[3] These increases have been especially noticeable in certain urban areas. The problem is acute in towns as well as larger cities. There is also an increase in seriousness of acts committed by boys and girls. The number of persons under 18 years of age involved in such offenses as burglaries, robberies, and automobile thefts has increased considerably since 1948.

As was pointed out earlier, juvenile court cases constitute only a part of the total cases handled by law enforcement and other agencies, and the total number of delinquents known to courts and other law enforcement agencies is only a fraction of delinquents. On the other hand, some of the cases handled by law enforcement agencies are not seriously delinquent, as is evidenced by the fact that many cases are dismissed and adjusted without using correctional facilities. The total number of juvenile courts in the United States has been variously estimated at from 2500 to 3000; possibly only a few hundred of these are juvenile courts in the full sense. In many of the smaller counties criminal courts may function also as juvenile courts. If the children brought to courts are to receive the minimum of assistance, these courts need sufficient probation service for the study of each child's background and for guiding those children that the courts place on probation. At least one half of the counties in the United States are without probation service for juvenile delinquents, according to the Children's Bureau, and the number of detention homes is only 174. Furthermore, a study of 177 cities, each with a population of more than 20,000, revealed that more than one third of them do not have special provision in their police departments for work with children.[4]

The volume of delinquency must be correlated with the juvenile population in order to ascertain the rate of law violation. Comparative studies over a period of time are not very meaningful unless the rates of delinquency are used for comparative purposes. Both the

---

3 Compare *Juvenile Court Statistics, 1950-1952* (published May 10, 1954) with *Juvenile Court Statistics, 1946-1949* (Statistical Series, No. 8, 1951). While no comparative statistics coming from the same courts are given, the report for 1952 indicates that 586 courts reported a total of 139,358 cases of delinquency (53,263 official and 70,427 unofficial cases). For a national survey of the problem of delinquency, see: *Juvenile Delinquency*, Interim Report of the Committee on the Judiciary, United States Senate, Eighty-Third Congress, Second Session (United States Printing Office, 1954). According to the Committee's estimate, "if the rate of juvenile delinquency continues to mount at the rate experienced during the past five years, the number of boys and girls going through juvenile courts will skyrocket to some 750,000 by that date." (p. 7.) This would include dependency and neglect, and special proceedings cases. By 1960, the child population 10-17 years of age will be about 40 per cent higher than it was in 1952, which will account for part of the anticipated increase in delinquency cases.

4 Cf. *The Child, op. cit.,* 64.

volume and the rate of delinquency have fluctuated, but the general trend during the past two decades has been an increase of the problem. However, these estimates are only partially accurate, owing to inadequate coverage and to other inadequacies of numerical data. The trends in juvenile delinquency will be indicated in the succeeding chapter.

Composition of the Delinquent Population

The analysis of the composition of the delinquent population shows variations as to age, sex, race, or nativity distributions in rates of delinquencies.

Age and Sex Factors. Age and sex factors are significant elements in juvenile delinquency. It is important to note whether there is a greater concentration of cases within certain age groups and what differences exist in sex ratios.

According to the cases of delinquency disposed of by 458 juvenile courts in 1951, the median age of the boys was 16.1, and of the girls it was 15.6. The following table indicates the age distribution of boys and girls when referred to court, including both official and unofficial cases. The statistics indicate that nearly eight out of ten

TABLE I. Juvenile Delinquency Cases, 1951: Ages of Boys and Girls When Referred to Court, in Cases Disposed of by 458 Courts.

Age of Child When Referred to Court	Juvenile Delinquency Cases									
	Number					Per Cent				
		Official		Unofficial			Official		Unofficial	
	Total	Boys	Girls	Boys	Girls	Total	Boys	Girls	Boys	Girls
Total cases..	100,360	35,301	7,818	46,886	10,355	—	—	—	—	—
Age reported......	83,430	27,528	6,034	41,205	8,663	100	100	100	100	100
Under 10 years..	2,474	538	74	1,633	229	3	2	1	4	3
10 years, under 12.	4,221	1,243	135	2,557	286	5	5	2	6	3
12 years, under 14.	10,260	3,086	736	5,212	1,226	12	11	12	13	14
14 years, under 16.	24,385	8,037	2,559	10,518	3,271	29	29	43	25	38
16 years, under 18.	36,977	13,065	2,220	18,554	3,138	45	47	37	45	36
18 years and over .	5,113	1,559	310	2,731	513	6	6	5	7	6
Age not reported..	16,930	7,773	1,784	5,681	1,692	—	—	—	—	—

Source: *Juvenile Court Statistics, 1950-1952*, Children's Bureau Statistical Series, No. 18, 1954. Compare *Juvenile Court Statistics, 1946-1949*, Statistical Series, No. 8, 1951. Official cases involve the filing of petitions for formal judicial hearing; unofficial cases are handled more informally.

delinquents were 14 years of age or over when referred to juvenile courts. The girls were slightly younger than the boys. It must be remembered that the age jurisdiction is established by state laws, which must be taken into consideration in interpretating the age distribution of cases under the jurisdiction of juvenile courts.

The Federal Bureau of Investigation (*Uniform Crime Reports*) has been analyzing the distribution of persons arrested, by age and sex; but since there is some variation in the number of cities reporting over a period of time and in the extent of reporting, it is difficult to make valid comparisons. However, the following table

TABLE II. NUMBER AND PERCENTAGE OF PERSONS ARRESTED
UNDER 21 AND 18 YEARS OF AGE, 1945-1951

Year	Under 21 Number of Arrests	Percentage of Total Arrests	Under 18 Number of Arrests	Percentage of Total Arrests
1945	113,996	21.0	49,566	9.1
1946	108,787	16.9	37,833	5.9
1947	117,861	16.1	34,376	4.7
1948	115,940	15.3	31,750	4.2
1949	117,562	14.8	32,922	4.2
1950	118,426	14.9	34,599	4.4
1951	119,676	14.4	37,259	4.5

SOURCE: *Uniform Crime Reports*, Vols. XVI-XXII (Washington, D. C.: United States Government Printing Office, 1946-1952). Since the data for 1952 and 1953 came from entirely different and much more complete sources than the data for the previous years, they are not comparable with previous reports, but represent the beginning of a new series. The arrest data by age groups for 1953 came from 1,174 cities over 2500 in population, involving a total of 1,791,160 arrests. Of these, 149,806 were under 18, and 113,594 were 18, 19, and 20 years of age. For 1952, reports were tabulated for 232 cities over 25,000 in population; but the data revealed that of the total of 1,110,675 arrests in these cities, 86,128 were under 18, and 61,504 were in the age bracket 18-20.

indicates in a general way the approximate extent of cases reported by these cities. The predominance of arrests by age groups during the same period indicates considerable fluctuation during the postwar periods, as Table III shows.

Sheldon and Eleanor Glueck,[5] in their study of 500 delinquents

5 Cf. *Unraveling Juvenile Delinquency* (New York: The Commonwealth Fund, 1950), 13, 27-28, 149, 154, 285, 293-294. In their earlier study (*One Thousand Delinquents*, 1939), the Gluecks found that the mean age of boys examined at the Judge Baker Foundation in Boston was 13 years and 5 months, and the time of their first delinquency was 9 years and 7 months. William Healy and Agusta F. Bronner (*Delinquents and Criminals: Their Making and Unmaking*, 1926, and *New Light on Delinquency and Its Treatment*, 1936), on the basis of the cases examined in New Haven and Detroit, as well as at the Judge Baker Foundation, found the modal age of delinquency

TABLE III. PREDOMINANCE OF ARRESTS BY AGE GROUPS, 1945-1951

Rank	1945	1946	1947	1948	1949	1950	1951
1.	17	21	21	21	21	21	23
2.	18	22	22	22	22	22	22
3.	21	23	23	23	23	23	21
4.	22	24	20	24	24	24	24
5.	19	20	24	20	20	25	26

SOURCE: Same as for Table II. Data for 1952 and 1953 are omitted since they were collected from different sources and are not comparable with the statistics of the earlier period.

and 500 nondelinquents, found that the average age at onset of misbehavior was 8.35 years and of first school misbehavior it was 9.5 years (for nondelinquents it was 12.54 years). The average age of their first court appearance proved to be 12.4 and of their first conviction, 12.5 years. The average age of their first probation was 12.7 years and commitment to correctional school, 13.9 years.

The dependency and neglect cases referred to juvenile courts are younger than the delinquents handled by these courts. In 1951, the 458 courts that submitted reports to the Children's Bureau reported 31,435 cases of dependency and neglect. Of the 24,435 cases for which the ages were reported, 46 per cent were under 6 years of age, and 23 per cent were 6 to 10 years old at the time of referral. The age distribution of the official and unofficial cases, also boys' and girls' cases, has been about the same over a period of time.

The sex distribution of delinquency cases varies a great deal from time to time, especially court cases as compared with juvenile arrests by the police. Edward E. Schwartz has indicated (see Table IV) the distribution of boys and girls cases from 1938 to 1947, which shows the wartime fluctuation in ratios, especially of arrests.

In 1948, the Children's Bureau started another series, using reports from more courts; and, as has already been indicated, the *Uniform Crime Reports* for 1952 and 1953 contain age and sex data which came from entirely different and much more complete sources than the data for the previous years. Hence, statistics of recent years

---

to be between 12 and 14 years. Walter C. Reckless (*Criminal Behavior,* 1940) maintains that the age curve of crime rises abruptly through adolescence, reaches a peak in young manhood (between 19 and 24 years), and declines with maturity. The Gluecks (*Juvenile Delinquents Grown Up,* 1940), 264-266, in a subsequent checkup of the 1000 cases studied, found that by the age of 29 almost 40 per cent had ceased to be offenders, and even among those who continued to commit crime, the proportion of serious offenses dropped from 75.6 per cent to 47.8 per cent during a fifteen-year period. They present the theory of maturation as the chief explanation of the decline in offenses, which theory will be examined further in Chapter V.

TABLE IV. BOYS' AND GIRLS' DELINQUENCY CASES DISPOSED OF BY
76 URBAN JUVENILE COURTS AND ALL FINGERPRINT RECORDS
RECEIVED BY THE FEDERAL BUREAU OF INVESTIGATION OF
BOYS AND GIRLS UNDER 18 YEARS OF AGE
ARRESTED BY THE POLICE, 1938-1947

	Police Arrests			Juvenile Court Cases		
	Number		Ratio of Girls' to Boys' Cases	Number		Ratio of Girls' to Boys' Cases
Year	Boys	Girls		Boys	Girls	
1938	33,907	1,897	1:18	42,500	7,951	1:5
1939	36,097	1,946	1:19	46,379	7,926	1:6
1940	33,111	2,221	1:15	43,687	8,591	1:5
1941	34,408	2,662	1:13	46,883	9,927	1:5
1942	33,746	4,176	1:8	49,814	12,042	1:4
1943	41,643	6,241	1:7	67,311	15,568	1:4
1944	40,892	5,798	1:7	65,780	14,936	1:4
1945	44,667	4,899	1:9	70,522	14,172	1:5
1946	34,393	3,440	1:10	60,722	12,726	1:5
1947	31,306	3,070	1:10	51,067	11,844	1:4

Cf. "Statistics of Juvenile Delinquency in the United States," *The Annals of The American Academy of Political and Social Science,* Vol. 261 (January, 1949), 9-20.

cannot be compared with similar data published earlier. Recognizing the differences in the sources of data, the reports show that the sex ratios of both arrest and court cases have remained fairly constant during the postwar period. The *Uniform Crime Reports* since 1947 indicate a fairly consistent ratio of 10 males to 1 female arrested by police and other law enforcement agencies. The new series of court cases, as reported to the Children's Bureau, indicates that the ratio of boys' to girls' cases was 4 to 1 from 1948 to 1951, and 5 to 1 during 1952.

The proportion of arrests of boys to girls has been consistently higher than the proportion of boys to girls who are filed on in juvenile courts. These ratios, however, may not be a true index of the differential in behavior patterns, for police practices and referral procedures account for part of the difference. It is a well-known fact that male police officers are often more reluctant to arrest girls than boys, except for the more serious types of offenses. And it should be noted also that proportionately a larger number of girls' than of boys' cases are referred to courts by nonpolice sources. In correctional institutions the ratio of boys to girls sometimes is 2 to 1, which indicates that courts in these areas institutionalize a relatively large proportion of the girls' cases disposed of by the courts.

There is a considerable variation in distribution of both juvenile delinquents and adult offenders by types of offenses. Except for cases of prostitution and commercialized vice, male arrests outnumbered female arrests in all types of offenses listed by FBI for 1953. However, females were arrested fairly extensively for drunkenness, larceny (theft), vagrancy, assault, disorderly conduct, and suspicion. Boys are more frequently referred to courts on the grounds of stealing, acts of carelessness or mischief, traffic violations, and injuries to persons than are girls; whereas girls seem to have relatively high rates of truancy, running away, being ungovernable, and sex offenses, as the following table shows.

TABLE V. JUVENILE DELINQUENCY CASES, 1945: REASONS FOR REFERENCE TO COURT, IN BOYS' AND IN GIRLS' CASES DISPOSED OF BY 374 COURTS

Reason for Reference to Court	Juvenile Delinquency Cases					
	Number			Per Cent		
	Total	Boys	Girls	Total	Boys	Girls
Total cases	122,851	101,240	21,611	...	...	...
Reason for Reference Reported	111,939	92,671	19,268	100	100	100
Stealing	40,879	38,610	2,269	37	42	12
Act of carelessness or mischief	19,241	17,779	1,462	17	19	8
Traffic violation...	9,852	9,659	193	9	10	1
Truancy	8,681	6,164	2,517	8	7	13
Running away ...	9,307	5,652	3,655	8	6	19
Being ungovernable	9,840	5,542	4,298	9	6	22
Sex offenses	5,990	2,579	3,411	5	3	18
Injury to person..	3,224	2,828	396	3	3	2
Other reason	4,925	3,858	1,067	4	4	5
Reason for reference not reported	10,912	8,569	2,343	...	...	...

SOURCE: *Social Statistics, loc. cit.* Used by permission of United States Children's Bureau. No later data are available, because this item was discontinued from the reporting plan after 1945.

There is no adequate way of ascertaining fluctuations of rates by age and sex over a period of time, but the fact that the adolescent and young adult age periods predominate in arrest and court cases and that males have consistently a higher rate of crime than females poses certain problems. These will be discussed in Chapter IV in connection with a consideration of age and sex as possible factors in law violations.

Race and Nationality. The problem of race and nationality as factors conditioning delinquency will be discussed later, but the distribution of the extent of law violation among the different racial and nationality groups will be considered here. Statistics of the racial composition of inmates in prisons and in correctional institutions do not give a true index of the differential rates of crime, for members of minority groups are likely to be institutionalized, proportionally, more extensively than members of the majority group. This may be because of the lack of other facilities of treatment for them as well as race discrimination in the disposition of cases, not to mention the differences in environmental influences in shaping the conduct of racial groups.

The *Uniform Crime Reports* [6] indicate that nearly 98 per cent of the fingerprints examined during 1953 to determine the racial composition were of the white and Negro races, and only 2.2 per cent represented Indians, Chinese, Japanese, and all other races. These percentages (and total statistics) are more meaningful if we compare them with the racial composition of the population in the United States for 1950 (Bureau of the Census, series PB-1, Table 36). For instance, in 1953, 26.9 per cent of those arrested in urban areas were Negroes, whereas only 9.9 per cent of the total population in 1950 were classified as Negroes. Since there were only 713,047 nonwhites (excluding Negroes), or about .5 per cent of the total population, and these had 2.2 per cent of the crime records, the percentage of criminality among them is higher than the proportion of people in this group, but this is chiefly because of the relatively high rate of delinquency and crime among Indians. The Japanese and Chinese have low criminal rates. The whites, constituting slightly under 90 per cent of the population, committed 70.9 per cent of the crimes.

The figures compiled for 1947 by the Children's Bureau show that 32 per cent of the reported children in public institutions for delinquents were nonwhite (predominantly Negro). It was estimated that 21 per cent of court delinquency cases were nonwhite, whereas less than 13 per cent of the United States child population

---

6 Annual Bulletin, Vol. XXIV, No. 2 (1954), 114. Of the 1,791,160 arrests by race in 1,174 cities over 2,500 population, 1,270,466 were whites, 481,095 were Negroes, 32,084 were Indians, 407 were Chinese, only 144 were Japanese, and 6,964 all others.

was nonwhite. Edward E. Schwartz, in analyzing these statistics, proceeds to explain that the relatively high institutionalized nonwhite cases are partly due to the inadequacy or absence of alternate facilities for this group, especially for the Negro children.[7]

Local studies of the racial and nationality composition of the delinquency population are somewhat limited and conditioned by the degree of ethnic heterogeneity and relations. Houston, Texas, may be used as an example of the ethnic distribution of delinquency in a southern city, for it has large Negro and Latin-American groups, although it has a relatively low percentage of foreign-born people, as compared with other cities.[8] This study shows that Negroes have a higher rate of delinquency than whites for the city as a whole. Of the 4,287 cases of delinquent children tabulated, 1,115 were classed as Latin-Americans. However, in using the 1940 census in computing the rates of delinquency by census tracts (10 to 16 years for the boys and 10 to 17 years for the girls), it was found that there was a great variation in rates by census tracts. In the four census tracts in which the Negro group constituted over 90 per cent of the total population, the delinquency rate was 21.8, whereas in 30 tracts in which Negroes constituted less than 10 per cent of the total, the rate was 49.7, or more than twice the rate in the four tracts in which most of the population was Negro.

The Baltimore study [9] included an analysis of delinquency rates for Negroes and whites, covering a four-year period (1939 to 1942). The mean annual tract delinquency rates per 1,000 population of the ages of 6 to 17 for unduplicated count of juvenile court cases was 10.6. On the comparative basis, the differential rates were: Negro boys, 43.8; white boys, 13.0 (ratio of about 4 to 1); Negro girls, 10.0; and white girls, 1.86 (ratio of about 5 to 1). A variation of differential rates by Census tracts was observed. The preponderance (88 per cent) of both white and Negro alleged delinquents lived within a radius of three miles from the city center. Differential juvenile delinquency rates were tabulated by areas and correlations were made between delinquency rates and such variables as housing and other socio-economic conditions, population composition, and related factors. Although the Negro children comprised

---

[7] *The Annals, op. cit.,* 17.

[8] See *Social Statistics: The Houston Delinquent in His Community,* Bureau of Research, Council of Social Agencies, Houston, Texas, Vol. II, No. 1 (June, 1945).

[9] Cf. Bernard Lander, *Towards an Understanding of Juvenile Delinquency.* A Study of 8,464 Cases of Juvenile Delinquency in Baltimore (New York: Columbia University Press, 1954), Chapter III. Compare Earl R. Moses, "Differentials in Crime Rates between Negroes and Whites, Based on Comparisons of Four Socio-Economically Equated Areas," *American Sociological Review,* Vol. XII (August, 1947), 411-420.

49 per cent of Baltimore's delinquents and only 20 per cent of the juvenile group in the general population, this study revealed that as the Negro population proportion increased beyond 50 per cent, the delinquency rate among them decreased, with the areas of 90 per cent or more Negro population concentration being characterized by the lowest delinquency rates. In other words, the most solidly populated Negro areas had the lowest Negro delinquency rates, which suggested a positive correlation between the percentage of Negroes in an area and the Negro delinquency rate.

It must be recognized that this type of equating objective data does not take into account subjective aspects. While the equating of areas by delineating socio-economic and other variables is an advance over other types of studies, more detailed comparisons are needed to give more complete explanations of the differences in delinquency rates between the predominantly Negro and the predominantly white areas. Also, comparative studies need to be made of southern and northern communities, and between stabilized and mobile areas. Attention should also be given to the age composition of ethnic groups, for variations in proportions of juveniles in the various groups may affect the delinquency rates.

As will be indicated in Chapter IX, interpretations of the data regarding the distribution of delinquency among racial and nativity groups need to be made carefully. The fact that Negro children, also those of Latin-American origin, seem to have higher rates of delinquency than whites (chiefly Anglo-Saxon) does not indicate that the tendency to crime is a matter of race or nationality. However, economic status, cultural inferiority, racial discrimination, and many other factors play an important part. Furthermore, there is a difference between the factors of race and culture in relation to delinquency. With respect to race, the elements of color and physical differences are significant. With respect to nativity, the country of origin and the culture of the group play a dominant part. Then, too, there are differences between the foreign born and the descendants of foreign born, whether born of foreign or mixed parents. The second and third generations of foreign born often experience cultural conflicts between the old and the new cultures, which tend to have disorganizing effects.

ECOLOGICAL DISTRIBUTION OF DELINQUENCY

One of the most outstanding characteristics of delinquency is its ecological distribution. This manifests itself chiefly in the differences between rural and urban rates and the phenomena of concentration and scatter in the various urban areas. By human or social ecology is meant the study of the spatial and temporal relations of social phenomena, especially in relation to the physical (geographic) setting. The usual procedure is to plot the distribution of cases of a city or county on a map (covering a specific period of time) to discover the sections in which concentrations have occurred, also the areas in which few cases have occurred. Having ascertained the patterns of concentration and scatter, the relative rates of delinquency can be obtained by correlating the number of delinquents living in a section with the population, especially the corresponding juvenile population, of the section. The rates of delinquency by areas may be further correlated with such conditions as housing, health and sanitation, general physical environmental factors, population composition and cultural groups, and economic factors. In other words, having ascertained the focal points of delinquency, it is possible to study the conditions of these areas in contrast with the areas in which few delinquents are found. By making a series of such studies over a period of time, it is possible to indicate the temporal changes in rates. The rates of delinquency may be very high in the slum and blighted areas of a city, whereas in other areas the rates may fluctuate a great deal.

Rural and Urban Differences. The growth of cities in the United States has been rapid, but the process of urbanization is by no means uniform throughout the country. By 1950, the urban population was 96,467,686, or 64.0 per cent of the total population. Of the urban growth, the most phenomenal increases have occurred in the metropolitan areas. The 168 standard metropolitan areas, each with one central city of 50,000 or more and the urban fringe territory, had 84,500,680 inhabitants, or more than half of the population of Continental United States. The twelve most highly urbanized areas had a combined population of 37,817,068, or about one fourth of the total population. The New York-Northwestern New Jersey area alone accounted for 12,296,117 people.[10]

The *Uniform Crime Reports* show that the criminal elements of the population are more active and concentrated in cities, especially in large cities, than in rural communities. This is particularly true of offenses against property. Urban and rural rates of offenses against persons are somewhat similar. By comparing the major offenses known to police in 2450 cities (total population 76,094,589,

---

10 Cf. *Advance Reports: 1950 Census of Population,* Bureau of the Census, Department of Commerce, Series PC-9, No. 6, November 24, 1952; Series PC-9, No. 4, October 7, 1952; and PC-9, No. 3, June 9, 1952.

based on the 1950 decennial census) with offenses known to and reported by 1615 sheriffs, 154 rural village officers, and 11 state police (the total population 40,691,017, based on the 1950 decennial census), it is possible to get an idea of the difference between urban and rural law violations. Since the urban population of these cities was nearly twice the total population of the rural areas, the differential rates per 100,000 people for the different types of offenses are better comparative indices.

TABLE VI. COMPARISON OF MAJOR URBAN AND RURAL CRIMES, 1952

Offense	Number of Offenses and Rate per 100,000 Population			
	Urban		Rural	
	Total	Rate	Total	Rate
Murder and nonnegligent manslaughter	3,846	5.05	2,025	4.98
Manslaughter by negligence	2,579	3.39	2,277	5.60
Rape	8,760	11.51	4,632	11.38
Robbery	45,320	59.6	7,017	17.2
Aggravated assault	61,985	81.5	13,804	33.9
Burglary—breaking or entering	297,912	391.5	70,683	173.7
Larceny—theft	731,724	961.6	104,863	257.7
Auto theft	142,308	187.0	23,517	57.8

SOURCE: Adaptation of Table 33 and Table 37, *Uniform Crime Reports*, Vol. XXIII, No. 2, 1953, 92 and 96. The distribution of crimes by types of offenses was somewhat similar in 1953, except that the statistics were taken from fewer jurisdictions. But increases occurred in nearly all categories of crime from 1952 to 1953.

The urban crimes (total and rate) are given by groups of similar sized cities, and the rates are given for the various states and geographic regions. These statistics show that the larger the cities the higher the crime rates. Variations in rates occur in respect to the different types of crimes, also by regions and size of cities; but, in general, Sutherland's [11] contention that the number of serious crimes increases with the size of the community is borne out by the crime reports. In certain respects, the number of crimes decreases as the distance from the large city increases. The rural territory as well as the urban fringe surrounding a large city usually has a crime rate higher than a rural area farther removed from the immediate influences of the urban environment.

We do not have comparable statistics for rural and urban juve-

---

[11] Edwin H. Sutherland, *Principles of Criminology* (New York: J. B. Lippincott Co., 1947), 44-45, 135-138.

nile delinquency, but local studies all seem to indicate the same trend—namely, that delinquency increases with the size of the community. The proportion of children committed to correctional institutions increases with the density of the population, with higher percentages coming from cities than from rural areas. Although all investigations have shown rural delinquency to be less than urban delinquency per unit of population, it must be remembered that urban law enforcement and other agencies give more careful attention to law violations. In rural areas many offenses go unnoticed by official authorities, which, if they had occurred in cities, would have been handled by law enforcement agencies. The family, the church, the school, and the neighborhood still exercise considerable control over the conduct of youth in rural communities—more so than in cities. The small community, because of its primary group relationship, exercises more intimate and direct influence than do urban areas, where more secondary types of relationships exist.

As was pointed out earlier, our statistical information regarding juvenile offenders comes chiefly from reports sent to the United States Children's Bureau by juvenile courts and probation departments. Since most of the reporting agencies are in cities, the chief information comes from this source. Even if juvenile courts were more extensive in rural counties, and a greater effort were made to deal with cases of offenders officially, it is doubtful if this would materially increase the reported delinquency rate.

Patterns of Distribution of Delinquency in Cities. As Carr [12] puts it, two facts stand out in the literature of juvenile delinquency everywhere in the United States. Juvenile delinquency appears in a pattern of scatter and concentration in space; and everywhere in the United States it appears in a pattern of ups and downs through time. In so far as the city is concerned, most of the attention has been given to the matter of concentration, for the focal point of delinquency requires the greatest attention. The most outstanding ecological studies of delinquency have been made by Shaw and Mc-Kay. [13]

---

[12] Lowell J. Carr, *Delinquency Control* (New York: Harper & Brothers, 1950), Chapter III.

[13] Clifford R. Shaw and Henry D. McKay, *Juvenile Delinquency and Urban Areas.* A study of Rates of Delinquents in Relation to Differential Characteristics of Local Communities in American Cities (Chicago: University of Chicago Press, 1942); cf. "Social Factors in Juvenile Delinquency," *Report on The Causes of Crime,* National Commission on Law Observance and Enforcement, Vol. II, No. 13 (1931); and *Delinquency Areas* (Chicago: University of Chicago Press, 1929).

The distribution of juvenile delinquents in space and time follows the pattern of the physical structure and the degree of social organization of the city. As the city expands, the greatest physical deterioration and social disorganization occur around the central business zone, and the least deterioration exists at the outskirts. Consequently, the delinquency rate is the highest in the most disorganized sections and the lowest in the most normal areas. Except for factory areas, which may be located in any zone, the rate of delinquency diminishes in proportion to the distance away from the central business zone.

The procedure used by Shaw and McKay in Chicago, and in other cities for comparison, is, simply stated, as follows. The distribution of places of residence of alleged delinquents brought before the juvenile court was plotted on a map. This plotting revealed the conditions of concentration and scatter, but it did not give an accurate picture of the distribution in terms of population densities of the various areas. The rates of delinquents were then computed on the square-mile area basis, representing the number of alleged delinquents taken to the juvenile court from each area during a specified period per hundred of those aged 10 to 16 in the population. For three series of male delinquents, the rate for each area was computed in terms of the male population in the corresponding age bracket. In the Chicago study several series of cases were used for comparative purposes, and in each case the rates were computed in terms of 140-square-mile areas. In these series of cases, the rates varied from less than one in the outlying sections to nearly twenty in the worst areas, and in the earliest series a few square-mile areas near the Loop had rates close to thirty.

Following these studies, three other methods were employed to determine the extent of variation in rates of delinquents in the several time series: (1) comparisons by zones, (2) area comparisons and correlations, and (3) extent of concentration. Rates of delinquents were calculated for each of five zones drawn at 2-mile intervals, with a focal point in the heart of the central business zone; and concentric circles were used to indicate the five zones. The rates were computed on the basis of the number of delinquents, and the total aged 10-16 male population in each zone. Again, the rates for the different series varied considerably, ranging from 1.7 to 11.9, 2.2 to 11.3 and 1.7 to 17.6 in the three series of cases. Furthermore, the critical ratios of selected zone rates were ascertained to get the zone rates of committed delinquents.

The concentration of committed delinquents in each series was analyzed by ranking the areas by rate of committed delinquents, then dividing the aged 10-16 male population into four equal parts and computing the proportion of total committed delinquents and of city area for each population quartile. It was found that more than half of the committed delinquents in each of three series came from the quarter of the population living in areas of highest rates, although these constitute less than one fifth of the total city area. At the other extreme, the quarter of the population in lowest-rate areas produced 7.3 per cent of the committed delinquents in 1900-1906, 7.2 per cent in the 1917-23 series, and only 4.3 per cent during 1927-33.[14]

In the earlier reports, efforts were made to show the gradations between the high rates near the center of the city and the low rates near the periphery by means of radial lines drawn from the center to the periphery, like spokes of a wheel. It was noted that the rates, with the exception of the radial lines running through industrial zones, decreased in proportion to the distance from the center of the city.

Community Patterns of Distribution. The distribution of delinquency indicates the focal points of trouble, but it does not show why this is so. The study of the distribution of other social problems reveals a close correlation between conditions existing in local communities of cities and differential rates of delinquents and criminals. These community factors will be discussed in connection with conditioning factors (causes) of delinquency. Shaw and McKay spotted the distributions of such problems as school truancy, rates of young adult offenders, infant mortality rates, tuberculosis cases, rates of insanity; and they gave special attention to recidivism and commitments. The delinquency rates were then correlated with such community conditions as population increases and decreases, also composition, percentage of foreign born and of Negroes, percentage of families on relief, rentals and home ownership, and differences in social values. The "spirit of delinquency" was considered, as well as objective characteristics of delinquency areas.

As Ernest W. Burgess points out in the introduction,[15] juvenile delinquency is shown to be highly correlated with a number of presumably separate factors, including population changes, poor housing, poverty, proportion of foreign born and Negroes, health conditions, adult crime, and mental disorders. If there is a high correlation existing uniformly between two sets of variables, with a small probable error, it is possible and valid to consider either series as the approximate index of the other. This is significant

---

14 Clifford R. Shaw and Henry McKay, *Juvenile Delinquency and Urban Areas, op. cit.*, 77. Used by permission of The University of Chicago Press.
15 *Ibid.*, xi.

from the point of view of the analysis of causation, as we shall see later, but it is also important to note that a study of the ecological distributions of social problems in a city reveals the general pattern of concentration and scatter.

The fluctuations through time, whether long-time trends, short-time cycles, seasonal variations, or more or less accidental fluctuations, reflect the conditions of the time and the area. The patterns of distribution vary from time to time in the same community and from community to community during a period of time. Hence, it is exceedingly difficult to indicate the exact extent of delinquency of an area or of a period of time.

MEASURING THE VOLUME OF DELINQUENCY

In spite of the progress made in the study of juvenile delinquency, no adequate ways have been devised to measure the volume and trends of delinquency. The improved system of reporting juvenile court cases to the United States Children's Bureau should produce good results in years to come. The greatest progress seems to have been made in keeping more adequate records and devising new methods of recording cases on the local level.

Community-wide statistics on delinquency and problem cases can be obtained by collecting records of children known to all agencies concerned with these problems. The establishment of a central register by all agencies of children referred to them because of delinquency or related problems is the best means of getting more adequate objective data. The efforts in local areas to gather more complete data regarding juvenile delinquency are a valuable aid in effective organization of a county or community program of treatment, control, and prevention.

In 1942, Los Angeles County established a Central Juvenile Index, commonly known as the CJI, for the registration of cases handled by the law enforcement agencies. It is maintained by the Probation Department, with the cooperation of 45 police departments in the county, the Sheriff's Office, the California Highway Patrol, the California Youth Authority, and the attendance offices of the county schools. When a law enforcement agency arrests or handles a case of delinquency, a report is submitted to the Index. The data include such items of information as the name, address, names of parents or guardians, sex, age, school grade, problem charged and the subdivision of the law violated, previous report of arrests, previous petition filed, agency (police or other) that has made a disposition of the case, juvenile employment (if any), father's and mother's occupation, marital status of parents, and cultural group. Data can be tabulated on the basis of these items and by census tracts, political subdivisions, and department. Over a period of time, it is possible to indicate trends. Juvenile traffic cases are reported and tabulated separately, but this information can be correlated with the regular reports. When a juvenile whose case record has been reported to the Index reaches the age of 18, the card in the central file is removed.

The Central Juvenile Index is a confidential file for cooperating agencies. Each agency has a code number and can call the Index for information regarding a juvenile who has been apprehended of a delinquency in order to check with respect to previous offenses and other data.

An experiment in Washington, D. C., by the Council of Social Agencies of the District of Columbia, in cooperation with the United States Children's Bureau, for the period from June, 1943, through May, 1944, demonstrated what can be done when all types of cases of juvenile misconduct that might be dealt with under the law are reported to a central register by all agencies dealing with such cases. Although the period of operation was too short for adequate conclusions regarding the volume and trends in delinquency, the counts of the total registration of juvenile delinquency for the report year show that: (1) less than half of all children registered for delinquency were known to the juvenile court; (2) the number of cases registered by the juvenile court was almost one fourth greater than the number of children brought to the court; and (3) the mere addition of cases results in a total almost double the number of children actually reported for alleged delinquency.[16]

The data on the extent and distribution of delinquency are admittedly not complete, yet they give an approximate indication of the problem. The general statistical tabulations, together with several special studies, can be used to indicate the trends in juvenile delinquency, which will be undertaken in the following chapter.

---

[16] Edward E. Schwartz, *A Community Experiment in the Measurement of Juvenile Delinquency,* reprinted for the Children's Bureau from the Yearbook of the National Probation Association (1945), 10. Used by permission of the National Probation Association, now the National Probation and Parole Association. For a discussion of the problem of measuring the extent of delinquency, consult: Sophia Robinson, *Can Delinquency Be Measured?* (New York: Columbia University Press, 1936).

QUESTIONS AND PROJECTS

For Class Discussion and Research

1. Make a study of the extent of delinquency in a specified area, such as a county, city, or community.

2. Plot on a map the distribution of delinquency, by ascertaining the addresses of the cases handled by the juvenile court or police or both.

3. If census statistics are available by census tracts, calculate the relative densities of the juvenile populations. Then ascertain the rates of delinquency by tracts in terms of population densities.

4. What difficulties are encountered in getting accurate numerical data regarding the volume of delinquency?

5. What is the chief delinquency age period?

6. To what extent do boys have a worse delinquency record than girls? Why?

7. Analyze the boys' and girls' cases to ascertain the differences in delinquency due to sex factors.

8. Test the hypothesis that delinquent behavior follows a line of progression from maladjustment in early childhood, truancy from school, minor delinquencies, recidivism, and serious crime.

9. Study the problem of the differential rate of delinquency among racial and nationality groups. Why do minority groups tend to have higher rates of delinquency than does the majority group?

10. Compare a rural and an urban county to ascertain the difference in the extent of delinquency and the possible reason for this difference.

11. To what extent do the rates of delinquents show similar variations among local communities in different types of cities?

12. To what extent do variations in rates of delinquencies in different communities reflect the social, cultural, economic, and physical environmental conditions of these communities?

13. Under what conditions does delinquency develop most rapidly?

14. When rates of delinquency are computed over a period of time, what do they reveal regarding the fluctuations in time?

15. Rural and urban differences in crime and delinquency.

16. Delinquency patterns in urban areas.

SELECTED REFERENCES

BARRON, MILTON L., *The Juvenile in Delinquent Society* (New York: Alfred A. Knopf, 1954), Chapter III.

CARR, LOWELL J., *Delinquency Control* (New York: Harper & Brothers, 1950, Chapter III).

CAVAN, RUTH SHONLE, *Criminology* (New York: Thomas Y. Crowell Co., 1948, Chapter II).

ELLIOTT, MABEL A., *Crime in Modern Society* (New York: Harper & Brothers, 1953, Chapter III).

Kefauver, Estes, *Crime in America* (Garden City: Doubleday, Doran and Co., 1951).

Lander, Bernard, *Toward an Understanding of Juvenile Delinquency* (New York: Columbia University Press, 1954).

Schwartz, Edward E., "Statistics of Juvenile Delinquency in the United States," *The Annals of the American Academy of Political and Social Science*, Vol. 261 (January, 1949), 9-20.

Tappan, Paul W., *Juvenile Delinquency* (New York: McGraw-Hill Book Co., Inc., 1949, Chapter II).

Teeters, Negley K., and John O. Reinemann, *The Challenge of Delinquency* (New York: Prentice-Hall, Inc., 1950, Chapter I).

The Child, Vol. 17, No. 4 (December, 1952) bulletin now published under the title of *Children;* and periodic issues of *Social Statistics,* dealing with "Juvenile-Court Statistics" (Washington, D. C.: Children's Bureau, United States Department of Health, Education, and Welfare).

Uniform Crime Reports. Washington, D. C.: Federal Bureau of Investigation, United States Department of Justice, latest issue.

III

DELINQUENCY TRENDS IN CONTEMPORARY AMERICAN SOCIETY

Most questions regarding the problems of delinquency could be answered quite satisfactorily by the available statistical, ecological, and case-study methods of research if they were fully applied. The official reports are largely statistical in nature. Improvements have been made in compiling numerical data, but even the best official reports give only a partial picture of the extent of, and trends in, juvenile delinquency, as was pointed out in the previous chapter. The limitations in determining trends need to be recognized.

It is possible, however, to indicate certain general trends in the nation, and probable trends in the future, based on available statistical and other data, and to present information regarding local conditions where information regarding trends is available. The main periods covered are the economic depression era of the 1930's, the period of World War II, and the postwar era. Special consideration will be given to the effects of the economic depression and war on the volume of delinquency. Changes in the composition of the delinquency population, types of offenses, conditioning factors, treatment, and control will likewise be noted.

56

ECONOMIC TRENDS AND JUVENILE DELINQUENCY

Of all the factors affecting trends in delinquency, economic conditions and the accompanying changes in society seem to exert the greatest influence. The business cycle, including the eras of economic depression and of prosperity, more specifically as these affect the economic conditions of families and communities, have far-reaching effects on delinquency trends, although the findings regarding this matter are too insufficient to be conclusive at this point.

Juvenile Delinquency in Relation to Business Cycles. Many studies have been made of business cycles and trends. Some have charted 54-, 18-, and 9-year cycles, with minor ones occurring at shorter intervals. During the 1930's we reached a low ebb in one or more of these cycles. Since the latter part of the 1930's the economic trend has been upward, with certain fluctuations in price and income levels during the war and postwar periods. A war acts as an inflationary force. Prices and wages tend to go up in spite of governmental and other efforts to control them. Upward trends in business cycles were noted during both of the world wars and the subsequent postwar periods. The slumps seem to be more difficult to explain and to control. While the upward and downward trends have been noted, there is no agreement as to exact nature and causes of business cycles.

Studies of the relationship between crime and economic trends have been made, but most of them have dealt with adult crime and not with juvenile delinquency. The criminal court and prison statistics that were used related principally, if not exclusively, to adult crime. The studies by Bonger,[1] Thomas,[2] Winslow,[3] and others [4] are in substantial agreement in concluding that certain types of crimes against property increase in periods of economic depression and extensive unemployment. The methods that have been used in these and other studies have seldom been carefully devised, and the indexes of both crime and business cycles have varied consid-

---

[1] William A. Bonger, *Criminality and Economic Conditions* (Boston: Little, Brown and Co., 1916).

[2] Dorothy Swain Thomas, *Social Consequences of the Business Cycle* (London: Routledge, 1925).

[3] Emma A. Winslow, "Relationship between Employment and Crime Fluctuations as Shown by Massachusetts Statistics," *Report of National Commission on Observance and Enforcement*, Vol. I, Part IV (1931).

[4] See Thorsten Sellin, *Research Memorandum on Crime in the Depression* (New York: Social Science Research Council, Bulletin 27, 1937), for a summary and appraisal of various studies.

erably, with the result that the generalizations may be questioned. Furthermore, since juvenile statistics were omitted for the most part, the studies do not indicate the relation of delinquency to economic trends.

Several studies of juvenile delinquency have shown that court cases tend to decrease in depressions and increase in prosperity.[5] Carr cites studies made in several counties in Michigan (Wayne County, counties with high population density as compared with nonindustrial counties, and up-state counties) to indicate that the delinquency rate per 1,000 population, aged 10-16, tends to follow the business trends. The rates were relatively high during the 1920's and fairly low during the early 1930's. However, the rural and up-state counties did not show the same fluctuation that occurred in the industrialized counties.

Possibly the most intensive study of the relation of juvenile court cases to economic trends was made in Los Angeles County by David Bogen.[6] This study indicates that during the years 1925 to 1941 juvenile delinquency increased in periods of prosperity and decreased in periods of widespread unemployment and economic distress. The index of business activity, as published by the Los Angeles Chamber of Commerce, represents a composite measure of bank debits, building permits, industrial employment, industrial power used, telephones in use, new car registrations, and department store sales. The index of school population covers the total number in elementary, junior high, and senior high schools of the county. The indices of the juvenile court petitions of boys and girls were computed on the basis of the annual number of cases handled as compared with the number of such cases in 1930. The index was calculated by dividing the number of cases (boys' and girls' cases tabulated separately) in a given year by the total in 1930, omitting traffic cases in each instance.

Inspection of the chart in Figure 1 reveals clearly that, while the index of the school population (y) showed a fairly continuous growth from 1925 to 1941, the business index (x) ascended gradually to a high peak in 1929, dropped sharply to a low point in 1933, after which it rose to a high level again. The indices of the boys' (B) and girls' (G) cases follow the index of business activity to a remarkable

---

5 Lowell J. Carr, *Delinquency Control* (New York: Harper & Brothers, 1940), 53-57; also 1950 edition, 86-92. Besides the studies in Michigan, Carr cites the study in Pennsylvania. Compare David Bogen, "Juvenile Delinquency and Economic Trend," *American Sociological Review*, Vol. IX (April, 1944), 178-184.

6 *Loc. cit.* Compare his article on "Trends in Juvenile Delinquency," *Federal Probation*, Vol. IX (January-March, 1945), 25-28.

extent and show practically no relation to the increase of the school population. Furthermore, the boys' and girls' delinquency indices run parallel to each other, except that the boys' cases increased slightly during 1933 and 1934, chiefly because of the fact that during those years there was a large group of transient boys brought

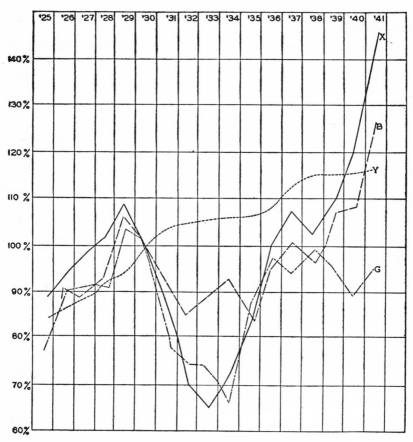

FIGURE I. JUVENILE DELINQUENCY COURT CASES (BOYS AND GIRLS), BUSINESS CYCLE, AND CHILD POPULATION IN LOS ANGELES COUNTY, 1925-1941

Used by permission of *American Sociological Review*. Article by Bogen, *op. cit.*, 180.

into court for the purpose of effecting their return to legal residences. The girls' index dropped as low as the business index. After 1939, boys' delinquencies increased more rapidly than did the girls', following the business index very closely. From 1940, the girls' cases increased and continued to increase rapidly for several years, as we shall see later.

Questions may be raised as to the validity of the methods used in calculating the business index, rates of delinquencies, and the child population curve, also the exclusive use of juvenile court cases, the types of cases included in the tabulations, and the possible effects of changes in administrative practices; but Bogen carefully checked all items to make sure that no outstanding discrepancies existed. It is recognized that available statistical data are not wholly accurate. However, allowing for possible variations in statistical data, the facts indicate a relationship between juvenile delinquency and business activity.

Several studies seem to contradict the findings of Bogen and others. Reed's [7] study of the children of relief clients in Hamilton County, Ohio, covering practically the same period used by Bogen, indicates that delinquency in this group about doubled during the period, but this applied to the relief clients only and should not be indicative of the trends in the total population. Maller's [8] study of delinquency cases in New York City during the early years of the depression (1930-1934) showed a 6 per cent gain in delinquency. This was practically equal to the population gain from 1930 to 1940 in the same area. These contradictions of results of studies are not easy to explain. Some of the differences may be accounted for by differences in areas studied, changes in population, types of cases used, differential methods of reporting cases, and various other factors. Reinemann [9] covered a longer period (1923-1945) than the other studies and he divided this into four subperiods: (a) 1923-1929, a period of reasonable prosperity, had an average proportion of delinquents; (b) 1930-1935, the worst depression years, had a relatively high delinquency rate; (c) 1936-1940, the period of economic recovery, had a fairly low rate of delinquency; and (d) 1940-1945, the war period, showed a high rate of delinquency. The war, as we shall indicate later, produced conditions quite apart from economic factors that unduly stimulated delinquency. Furthermore, it was difficult to correlate delinquency rates with the business cycle, for price controls and other restrictions affected economic trends.

In view of the fact that economic factors cannot be separated from other causes, no one economic trend or condition is a decisive element in changing the course of delinquency. Furthermore, the

---

7 Ellery F. Reed, "Relation of Relief to Increase of Juvenile Court Cases," *The Social Service Review*, Vol. 15 (1941), 104-115.

8 J. B. Maller, "Juvenile Delinquency in New York," *The Journal of Psychology*, Vol. 3 (1935), 1-25.

9 John O. Reinemann, "Juvenile Delinquency in Philadelphia and Economic Trends," *Temple University Law Quarterly* (Philadelphia: April, 1947), Vol. 20, No. 4.

studies of economic trends in relation to delinquency do not cover
a long enough period, and the investigators did not use the same
methods of research. Economic trends are variously ascertained,
and the law enforcing agencies use different methods in handling
cases; also they may change the methods of procedure, which would
affect delinquency trends. Nevertheless, certain general effects of
both economic depressions and periods of economic prosperity may
be noted.

Effects of Economic Depressions and Prosperity. Assuming that
in some areas delinquency rates went down considerably during the
depression years, why should a period of extensive economic want
and poverty result in a reduction of law violations, especially in
view of the widespread opinion that poverty is an important cause of
delinquent behavior?

Various reasons have been given in explanation of the decline
of delinquency, especially of certain types of offenses, during depression years.[10] Many factors may work together to produce the result.
Families with reduced income spend more time at home. Being
more at home, parents are likely to supervise their children's behavior more continuously; and, being thrown more closely together,
primary group influences and controls become more effective. Discipline may also be intensified. Some families become more unified,
and there is less overt family disorganization. Divorce, marriage,
and birth rates tend to go down with the downward curve of the
business cycle. Since families have less money for recreation, they
tend to spend more of their leisure time at home instead of going
to commercial amusement centers. Decreased deviation pressures
and relaxed law enforcement may likewise affect the extent of delinquency. Townspeople and officials take a more lenient view of
petty thieving by poor children. The reluctance of complainants
to press charges involving children from poverty-stricken families
suspected of petty thefts affects the statistical rate of delinquency.
Likewise, the reduction of police personnel and resources for effective law enforcement may affect the volume of cases handled.

Certain constructive forces were put into operation during the
depression period. The constructive benefits of such government
sponsored programs as the Civilian Conservation Corp (CCC), National Youth Administration (NYA), Works Progress Administration (WPA), and other measures have been pointed out by those
who have analyzed these programs. Community agencies likewise

---

[10] Lowell J. Carr, *op. cit.*, 88-89. Compare Philip M. Smith, "Criminality and the
Economic Factor," *Sociology and Social Research*, XXII (January-February, 1948), 720.

endeavored to meet the needs of the people on relief in a more effective manner, including many forms of services other than financial. However, one must be careful not to overemphasize the beneficial effects of relief and welfare programs, for, in spite of the vast amount of government aid provided for millions of people, a large percentage of families, as will be indicated later, lived below the poverty line and suffered greatly from want and humiliation. As Cavan and Ranck [11] have pointed out, the external effects of the depression are well known but the more personal effects are less known. Lessened income changed the family plans of living and often resulted in a loss of status and the thwarting of lifelong ambitions. Some families became disorganized as the result of these conditions; yet there were certain stabilizing influences.

The increase of delinquency during periods of prosperity suggests that certain conditions of the increase of wealth and income have undesirable effects on juvenile behavior. Marriage, divorce, birth, and delinquency rates all seem to rise proportionately, and they tend to follow the business cycle. Bogen [12] suggests that family disorganization, which is characteristic of periods of prosperity, helps to explain the delinquency trend. When jobs are plentiful and money flows freely, and more women and children work, the family relaxes parental supervision, parents and children are away from home and from each other, and the family ties seem to weaken. Furthermore, patronage of commercialized recreation reaches a higher level, more liquor is consumed, and people live a more carefree life. The carelessness with which people handle their property, the emphasis on money matters, and similar conditions that seem to be associated with prosperity may likewise have an influence.

It appears that juvenile delinquency rates do not react to economic conditions, whether during depressions or periods of prosperity, in the same way as adult criminality. This fact needs further explanation. The combination of enforced idleness, financial needs, and excessive worry may result in the increase of adult offenses, especially against property, in periods of economic depression, whereas eras of prosperity remove or reduce somewhat these conditions. Parental supervision, of course, is not an important factor in adult behavior, as it is in that of children, although there is no fixed age at which parental supervision gives way to adult responsibilities.

If economic conditions are important factors in affecting the incidence of juvenile delinquency, it can be anticipated that rates

11 Ruth S. Cavan and Katherine H. Ranck, *The Family and the Depression* (Chicago: The University of Chicago Press, 1939), 1.
12 *Op. cit.*, 183.

of delinquency will remain relatively high as long as industrial and business activity remains at a high peak.[13] There is some difficulty in verifying the correlation between economic conditions and delinquency rates during wartime, for abnormal conditions of industry, business, employment, housing, and other factors are more rigidly controlled and have varying degrees of effects. Many factors other than economic conditions exert great influences. The usual index of business activity relies upon such factors as automobile registrations, telephone users, building construction, and retail store sales, all of which are more or less invalidated because of the shortages of materials, government controls of prices and rationing of purchases, and other conditions peculiar to these years. Even employment figures do not give a reliable index. The peak of juvenile delinquency during World War II was from 1943 to 1945, which was to some extent also the peak of economic activity; but after the war the delinquency curve declined much faster than the economic trend. The delinquency curve declined for several years following the war, but the business index remained on a relatively high level, even though some fluctuations occurred. Further discussions of the influence of economic conditions as possible causal factors will be discussed in Chapter X.

Seasonal Variations in Delinquency. Besides the cyclical trends, the ups and downs of the business cycle, and their effects on delinquency rates, certain seasonal fluctuations can be observed. As Carr and Wattenberg [14] have pointed out, seasonal differences in delinquency are somewhat puzzling, for in a given area (state, county, or city) the peaks and low ebbs seldom are the same from year to year, and the illustrations from Michigan that Carr gives indicate this point. While the increases and decreases of cases in monthly periods tend to follow a seasonal pattern, this pattern differs from year to year and from community to community in the same year. Thus the explanations are more speculative and less factual than in the case of the cyclical trends.

Attention has been given to delinquency trends during summer

---

13 See David Bogen, "Trends in Juvenile Delinquency," *Federal Probation*, IX (January-March, 1945), 25-28.

14 Cf. Lowell J. Carr, *op. cit.*, 77-83; and William W. Wattenberg, "Delinquency during Summer Months," *Journal of Educational Research* (December, 1948), 253-267. For a review of earlier studies and data of crime rates of eight cities (Buffalo, Cincinnati, Denver, Detroit, Ft. Worth, Los Angeles, Rochester, and St. Louis) using ten consecutive annual reports (1928-1946), see: Gerhard J. Falk, "The Influence of the Seasons on the Crime Rate," *The Journal of Criminal Law, Criminology, and Police Science.* Vol. 43, No. 2 (July-August, 1952), 199-213.

months, especially as compared with the other seasons of the year. Some investigators have been surprised to discover that delinquency rates appear to drop or remain steady during the summer vacation period. Wattenberg cites studies made in such widely separated areas as Passaic (New Jersey), Houston, Detroit, and New York to indicate that delinquency tends to go down during the summer season, especially during the early part. In New Jersey a significant falling off in the delinquency rate during summer months was noted over a five-year period, according to reports of cases referred to the Passaic Children's Bureau. Similar trends have been observed in other cities, but this pattern may not be true for all American cities. For instance, a study made in Philadelphia shows that the most striking troughs in the delinquency curves for 1946 occurred in June and December for school-age boys and in May and December for girls. The *Uniform Crime Reports* do not seem to show summer drops in crime; but, as noted earlier, these reports pertain chiefly to adult offenders. The *Uniform Crime Reports* show monthly variations, but there is no uniform pattern of variation from year to year.

Certain hypotheses and theories have been advanced to explain the possible reduction of delinquency during the summer months. Many juveniles leave cities to go with parents to summer resorts or are sent to camps. Fewer complaints arise from truancy or other school-connected misconduct. Since the school is not in session, boys and girls do not have the same opportunities to get together to form cliques or gangs and to plan exploits. The heaviest drop in offenses charged against boys during the summer includes forms of deviant behavior that are usually committed in groups rather than by individuals alone. While these and similar conditions may explain some reductions in delinquency rates, they do not seem to be altogether valid explanations, for certain contradictory tendencies exist. At best, they would account for only a part of the reduction of delinquency summer season.

DELINQUENCY IN WARTIME AND POSTWAR TRENDS

Delinquency did not emerge as a wartime problem, for its increase was noticeable before the war. But as indicated in the previous chapter, national statistics are somewhat inadequate. For this reason, it is difficult to indicate long-range trends in the volume of delinquency. Local reports of wartime increases are statistically on a somewhat shaky foundation. Comparative local statistics are inadequate when the system of reporting is not uniform over a period of time and when delinquency data are not correlated with changes of the population. For instance, the rapid increases in delinquency during World War II occurred in regions of rapid increases of the population. For that reason it is better to compare rates of delinquency rather than totals, and the rates should be calculated on the basis of the juvenile population changes.

That new and disorganizing conditions are created during wartime is evident to any casual observer. Some observers have contended that the chief effect of the war is not that it creates new conditions of delinquency but rather that it accentuates and intensifies the existing causal factors. Perhaps the most significant development during the war was not the fact that delinquency increased but that there emerged an increased awareness of the problem.[15]

Wartime and Postwar Trends in the Volume of Delinquency. In order to make valid comparisons and to indicate long-range trends, it is necessary to have comparable statistics. Herein lies the difficulty. The United States Children's Bureau has been gathering statistics of delinquency since 1927, but because of the wide variations in court practices with respect to the method of handling cases and in reporting them it has been difficult to ascertain the exact extent of delinquency. Court cases represent only a fraction of the total number of delinquents known to law enforcing agencies. The Children's Bureau has recognized the limitations of delinquency data and has been cautious in indicating trends. Beginning with data for 1946, the Bureau has included only those courts in the tabulations that reported on both official and unofficial cases, believing that a count of both types of cases gives a more reliable index of children brought to courts than does a count of official cases only. This has made it possible to chart trends more accurately. A new trend series was started that year, but because of the great interest in wartime increase of delinquency, the Bureau has estimated the trend for the period 1940-1945 on the basis of fairly reliable data. However, it is not possible to estimate the trend for the years prior to 1940 with the same degree of accuracy because of the limitations of court statistics.

The eleventh report in the series of juvenile court statistics, and

15 For reports of wartime trends in delinquency, consult: Charles L. Chute, "Juvenile Delinquency in Wartime," *Probation* (June, 1943); Frederick W. Killian, "Juvenile Delinquency: Wartime Trends," *Probation* (June, 1944); and Martin H. Neumeyer, "Delinquency Trends in Wartime," *Sociology and Social Research*, Vol. XXIX (March-April, 1945), 262-275.

the sixth in the series on Federal juvenile offenders,[16] indicates that the number of courts reporting increased from 43 in 1927 to 473 in 1939. By using the data of 67 courts that reported continuously from 1933 to 1939, which courts served specific areas of 100,000 or more population, it was possible to indicate the fluctuations from year to year in the number of delinquency cases handled by these courts. While the number of cases reported increased or decreased from year to year, no marked changes occurred, except that there was a slight decline of 4 per cent during the period (from 53,925 cases in 1933 to 51,994 cases in 1939). The number of delinquency cases in 1939 was 6 per cent greater than in 1938 and approximately equal to the number disposed of in 1937, indicating the fluctuation in number of cases handled from year to year. The preliminary statement of *Juvenile Court Statistics, 1947* (published in 1948) likewise indicates that the courts began to report more cases of delinquency after 1938, with a rapid upward swing during the early years of the war.

The wartime increases and the postwar changes in court cases and in arrests of juveniles under 18 years of age can be indicated by means of a chart with a fair degree of accuracy, provided it is recognized that the index of court cases is based on reports submitted voluntarily to the Children's Bureau by a limited number of courts and the index of arrests of juveniles is based chiefly on fingerprints sent to the Federal Bureau of Investigation by police, sheriff, and other law enforcement agencies, also on a voluntary basis. Beginning with 1952, data regarding age, sex, and race of persons arrested are from special reports.

The Children's Bureau has been constructing charts, based on available data, to indicate general trends. These charts compare delinquency rates with changes in the child population from 10 to 17 years of age, omitting children under 10 years old since only a small percentage of children in this age group are involved in delinquency cases and this is the group that increased greatly because of the high birth rate since the early part of World War II. If all children under 18 years of age were included, the child population curve would show a decided increase in number. By 1960, the child population 10 to 17 years of age will probably be at least 40 per cent higher than it was in 1952. While the juvenile court cases were reported by courts located in specific areas, the police arrest data are not related to specific areas but are for the United States as a whole.

As the figure indicates, the increases of delinquency during

---

16 *Children in the Courts, 1938 and 1939*, publication No. 280 of the Children's Bureau. See tables 4 and 5, pages 6 and 7.

World War II occurred during the early period of the war. However, these increases were by no means uniform throughout the United States, and some areas actually reported decreases. For instance, 83 juvenile courts serving areas of 100,000 or more people reported a 16 per cent increase of cases handled from 1940 to 1942

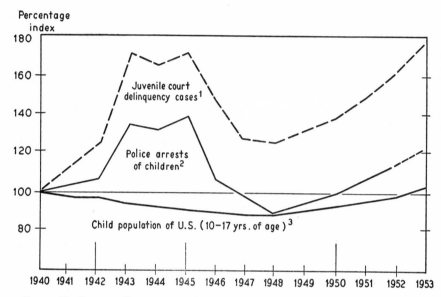

FIGURE II. JUVENILE DELINQUENCY COURT CASES, POLICE ARRESTS OF CHILDREN, AND U. S. CHILD POPULATION, 1940-1953
$(1940 = 100)$

[1] Data for 1940-1945 estimated by the Children's Bureau; data for 1946-1952 based on official and unofficial cases disposed of by 206 courts; the total for 1953 (435,000 cases) is a preliminary estimate received to date.
SOURCES: *Juvenile Court Statistics, 1950-1952,* Statistical Series No. 18, 1954, p. 3, and *Juvenile Court Statistics, 1946-1949,* Statistical Series No. 8, 1951, p. 11 (United States Children's Bureau). See also *News Notes on Juvenile Delinquency,* May 10, 1954 and October 13, 1953; and *The Child,* Vol. 17, No. 4, December, 1952.
[2] Based on fingerprint records of children under 18 years of age reported in *Uniform Crime Reports* (Annual Bulletin), Federal Bureau of Investigation, for the years 1940-1951. No comparable data on police arrests of children from FBI fingerprint records are available for 1952 and 1953. The trend for these two years is an estimate.
[3] *Current Population Reports,* Bureau of the Census, Series P-25, Nos. 41, 73 and 78.

(chiefly the prewar period), of which 41 areas with population increases reported an increase of 18 per cent and 42 with population decline reported only 9 per cent increase. A special study was made of 130 courts in small cities, towns, and rural communities in four states, of which 73 reported increases, 49 reported decreases, and 8 handled the same number of cases. A later report showed that the number of delinquency cases handled by 304 courts in various sections of the nation increased 31 per cent in one year (1942 to 1943). Similar increases were noted by the National Probation Association (now the National Probation and Parole Association) in its annual reports covering 117 jurisdictions. Except for the slight decrease in both juvenile court cases and police arrests of juveniles in 1944, the volume of delinquency remained on a high level during the period of the war, after which a marked decline occurred. Unfortunately, changes in the volume of delinquency were not sufficiently correlated with population changes in the areas submitting reports. Since a considerable number of the juvenile courts that have sent in reports are in urban areas, most of which experienced considerable increases in population, with attendant changes in the number of children subject to the jurisdictions of the various courts, the statistics of increases of cases handled must be discounted in part. The greatest increases occurred in areas that gained extensively in population, which may be the result not only of an increase in the juvenile population but also of the conditions of living in overcrowded cities with inadequate educational and recreational facilities to meet the needs of boys and girls.

Austin L. Porterfield [17] analyzed the trends of serious crimes in the United States during the ten-year period from 1937 to 1946, using the *Uniform Crime Reports* as the source of the basic data. While this study pertained chiefly to adult crime, it indicates the value of correlating crime data with population changes. Using 1937-1939 as the base period, he computed the increases or decreases for the war year 1943 and the postwar year 1946. He recognized the difficulties involved in making such comparisons, chiefly because of the limited reliability of the basic data. Not all law enforcement agencies send in reports, some departments do not report all crimes known to them, police departments are not aware of all crimes committed, uniform definitions of crime are hard to achieve, and there are difficulties in interpreting the data.

Although the juvenile crime statistics are not segregated from the crime rates of the total population, the statistics of arrests for serious offenses reveal certain trends, differing from the trends of juvenile offenses, as noted previously. This seems to imply that the trends for adult offenses during the war period did not follow quite the same pattern as those for juvenile offenses. Porterfield points out the trends as revealed by arrests for serious offenses of all age

---

[17] "A Decade of Serious Crimes in the United States: Some Trends and Hypotheses," *American Sociological Review*, Vol. XIII, No. 1 (February, 1948), 44-54.

groups as a whole and he indicates some possible hypotheses emerging from the study.

The first trend observable is that the rates for serious crimes in a majority of the states were down from the base period to 1943, but in some of the states they were sharply up with the result that the trend for the nation as a whole did not change significantly. The second is that the rates came up in the main from the base period to 1946. For the nation as a whole there was a great increase. Yet in a few states the rates remained lower than for the prewar years or even continued to decline from 1943.[18]

Certain hypotheses are offered in explanation of these trends. The absence of a great number of men of crime-committing age who were in military service tended to hold the crime rate down, or prevented its increase, although there was a growth in serious criminal behavior among civilians; but when the men returned from military service after the war they probably affected the increase of the crime rate. The influx of outside population into the war-industrialized areas apparently was responsible in part for the increase of criminal behavior among civilians. The growth of crime is related to the increase of social disorganization, occasioned in part by the increased mobility and heterogeneity of the population. The states vary in rank by kinds of serious crimes committed with the variations in social structure and general social well-being. Porterfield indicates the indices of shift in rates of serious offenses by states from the prewar base period to 1943 as compared with the rates for the postwar period of 1946. These rates in turn are correlated with the shifts in population, the possible effects of the heterogeneity of the population in certain states being especially noted. The patterns of crime by regions and states are noted and they indicate that the same variations in patterns of criminal behavior are found in the nation as a whole as was found by Clifford Shaw in his Chicago studies. In other words, the variations in social structure and general social well-being, whether by states or by areas in a city, tend to affect the crime rates. The degree of urbanization of a state has a bearing on the crime rate; most of the crime reports come from towns and cities. Urban areas have higher crime rates for most offenses than have rural areas. Therefore, the recent increase of serious crimes in the more rural states is difficult to explain, except that the impact of urbanization and changes in social well-being may have affected the rate of change, but these in turn are influenced by other factors.

---

18 *Ibid.*, 44. Used by permission of *American Sociological Review*.

Changes in Composition of the Delinquency Population and in Types of Offenses. The sex, age, race, and nationality factors were indicated in the previous chapter. Although the volume and rate of delinquency fluctuated considerably, less pronounced changes have taken place in the composition of the delinquency population during the war and postwar periods, except that delinquency among girls and in minority groups apparently increased more rapidly during the early years of the war than was true among boys and in the white (majority) group. The increase of girls' cases was halted earlier than the increase of boys' cases, apparently the result of changing conditions and a more concerted effort to deal with the problem. Offenses among boys apparently continued to increase during the entire war period, even though the increase was halted somewhat during the last two years of the war, after which there was a fairly rapid decline for several years. Offenses among girls declined gradually from 1943 until the recent rise. Since 1948, offenses of both boys and girls have been on the increase.

Statistics relating to age composition of the delinquent population are less reliable than those pertaining to sex differences in rates of delinquency. The *Uniform Crime Reports* have shown that the predominant age for arrests fluctuates considerably. During the prewar period (1939-1941) the age at which the greatest number of arrests was made was 19, the peak age dropped to 17 during the war (1944-1945), and rose to 21 by 1946 and to 23 by 1951. This fluctuation is largely accounted for by the extent to which youth is enlisted or drafted for military service. When many of the young men and boys are in military service, their misconduct is handled mainly by military authorities rather than by the regular law enforcement agencies, a fact which tends to affect the statistics of arrests in the military age bracket.

Even though many of the males and some of the females under 21 years of age were in military service during the war, over a fifth of all persons arrested were under voting age. During 1943, more boys 17 years of age and more girls 18 years of age were arrested than from any other age group, and the largest increase of arrests for individual age groups was age 17 among boys and age 16 among girls. Since it has been the practice in some jurisdictions not to fingerprint youthful offenders, the fingerprint arrest figures in the lower age group are incomplete to that extent.

The Children's Bureau reports of juvenile court cases do not show great fluctuations in the age composition of the cases handled, which is accounted for by the fact that state laws restrict the jurisdictions of juvenile courts, for each state has established an age ceiling and some have set age floors for court jurisdiction. Hence, the peak ages of cases handled by juvenile courts range from 15 to 17. Juvenile court statistics in certain cities have indicated a general decline in the age of offenders, with noticeable increases in the age group from 12 to 15.

Considerable fluctuations have occurred in the types of offenses during the past decade or so. The *Uniform Crime Reports* emphasize the annual changes in types of offenses, noting increases and

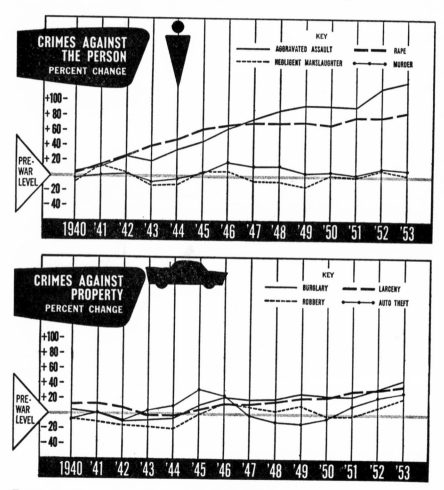

FIGURE III. URBAN CRIME TRENDS, 1940-53 TREND VERSUS 1937-39 AVERAGE. OFFENSES KNOWN TO THE POLICE.

363 CITIES—TOTAL POPULATION 47,586,584

SOURCE: *Uniform Crime Reports*, Vol. XXIV, No. 2, 1953, Fig. 10, p. 79, Federal Bureau of Investigation, 1954.

decreases in the various categories. Offenses against persons, although relatively few in number, increased during the war period, except for occasional declines in certain categories. While offenses against property increased also, decreases occurred in certain instances. The tables showing the percentages of increases or decreases of the various offenses known to the police indicate that increases occurred in such offenses as murder, negligent manslaughter, robbery, aggravated assault, burglary, and to a lesser extent in larceny, auto theft, and rape, during the war period; and decreases occurred in some of these categories following the war. During 1952, increases occurred in almost all categories of crime, but chiefly in aggravated assault, robbery, auto theft, burglary, and larceny. The following figure presents a graphic picture of the trends of eight major crimes.

It is difficult to ascertain changes in types of offenses by juveniles, for only a certain number of juvenile courts have reported regularly over a period of time and some of them do not report accurately the types of offenses for which juveniles are referred to courts. The available reports indicate that the reasons for which boys are most frequently referred to courts differ considerably from those for which girls are most commonly referred. The boys' cases for which the reasons for referral are given show that the chief offenses are stealing (including auto theft, petty larceny, burglary or unlawful entry, and robbery), destroying of property, malicious mischief and acts of carelessness, with relatively fewer referrals for truancy, running away, being ungovernable, sex offenses, and injuries to persons. Traffic offenses are extensive among boys, but in many jurisdictions the cases are handled separately and no complete statistics are available. Among girls, being ungovernable, running away, and sex offenses account for nearly six out of ten referrals; with truancy and stealing fairly extensive, although not as prevalent as among boys. Fewer girls are referred to court for acts of carelessness and mischief, injury to persons, and traffic offenses.

Periodically, certain types of offenses are more prevalent than at other times. Today, vandalism seems to be the vogue, as evidenced by the destruction of school property in many cities. A few years ago various types of gang activities were extensive in some areas, of which the Zoot Suit activities were a conspicuous example.

Changes in Conditioning Factors. The trends in the volume of delinquency and in the composition of the delinquent population are rooted in the changes in conditioning factors. The complexity of factors that produce delinquency is now generally recognized.

There is no agreement as to the exact causes of law violation or the relative importance of the various types of contributing factors, as will be indicated in Part Two. However, certain more or less obvious factors can be observed in wartime which have detrimental effects on children as well as adults, and which affect delinquency rates. Wars, revolutions, depressions, and other periods of great upheaval seriously disturb the normal way of life. In wartime, standards of behavior are confused, social controls are weakened, moral values are shaken, attitudes of hate and destructiveness are encouraged, and life is full of uncertainty. The tensions and emotional stresses of war affect adolescents, possibly more than adults, for the youth of the country must bear the brunt of the military tragedies. Family life tends to become disorganized, with fathers, mothers, the older boys and some of the older girls in defense industries or in military services. Increased numbers of mothers and children are gainfully employed. The lack of consistent guidance and supervision by the parents gives children opportunities to indulge in unacceptable behavior. The widespread migration of families to crowded centers of war industries uproots children and subjects them to conditions in new communities that tend to expose them to moral hazards.[19]

Conditions outside the home often have more far-reaching consequences than is sometimes supposed. During wartime, the schools, churches, recreation centers, group work agencies, and other community forces are faced with new conditions and tend to lag in effective functions. The constant mobility of certain families makes it difficult for the children to experience regular school life, necessitating many adjustments to strange places. Many of the adult leaders of children in churches, recreation centers, and youth-serving agencies go to war or move to other communities, thus upsetting the continuity of leadership. On the other hand, commercial amusements and other new attractions may exert harmful effects. The general spirit of excitement and uncertainty aroused by war tensions and upheavals is reflected in the anxiety, restlessness, emotional upsets, and often defiance and other negative forms of behavior on the part of children and young people.

While it is evident that wartime conditions produce dislocations and tensions, which in turn may result in maladjustments and misconduct, possibly the most notable effect of the war on delinquency

---

19 Cf. *Understanding Juvenile Delinquency* and *Controlling Juvenile Delinquency*, Children's Bureau Publications 300 and 301, 1943. These pamphlets were designed to call attention to the conditions of war that were likely to result in the increase of delinquency and to suggest ways of controlling the situation.

is that it accentuates the already existing conditioning factors, including personal elements, family conditions, gang life, and disorganized community conditions. However, the effects of these factors have not been fully measured. It must be noted also that the dislocations of war are in time adjusted. Some adjustments to wartime conditions are made long before the war is over. During the postwar period, the upsetting forces that were unleashed during the war tend to subside; and, as they do, more normal existence reduces the incidences of law violation. On the other hand, family disorganization, inadequate housing, child labor, mental illness, excessive consumption of liquor, and similar conditions are more prevalent, offsetting to some extent the positive social forces.

Changes in the Treatment Process, Law Enforcement, and Social Controls. Changes in law enforcement, methods of treatment of juvenile offenders, and preventive measures have accompanied increased knowledge of deviant behavior and of conditioning factors, also changed attitudes toward the problem of delinquency. Possibly no movement has more clearly demonstrated the new approach to the problem than the development of the juvenile court. Since the establishment of the first juvenile court in 1899, there have been continuous expansion and specialization in juvenile courts. Although the specialized courts for juveniles vary considerably in organization and operation, the main types may be classified as follows: independent courts with jurisdiction over children (city, county, or state-wide); courts as sections or parts of courts with more general jurisdiction, but with attached or separate services; family courts, including jurisdiction over children; and juvenile and domestic relations courts, either independent or attached courts, but with jurisdiction over children.[20] Informality of procedure, dependence on probation service for investigation and treatment, and specialized treatment of cases have become fairly standard phases of the specialized courts for children. Some courts have expanded their functions considerably, operating more like a social agency than a judicial tribunal. Furthermore, approximately 50 per cent of the children's cases in some urban courts are being handled extralegally and unofficially. Another significant move has been the growth of police juvenile bureaus and similar bureaus in sheriff offices. These and similar developments have played a major role in the application

---

20 *Comparative Survey on Juvenile Delinquency.* Part I. North America, prepared by Paul W. Tappan (New York: Division of Social Welfare, Department of Social Affairs, United Nations, 1952), 25.

of a more scientific approach to children's behavior problems and the treatment of young offenders.

The expansion of some of the urban juvenile courts to include the handling of cases of neglect, dependency, health, and maladjustment, especially if they do not involve offenses, has been questioned by some investigators and authorities. It has been suggested that juvenile courts should not be overloaded as case-work agencies, even though some of the cases require legal decisions. Courts for children, of course, must use case-work procedures in handling offenders, but they have functions quite apart from case work. Further discussion of this problem will be reserved for Part Three.

Juvenile detention and correction institutions are woefully inadequate. The depression and war periods impeded the construction of new facilities. With the increased number of delinquency cases during the war, the available facilities become overcrowded. According to Sherwood and Helen Norman,[21] detention should provide physical care and custody of children, under safe and healthful conditions, including sound medical programs, meet nonphysical needs, and provide information for the court. They conclude that throughout the country the increasing problems of juvenile delinquency, a growing recognition of these problems, and widespread publicity on the destructive use of jail detention for children, together with the wartime suspension of building operations, have contributed to a greatly increased demand for postwar improvements of detention facilities. The construction of such facilities has progressed fairly rapidly during recent years, but there are still many areas in which the facilities are inadequate.

Another trend is the growing demand for trained personnel in courts, probation and police departments, sheriff offices, and other law enforcement agencies, as well as in detention and correction institutions. Since the war, many of these agencies have added to their staffs persons who are especially trained for juvenile work. So great has been the demand for more adequately trained personnel that educational institutions have been requested to provide special training for those already employed in law enforcement agencies and to offer courses that lead to specialized training for future personnel. For instance, The University of Southern California established a special Delinquency Control Institute in 1946, after more than two years of planning by California peace officers and staff members of

---

[21] *Detention for the Juvenile Court.* A Discussion of Principles and Practices, National Probation Association (March, 1946), now the National Probation and Parole Association. See Part Three of the present text for further discussion of detention and correction institutions and agencies.

the University. This DCI, as it is commonly called, has offered each year intensive training to a selected number of officers employed by police departments, sheriff offices, and other law enforcing agencies.[22] While this is the only organization of its kind, special courses for the training of personnel in various types of juvenile bureaus are offered in a number of universities.

California has also pioneered in the establishment of state-wide programs for improved treatment and control of delinquency. In 1941, the California Youth Authority was established, patterned on the widely publicized model act recommended by the American Law Institute. Since its inception, the Authority has expanded the correctional schools and set up camps for the treatment of juvenile offenders, reorganized juvenile parole work, provided consultation services for juvenile courts and other agencies dealing with delinquents, and carried on extensive programs of preventive work, especially through community organization and the strengthening of local agencies. Now five other states (Minnesota, Wisconsin, Massachusetts, Texas, and Illinois) have made similar youth authority provisions.

There seems to be a renewed effort to organize communities on the local level for the purpose of helping children and young people by making residential areas better places in which to live. Community coordinating councils, such as those organized in Los Angeles County, are examples of this trend. There is a growing feeling that the small community, as it existed in early America, is disappearing or at least is less a functional unit than it formerly was. Consequently, local control of behavior problems has lessened. To meet the needs of youth and to stem the tide of law violation, some communities have mobilized local forces and organized the institutions and agencies of the areas into a coordinated unit.

Perhaps the most important trend during recent years has been the growing public interest in the problem of delinquency and its control. Public interest has been aroused, and there is an increasing demand that something be done to improve the treatment of delinquents and to prevent the spread of delinquency. The proper treatment of delinquents and better facilities for handling them, including facilities for more extensive case analysis and diagnostic treatment, as well as better methods of law enforcement, are important in dealing with the problem; but the social environment of

---

22 Cf. Dan G. Pursuit, "A University and Law Enforcement Work Together in the Control of Juvenile Delinquency," *Journal of Criminal Law and Criminology,* XXXVIII (November-December, 1947).

children must be improved if we are to get at the roots of delinquency.

The so-called "junior crime wave" lead the United States Senate at its 1953 session to authorize the first congressional investigation of the problem of juvenile delinquency.[23] The inquiry opened in November and the report was ordered published in March, 1954. While the report summarizes testimonies and reports by prominent authorities, the investigating committee apparently was baffled in trying to get at the root of the problem. The investigators found specifically grave problems in certain urban areas and noted the increase of certain types of offenses. No conclusion was reached with respect to the fundamental causes of delinquency, except that there is no one type of cause that has produced the apparent increase in juvenile offenses. The Senators recommended that no legislative action be taken until the problem had been studied further.

The social scientists are interested in research. Although many studies of delinquency have been made, especially for the purpose of improving treatment of offenders or promoting programs of prevention, much research work needs to be done before the problem of delinquency can be fully understood. Studies of the conditioning factors of delinquency are needed in particular, for few comprehensive studies of this kind have been made. Before it is possible to solve a problem, it is necessary to know what causes it and what forces contribute to its increase.

QUESTIONS AND PROJECTS

For Class Discussion and Research

1. What are the chief effects of the business cycle on delinquency?

2. Give reasons for the decline of juvenile delinquency during the depression years.

3. Show how the effect of a depression may affect juvenile behavior as contrasted to adult conduct.

4. Why should economic prosperity and economic depression have different effects on delinquency rates?

5. Make a list of the main wartime trends in juvenile delinquency. Which of these are subject to objective measurements?

6. On the basis of available statistical material, what were the trends in delinquency immediately following the war?

7. What factors account largely for the variations in increases and decreases of delinquencies by boys and girls?

23 *Juvenile Delinquency:* Interim Report of the Committee on the Judiciary, United States Senate, Eighty-Third Congress, Second Session (United States: Government Printing Office, 1954).

8. Why should some areas experience increases in delinquency during wartime, while others experience decreases or no change in the rate?

9. What are the advantages of using local statistics to show trends in delinquency?

10. Why are statistics of the volume and changes of delinquency relatively meaningless unless correlated with the population? Why is it necessary to use juvenile population rather than total population statistics for comparative purposes?

11. What changes have taken place in the nature and types of offenses?

12. Analyze changes in treatment of juvenile offenders, in law enforcement and observance, and in methods of control since the beginning of World War II.

SELECTED REFERENCES

BOGEN, DAVID, "Juvenile Delinquency and Economic Trend," *American Sociological Review,* IX (April, 1944), 178-184.

CARR, LOWELL J., *Delinquency Control* (New York: Harper & Brothers, 1950), especially Chapters IV and V.

CHUTE, CHARLES L., "Juvenile Delinquency in Wartime," *Probation* (June, 1943).

KILLIAN, W., "Juvenile Delinquency: Wartime Trends," *Probation* (June, 1944).

NEUMEYER, MARTIN H., "Delinquency Trends in Wartime," *Sociology and Social Research,* XXIX (March-April, 1945), 262-275.

UNITED STATES CHILDREN'S BUREAU, *Understanding Juvenile Delinquency.* Publication 300, 1943.

———, *Controlling Juvenile Delinquency,* Publication 301, 1943.

For bibliographies regarding delinquency and crime trends, consult:

CABOT, P. S. DEQ., *Juvenile Delinquency.* An Annotated Bibliography (New York: The H. W. Wilson Co., 1946); and *Comparative Survey of Juvenile Delinquency.* Part I. North America, prepared by Paul W. Tappan (New York: Division of Social Welfare, Department of Social Affairs, United Nations, 1952), bibliography 126-132; and *International Review of Criminal Policy* (New York: Department of Social Affairs, United Nations, published semi-annually, beginning with No. 1, 1952).

PART TWO

BASIC FACTORS AND CONDITIONS OF JUVENILE DELINQUENCY

It is more difficult to determine the causes of delinquency than to ascertain the extent of law violation among juveniles. Any etiological research is beset with difficulties. Deviant behavior is a part of a dynamic social process that can be understood only in relation to the personal-social situation and the sequence of events and experiences of which it is a part. Hence, to explain juvenile misbehavior, or any form of behavior, one must study the conditions of the individual, the main factors and influences of the social world in which the individual lives, and the series of occurrences that precede action. As Shaw and McKay have put it,

. . . It is generally assumed among students of human behavior that the attitudes and habits underlying the behavior of the child are built up in the course of his experiences, developing in the process of interaction between the child and successive situations in which he lives. The character of this process is determined, therefore, both by the condition in the organism and by the nature of the social and cultural situations to which the child is responsive. The child is born into the world a physical organism endowed with certain physical characteristics, reflexes, capacities, and undefined impulses. Furthermore, he is always born into a social world in which certain personalities, traditions, cultural forms, activities, and social relationships already exist. The social world thus precedes the child and has certain expectations with reference to him. It functions in relation to the original impulses as a defining agency, giving meaning to these impulses and largely determining the course of their development.

If the attitudes underlying behavior traits are formed in the process of social interaction, it follows that an understanding of the behavior of the child necessitates a knowledge of the social world in which he lives. Children always live and act in association with other persons. They live as members of groups, as participants in the activities of a dynamic social world; it is artificial to view them and their behavior apart from the various groups of which they are members.[1]

Students of human behavior must reckon with the phenomena of early established reaction patterns and tendencies. Children live and act in association with other persons, chiefly adults at first, and these intimate relationships are the source of some of the basic tendencies to act. Most of the early associations of a child are in the family, the play groups, and the immediate neighborhood. These groups are particularly significant, not only because they are the first groups to which the child belongs, but because they are primary groups. The relationships in these groups are face-to-face, the individual members have a sense of belonging (a we-feeling), and they are fundamental in the formation of the social ideas and ideals of the individual. Since the basic tendencies of behavior are formed so early in life, it is all the more difficult to ascertain the causes of misbehavior, for some of the social drives motivating behavior or misbehavior may have been formed many years prior to the particular act of delinquency.

Studies have shown that there is no single, unilateral cause of juvenile delinquency or of adult crime. Deviant behavior is not assignable to one universal source, nor yet to two or three. It springs from a wide variety, and usually a multiplicity, of converging influences. Even one act of delinquency may involve multifarious conditioning factors, some of which are difficult to discover. A number of factors usually occur together in a situation, some of which are more or less directly related to deviant behavior and may constitute the most conspicuous influences, whereas others have an indirect relationship to the behavior of the individual. The indirect conditions may at times become the chief cooperating factors, or they may remain as minor predisposing or aggravating factors. Sometimes otherwise disorganizing conditions exist in the situation, but they are inoperative in so far as a given act of delinquency is concerned. If a number of factors are merely concomitant elements, it is difficult to ascertain the exact connection between them and a given act of delinquency, for there may be no observable relationship between them. Existing or occurring together in a situation does not mean that some of the apparently disorganizing factors necessarily consti-

---

1 Clifford R. Shaw and Henry D. McKay, "Social Factors in Juvenile Delinquency: A Study of the Community, the Family, and the Gang in Relation to Delinquent Behavior," *Report on the Causes of Crime*, Vol. II, prepared for the National Commission on Law Observance and Enforcement (Washington, D. C.: United States Printing Office, No. 13, Vol. II, 1931), 3-4. Used by permission of United States Printing Office.

tute the causes of a given action. The relationship between concomitant factors may be incidental.

Thus, the complexity of the human organism and of the social world in which behavior takes place makes it confusing to ascertain the major reasons for delinquent behavior. The immediate and most apparent factors may root in deeper causes. The real causes sometimes are hidden beneath external and more easily observable factors. A cause is an agent or condition that determines by its incidence the appearance of a new force or action. It, therefore, precedes the effect. Herein lies the difficulty, for the cause-and-effect relationship is not clearly evident. For instance, sickness, poverty, poor housing, family disorganization, cultural conflicts, and delinquent behavior may occur together in a situation. While the other forms of disorganization have a bearing on delinquency, they do not necessarily constitute the decisive causes of the deviant conduct, even though some may have considerable influence. However, when two or more series of factors occur together, such as dependency and delinquency rates, one series can be regarded as the approximate index of the other, especially if such concomitant occurrences have been confirmed by a number of studies.

In approaching the causes of delinquency one must avoid both the older dogmatism and the more recent skepticism that sometimes verges on intellectual snobbery. Many prescientific views of the causes of delinquency and crime have been held, as indicated in Chapter I. Some of the early theorists held that criminal behavior was caused by innate depravity or was the instigation of the devil. This was followed by "schools of criminology," each with a specific emphasis, such as the hedonistic notion of the classical school, the economic determinism of the socialists, and the morphological or born-criminal theory of the Lombrosians. More recently, various theorists have attributed delinquency to such factors as biological or constitutional condition, to mental inferiority, to emotional immaturity, or to specific demographic or cultural conditions, omitting or greatly minimizing other important factors. These disagreements among theorists, as well as the obvious difficulties in getting at the true causes of a given phenomenon, have led some to despair of the possibilities of ever discovering the true causes of a given problem.

The multiple causation explanation is now quite generally subscribed to, but without some kind of theoretical frame of reference it leaves us somewhat "up in the air." It is true that the causes of delinquency are multifarious, ever changing, and deeply rooted. The total process, in which numerous and sometimes imponderable variables exist, is exceedingly complex. The relative roles of the variables differ from case to case, and from time to time, both as to the component elements and in the way the elements interact. But the multiple causation theory or explanation of delinquency does not mean that it is impossible to ascertain the important types or groups of factors that play a part in the process. A theoretical frame of reference is useful in discovering and in appraising the relative merits of the types of dynamic factors that play a part in a given situation.

Broadly stated, the frame of reference employed in this text is postulated on the theory that there is no single or well-established set of causes of delinquency. Delinquent behavior is the result of a multiplicity of associated factors rather than the product of a few apparent causes. More specifically, it is the product of both personal and social disorganization, which, in turn is rooted in various conditions. It is an integral part of a process in which disintegrating tendencies exist. As previously stated, this process involves the conditions of the individual personality of the delinquent, the pressures of the social environment, and the sequence of experiences preceding the act.

Since delinquency appears to be the product of the interaction of many associated factors and variables, and not the impact of any single cause or group of causes, "a functional frame of reference seems to be the desirable method of analysis for unraveling the multiplicity of relationships and the system of intricate associations between the factors and variables connected with crime and delinquency." [2] To disentangle the functional relationships of the conditioning factors requires careful research. Specific studies, limited to the analysis and correlation of selected factors and variables, enable one to measure their relative influence. The combined results of many such studies, using different kinds of variables, will give a more accurate indication of both primary and secondary causal factors.

It must be remembered that the personal and social disorganizing tendencies may not always culminate in delinquency, provided they are kept in check or are overcome by personal and social controls. To some extent delinquency is a failure of personal and social controls. Juvenile delinquents are usually not handicapped by one or a few adverse conditions, but by a number of them in combination. Most juveniles can overcome a few handicaps; but, if they are forced to face a series of difficulties involving various personal de-

---

2 Cf. Morris G. Caldwell, "The Youthful Male Offender in Alabama: A Study in Delinquency Causation," *Sociology and Social Research,* Vol. 37, No. 4 (March-April, 1953), 242.

fects, and social pressures and circumstances, they are likely to get into trouble, unless they are aided in their effort to overcome them by group influences and services. Thus, segmented data should be avoided, for delinquents are usually affected by numerous deleterious factors.

Some writers have maintained that the causes of crime and delinquency should be analyzed in terms of types of offenses. One way of avoiding the too comprehensive meanings attached to such terms as "criminals" and "delinquents" is to classify law violators into subtypes. Attempts to classify criminals go far back in the history of criminological research.[3] It seems obvious that the causes of offenses against property (larceny, auto theft, burglary, and possibly robbery) may differ markedly from offenses against persons (aggravated assault, murder). Also, sex offenses differ from the above-mentioned types of crimes in motivation. Habit-forming activities (drug addiction, alcoholism) belong in a special category. But there are difficulties in analyzing delinquents in accordance with types of offenses, for there are no fixed types of rigid and mutually exclusive categories. However, one way to avoid a too inclusive view of delinquency causation is to select relatively homogeneous groups, on the basis either of types of offenses as defined by law or of types of behavior involved, recognizing that individual variability often complicates any attempt to classify offenders. As a research device, a tentative classification of cases on the basis of types of offenses has considerable merit.

In spite of the difficulties encountered in the search for basic factors and conditions of delinquency, it is desirable to simplify the analysis by classifying the various items under certain general headings. These items do not necessarily cover the entire gamut of possible causal factors, but they do call attention to the ramifications of the problem. They represent a general frame of analysis rather than a system of verifiable causes. Furthermore, these items have been investigated and the order in which they are given represents

---

3 Men like Lombroso, Ferri, Garofalo, Mayhew, and Moreau have attempted various types of classification of criminals. In Chapter III of this text are given some of the types of offenses for which we have statistical information. For a discussion of criminal typology, see: Alfred R. Lindesmith and H. Warren Dunham, "Some Principles of Criminal Typology," *Social Forces*, Vol. 19, No. 3 (March, 1941), 307-314. Compare: Charles J. Browning, "Differential Social Relationships and Personality Factors of Parents and Boys in Two Delinquent Groups and One Nondelinquent Group," Doctor of Philosophy Dissertation, University of Southern California, 1954. Browning's contention is that the delinquent population is not a homogeneous and unitary group, but that there are more or less distinct subgroups of the delinquent population. He made a comparative study of auto thieves and truants, and compared them with a control group of perfect attenders in school.

to some extent the historical development of the analysis of the etiology of delinquency.[4]

The conditioning factors will be treated, for convenience and to simplify the analysis, under the following headings: (1) personality factors, including (a) biological, mental, and emotional conditions and (b) character and behavior traits; (2) home and family conditions, especially broken homes, inadequate or maladjusted families; (3) companionship relationships and gang activities; (4) the influence of community institutions and agencies, especially the deleterious effects of certain types of amusements; (5) population factors and cultural differences, including the composition, distribution, and changes of the population, as well as racial and nationality factors, cultural conflicts, and the succession of cultural groups; (6) economic and physical environmental factors, especially poverty, unemployment, economic exploitation of youth, slums and blighted areas, poor housing, and certain ecological elements; and (7) inadequate controls, law observance and enforcement, and the treatment of offenders.

These classes of factors could be variously grouped, such as those that have their roots chiefly in the personality of the delinquent, the factors associated with such intimate groups as the family and the play or gang group, and the community influences.[5]

---

[4] For discussions and classifications of the causes or conditions of delinquency and crime, consult Paul W. Tappan, *Juvenile Delinquency* (New York: McGraw-Hill Book Co., Inc., 1949), Part II; Negley K. Teeters and John O. Reinemann, *The Challenge of Delinquency* (New York: Prentice-Hall, Inc., 1950), Chapters III-VI; Sheldon and Eleanor Glueck, *Unraveling Juvenile Delinquency* (New York: The Commonwealth Fund, 1950) or *Delinquency in the Making* (New York: Harper & Brothers, 1952); Harry Elmer Barnes and Negley K. Teeters, *New Horizons in Criminology* (New York: Prentice-Hall, Inc., 1951); Ruth Shonle Cavan, *Criminology* (New York: Thomas Y. Crowell Co., 1948); Mabel A. Elliott, *Crime in Modern Society* (New York: Harper & Brothers, 1952), and Donald R. Taft, *Criminology* (New York: The Macmillan Co., 1950). For a brief review of the literature on phases of the problem, see: Marshall B. Clinard, "Sociologists and American Criminology," *The Journal of Criminal Law, Criminology, and Police Science,* Vol. 41, No. 5 (January-February, 1951), 549-557. For readings on causes of delinquency, consult Clyde B. Vedder, *The Juvenile Offender* (Garden City, N. Y.: Doubleday and Co., 1954).

[5] The outline and much of the material in this book are the outgrowth of several years of experience in teaching courses on juvenile delinquency. However, the writer is indebted to a special committee of the Delinquency Control Institute of the University of Southern California, which was composed of faculty members and experienced officers of law enforcement agencies of the Los Angeles area, for contributions in formulating the important items to be included and the types of data to use. This committee, of which the writer was a part, prepared the prospectus, the course outlines, and the syllabi used in the Institute. A group of graduate students did much of the library work in gathering material for the syllabi. The syllabus on *Conditioning Factors in Delinquency* (1946), prepared by Dr. Esther Pencheff under the writer's supervision, was of special help in formulating the details of Part Two.

Although many authorities now recognize that the causes of delinquency are multifarious, yet one-sided emphases are still prevalent and the functional relationships of variables are not recognized. Some of the best-known authorities who stress personality factors as of primary importance will be cited in Chapters IV and V, and the studies of environmental influences will be cited in the subsequent chapters of Part Two. Social scientists subscribe to the position that the causes of delinquency root chiefly in the society in which delinquents live. Some are inclined to overemphasize societary factors in their analysis of the causation of social problems, omitting important personality traits as dynamic forces behind conduct.[6]

---

[6] See Milton L. Barron, *The Juvenile in Delinquent Society* (New York: Alfred A. Knopf, 1954), especially Chapter XII. The central theme of this book is implicit in its title. The author maintains that "the theory of a delinquent society simply implies that society plays an incredibly greater role in making the individual juvenile delinquent than the individual freely determines for himself." (p. 202.) Society, culture, and social values are primarily the conditioners of juvenile conduct. Juveniles acquire both official and unofficial social values from adults. Socients have posed provocative theories with respect to conflict of culture and value differentials between delinquents and nondelinquents.

IV

PERSONALITY FACTORS: BIOLOGICAL AND PSYCHOLOGICAL

Personality may be defined, in a broad sense, as all the traits that make up the person and that condition his role in the group. For practical purposes, the chief traits may be classified as follows: (1) physical features and biological conditions (color, features, shape, size, general appearance, health and vitality, and the various biologic factors, whether inherited or acquired); (2) intelligence and mental reactions, including both mental ability and training; (3) emotional make-up and temperament, and the resultant feelings, emotional responses, sentiments, disposition, and the degree of emotional stability; (4) social drives, notably wishes, attitudes, habits, and interests; (5) character and moral or spiritual ideals, standards, and life's values; (6) modes of expression and skills; and (7) the conception the person has of himself and of his role in the group, and, the counterpart, his social status and prestige. These items overlap considerably and tend to merge into a unified whole.

This classification of personality traits indicates the make-up of a person. The topical arrangement of the present and the following chapters, however, is designed to call attention to only the personality factors that have been given attention in the studies of the problem of delinquency. Not all personality traits have been studied carefully in relation to conduct. Also, some of the conclusions presented need further testing. Nevertheless, it is desirable to review briefly the findings of previous studies in order to appraise personality factors as conditions of delinquency. The outline represents a convenient framework for the purpose of analysis and constitutes a logical sequence of items.

The roots of personality are found in the individual's organic inheritance, that is, in an organism endowed with physical, mental, and emotional conditions and capacities; but acquired traits, notably wishes, attitudes, habits, and behavior traits, are developed by the interplay of the individual with his environment. Inheritance may play an important part in certain biological and psychological conditions of the organism, but physical, mental, and emotional traits are affected early and more or less continuously throughout life by experience and by social influences. From a sociological point of view, personality is the totality of the individual as he is oriented for social participation.

Personality becomes oriented to and is molded by the natural setting, by the process of social interaction in the group, and by the nature of society. It is the product of the reciprocal relationship between the individual and the environment. To function efficiently, the many-segmented personality must be adjusted to the changing conditions of the environment.

Although personality traits are considered separately, it must be remembered that the total personality means an integration of the individual into his whole life and into the social milieu. In a way, a person as a unit is self-sufficient; that is, we can think of a person as apart from other persons. Yet no person lives unto himself and no one is a static entity. Personality is fundamentally behaving in a characteristic manner. This behaving takes place in a group. To function efficiently, personality must be integrated with the environment. One must view a person, then, in relation to other persons and as a part of a social situation. People are pliable and subject to social influences.

The individual approach to the study of delinquent behavior was the first to receive considerable attention on the part of those who endeavored to apply scientific methods to the analysis of conditioning factors. Psychologists and psychiatrists made the major contributions in this field. William Healy was one of the first to emphasize that the dynamic center of the whole problem of delin-

quency is the individual offender.[1] In his early work he overstressed
the point of view that all conduct is directly the expression of mental
life, but this view was somewhat corrected in his later studies.[2] The
case studies made by Healy and Bronner revealed the presence of
numerous personality factors as possible causes of delinquency, including underdeveloped physical organisms, glandular weaknesses,
constitutional inferiority, temperamental and dispositional weaknesses, neurotic and psychotic disorders, strongly self-assertive tendencies, precocious sex development and aggressive sex activities,
inferiority complexes, abnormal habits and attitudes, character defects, and a variety of other conditions. However, these cases likewise revealed certain environmental influences, notably family
disorganization, domineering parents, bad companionship, and
cultural conflicts.

Literally hundreds of studies have been made of individual
factors in crime, many of which have dealt with physical and biological conditions of criminals. Physical characteristics and handicaps, illnesses, and disorders have been emphasized.

Physical and Biological Factors

Experts do not agree regarding the physical characteristics
of delinquents or the effects of biological conditions on the incidence
of delinquency. Various conclusions with reference to the physical
characteristics of criminals have been summarized by Arthur E.
Fink [3] and Hans Von Hentig.[4] Other summaries [5] can be found in
recent books on delinquency and crime.

---

1 *The Individual Delinquent* (Boston: Little Brown and Co., 1915).

2 See William Healy and Augusta F. Bronner, Judge Baker Foundation, *Case
Studies* (1922-1923); *Delinquents and Criminals: Their Making and Unmaking* (New
York: The Macmillan Co., 1926); *New Light on Delinquency and Its Treatment* (New
Haven: Yale University Press, 1936). Compare Franz Alexander and William Healy,
Roots of Crime: Psychoanalytic Studies (New York: Alfred A. Knopf, 1935). Healy and
Bronner discuss "What Makes a Child Delinquent," in *Juvenile Delinquency and the
Schools:* Forty-Seventh Yearbook of the National Society for the Study of Education,
edited by Nelson B. Henry (Chicago: University of Chicago Press, 1948), 30-47. In
this latest résumé of causation they stress the complexity of factors that contribute to
delinquency; emphasizing that both acceptable and unacceptable forms of behavior are
the product of diverse personality components, the early and current experiences, and
the influence of the larger social scene. They believe that delinquents more than nondelinquents are dissatisfied with themselves and with their life situations, have stronger
unsatisfied urges, are often more active and restless, and suffer from inner conflicts.

3 *Causes of Crime* (Philadelphia: University of Pennsylvania Press, 1938).

4 *The Criminal and His Victim* (New Haven: Yale University Press, 1948) and
Crime: Causes and Conditions (New York: McGraw-Hill Book Co., 1947).

5 Mabel A. Elliott, *Crime in Modern Society* (New York: Harper & Brothers, 1952),
Chapter 12; Negley K. Teeters and John O. Reinemann, *The Challenge of Delin-*

The notion that criminality is due primarily to the physical inadequacy of the individual preceded Lombroso, but it was Cesare Lombroso, a prison physician, who popularized the theory. On the basis of what now seems rather naïve and superficial evidence, he concluded that the typical criminal is characterized by such physical traits as low forehead, ear deformation, receding chin, and other marked asymmetry. He measured the physical traits with great care and amassed sufficient data to make his theory impressive. But he was severely criticized, and his theory that criminals possessed biological inferiority fell into disrepute.

More recently, Earnest A. Hooton [6] has revived the early interest in the measurement of the physical traits of criminals. He tried to avoid what he regarded as Lombroso's "great error" by getting a larger sample and by recognizing racial and nationality differences, also by using a control group. He obtained measurements of 107 different anthropometric characteristics of 13,873 male convicts in ten states. Even though this was a relatively large sample, convicts are not a good measure of all criminals; and the study of 3,205 noncriminals was, by comparison, a small sample. He did not include corrections of all variables. Nevertheless, he concluded that criminals as a group are sociologically and biologically inferior individuals, with marked deficiency in gross bodily dimensions and in face and head diameters. They have broad noses and poorly developed facial dimensions, low foreheads, narrow jaws, and other abnormal features. Criminals are organically inferior, which inferiority is inherited. His general argument is that crime is the resultant of the impact of environment upon low-grade organisms. Social characteristics do not cause crime unless they are associated with physical characteristics. He did not explain the method of translating physical deviations into physical inferiority. In fact, there seems to be a lack of connection between his conclusions and his data. Apparently he started with the hypothesis that criminals are biologically inferior, and he continued to believe this even though the facts did not substantiate it. Certainly, there is meager evidence to support his notion of "primitivism" and "degeneracy."

A more recent and widely publicized study of the relation of bodily structure to the behavior of an individual was made by

---

quency (New York: Prentice-Hall, Inc., 1950), Chapter III; and Paul W. Tappan, *Juvenile Delinquency* (New York: McGraw-Hill Book Co., 1949). Compare: Walter C. Reckless and Mapheus Smith, *Juvenile Delinquency* (New York: McGraw-Hill Book Co., 1932), Chapter IV.

6 *Crime and the Man* (Cambridge: Harvard University Press, 1939).

William H. Sheldon.[7] His main thesis is that behavior is the function of structure. Life is a structure-behavior continuum. He presents descriptions and pictures of 200 young offenders referred to the Hayden Goodwill Inn in Boston. The 200 biographs, or micrographs as he prefers to call them, include descriptions, in each case, of the physique (the somatotype), with three photographs, and an analysis of temperamental patterns, the delinquency record, family background, medical and mental history, a running record of the boy's activities, a brief summary of his personality, the I.D. (Index of Delinquency), and comments in regard to the outlook of the case. By constitution, according to Sheldon, is meant the organizational or underlying pattern (the way things stand together), and somatotype refers to a quantification of the primary component determining the morphological structure of an individual. His earlier studies led to the conclusions that the somatotypes may be classified as endomorphic, mesomorphic, and ectomorphic, and that with these are closely correlated three temperamental and three psychiatric types. The major conclusions of his analysis of the 200 so-called delinquents indicate that they tend to be mesomorphic; that is, they are the solid and muscular type, with thick neck, broad shoulders, tapering torso, and a little on the "hefty and meaty" side.

As Sutherland has pointed out, Sheldon's definition of delinquency as "disappointingness" removes his study from the area of empirical research. His manner of selecting cases was inadequate, his scoring method was highly subjective and unreliable, his classification of cases was arbitrary, for it is difficult to distinguish the various types of delinquents (or rather cases studied), and his somatotypal and psychiatric indexes of the 200 youths have little meaning. Possibly the greatest objections to his study are not in respect to the descriptive material but to the interpretation of the data and to the theoretical excursions into bypaths of interpretation.

No studies in recent years have received more attention, both praise and criticism, than the studies of Sheldon and Eleanor Glueck. Famous for over a quarter century for their studies in juvenile delinquency and criminology, the Gluecks devoted the first fifteen years of their criminological research (1925-1939) to a study

---

[7] *Varieties of Delinquent Youth: An Introduction to Constitutional Psychiatry*, with the collaboration of Emil M. Hartl and Eugene McDermott (New York: Harper & Brothers, 1949). Compare the first two studies in the Human Constitution Series, *The Varieties of Human Physiques* (1940) and *The Varieties of Temperament* (1942). For a critical analysis of methods and conclusions, see "Critique of Sheldon's *Varieties of Delinquent Youth*," by Edwin H. Sutherland, *American Sociological Review*, Vol. 16 (February, 1951), 10-13.

of the effectiveness of various forms of peno-correctional treatment.[8] Since 1939 the Gluecks have shifted from the study of the effectiveness of various types of peno-correctional treatment to the study of causation, with the view of determining the most effective therapy and crime-preventive programs.[9]

Since these studies by the Gluecks will be referred to a number of times in this text, it is desirable to present a brief appraisal of them at this point. For comprehensiveness, no group of studies has equaled their criminological research. By taking 500 or 1,000 cases, each study was based on a relatively large sample. The earlier samples were institutionalized cases or general run of juvenile court cases. The more recent study included 500 delinquents and 500 nondelinquents. Furthermore, the Gluecks used a variety of methods in analyzing the cases. The criticisms of their recent study have been directed chiefly toward the methodology and the interpretations.[10] The matching of the delinquents with the control group was good on ethnic, intelligence, and several other grounds, but it was defective in age matching and to some extent in neighborhood matching. There is a strong possibility that the institutionalized life of the delinquents had a bearing on some of the behavior traits, as compared with the control group, which had no experience in institutions. The Gluecks relied too much on the examination of physical traits (see Sheldon) and the use of the Rorshach test, although they are a little dubious about the use of the latter. Since the methodology was somewhat defective, some of the findings must be questioned. Some of the reviewers feel that the "causal formula

8 Cf. *500 Criminal Careers* (New York: Alfred A. Knopf, 1930); *Later Criminal Careers* (New York: The Commonwealth Club, 1937); and *Juvenile Delinquents Grown Up* (New York: The Commonwealth Club, 1940). This series embraced the criminal careers of 500 male graduates of the Massachusetts Reformatory, the latter two constituting follow-up studies. The study of 500 former inmates of the Women's Reformatory at Farmingham, Massachusetts, is reported in *Five Hundred Delinquent Women* (New York: Alfred A. Knopf, 1934). The study of 1,000 juvenile offenders who passed through the Boston Juvenile Court and the Judge Baker Foundation Center is reported in *One Thousand Juvenile Delinquents* (Cambridge: Harvard University Press, 1934), and the subsequent report *After-Conduct of Discharged Offenders* (London: Macmillan and Company, Ltd., 1945).

9 Cf. Sheldon and Eleanor Glueck, *Unraveling Juvenile Delinquency* (New York: The Commonwealth Fund, 1950) and *Delinquents in the Making: Paths to Prevention* (New York: Harper & Brothers, 1952).

10 Cf. Sol Rubin, "Unraveling Juvenile Delinquency: I. Illusions in a Research Project Using Matched Pairs," and Albert J. Reiss, Jr., "Unraveling Juvenile Delinquency: II. An Appraisal of the Research Methods," *The American Journal of Sociology*, Vol. 57 (September, 1951), 107-120; "Symposium on the Gluecks' *Unraveling Juvenile Delinquency*," by a federal judge, several sociologists, psychiatrists, and psychologists, in *Federal Probation*, Vol. 15, No. 1 (March, 1951). Similar reviews and symposia are found in other journals.

or law" is oversimplified. A cross-sectional analysis of preselected factors tends to lend itself to one-sided interpretation. Although the Gluecks reject any unitary explanation, such as the cultural, they have a strong leaning toward the biological or constitutional determinants.

In summarizing the "causal complex" and taking into account the dynamic interplay of the various levels and channels of influence, the Gluecks present a tentative "causal formula or law," as follows:

. . . The delinquents as a group are distinguishable from the nondelinquents: (1) physically, in being essentially mesomorphic in constitution (solid, closely knit, muscular); (2) temperamentally, in being restlessly energetic, impulsive, extroverted, aggressive, destructive (often sadistic) —traits which may be related more or less to the erratic growth pattern and its physiologic correlates or consequences; (3) in attitude, by being hostile, defiant, resentful, suspicious, stubborn, socially assertive, adventurous, unconventional, non-submissive to authority; (4) psychologically, in tending to direct and concrete, rather than symbolic, intellectual expression, and in being less methodical in their approach to problems; (5) socio-culturally, in having been reared to a far greater extent than the control group in homes of little understanding, affection, stability, or moral fibre by parents usually unfit to be effective guides and protectors or, according to psychoanalytic theory, desirable sources for emulation and the construction of a consistent, well-balanced, and socially normal superego during the early stages of character development. While in individual cases the stresses contributed by any one of the above pressure-areas of dissocial-behavior tendency may adequately account for persistence in delinquency, in general the high probability of delinquency is dependent upon the interplay of the conditions and forces from all these areas.[11]

While it is a daring thing to formulate a law of crime causation, the Gluecks' formula has not been tested enough to use as a law. It emphasizes chiefly the personality aspects.

Without further review of the theories and studies of the biological basis of crime and delinquency, certain findings with respect to heredity, diseases, and physical handicaps may now be analyzed. It must be remembered that most of the studies of the physical and mental conditions of delinquents have been made of institutionalized cases. One of the most elementary cautions in criminological research is the recognition that an examination of institutionalized offenders does not necessarily give a true picture of delinquents in general. Usually, only the more serious cases are institutionalized, and often only after all other methods of treatment have been tried

---

11 *Unraveling Juvenile Delinquency, op. cit.,* 281-282. Used by permission of the Commonwealth Fund and Harvard University Press.

and have failed. Furthermore, some individuals are institutionalized not only because of their delinquencies but also because they need treatment for certain ailments or defects. After a person has been institutionalized for some time, he sometimes acquires certain traits characteristic of institutional associations, particularly from contacts with certain types of offenders. These and other factors associated with them may unduly affect the personalities of individual cases; hence the analysis of institutionalized cases may give an exaggerated picture of the extent of physical diseases and handicaps among delinquents.

Innate versus Acquired Traits. This is not the place to debate the question of the relative importance of innate versus acquired traits. It is obvious that every individual inherits an organism endowed with certain characteristics and potentialities. All of us have inherited human traits, sex characteristics, racial features and color, and various consanguineal and individual traits. No two individuals are born with exactly the same type of organisms. Likewise, every individual possesses acquired traits, some of which are developed early in life. So it is not a manner of either inherited or acquired characteristics, for both influence conduct.

Delinquency as such is not inherited, but some theorists have maintained that delinquents possess certain biological traits which predisposes them to delinquent behavior. As has already been indicated, writers like Lombroso have maintained that criminals can be identified by certain biological traits which for the most part are inherited. It is now generally believed that the hereditary constitution of a person has but an indirect effect upon his behavior. The delinquent is not by organic make-up, temperament, or predisposition criminal in nature. However, weaknesses in native equipment. such as deformities and other abnormalities of the body, which handicap the person in his social relationships, may be an important factor in deviant behavior.

The part played by heredity is usually in conjunction with adverse environmental influences and pressures. Heredity conditions what a person can do, whereas environment conditions what he does. Heredity places certain limitations upon a person's activities and achievements. Some hereditary traits are great handicaps. Thus, it can be assumed that hereditary factors establish a condition within which framework environmental influences operate. Behavior is biosocial; that is, the biological equipment of a person and the environment in which a person lives operate jointly in the process of behavior. Both are important factors, and in a given situation it is sometimes impossible to know which set of influences is more important.

Studies of delinquency have not proved that abnormal behavior is attributable to defective germ plasm; but, nevertheless, heredity plays a considerable role in maladjustment. Deficiencies of the body, of the mind, and of the temperamental or emotional make-up are bound to have a bearing on conduct. The term "defective delinquent" [12] has been coined to describe individuals who are mentally defective and morally delinquent. At first they were known as "moral imbeciles," but later they were usually referred to as "defective delinquents." This, however, does not mean, necessarily, that the defectiveness is the cause of their delinquency. Dr. Walter E. Fernald recognized the defective delinquent type as early as 1910. He felt that they should not be placed in institutions for the feeble-minded, for they had behavior traits and problems that had a bad influence on the ordinary defectives. Even though numerically they constitute only a small part of the defectives—probably not more than 10 per cent of the total feeble-minded population—they are a great problem from the point of view of treatment. Being both defective and criminalistic, it is sometimes difficult to decide into what type of institution such a person should be placed. If the subnormal intelligence and antisocial tendencies are so deep-seated as to require care and treatment, they probably should be institutionalized; but they require a special type of treatment quite apart from that of the usual mental deficiency institutions. They cannot easily be handled in institutions for delinquents, for most correctional institutions do not have special facilities for the treatment of the mentally deficient or diseased.

The term "psychopath" has been applied to some delinquents. Hirsch [13] lists psychopathic personality, constitutional inferiority, schizoid condition, cyclothymic personality, constitutional homosexualism, and compulsion neuroticism as possible hereditary causes of delinquency. Those who have emphasized that some of the delinquents are "psychopaths" or possess similar conditions of personality have pointed out that they are unstable, irresponsible, and egocentric, lack ambition, and are unable to learn from experience. Their deficiency is not one of intellect, necessarily, but pertains to matters of decency, honesty, and other character traits.

---

[12] Consult Samuel B. Kutash, "Defective Delinquent," *Encyclopedia of Criminology*, edited by Vernon C. Branham and Samuel B. Kutash (New York: Philosophical Library, 1949), 124-127.

[13] Nathaniel Hirsch, *Dynamic Causes of Juvenile Crime* (Cambridge: Science-Art Publishers, 1937), 12.

That some delinquents are emotionally unstable and show evidence of mental disorders is evident, but it is quite another thing to classify them as "born psychopaths." Character, as will be pointed out in the subsequent chapter, is definitely acquired. Mental and emotional conditions may affect character development, but the basic elements of character grow out of experience. The term "psychopathic" has acquired the function of a wastebasket, for there is a tendency among some psychiatrists to include under it all the cases that do not clearly fit the categories of psychosis and psychoneurosis.[14] For this reason, some have questioned the use of the term. To include such types of cases as antisocial persons, moral degenerates, pathological liars, swindlers, kleptomaniacs, eccentrics, drug addicts, and the like, is obviously using the concept "pathological" loosely. Furthermore, to attribute their condition fundamentally to heredity is largely a matter of conjecture, not of science.

It should be noted that heredity plays a part in such matters as general physique, intelligence, sex, race, and various individual peculiarities. These matters are given consideration in other parts of this text and need not be emphasized here. None of the hereditary factors, although significant, predestine the individual to criminal behavior independent of experience. The chief difficulty in determining the relative merits of innate and acquired traits is that it is not possible to control completely either the factors of heredity or those of environment and experience for the purpose of accurate measurement.

Physical Abnormalities and Poor Health. Possibly no phase of delinquency has been more investigated than the health conditions of delinquents, especially medical examinations to determine the extent of diseases, physical weaknesses and defects, and other physical handicaps. The medical examination of delinquents, especially of the institutionalized cases, is now considered a necessary part of the treatment process. When juveniles are admitted to detention homes or to correctional institutions, one of the first steps in the intake process is the medical examination. And in the larger institutions, the medical staff includes a psychiatrist to examine the mental conditions of individuals who need such examination. From the point of view of treatment, it is important to detect and to correct health defects regardless of the effects these conditions may have had on their conduct, for ill health or physical defectiveness in itself is

---

14 For a discussion of this point, consult: Norman Q. Brill and John H. Baird, chapter on "Psychopathic Personality," in *Modern Abnormal Psychology: A Symposium*, edited by William H. Mikesell (New York: Philosophical Library, 1950), 663.

a problem that must be dealt with if the inmates in institutions are to receive adequate care and treatment.

Although medical staffs of detention and correction institutions have found numerous major and minor physical ailments and defects among the clients, the relationship between these conditions and their behavior is not always ascertainable. Many with physical defects and inferior biological conditions or diseases have made their way through life without excessive disturbance or antisocial conduct, even playing a useful part in life's work; but others become delinquent. Physical shortcomings are accessory and aggravating influences, and sometimes primary factors, in delinquency. No significant statistical comparison of the frequency of physical defects and abnormalities in the criminal and noncriminal population has been made, but in some cases they are undoubtedly significant. The significance depends largely on the reactions of other persons toward those defects and the effect that they have on the desired activities of the individuals. Physical defects and illnesses go along with poor economic and social conditions. Physical conditions or economic poverty, or both, tend to produce negative social reactions, even disapproval, which affects the person's status and can, at least indirectly, condition a person's criminal behavior. Crime may be motivated by the desire to compensate for frustrations growing out of such conditions.

As the literature on delinquency is reviewed, one finds many statements and references to the extent of physical defects and diseases of the delinquents studied and of the possible effects of biological conditions on the incidence of delinquency.[15] Burt found that 70 per cent of the delinquents studied had some physical defects, but the majority of them were otherwise fairly normal, not diseased. Healy and Bronner, and the Gluecks (in the earlier studies), on the basis of case studies, found a considerable proportion of the delinquents in poor physical condition, but they also found that many were in good physical condition. The later study by the Gluecks and the study by Sheldon seem to indicate that the typical delinquent is not the physically defective type as was formerly assumed. In *Unraveling Juvenile Delinquency* (Chapter XIV), the Gluecks

---

15 Cf. Cyril Burt, *The Young Delinquent* (New York: D. Appleton and Co., 1925 and 1938). Compare Maud A. Merrill, *Problems of Child Delinquency* (Boston and New York: Houghton Mifflin Co., 1947); Ralph S. Banay, "Physical Disfigurement as a Factor in Delinquency and Crime," *Federal Probation*, Vol. VII (January-March, 1943), 20-24; and the books previously referred to in this chapter, such as those by William Healy and Augusta F. Bronner, Sheldon and Eleanor Glueck, Earnest A. Hooton, and William H. Sheldon. See summaries in the references given in footnotes 3, 4, and 5. See also Ralph S. Banay, *Youth in Despair* (New York: Coward-McCann, 1947).

emphasize that their studies show that there was little difference in the health of the 500 delinquents and the 500 nondelinquents. Physiologically the delinquents were found to be superior to the nondelinquents in gross bodily size; that is, they were more muscular, with heavy arms, broad shoulders, strong neck, and tapering torso, but with a small face. Otherwise they did not find strong bodily disproportions. The differences were chiefly in the functional deviation field.

Those who have paid special attention to physical conditions of the inmates in institutions or of children brought into courts have pointed out certain types of health conditions that seem to them to be especially prevalent. Malnutrition is frequently mentioned. Thurston,[16] who studied many aspects of delinquency, cites a New York study which shows that 42 per cent of the children in a high delinquency area were suffering from malnutrition as compared with only 19 per cent in the general population who were malnourished. Deviation from the normal weight and height norms is another factor that has been extensively noted among delinquents. An oversized or an underdeveloped child, especially if the deviation from the norm is conspicuous, may make the child feel out of place. Some studies have shown that sex delinquents, especially girls, are physically overdeveloped. Enuresis (bed wetting) has been found by some to be more extensive among delinquents than among nondelinquents. Medical staffs of detention and other institutions for deviation children have noted the types of diseases that seem to be most prevalent among delinquents, as the medical histories of cases have revealed them; but the results of such studies vary a great deal.

The relationship of glandular functioning to emotions and behavior has been known for some time. Hormone imbalance, endocrine disturbance, and other glandular conditions may affect behavior in a number of ways. Hormones, as chemical products, may disturb the internal make-up of an individual. Indirectly, hereditary factors and the external environment can produce changes in the hormone pattern. Endocrine disorders, as hyperthyroidism, hyperadrenalism, hyperpituitarism, or deficiency in pancreatic hormone secretion (insulin), affect both the bodily and mental conditions of the child. The disorder may be relatively localized in one or two glands, or the whole interacting endocrine system may be disfunctioning. Deficiency in glandular functions results in stunted growth, delayed puberty, fat formation, inertia, and even mental retardation. Hypersecretion may promote excessive growth and re-

16 Henry W. Thurston, *Concerning Juvenile Delinquency* (New York: Columbia University Press, 1942), 26.

sult in excessive activity or excitability. It may lead to quick, impulsive behavior and lack of caution. Some have taken an extreme view of glandular influences on conduct, asserting that nearly all misbehavior involves some form of glandular dysfunctioning. Glandular influences result chiefly from the interfunctioning of several glands, rather than from a single gland functioning independently. But as impressive as the findings of endocrinology are, the studies of glandular dysfunctions do not provide a clue to criminal causation, noncriminals as well as criminals have malfunctioning glands. Excellent work is done in relieving tensions and discomforts of persons suffering from glandular imbalance; but it is another thing to say that if such imbalance is allowed to exist it will produce delinquency. Glandular treatment may clear up some atypical behavior, but delinquents may suffer no more from glandular dysfunctioning than do members of the general population, although it must be admitted that insufficient comparative studies have been made to prove or to disprove a direct connection between the dysfunctioning of glands and acts of law violation.

Defects, such as blindness, deafness and hard of hearing, lameness, stammering, hideous scars, or other malformations and deformities of the body, tend to set children apart from the group and may directly or indirectly contribute to delinquent behavior, especially if the child is very unhappy about the situation and feels that something needs to be done to compensate for the misfortune. Speech defects may cause, or be caused by, emotional conflicts. They sometimes result in teasing and other unfavorable reactions on the part of playmates. Sensory defects sometimes have similar effects. Inferior stature or conspicuous bulkiness of the body may likewise call forth teasing. Although it is difficult to show a direct connection between physical deformity or ugliness and behavior, when individuals have repulsive features they face untoward reactions on the part of others. Frustration, disappointment, and even antisocial behavior may be the consequence of such biosocial conditions. Some investigators have reported that delinquents more than nondelinquents suffer from bodily weaknesses. Such conditions may thwart activities and ambitions.

It is not necessary for our purpose to cite further illustrations of studies of physical and biological conditions of delinquents. Although many investigators have discovered excessive incidences of abnormal conditions among the delinquents, few have maintained that the delinquents are a special type from the physical point of view. The studies reviewed earlier in this chapter are exceptions, but their findings have been questioned by many authorities. It is safer to assume that both delinquency and certain physical or biological conditions occur concomitantly in situations, and both may be the result of deeper causes. That there may be a reciprocal relationship between certain variables is fairly obvious, but the difficulty arises when the relationship has to be demonstrated.

Although it is difficult to measure precisely the possible effects of physical illness and defectiveness on conduct, they represent health problems irrespective of their relationship to subsequent behavior. Health is a measure of physical well-being and is a prized possession. Sickness is rated as one of the great social problems of society. It is estimated that as of June, 1950, over 10,000,000 persons in the United States were suffering from chronic illness and disabling conditions, and the number of handicapped individuals exceeded 18,500,000. The total admissions to registered hospitals during the preceding years exceeded 16,500,000, and the total expenditure for medical care during that year was about $10,000,000,-000.[17] Great progress has been made in medical care and in the control of diseases, but much needs to be done to keep the population healthy.

PSYCHOLOGICAL FACTORS

Psychological factors are closely interwined with physical conditions. The division is somewhat arbitrary and of value chiefly for the purpose of analysis. Health conditions and physical handicaps affect the mental and emotional functioning of the individual, and psychological disturbances may upset the physical organism, as recent studies of psychosomatic medicine have clearly shown. The thinking, feeling, and acting processes are significant factors to consider in the understanding of the behavior of individuals. The psychological factors studied most extensively, in so far as delinquent behavior of juveniles and adult crime are concerned, may be classed as mental deficiency and retardation, mental diseases and functional disorders, and emotional conflicts and instabilities. Individuals whose personalities have not developed evenly in these matters are especially prone to cause trouble. Uneven mental growth, under- or overdevelopment of the mental processes, lack of emotional control, mental defects and disorders, or a combination of these factors may be associated with delinquent behavior.

---

[17] See the author's book on *Social Problems and the Changing Society* (New York: D. Van Nostrand Co., 1953), 150-155.

Mental Deficiency and Retardation. Mental deficiency refers to defective intellect or the lack of learning capacity. It generally implies an inherited defect, although injury to a normal brain may result in feeble-mindedness. Feeble-minded persons are sometimes classified as idiots, imbeciles, and morons. A feeble-minded person lacks the intelligence or training required to take care of his own needs properly. In children, low intelligence means that they are incapable by reason of such defectiveness of receiving proper benefits from instruction at home or in school. Mental retardation is an arrested development of the mind because of neglect or lack of training in thinking. These conditions result in low mental efficiency.

The exact relationship between lack of intelligence and misconduct has not been proved. There is nothing in the make-up of a feeble-minded person that makes delinquency inevitable, though he may be more open to suggestion, more easily led, and less clever in escaping law enforcement officers. Extreme cases of mental deficiency are not often found among delinquents, because, as a rule, such cases become institutionalized rather early, and are not held responsible for their behavior, or their intelligence is so low as to be incapable of gross and deliberate violation of law.

Carr [18] summarizes studies made by Burt, Beans, Armstrong, the Gluecks, Fenton, and Livingston of the range of intelligence (I.Q. distribution) of juvenile delinquents as compared with the theoretical distribution. A total of 4314 cases was reported in these six studies. The average percentage below 70 in these studies is 24.6 as compared with the theoretical 1 per cent in the general population. But since these were institutionalized cases, the degree of mental retardation or inferiority is much higher than would be found among the "run of the mine" cases in the juvenile courts.

Although low or uneven intelligence or aptitude may seriously affect a person in conforming to socially sanctioned behavior norms, the lack of intelligence is not overwhelmingly causal in cases of delinquency. Healy found that, of 4,000 recidivists in the juvenile courts of Chicago and Boston, over 70 per cent were mentally normal. However, Healy and Bronner [19] concluded that serious delin-

---

[18] Lowell J. Carr, *Delinquency Control* (New York: Harper & Brothers, 1951), 133. For a review of important studies of the incidence of feeble-mindedness among offenders, intelligence test scores of offenders, intelligence in relation to age and sex of offenders and to types of crime and to recidivism, see Milton Metfessel and Constance Lovell, "Recent Literature on Individual Correlates of Crime," *Psychological Bulletin,* Vol. 38, No. 3 (March, 1942).

[19] William Healy and Augusta F. Bronner, *Delinquents and Criminals, Their Making and Unmaking, op. cit.,* 151.

quency is five to ten times more frequent among the feeble-minded than among the general population. Burt recognizes that the relationship between delinquency and feeble-mindedness is negligible, but he stresses the point that there are indications of high incidence of dullness among delinquents.

Sutherland [20] analyzed 350 reports, which included mental tests of approximately 175,000 criminals and delinquents. The proportion of delinquents diagnosed as feeble-minded decreased from more than 50 per cent in the average study made in the early period, 1910-1914, to 20 per cent in the later period, 1925-1928. Sutherland thinks that the decrease was due chiefly to changes in the methods of making and scoring the tests. As the ability to compose and administer intelligence tests increased, the trend was to find less mental deficiency among the inmates of correctional schools and penal institutions. This survey demonstrated that feeble-mindedness is a less significant factor in delinquency than had been supposed. However, the relation of feeble-mindedness to delinquency cannot be determined by dealing with it in isolation from other factors. It has significance only if considered in relation to many other personal and situational factors. Whatever relation the lack of intelligence bears to misconduct, it cannot be considered as overwhelmingly causal. This is particularly true of adult criminals—more so than of juvenile delinquents.

In certain types of offenses, such as sex crimes, low intelligence seems to be a more common factor than in cases of forgery and the gangster types of crimes. It is recognized that among sex offenders the mental status of the girls may be low; but this may not be the prime cause of their difficulties, for other factors play an important part. Equally defective and vicious males with whom they come in contact, or who make it a practice to prey upon such girls, are in substantial measure responsible for their sex involvements. The feeble-minded are more easily led into delinquency; and once they have formed habits, they are slow to change. The cause is both hereditary and acquired.

When intelligence testing experienced a great vogue a few decades ago, no trait of delinquents and criminals was more investigated than was their intelligence. It was generally assumed that low intelligence per se was responsible for their misconduct. Later, more refined research revealed the difficulties involved in unrestricted correlation of intelligence and delinquency. Test results

---

[20] Edwin H. Sutherland, *Principles of Criminology* (New York: J. B. Lippincott Co., 1947), 103-105.

have varied according to what they are designed to measure and the methods used in the measurement process. It is difficult to separate intelligence from physical conditions, emotional qualities, education, and environmental influences in the matter of conduct. Low intelligence seems likely to increase frustration experienced by individuals and to diminish the effectiveness of socializing forces, in that the lowered capacity makes it less likely to understand and appreciate the consequences of specific acts. On the other hand, those with low intelligence may lack aspirations and adjust themselves to situations considered less tolerable by the more intelligent boys and girls. The adjustment or the lack of adjustment of the individual to social situations is conditioned by the way people react to the individual thus afflicted.

Metfessel and Lovell, after surveying the relationship between intelligence and crime, especially the incidence of feeble-mindedness and the intelligence test scores of offenders, and reviewing the basic studies of this subject, conclude that intelligence is not considered so important a cause of crime as it was formerly.

> There is considerable disagreement as to just how important this correlate is, but studies do, in the main, support placing the typical delinquent in the dull normal class. Any general statement as to the relative intelligence of offenders and nonoffenders is difficult. It appears safe to say that most results show inferiority of the test scores of criminals in comparison to the theoretical distribution of the population (the validity of which is doubtful). Smaller differences have been found between offenders and such samples of the population as the Army draft, but no clear-cut conclusion can be drawn even from these, because the representative quality of these noncriminal groups is questionable.[21]

The authors point out, in reviewing the studies of intelligence in relation to the age factor, that intelligence is a more significant factor among juvenile delinquents than among adult prisoners. The influence of intelligence as a factor in crime varies also with the type of crime.

Mental Diseases and Functional Disorders. The more extreme forms of mental disorders develop chiefly during adult life, but the early manifestations of certain types of mental conditions are discernible during childhood. The psychoanalysts, in particular, have called attention to the fact that delinquency tendencies may develop early in a child's life and that certain mental conditions precede or

---

21 Metfessel and Lovell, *op. cit.*, 148. Used by permission of *Psychological Bulletin*.

accompany delinquent behavior.[22] In order to evaluate the possible effects of mental disorders on juvenile conduct, it is necessary to understand the major types of mental disorders.[23] The following simplified grouping of abnormal psychological problems may be used: (1) feeble-minded and low mental efficiency (already discussed); (2) psychoneuroses; (3) psychoses and associated personality disorders; (4) minor forms of personality disorders and borderlands of abnormality, including emotional conflicts and instability, also various forms of frustrations. Psychiatrists have described other forms of mental disorders usually not classified under the foregoing captions.

Psychoneurosis, or simply neurosis, manifests itself in various forms, although the types overlap. They are chiefly emotional disorders that involve some degree of inefficiency. Not all forms of emotional conflicts and frustrations, as will be indicated later, should be classified under neurosis. There is no agreement with respect to the exact types of psychoneurosis (or neurosis), but five fairly clear-cut groups of symptoms (syndromes) have been identified: (1) neurasthenia, accompanied by headaches, dizziness, chronic fatigue, irritability, and weakness or discomfort (the term has been so misused that it has fallen into disrepute); (2) psychasthenia, characterized by abnormal fears (phobia), obsessions, and compulsions;

---

22 Cf. K. R. Eissler, Editor, *Searchlights on Delinquency: New Psychoanalytic Studies* (New York: International Universities Press, Inc., 1949). This book consists of a series of papers by thirty-eight psychoanalysts from all parts of the world, dedicated to August Aichhorn, president of the re-established Psychoanalytic Society in Vienna, on his seventieth birthday. Compare Aichhorn's own book, *Wayward Youth* (1935), or the original German edition, *Verwährloste Jugend* (1925). See also Kate Friedlander, *The Psycho-Analytical Approach to Juvenile Delinquency* (New York: International Universities Press, Inc., 1947), and Eugene Davidoff and Elinor S. Noetzel, *Juvenile Delinquency: The Child Guidance Approach* (New York: Child Care Publications, 1951). The latter book is based upon experimental work conducted at the Syracuse Psychopathic Outpatient Department and Hospital. It is not just a programmatic endeavor, for the discussion of the cases includes the social, mental and medical aspects of the larger problem of juvenile delinquency, and the authors present the broader psychiatric and mental hygiene approach to juvenile conduct disorders.

23 For a classification of personality disorders, see Louis P. Thorpe and Barney Katz, *The Psychology of Abnormal Behavior: A Dynamic Approach* (New York: The Ronald Press Co., 1948), 208-210, 211-224. Thorpe and Katz give the classification of types of mental disorders prepared by the American Psychiatric Association and discuss in greater detail their own classification. See also Louis P. Thorpe, *The Psychology of Mental Health* (New York: The Ronald Press Co., 1950). For a biosocial classification, see Norman Cameron, *The Psychology of Mental Disorders: A Biosocial Interpretation* (New York: Houghton Mifflin Co., 1947). For concise description of problems of mental hygiene, see D. B. Klein, *Mental Hygiene: The Physiology of Personal Adjustment* (New York: Henry Holt and Co., 1944), and Herbert A. Carroll, *Mental Hygiene: The Dynamics of Adjustment* (New York: Prentice-Hall, Inc., 1951). The author's book on *Social Problems and The Changing Society, op. cit.,* 155-168, is a concise summary of the various types of psychological deficiencies and disorders.

(3) hysteria, including a wide variety of symptoms, such as paralysis, heart attack, headache, and nonfunctioning of one or more of the senses; (4) anxiety neurosis, involving marked apprehensiveness regarding impending dangers and a variety of psychosomatic symptoms; and (5) hypochondria, an excessive preoccupation with the state of health. Psychoneurotic persons usually have failed to mature emotionally. When frustrated, they lack self-reliance and self-confidence to face the situation. Otherwise, the psychoneurotics may possess desirable personality traits. Wartime neuroses are not essentially different from the usual types, except that the individuals are under unusual stress, which may lead to "crack-ups."

The types of psychoses and associated personality disorders have been variously classified. They may be organic or functional, but usually they are both. Psychoses that are chiefly organic in nature are due to structural (physical) alternation or disturbed physiology of the body; whereas the functional disorders grow out of experience in frustrating, emotionally disturbing, extremely conflicting, and disorganizing situations, although they frequently involve certain organic dysfunctions also. The most pronounced functional disorders include schizophrenia (dementia praecox), paranoia, manic-depressive, and involutional melancholia types, each of which can be further subdivided into special classes. The schizophrenes range from the simple type to the hebephrenic (bizarre symptoms like hilarious laughter, silly gestures, or grotesque facial expression), catatonic (psychomotor abnormalities, ranging from stupor to excitement), and paranoid kinds. Paranoia is characterized by persecution complexes and grandiose delusions. The paranoiac pattern includes suspicious attitude, logic-tight delusion, and intensity of reaction. The paranoia cases sometimes exhibit contradictory patterns, showing evidence of intelligence and social acceptability, on the one hand, and at other times being litigious (wanting to bring the persecutor to trial and have him punished), erotic, jealous, or the exalted crusader type. Once having developed strong delusions, the patient is difficult to treat successfully.

The manic-depressive patient has periodic attacks of elation or depression, usually with relatively normal periods between such attacks. The emotional reactions are strongly in evidence. This form is very rare before the age of 18.

It is difficult to show the exact relationship between these forms of mental disorders and delinquent behavior. Dunham [24] concludes

---

24 H. W. Dunham, "The Schizophrene and Criminal Behavior," *American Sociological Review*, Vol. IV (June, 1939), 356. Compare Robert E. L. Faris and H. W. Dunham, *Mental Disorders in Urban Areas* (Chicago: University of Chicago Press, 1939).

that the schizophrenes show almost complete absence of delinquent behavior during their early adolescent period. The paranoid type is probably a greater threat to life and property, but it is difficult to detect the early tendency toward delinquency. The delusion of persecution involves the desire to kill the supposed persecutors. In fact, both the schizophrenic and the paranoid types may have strong persecution delusions and complexes, which may lead to homicidal attacks upon the supposed persecutors.

In reviewing the etiology of delinquency, Bovet [25] cites examples and gives illustration of how various forms of mental and emotional disorders may affect conduct, but he also discusses the differences of opinion in regard to the possible effects of such conditions on conduct. He thinks that, of the functional psychoses types, schizophrenia is of special interest here. He recognizes that the relative importance assigned to schizophrenia in the causation of juvenile delinquency varies from one side of the Atlantic to the other. The psychiatrists of the European school have considered infantile schizophrenia a rarity. Bovet thinks that it is not difficult to understand how some forms of psychoneuroses may predispose to delinquent behavior, for like other forms of mental illness they may result in severe "dis-adaption" and can lead to a kind of compulsive need to commit crimes. This is particularly true of some sexual crimes and also thefts and related offenses. On the other hand, although certain psychoneurotic reactions may favor delinquent behavior, more often the suppressions and repressions which typify a fully developed psychoneurosis may protect the neurotic from his antisocial impulses. However, isolated neurotic symptoms are often found among the etiological factors in a juvenile's social "dis-adaptation." Bovet has a lengthy discussion of the "constitutional psychopaths," which designation is now somewhat in disrepute, especially in America. According to the usual description of this type, the psychopath is supposed to be egocentric, unable to profit by experience, emotionally unstable, lacking in feeling, lacking in moral scruples and insensitive to the rights of others, and in general erratic and

---

The Yale University study of the relationship between psychiatric disorders and social stratification may be noted in this connection. See August B. Hollingshead, "Trends in Social Stratification: A Case Study," *American Sociological Review*, Vol. 17, No. 6 (December, 1952), 679-686, and A. B. Hollingshead and Frederick C. Pedlich, "Social Stratification and Psychiatric Disorders," *American Sociological Review*, Vol. 18, No. 2 (April, 1953), 163-169.

25 Cf. L. Bovet, *Psychiatric Aspects of Juvenile Delinquency* (a study prepared on behalf of the World Health Organization as a contribution to the United Nations programme for the prevention of crime and treatment of offenders) (Geneva: World Health Organization, 1951).

purposeless in his way of living. According to this view, psychotic traits are permanent character abnormalities, of constitutional origin, which are not derived from psychoses, neuroses, or mental deficiency, but which predispose the individual to behavioral disorders from which he suffers and may cause society to suffer.

Borderlands of Abnormality, Minor Personality Maladjustments, and Emotional Tensions. Personality disorders include physical, mental, emotional, and behavior traits; and the symptoms involve both organic and functional conditions. Some of the disorders already discussed may be classified as minor or borderland. However, certain borderland and minor personality disorders do not involve psychoneurotic and psychotic conditions. An individual may suffer from a variety of subnormal conditions. Borderland types of maladjustments include emotional deficiency (apathy) and inadequacy, or excesses and disharmonies; defects of the cognitive processes (attention, perception, memory, judgment); motor disorders (mobility, volition, speech, writing); and a variety of other forms of deviations. Feelings of insecurity, inferiority, and guilt; forms of nervousness and excitability; stuttering and other speech defects are all forms of maladjustments or defects. Intellectual deficiencies, already discussed, are also forms of borderland abnormalities. Psychosomatic maladjustments are numerous and varied.

Although emotional disorders accompany physical and mental maladjustments, they constitute problems of their own. Emotional tensions among children are far more extensive than most people suppose. They range from vague fears and anxieties to serious disorders. Feelings, emotions, temperamental traits, and disposition are closely related. Emotions make up the feeling tones, involve perception and sensation, and are accompanied by organic disturbances. They occur particularly in conflict situations and involve elements of tension. They localize and objectivate the stimuli, yet the whole organism may be affected. Feelings are largely subjective and temperament is a more or less permanent predisposition to certain forms of feeling and thinking. Disposition, although related to temperament, is more modifiable.

Most people at times are subjected to situations of excessive competition, conflict, and unmet wants, and are thwarted in freedom of action. Failure to achieve desired objectives is often a difficult and disillusioning experience. Emotionally and otherwise stable people can usually face trying situations with confidence and courage, and without becoming disorganized. Weak individuals are more likely to succumb to untoward circumstances. When such a person is unable to achieve superiority or to realize his objectives because of real or imagined deficiencies or perverse circumstances, he tends to develop a feeling of inferiority, incompetence, and unworthiness. Feelings of insecurity may grow out of many kinds of threats in the environment which are viewed with alarm. A person may suffer from a feeling of insecurity, a fear of disapproval or condemnation, humiliation, and uncertainty. Feelings of guilt grow out of the evaluation of one's own acts, a sense of unworthiness arising from conduct that is socially unacceptable. A person may also suffer from a sense of inadequacy that affects his self-esteem and status in the group. The symptoms and effects of these forms of reactions vary considerably.

Closely related to these forms of social maladjustment are the thwarting of the basic social drives, especially the wishes. Besides the elementary impulses and urges that press for action, which may at times dominate behavior, the most persistent drives are the wishes (desires). Wishes are impulses plus images of objects. W. I. Thomas [26] has classified the fundamental wishes under four main classes: (1) the wish for new experience, including curiosity, adventure, craving for excitement and sensations: (2) the wish for security, based on fear, apprehensiveness, and avoidance; (3) the wish for response, as expressed in love, friendship, and affection; and (4) the wish for recognition, expressed in the struggle for status, prestige, and social approval. Emory S. Bogardus [27] has added the wish to aid or serve, and Ellsworth Faris has added the wish for participation. Whatever classification of wishes we may accept, the important thing to remember is that the basic wishes represent powerful drives behind action. We become especially conscious of them when activities designed to meet human needs and wants are not satisfied. When wishes cannot be met in normal ways, children and adults alike may resort to various devices to secure satisfaction. For instance, the unsatisfied desire for recognition may lead to temper tantrums, impudence, and various tricks and devices to get attention. When the wish for response is not satisfied, children often feel uncertain and unwanted. The wish for new experience, if thwarted, may find outlets in running away, in gang activities, and in various forms of dangerous adventures. The feeling of insecurity is all too common among children, especially if the home situation is full of conflicts and uncertainty.

---

26 *The Unadjusted Girl* (Boston: Little, Brown, and Co., 1923), 4-40.
27 "The Fifth Wish," *Sociology and Social Research,* Vol. XIV (September-October, 1931), 75-77.

Healy and Bronner [28] present a diagram to show how urges and wishes, if they find expression in socially acceptable activities, produce normal consequences; but when they are thwarted by unsatisfactory human relationships, feelings of inadequacy, urges for substitute forms of satisfaction and the acceptance of the idea of delinquency may be the consequences. The obstructive relationships are mainly those within the family group. The great driving forces that have strong emotional concomitants are the desires for ego and affectional satisfactions. It is their contention that the delinquent is typically a child who is unhappy because of thwarted wishes. From the resulting emotional stress the child seeks relief in various ways, among which the resort to delinquency or joining a delinquent gang may be the outcome. The individual finds escape from frustration or he may seek revenge through delinquency.

Dollard and associates of the Yale Institute of Human Relations [29] have emphasized that aggression is the consequence of frustration. For instance, a child may desire ice cream. He looks at his mother appealingly, puckers his lips, and tries to coax her into buying an ice cream cone. The mother refuses. The child is frustrated. He may look for substitute response and satisfaction. There is a conflict between the stimulus or instigation and the inhibition. These investigators conclude that the strength of the instigation to aggression varies directly with the amount of frustration, provided the anticipation or threat of punishment is held constant. If the strength of frustration is held constant, then the greater the anticipation of punishment for a given act of aggression, the less likely the act is to occur. While this theory has certain weaknesses, it explains some acts of aggression, and it also indicates how aggression may be kept in check.

Emotional disturbances and various forms of frustrations are not per se causes of delinquency, although they may constitute significant contributing factors, especially if they occur concomitantly with other aggravating factors. It must be recognized, also, that delinquent behavior itself produces emotional disturbances, as we shall note in the next chapter.

Redl and Wineman [30] have made a study of the disorganization and

---

28 William Healy and Augusta F. Bronner, *New Light on Delinquency and Its Treatment, op. cit.,* 4. Franz Alexander and William Healy, in *Roots of Crime, op. cit.,* point out the relationship of inner conflicts to crime.

29 John Dollard, Neal E. Miller, Leonard W. Doob, O. H. Mowrer, and Robert S. Sears, *Frustration and Aggression* (New Haven: Yale University Press, 1939 and 1945).

30 Fritz Redl and David Wineman, *Children Who Hate* (Glencoe, Illinois: The Free Press, 1951).

breakdown of behavior controls of preadolescent children (predominant ages 8, 9, and 10) with normal health and intelligence, and free from physical handicaps, but who were in conflict with the adult world, chiefly their parents, and who had developed an unusual amount of hatred. They used the psychoanalytic approach in their studies of cases, inspired by the works of August Aichhorn and Kurt B. Eissler. As basic material, they used the cases, experiences, and observations of the Detroit Group Project, the Detroit Group Project Summer Camp, and Pioneer House. Their main goal was to discover why children's controls break down, how some defend themselves against adults, and what can be done to treat and prevent child disorganization. Since these children were referred by agencies they had at least some predelinquent symptoms, such as destructiveness, hypro-aggression, temper tantrums, lying, sassiness toward adults, bad language, and patterns of "touchy" behavior. Some had records of running away from home, truancy from school, and stealing.

In analyzing the cases it was found that the adult-child relationship was the chief source of difficulty. Some were brutalized by their fathers, hated by their mothers or stepmothers, and were the targets of sibling rivalries. Invariably the children reared in an atmosphere of hate, brutality, neglect, cold treatment, and unfeeling attitude made poor adjustments in the school and in the community. They developed persecutionary attitudes toward rules and routines, as well as toward adults who abused them. Even after they were referred to an institution in which the workers treated them with understanding and kindliness, the inner rebellion was still present. Their hate complex was deeply rooted. The excuses and justifications which they gave for their behavior made it difficult to provide a corrective influence. The delinquency-prone ego ideals persisted. The workers were able to overcome many of the defense attitudes and antisocial behavior tendencies by careful case analysis and treatment procedures.

The Orthopsychiatric Approach to Delinquency. One of the recent approaches to the etiology of maladjustment, including delinquency, is known as orthopsychiatry. It is a subdivision of psychiatry that concerns itself with the diagnosis and treatment of the borderline cases of mental and emotional deviations of personality rather than with the deep-seated psychoses and psychoneuroses cases. Since it is especially concerned with conduct disorders and incipient maladjustments in children and adolescents, a review of some of the contributions of orthopsychiatry will be given here. Teeters and

Reinemann [31] devote an entire chapter to this subject in connection with the discussions of the etiology of delinquency, which is probably an overemphasis of this specialized approach, but they cover the basic material in this field. The movement has grown sufficiently to form an organization, known as The American Orthopsychiatric Association (organized in 1923), which publishes the *American Journal of Orthopsychiatry*. Psychiatrists, psychologists, social workers, and others who belong to the organization seem to be enthusiastic about this approach to personal maladjustments. Although much has been accomplished by those who are dedicated to this approach to delinquency, it must be kept in mind that there is no magic formula for the cure or prevention of maladjusted persons. And as Teeters and Reinemann state, while orthopsychiatry has become somewhat of a fashion, this approach is based on the earlier work by such men as Healy in America and Aichhorn in Europe. It has its roots in the earlier developments in psychiatry and psychoanalysis. Much of the literature on this subject is cast in technical jargon, which is somewhat confusing to a layman. [32]

Children tend to be aggressive and assertive. They have many wants and desires. This requires some form of control. Parents usually are the first to attempt the exercise of control. Children sometimes rebel and protest. Every child is compelled to live in several groups, first the family and later in other primary groups. Wise parents and other adult leaders know how to help children make adjustments to various situations that they face, and children become socialized and participate in group life with a minimum of friction. If children are rebellious, they may have to learn by bitter experience that they cannot always have their own way of doing things. If they are severely disciplined and penalized, rebellion often is the natural consequence.

The psychiatrists, psychoanalysts, and now the orthopsychiatrists have described various mechanisms of adjustment, ranging from suppression or repression to identification and various compensatory forms of adjustments. Suppression or repression affects control over a situation or prevents an outburst of expression, but it may produce

---

[31] Negley K. Teeters and John O. Reinemann, *op. cit.*, Chapter VII. Compare Harry Elmer Barnes and Negley K. Teeters, *New Horizons of Criminology* (New York: Prentice-Hall, Inc., 1951), Chapter XI.

[32] Besides the books by Healy, Aichhorn, Eissler (Editor), and Friendlander, previously referred to, readers may consult issues of the *American Journal of Orthopsychiatry*, and the references given by Negley K. Teeters and John O. Reinemann, *op. cit.*, 752-754. Numerous articles have been written on the psychiatric and psychological aspects of delinquency and crime.

other forms of disorganization, which sometimes have long-lasting consequences. In the struggle between a wish and social controls or inhibitions, the situation may be corrected by the process of sublimation, provided it is not carried too far. Overcompensation may play a considerable role if the individual feels keenly the lack of physical impressiveness or social status, or in other ways feels frustrated; but an exaggerated defense mechanism may in the end produce other problems. The other processes of adjustment that have been observed and described include projection, rationalization, fixation, symbolization, and ambivalence. In sociology, the social processes have been broadly classified as those of social disintegration and opposition, including conflict, competition, social differentiation, and maladjustment and the processes of social integration and cooperation, such as accommodation, assimilation, socialization, social organization and control, and social planning or societal self-direction. These have individual and social aspects and consequences. The individual can be said to be integrated and adjusted if he can overcome conflict and other processes of disintegration, and is adjusted to the group, has assimilated its culture, has become socialized, and has become an integral part of a cooperative society.

Mental Health and Personality Adjustment. Fortunately, various movements are designed to improve the mental health of the population. The literature on mental health or hygiene and personality adjustment is extensive.[33] As aids in the analysis of mental, temperament, and personality adjustment, a variety of tests and inventories have been devised.[34] Many professional workers, in at-

---

33 For examples of sources, consult the references already mentioned in this chapter, especially those by Bovet, Cameron, Carroll, Klein, and Thorpe. See also John E. Anderson, *The Psychology of Development and Personality Adjustment* (New York: Henry Holt & Co., 1949); James H. S. Bossard, *The Sociology of Child Development* (New York: Harper & Brothers, 1948); Robert J. Havighurst and Hilda Taba, *Adolescent Character and Personality* (New York: John Wiley & Sons, Inc., 1949); Clyde Kluckhohn and Henry A. Murphy (Editors), *Personality: In Nature, Society, and Culture* (New York: Alfred A. Knopf, Inc., 1948); Fred McKinney, *The Psychology of Personal Adjustment* (New York: John Wiley & Sons, Inc., 1949); Helen L. Witmer and Ruth Kotinsky, *Personality in the Making: The Fact-Finding Report of the Midcentury White House Conference on Children and Youth* (New York: Harper & Brothers, 1952); and Kimball Young, *Personality and Problems of Adjustment* (New York: Appleton-Century-Crofts, Inc., 1952).

34 Cf. H. M. Bell, *The Adjustment Inventory* (Stanford, California: Stanford University Press, 1934); R. G. Bernreuter, *The Personality Inventory* (Stanford, California: Stanford University Press, 1931); J. P. Guilford and W. S. Zimmerman, *The Guilford-Zimmerman Temperament Survey* (Beverly Hills, California: Sheridan Supply Co., 1949); S. R. Hathaway and J. C. McKinley, *The Minnesota Multiphasic Personality Inventory* (*Journal of Psychology*, 1940, Vol. 10, 249-254, and *Manual for the Minnesota Multiphasic Personality Inventory;* and Ernest W. Tiegs, Willis W. Clark, and Louis P.

tempting to help juvenile delinquents or in preventing delinquent behavior, have felt the need for objective instruments to help identify the traits of personality that are likely, or unlikely, to lead to delinquency. By using some of the tests indicated (the selection of the instruments being made in view of the objectives of the study), it is possible to get a clearer and more objective picture of the personality factors involved in behavior problems than can be obtained by other means.

The studies made in Ohio may be cited as examples of community or county-wide surveys of mental health and personality adjustment (or maladjustment).[35] These studies revealed the extent of personality difficulties among school children. Such studies are important for a constructive program of mental hygiene and personality adjustment work.

That the problem of mental health is increasingly being recognized is indicated by the growth of mental hygiene clinics, hospitals, institutes, and educational programs. The National Mental Hygiene Act of 1946 has provided funds for financing research and training programs, and to assist the states in establishing mental health services. The National Institute of Mental Health has made grants to support training institutes. Psychiatrists, psychiatric social workers, psychoanalysts, psychologists, doctors, and others have been successful in treating the developing cases of mental disorders among children. The difficulty is that so few of them have been adequately trained, and public apathy prevents the trained workers from getting the cases in time to do the most effective work.[36]

Thorpe, *California Test of Personality* (Los Angeles: California Test Bureau) and *Journal of Educational Research,* Vol. 35, 1941, 102-108. For use of the Minnesota Multiphasic Personality Inventory (MMPI) in the analysis and prediction of delinquency, see S. R. Hathaway and Elio D. Monachesi, (Editors), *Analyzing and Predicting Juvenile Delinquency with the MMPI* (Minneapolis: The University of Minnesota Press, 1953). Compare Elio D. Monachesi, "Personality Characteristics and Socio-economic Status of Delinquents and Nondelinquents," *Journal of Criminal Law, Criminology, and Police Science,* Vol. 15, No. 5 (January-February, 1950), 570-583.

[35] Cf. Reports of studies conducted jointly by the Division of Mental Hygiene of the Ohio State Department of Public Welfare, the Ohio State University, and the Ohio Agricultural Experiment Station. A. R. Mangus, *Personality Adjustment of School Children,* July, 1948; A. R. Mangus and R. H. Woodward, *An Analysis of the Mental Health of High School Children,* July, 1949, and *An Analysis of the Mental Health of Elementary School Children,* July, 1949; also R. H. Woodward and A. R. Mangus, *Nervous Traits among First Grade Children in Butler County Schools,* in cooperation with the Butler County Mental Hygiene Association, July, 1949. One of the instruments used in these studies was the *California Test of Personality.*

[36] For a description of a Mental Hygiene Clinic and psychiatric approach to juveniles with conduct disorders, including concrete case material, consult: Eugene Davidoff and Elinor S. Noetzel, *Juvenile Delinquency: The Child Guidance Approach to Juvenile Delinquency, loc. cit.*

COMPARATIVE PERSONALITY AND PREDICTION STUDIES

In most of the earlier studies of personality traits as conditioners of delinquency and crime, no effort was made to compare the extent of personal maladjustments among law violators with similar conditions in the general population or in control groups. Delinquents, especially those in institutions, were found to have numerous physical and mental defects. Hence, the general conclusion was that delinquents by and large were defective individuals. However, more refined studies, using the comparative method, have necessitated somewhat a revision of the earlier contention, although the results of recent studies are not conclusive with respect to differential personality traits.

The simple design of a comparative study is to divide the sample into two groups, one called the "experimental" group, and the other the "control" group. These two groups should be as much alike as possible in all relevant aspects, except in the variables to be studied, and both should be representative samples. After the two groups are decided upon and have been formed, every individual in each group is then carefully studied with respect to the index of the variable, or groups of variables, under study. If a treatment procedure is followed, as in the Cambridge-Somerville Youth Study, the experimental group, but not the control group, is subjected to the treatment process under controlled conditions. After the experimental group has undergone the treatment, measures are obtained from both groups with respect to the variables about which the experiment is concerned. By using comparative measuring devices, whether they pertain to personality factors, family conditions, or other factors, it is possible not only to ascertain the extent of a given set of conditions influencing the experimental group, to get a comparative picture of delinquents and nondelinquents, which comparison can be stated in statistical terms.

Schuessler and Cressey [37] have evaluated 113 studies of personality differences between criminals and noncriminals as determined by objective tests of personality. Some testing was done for screening purposes and only incidentally as a means of contrasting criminals and noncriminals; but the usual procedure was to compare a group of prisoners with a control group. The material is discussed under emotionality, temperament, character, total personality, and miscel-

---

[37] Karl F. Schuessler and Donald R. Cressey, "Personality Characteristics of Criminals," *American Journal of Sociology*, Vol. 55 (March, 1950), 475-484. Reprinted without footnotes and tables in *Criminology: A Book of Readings*, by Clyde B. Vedder, Samuel Koenig, and Robert R. Clark (New York: The Dryden Press, 1953), 59-68.

laneous items. Various well-known questionnaires or tests were used in these studies, such as those by Woodworth, Thurstone, Bernreuter, Hartshorne and May, and the Rorshach method, the Minnesota Multiphasic Personality Inventory, and California Test of Personality. Recognizing the popularity of personality tests of criminals, Schuessler and Cressey conclude, however, that when the results are considered chronologically there is nothing to indicate that the personality components of criminals are established by this method, for the distribution of scores in the criminal population is about the same as in the general population. Furthermore, the tests do not demonstrate whether criminal behavior is the result of certain personality traits or the traits are the result of criminal behavior. The prison group is not representative of the criminal population, and the criminal group is not a homogeneous one. Thus, they conclude that the various types of personality tests are useful chiefly for diagnostic purposes rather than as techniques of criminological research.

Prediction studies are of several kinds. Some [38] are concerned with predicting success or failure of persons on parole or on probation, whereas others are concerned with the perfection of instruments of research that can be used in predicting in advance the behavior of juveniles. The most recent summary of studies dealing with the analysis and prediction of delinquency is contained in the book edited by S. R. Hathaway and Elio D. Monachesi, previously referred to. In these studies the chief focus of attention is personality traits. The investigators used as their main instrument of research the Minnesota Multiphasic Personality Inventory, hoping that the data might reveal personality patterns likely to lead to delinquency. The stand taken by the investigators is that individual cases manifest multiple personality patterns that can be isolated and the various types of deviant traits can be detected. The tasks of analyzing the various types of personality problems that often lead to delinquency and of predicting the delinquency by a probable number are closely related but not identical endeavors. Although the limitations of such procedure are recognized, it is believed that objective tests of personalities

---

[38] For a brief summary of prediction studies, with bibliography, see Elio D. Monachesi, "Prediction of Criminal Behavior," *Encyclopedia of Criminology*, edited by Vernon C. Branham and Samuel B. Kutash (New York: Philosophical Library, 1949), 324-330. Compare Floyd E. Ohlin, *Selection for Parole* (New York: Russell Sage Foundation, 1951), which reviews studies of 17,000 Illinois prisoners, over a period of twenty years, who were paroled; also studies of parolees and persons placed on probation, including some juveniles, in Wisconsin, and a comparison of the results of these studies with findings of other prediction studies, made by John L. Gillin and Associates, *Predicting Criminal Behavior* (Madison, Wisconsin: University of Wisconsin Press, 1952), in micro-card form.

provide a better method of analyzing difficulties and of possibly predicting behavior than other methods of study. They summarize five
studies that preceded their own study of 4,048 ninth graders. In
these, a positive relationship was discovered between recognized
scale meanings and delinquency. The results on these scales led
them to conclude that the asocial, amoral psychopath and the hypo-
manic among the patterns of adult maladjustment are those chiefly
represented among adolescents. Those adolescents who do not show
high deviation are unlikely to be found delinquent.

Comparative studies of delinquents and nondelinquents designed
to ascertain possible future behavior tendencies should cover a wider
scope of data than the studies of personality traits. Maud A. Miller [39]
used social frames of reference as well as personality tests to obtain
the basic data for a comparative study of 300 delinquents and 300
nondelinquents. The Gluecks, as previously indicated, likewise
studied their delinquent group (500) and their control group (500)
from a variety of angles. However, in their prediction scale they
narrowed down the items to only five main categories with their
weighted subcategories, and they indicated the failure score.[40] The
five categories are: (1) discipline of boy by the father, (2) supervision
of the boy by the mother, (3) affection of the father for the boy,
(4) affection of the mother for the boy, and (5) the degree of cohesiveness of the family. All of these traits pertain to the family situation,
omitting important personality and other factors. However, their
prediction scores are high; and the more recent attempt to validate
the Gluecks' prediction scale by Thompson [41] seems to indicate a
certain degree of reliability, although the critics do not place much
confidence in the method of scoring. Thompson selected case records
made in connection with the Cambridge-Somerville Youth Study.[42]
By using the Glueck scale his prediction score was 91.0 (per cent), as
compared with the scores of the three members of the selections
group, which were 65.3, 61.5 and 65.1. But the critics of the Glueck
scale have called attention to the inadequacies of the items used in

[39] *Problems of Child Delinquency* (New York: Houghton Mifflin Co., 1947).

[40] Cf. *Unraveling Juvenile Delinquency, op. cit.,* table on p. 261 and the description on pp. 257-271.

[41] Cf. Richard E. Thompson, "A Validation of the Glueck Social Prediction Scale
for Proneness to Delinquency," *The Journal of Criminal Law, Criminology, and Police
Science,* Vol. 43, No. 4 (November-December, 1952), 451-470. For criticism of the scale,
see: Ernest W. Burgess, in "Symposium on the Gluecks' *Unraveling Juvenile Delinquency,*" *Federal Probation,* Vol. 15, No. 1 (March, 1951). See also Sidney Axelrad and
Selma J. Glick, "Application of the Glueck Social Prediction Table to 100 Jewish Delinquent Boys," *The Jewish Social Quarterly,* Vol. XXX, No. 2 (winter, 1953), 127-136.

[42] Edwin Powers and Helen Witmer, *An Experiment in the Prevention of Delinquency* (New York: Columbia University Press, 1951).

the prediction scale and in the methods of scoring. The items used undoubtedly are present, but they are not sufficient for prediction purposes. Besides, it is often difficult to determine which of the items are causes and which are effects.

The material covered thus far has pertained mainly to the physical and psychological characteristics of delinquents, although many of the studies cited are more comprehensive and the personality studies used include items pertaining to character and behavior, which will be treated in the subsequent chapter. Medical examinations of delinquents have revealed physical defects and diseases, which are problems by themselves regardless of their possible relationship to delinquent behavior. The mental testing of delinquents, the diagnosis of mental disorders and diseases, and the various tests of personality adjustment or maladjustment have contributed much to the understanding of delinquency. The extravagant claims of some investigators as to the relative importance of certain physical or mental factors in delinquency may be discounted. Only a small number of the delinquents suffer from the extreme abnormalities of personality indicated by some writers. It is true that the institutionalized cases show an unusual prevalence of abnormalities. Nevertheless, child guidance and behavior clinics, juvenile courts, probation and police departments, and correctional and detention institutions are relying heavily upon the findings of the physicians, psychologists, psychiatrists, social workers, and sociologists for guidance in dealing with offenders. Their findings are important also for the development of preventive programs.

QUESTIONS AND PROJECTS

For Class Discussion and Research

1. What is meant by "cause"? What are the chief difficulties in ascertaining the causes of a social problem?

2. Apropos of the statement that causation is multiple, compound, and complex rather than single, make a list of the items given as causes of delinquency by authors cited in this chapter.

3. Analyze the Judge Baker Foundation *Case Studies,* cases 1 to 20, giving background of cases; enumerate causal factors and the chief element in the diagnosis and prognosis procedures.

4. Study, in detail, longer case studies of delinquencies, such as *The Jack-Roller* (1930), *The Natural History of a Delinquent Career* (1931), and *Brothers in Crime* (1938), by Clifford Shaw.

5. Enumerate the different kinds of diseases and physical handicaps that have been found among delinquents.

6. If delinquency is not inherited, what inherited conditions may contribute to the incidence of delinquency?

7. Analyze the pros and cons of the influence of heredity. Apply the conclusions to cases of delinquency.

8. Discuss the pros and cons of mental deficiencies as factors in delinquency. What evidences are there in support of the notion that children with mental deficiencies are more likely to have delinquency records than normal children, because the brighter ones are more clever in avoiding being caught?

9. Compare mental deficiencies with mental diseases or disorders as possible causes of delinquency. Compare the proportions of feeble-minded and the mentally disorganized in the population under the age of 15.

10. Discuss mental diseases and functional disorders in relation to deviant behavior. Suggest ways in which parents, teachers, and others may be of service in preventing the development of delinquent behavior brought on by mental disorders.

11. Discuss the place of emotional disturbances in the conduct of children. What is the role of social environment in the emotional stresses of children? The role of emotional immaturity in delinquent behavior.

12. Discuss mental and emotional conflicts in relation to delinquency.

13. Make a study of the personality and prediction research methods with the view of determining which devices or approaches yield the most accurate results.

14. Discuss personality differences between delinquents and non-delinquents.

SELECTED REFERENCES

BIRNBAUM, KARL, "A Court Psychiatrist's View on Juvenile Delinquents," *The Annals of the American Academy of Political and Social Science,* Vol. 261 (January, 1949), 55-63.

BOVET, L., *Psychiatric Aspects of Juvenile Delinquency* (Geneva: World Health Organization, 1951).

BURT, CYRIL, *The Young Delinquent* (New York: D. Appleton and Co., 1925 and 1938).

CAMERON, NORMAN, *The Psychology of Behavior Disorder: A Biosocial Interpretation* (New York: Houghton Mifflin Co., 1947).

DAVIDOFF, EUGENE, AND ELINOR S. NOETZEL, *The Child Guidance Approach to Juvenile Delinquency* (New York: Child Care Publications, 1951).

DOLLARD, JOHN, NEAL E. MILLER, LEONARD W. DOOB, O. H. MOWRER, AND ROBERT SEARS, *Frustration and Aggression* (New Haven: Yale University Press, 1939 and 1945).

EISSLER, K. R., Editor, *Searchlights on Delinquency: New Psychoanalytic Studies* (New York: International Universities Press, Inc., 1949).

ELLIOTT, MABEL A., *Crime in Modern Society* (New York: Harper & Brothers, 1953), Chapters IV, XII, and XIV.

GILLIN, JOHN L., *Criminology and Penology* (New York: D. Appleton-Century Co., 1945), Part II.

GLUECK, SHELDON AND ELEANOR, *Unraveling Juvenile Delinquency* (New York: The Commonwealth Fund, 1950), Chapters XIV-XIX.

———, *One Thousand Juvenile Delinquents* (Cambridge: Harvard University Press, 1934).

HARRISON, LEONARD V., AND PRYOR GRANT, *Youth in the Toils* (New York: The Macmillan Co., 1938).

HARTWELL, SAMUEL W., *Fifty-five Bad Boys* (New York: A. A. Knopf, 1931).

HATHAWAY, STARKE R., AND ELIO D. MONACHESI, *Analyzing and Predicting Juvenile Delinquency* (Minneapolis: The University of Minnesota Press, 1953).

HEALY, WILLIAM, AND AUGUSTA F. BRONNER, *Delinquents and Criminals: Their Making and Unmaking* (New York: The Macmillan Co., 1926).

———, *New Light on Delinquency and Its Treatment* (New Haven: Yale University Press, 1936).

HIRSCH, NATHANIEL, *Dynamic Causes of Juvenile Crime* (Cambridge: Science-Art Publishers, 1937).

KVARACEUS, WILLIAM C., *Juvenile Delinquency and the School* (New York: World Book Co., 1945).

MERRILL, MAUD A., *Problems of Child Delinquency* (New York: Houghton Mifflin Co., 1947).

SLAWSON, JOHN, *The Delinquent Boy* (Boston: R. G. Badger, 1926).

TAPPAN, PAUL W., *Juvenile Delinquency* (New York: McGraw-Hill Book Co., Inc., 1949), Chapters V and VI.

TEETERS, NEGLEY K., AND JOHN O. REINEMANN, *The Challenge of Delinquency* (New York: Prentice-Hall, Inc., 1950), Chapters III and VII.

VEDDER, CLYDE B., SAMUEL KOENIG, AND ROBERT E. CLARK, *Criminology: A Book of Readings* (New York: The Dryden Press, 1953), sections III, VI, and VII.

V

PERSONALITY FACTORS: CHARACTER AND BEHAVIOR TRAITS

The biological and psychological factors, as indicated in the previous chapter, have varying degrees of influence in shaping conduct, most of which are background conditions and not directly causal in nature. Defective character and certain behavior traits have a more direct bearing on the responses of an individual to situations; these often lead to misconduct. The wishes, attitudes, sentiments, interests, habits, and social values of an individual are the dynamic drives that impel him to action. Although these drives may have a biological base, they are chiefly the results of experience, developing in the process of interaction between the individual and the successive situations that he faces. People are not born with antisocial traits and tendencies. Behavior tendencies develop as the result of innumerable influences that emanate from the social environment and that are brought to bear upon the individual.

As stated in the previous chapter, personality is the sum and organization of all traits that make up the person and that condition his role in society. It is the outgrowth of the development of the individual in relation to his environment. Physical, mental, and emotional conditions, the social drives, character, and modes of social expression are all parts of personality. The conception the individual has of himself and of his role in society and his social status likewise are integral parts of personality. It is in this connection that the intimate relations between personality factors and environmental influences can be seen in a child's conduct.

Greatness of personality depends upon the integration and balance of traits, impressiveness of personal appearance, the genuineness of his purpose, the effectiveness of his expression, and the usefulness of his life. Personality enrichment is one of the major functions of education, group work, organized community recreation, and all other efforts to contribute to abundant living.

In a way, the *summum bonum* (greatest good) in life is the development in ourselves, and in others, of enriched, well-balanced, and integrated personality, functioning with efficiency and satisfaction in wholesome cooperative living; and the establishment of a social order conducive to this end.[1] The final test of the efficiency of human endeavor is the degree to which it serves life, and the extent to which it makes possible the full realization of personality.

Through juvenile delinquents there often runs a persistent pattern: they appear to be under stress. Some of them are indecisive, uncertain of themselves, frustrated, or maladjusted. At the root of this pattern is often a state of planlessness. Because of the insecurity of their childhood, the lack of training in character, and often the inconsistency and dishonesty of parental instruction and behavior, some are not positive of what is "right" or what is "wrong." The result is that the "bad" is mixed up with the "good," and they exhibit a mixture of kindness and viciousness, sentimentality and morbidity. Irrational behavior is the natural consequence. Others know fully the difference between right and wrong, and they are consciously aware of their deviant behavior; but, either because of too strict discipline or because of laxity in supervision and control at home, they have not learned to exercise self-control. Their attitudes and values, character and conscience have not become thoroughly formed and integrated.

Youth growing up in a social setting of cultural disorganization sometimes have great difficulty in finding clear-cut norms for behavior that provide a sound basis for personality integration. In a

---

[1] See Loran D. Osborn and Martin H. Neumeyer, *The Community and Society* (New York: American Book Co., 1933), Chapters XXVI and XXVII; Martin H. and Esther S. Neumeyer, *Leisure and Recreation* (New York: A. S. Barnes and Co., 1936 and 1949), Chapter VII.

more stabilized society, the ready-made patterns of conduct provide a background for choices, involving little disturbance of personality. Young people are allowed greater initiative and a greater latitude of choices, but they are sometimes not prepared for the complexity of factors involved in moral choices. Adults blame them for losing their way, not realizing that they themselves have produced the confused environment in which the children are being reared. They expect youth to make decisions for themselves, when the adult generation has failed to define adequately situations for them, or has failed to practice the accepted mores of the group.

Delinquency involves character problems. Behavior traits and habits may deviate far from the prevailing mores and standards. The habits that pertain to the use of alcohol and drugs, and sexual misconduct are outstanding forms of deviant behavior. Personality maladjustment may be both a cause and a result of deviant conduct.

CHARACTER PROBLEMS

Attitudes, habits, and interests, as well as character and conscience, including the morals and spiritual ideals, standards, life's values, and the modes of social expression, are integral parts of personality. The antisocial attitudes and behavior of delinquents clearly indicate a breakdown or maladjustment of personality, especially the aspect of personality known as character or as conscience. Delinquency represents a deviation from the prevailing mores and laws of society. Whether deviation expresses itself in overt behavior or in attitudes, or in both, the significance of this condition is that the individual fails to "fit in." Carr thinks that emotional conflicts and the acceptance of antisocial behavior patterns are the chief reasons why individuals fail to "fit in." They deviate from the traditional mores because of these conflicts within and because their character has become disintegrated or adjusted to a delinquency standard.

Attitudes, Interests, and Social Values. Human hungers and wishes demand satisfaction. Every activity produces changes in the organism, calling for adjustment, balance, and replenishment. To defy one's needs is to invite inefficiency and to accelerate deterioration. The wholeness of man requires a balance and satisfying exercise of all parts of the total being. The satisfaction of biological urges and wishes, the development of wholesome attitudes and interests, and the formation of habits that are in harmony with the prevailing social values are necessary for an integrated personality and for successful living.

Attitudes are acquired, learned, and establish tendencies to react toward or against somebody or something. They are evidenced by approaching and withdrawing tendencies and are accompanied by social values. Attitudes and social values are the subjective and objective phases of the same process. Social values are meaningful objects. Each individual has a system of values, things that he regards as having positive or negative worth, ranging from the objects or situations that he most desires to those that he wishes to avoid.

Habits are closely associated with attitudes and interests. They are fundamentally acquired ways of acting or modes of responding, constituting a repetition of acts and relatively stabilized forms of conduct. But habits are not mere recurrences of specific acts, for running through these acts are tendencies or predispositions to function according to certain patterns of action. Boys fly kites, play football, dig caves, and indulge in rough-and-tumble games; and girls play with dolls, play house, and indulge in more sedentary activities because they have formed certain habits, which in turn are conditioned by past performances and by the traditions of the group.

The things that people are interested in and that they desire, and the attitudes that they have developed toward them, condition to a large extent what they will do. Children experience little difficulty in their conduct if their wishes, interests, attitudes, and habits are socially desirable. They behave in accordance with the established patterns of conduct. But it is common knowledge that this is not always the case. All children are guilty of some deviant behavior. They are often rebellious, disobedient, and hostile. If the conduct is not a serious breach of ethics, or if it is not in violation of a law or of one of the mores of society, the behavior is not considered as delinquency—although it may constitute a problem.

Character and Conscience. In a broad sense, the term "character" has reference to

a quality, trait or sum of traits, attributes or characteristics which serve to indicate the essential nature of a person or a thing. As a moral quality, the sum and organization of traits, attitudes, and habits oriented with reference to an objective standard of conduct. The life-organization of a person; the motives, attitudes, habits, sentiments, ideals, and values that condition or determine the course of action in a situation requiring choices of conduct. The character of a person ranges from exemplary conduct or standard of conduct, deserving imitation, to misconduct and socially tabooed forms of behavior or plane of living.[2]

[2] *Dictionary of Sociology* (New York: Philosophical Library, 1944), 37.

Conscience has reference to a system of attitudes, habits, and forms of action that involve standards of values and a consideration of right and wrong in conduct. No one is born with a conscience and it is not intuitive, although human beings have the potentialities for conscience. Conscience is the outgrowth of experience and of instruction and social influence. It is the gradual outgrowth of a succession of experiences in social situations in which the elements of right and wrong exist.

Character and conscience are built up by developing ideals of behavior. Character training is a process of developing personal attitudes, habits, moral values, and ideals of conduct through instruction, guidance, and example, and by giving children opportunities of experience in situations that require moral decisions. Character building is a continuous process, but it occurs chiefly during childhood.

It is not known at what age a child experiences the earliest consciousness of the difference between right and wrong in conduct. It is obvious that the process of character training is a gradual one. Small children accept regulations of conduct and distinctions between right and wrong without much thought and without knowing the reasons for such distinctions. The growth of moral sensitivity and a sense of personal responsibility is a slow and by no means smooth and even process. Gradually, concepts of right and wrong are made an integral part of a child's thinking, although revolts occur frequently.

Because of the close relations between the child's play life and character growth, recreation leaders and group workers have considered directed play as an important means of character training. With proper supervision, a child can learn to play fairly, honestly, and with initiative. Such moral and social qualities as courage, decision, self-control, reliability, good sportsmanship, kindness, unselfishness, truthfulness, tolerance, and sociability can be developed through play. Leisure activities have vast potentialities for character building and the growth of socialized personality.

Character develops chiefly during the impressive years of childhood, in which parents and playmates play a conspicuous part. Teachers and other adult leaders also contribute to this development throughout the years. From experience and adult influences, children learn that distinctions are made between different forms of conduct. Some acts are approved and emphasized. Compliance brings praise and rewards; violation brings censure, reprimand, and sometimes physical punishment. In this way certain inhibitions are built up to such an extent that uneasiness may accompany violations of parental teachings and societal mores, even if the act is not detected. Knowledge that an act is condemned and that the individual is likely to suffer the consequences of violation at some time is usually sufficient to support the ideal of correct conduct. It is in the many informal situations that the formation of character and conscience takes place. Many questions may be asked by the child as to why certain acts are considered undesirable, and on occasions the child may wish to indulge in the "forbidden pleasure," and sometimes does so; but if well trained, the corrective process will overcome the deviant tendency.

How does the conscience of a person work in specific situations? What part does character play in meeting situations that involve decisions and actions in terms of the rightness or the wrongness of the several possible courses of action? Conscience tends to work well when faced with familiar problems. Simple situations that are predefined for them by parents and by society give children fairly ready-made approaches to them. But in new and complex situations, such as occur in a rapidly changing society, previous training is frequently inadequate in providng clearly defined definitions of them. Parents may not even know the answers to the problems faced by their children. Conscience may not provide a ready-made solution. The individual may be faced with several alternatives, some of which are vaguely defined.

Piaget,[3] in discussing the process by which moral judgment develops in a child's life, points out that the morality prescribed for the individual by society is not homogeneous, because society is not just one thing. It is the sum of relationships. In these relationships there are wide extremes of control. Society may impose rigid constraints and enforce upon the individual a system of rules with obligatory content. On the other hand, the relationship between the individual and society may be one of cooperation, in which case the child learns about norms and the ideals back of them through experience in a cooperative atmosphere. It should be noted that between these extremes of rigidly imposed rules and cooperative permissiveness the child has a variety of experiences.

The way character and conscience function in specific situations may be illustrated by picturing a scale of values that may be used in making decisions with respect to forms or levels of conduct. When a person is confronted with a situation that involves a decision as to the right or wrong course to pursue, he is faced not only with the alternates—"right" and "wrong"—but with a number of possible

---

[3] Jean Piaget, *The Moral Judgment of the Child* (New York: Harcourt, Brace & Co., 1932), 412.

courses of action, ranging all the way from the highest ideal of which the person is aware to the lowest form of conduct of which he can conceive. It is not so simple as choosing between white and black, although even in matters of color there are degrees of whiteness and blackness. An individual develops a system of values and he may function more or less unconsciously, nonreflectively, and habitually on a plane of acting that is his accepted mode of living. Then he faces a situation that requires a decision. The situation involves a moral element when a choice is made as to a course of action that necessitates a consideration of right and wrong in conduct. For a while, the individual experiences inner conflict while appraising the factors involved in the situation and the possible consequences of different courses of action. A person may be challenged by a higher value than he is accustomed to, or by a series of values above the level of previous performance, thus necessitating a choice between his previous level of conduct and the challenging ideal. Or, a person may be tempted to deviate from the accepted and accustomed mode of behavior, in which case the conflict is between his new inner desire stimulated by the tempting situation and his better judgment based on past experience. If a person yields to the temptation and deviates in his conduct from the established mores which he has accepted, he probably will experience regret, remorse, and even disorganization. Of course, a person may be either challenged or tempted and yet continue to function on the accustomed plane of conduct, without serious deviation in either direction.

While the above illustration presents the broad outlines of decisions and behavior situations involving a person's conscience and character, concrete situations and experiences are often more complicated, involving many personal factors and environmental conditions. A person is likely to face numerous new and conflicting situations if he migrates from one group to another, especially if the new group lives by standards different from those he is accustomed to, some of which seem to him to be wrong. Immigrants are constantly facing this type of problem, as are those who go from one religious group to another, or from a group in which high religious ideals and moral values are maintained to a community in which there is considerable religious indifference and deviation from his accepted moral standards.

Aichhorn [4] presents a number of cases of dissocial behavior of children, using the psychoanalytical approach in analyzing the background factors. By "Wayward Youth" Aichhorn means not merely

---

4 August Aichhorn, *Wayward Youth* (New York: Viking Press, 1935), 31-33.

delinquent and dissocial children, but also so-called problem children and those suffering from neurotic symptoms. As a part of his analysis, he cites cases of the possible reactions of children to eating candy. A child standing beside a table on which there is a box of candy may help himself to a piece and enjoy eating it without conflict, if he has never been told that it was wrong to take candy without permission. Another child has been forbidden to eat candy, but he has forgotten this. A vague feeling of uneasiness may make him hesitate, but he finally takes the candy and eats it without a bad conscience. In this latter case, the wish is stronger than the vague opposition. A third child understands clearly that he should not take candy, but he wants it so much that he takes it anyway and suffers guilty feelings. The wish overcame the restraint, but the no-candy rule had become so firm a part of his standard of action that he suffered remorse following the action. Another possible reaction is that an inhibiting force (conscience, or a censor as some prefer to call it), the result of the child's experience and training, drives the wish back into the unconscious or even prevents it from becoming conscious.

When some parents are asked why their child has misbehaved, they may say that it resulted from bad company and running around on the street. To a certain extent this is true, as we shall show later. But this does not explain why it is that not all children in the group are thus affected. There must be something in the make-up and training of this particular child that the environment brings out, whereas other children in a similar situation refrain from misconduct. Conversely, sometimes children may have strong desires to commit delinquencies, but the occasions for such conduct do not present themselves, or the social restraints are so uniform and strong that the tendencies are overcome.

The conscience (moral) situation involves some kind of intentional or responsible behavior. Unintentional or accidental (or thoughtless) behavior, for which no personal responsibility is recognized and which does not entail a sense of guilt or innocence, usually does not involve the element of conscience—although one's action may be regretted. Not all intentional behavior, of course, involves the element of conscience. It is difficult to draw a hard and fast line between a moral and a nonmoral situation. The factor of conflict must invariably be reckoned with, and often plays a dominant role. Conflict ensues when overt action is blocked or checked and a person is compelled to choose between various possible lines of action, or at least has alternate possibilities presented to him. This situation necessitates deliberation before a choice is made. At times, however, behavior is accompanied by a small amount of re-flection. Actions are impulsive, emotional, or habitual.

Conflicts may be inner (within the personality) or social (between persons or between groups). Inner conflicts arise from the blocking of overt action, owing to the injection of some newly released impulse or desire into the process of acquired and habitual or cus-tomary behavior. The conflicting elements may produce consider-able confusion and be emotionally upsetting. Inner conflicts are due to a variety of causes. When they occur, a contradiction between motor tendencies, or between social drives and social restraints, ex-ists. Incompatible elements present themselves. The conflict may be so intense that it constitutes a real crisis. When the conflict is chiefly between the desires of the individual and the mores and con-trols of society, the individual may be better integrated as the result of the social conflict; but it is a disturbing experience, which may involve inner conflicts of considerable intensity.

Once a person has accepted certain moral and spiritual values, and firmly believes in maintaining what he conceives to be the right course of action, any subsequent deviation, such as yielding to a temptation, results in distress over his conduct, sometimes even deep remorse. The conflicts preceding or accompanying misconduct do not always reveal conscience behavior so clearly as do the reactions after misbehavior has occurred. Conscience functions more inex-orably in afterthought, in the form of a sense of guilt or the emo-tions of remorse, shame, and sorrow. When these disappear, the conscience situation can be said to have come to an end.

Reactions to moral situations may involve the entire gamut of mental conflicts, emotional disturbances, inferiority complexes, and maladjustments. The breakdown of character tends to occur or manifest itself in situations that evoke strong desires and in which the deviant pressures are especially strong.

Behavior Traits and Habits

The behavior traits and habits that have caused special con-cern are those pertaining to the use of alcohol and drugs, and homo-sexuality and sex offenses. These are overt expressions of inner conflicts and environmental pressures. Habitual cases come under the general designation of delinquent and antisocial behavior and call for official action. To be sure, these are not merely personality problems, but they usually have a large component of personality conditions.

The extent of alcoholism and drug addiction among juveniles is not exactly known, but these are habit-forming activities that may have dire consequences. This is particularly true of alcoholism and drug addiction.

Alcoholism and Intemperance.[5] The consumption of distilled spirits and fermented malt liquor has increased enormously since the period of prohibition. McCarthy and Douglass [6] compare the average per capita consumption per year of absolute alcohol in beverages (in U. S. gallons) of the different countries. Only four countries (France, Spain, Belgium, and Italy) consume more liquor per capita of the population fifteen years old and over than the United States. From 1934 to 1946 the consumption of distilled spirits in the United States increased from 58,000,000 (wine) gallons to 231,000,000 gallons; while wine consumption increased from 33,-000,000 to 133,000,000 gallons, after which there was a slight drop in consumption of both types of liquor. Beer consumption increased from 40,000,000 to 87,000,000 barrels from 1934 to 1947, with only a slight drop during the next year. Total expenditure for all three types of alcoholic beverages increased from $2,080,000,000 in 1934 to $9,640,000,000 in 1947 and $9,885,000,000 in 1953.

But figuring the increases in total consumption of and in expenditures for alcoholic beverages is not the most exact way of measuring changes, for the population and prices of commodities both have increased during that period. The federal government has a fairly accurate statistical summary of year by year consumption of

---

[5] The literature on alcoholism and drinking is voluminous. For data regarding the extent of drinking, consult the latest issue of the *Statistical Abstract of the United States,* Bureau of the Census, Department of Commerce. For reports of current studies, consult the *Quarterly Journal of Studies on Alcohol,* published by Yale University Press, New Haven, Connecticut. The following books contain comprehensive material and bibliographies: Clarence H. Patrick, *Alcohol, Culture, and Society* (Durham, North Carolina: Duke University Press, 1952); Raymond G. McCarthy and Edgar M. Douglass, *Alcohol and Social Responsibility: A New Educational Approach* (New York: Thomas Y. Crowell Co., 1949); E. M. Jellinek (Editor), *Recent Trends in Alcoholism and in Alcohol Consumption* (New Haven: Hillhouse Press, 1947); and Howard W. Haggard and E. M. Jellinek, *Alcohol Explored* (New York: Doubleday, Doran and Co., 1942). In *Criminology: A Book of Readings,* by Clyde B. Vedder, Samuel Koenig, and Robert E. Clark (New York: The Dryden Press, 1953), are reprints of articles on: "A Psychocultural Analysis of the Alcoholic," by Harriet R. Mowrer; "Alcohol and Crime," by Robert V. Seliger; and "Alcoholics Anonymous," by Charles H. Upton. Alcoholics Anonymous has published considerable literature. Among recent references dealing more directly with drinking among juveniles and young adults, see J. L. Block, "Alcohol and the Adolescent," *Parent's Magazine* (December, 1951), 40-41; "Drinking at College," *Science News Letter* (July 26, 1952); "Teen-Agers and Alcoholism: Utah School Program," *Ladies' Home Journal* (April, 1952); and Robert Strauss, and Sheldon D. Bacon, *Drinking in College* (New Haven: Yale University Press, 1953).

[6] *Ibid.,* i.e., 44-46.

liquor. The reports are published in various sources, principally in the *Statistical Abstract of the United States,* published annually. From 1850 to 1921 the apparent average annual per capita consumption of alcoholic beverages in the Continental United States fluctuated considerably, but there was a noticeable decline in consumption even before the era of prohibition. From 1921 to 1932, the prohibition era, the consumption of distilled spirits and wines (no data are given for malt liquor) was very low. The consumption of distilled spirits ranged from .32 gallon per capita in 1921 to .06 gallon in 1932; and wine consumption ranged from .19 gallon per capita in 1921 to .03 in 1930, the lowest point. The following table indicates the increases in consumption of the various types of alcoholic beverages from 1933 to 1952.

TABLE VI. THE APPARENT AVERAGE ANNUAL PER CAPITA CONSUMPTION
OF DISTILLED SPIRITS, MALT LIQUORS, AND WINES IN THE
CONTINENTAL UNITED STATES: 1933 TO 1951

(In gallons, except distilled spirits, which is shown in tax gallons)

Fiscal Year	Distilled Spirits	Malt Liquors	Wines
1933	.05	1.56	.01
1934	.33	7.90	.14
1935	.70	10.45	.30
1936	.81	11.93	.39
1937	1.03	13.47	.52
1938	1.00	13.02	.51
1939	.93	12.41	.55
1940	1.02	12.58	.66
1941	1.04	12.42	.70
1942	1.13	14.18	.79
1943	1.11	15.96	.84
1944	1.03	17.97	.73
1945	1.22	18.86	.73
1946	1.39	18.56	.87
1947	1.28	18.08	.77
1948	1.06	18.58	.79
1949	1.02	18.05	.85
1950	1.02	17.26	.93
1951	1.23	16.97	.87
1952	1.00	16.94	.85

SOURCE: *Statistical Abstract of the United States* (Bureau of the Census, United States Department of Commerce, 1953), 811.

The increase in the consumption of intoxicating liquor since the prohibition era is explained in part by the increase of the per capita consumption and also by the increase in the number of drinkers, although data regarding the latter are limited. Apparently the peak of drinking was reached toward the end of the war or during the early years of the postwar era. According to reports of the American Institute of Public Opinion (Gallup Poll), 67 per cent of the adult population 15 years old and over were drinking in 1945, whereas the 1951 poll indicates that 57 per cent were drinking. It was estimated that 57,500,000 people were drinking in 1951, but some estimates put the figure at 65,000,000 or even higher.

The patterns and attitudes involved in drinking are many and varied. According to the 1951 Gallup Poll, 70 per cent of the males and 46 per cent of the females were drinking. It seems that the highest percentages of drinking occur in the age brackets from 20 to 30, 30 to 50, over 50, and under 20, in that order; but it is not known exactly how extensive drinking is during the adolescent period. The percentage of drinking seems to increase from lower to higher economic levels, but this may be because people with larger income can afford to buy more liquor. Striking differences are noted according to broad religious groups, with the Jewish group having the highest proportion of drinkers; next in order being the Catholics, Protestants, and Mormons. The stronger the opposition to drinking by a religious group, the lower the percentage of drinkers in the group.

There are many motives for drinking. According to various studies of drinking, the following reasons seem to occur frequently. Some people like liquor as a thirst-quenching drink or simply to add color at meals and social gatherings. This is particularly true in such countries as France, Italy, and Germany. The custom of serving drinks with meals has undoubtedly increased the amount of consumption. Some like drinks as stimulants, especially when they wish to have a feeling of exaltation or to celebrate an event or simply to get a "kick." Others consume liquor because of the depressant or narcotic effect. They desire to escape from something—frustration, tension, pain, boredom, and the like. Some are social drinkers. They desire to conform to a custom or to be sociable. They go along with the crowd. Once the habit of drinking is formed, the withdrawal distress is great, and they may keep on drinking long after social stimulations cease. As important as geographic, physiological, and psychological factors may be in the causative process. It seems that culture largely determines the function of the consumption of alcohol, for social tradition and social pressure condition drinking or abstinence. Public opinion, advertising, educating people to drink, and many other factors in the social environment of an individual may lead one to form the habit of drinking.

It is not exactly known how many people are heavy drinkers. The National Committee on Alcohol has estimated that some 4,000,-000 of the 65,000,000 drinkers have found that the use of alcohol is more or less a problem with them, of whom 750,000 are uncontrollable drinkers to such an extent that they have impaired their physical and mental health. In medical parlance, alcoholism is a condition of uncontrollable or compulsive drinking and its victims are called alcoholics. The heavy drinkers have been classified as chronic drinkers, alcoholics, or just plain drunks. Until recently they were shunned, reproached, and ostracized. But nowadays physicians and others who have made studies of alcoholism regard it as a problem that must be dealt with in more constructive ways. The victims need treatment and protection. Various types of medical treatment are now available. Psychotherapy is helpful, as are other methods. Alcoholics Anonymous has demonstrated what can be done by sympathetic understanding and mutual helpfulness, provided the individuals are honestly willing to stop drinking and to follow the program for recovery.

The extent and intensity of juvenile drinking are difficult to determine statistically, but it is well known that drinking by teen-agers and young people is a serious problem in many communities. Even though minors are not permitted to purchase liquor, sometimes liquor dealers make it easy for them to obtain it, and parents or other adults provide it for them. In many circles it is no longer considered bad etiquette for high school boys and girls to drink alcoholic beverages. In the Utah survey, reported in the *Ladies' Home Journal* (*op. cit.*, 25 f.), it was found that, of 1,177 high school students who filled out questionnaires, 30 per cent said that they drank and that they took their first drink before they were 16 years of age. Some have estimated that approximately three fourths of the alcoholics began drinking when they were in their teens.

Drinking among college students has been the subject of extensive studies. The study of college drinking conducted by the Yale Laboratory of Applied Physiology in twenty-seven colleges and universities included replies from 15,747 students. Information has been obtained on a somewhat limited basis of the extent of drinking among students, why and when they drink, under what circumstances, with what resulting effects, and the interrelationships between drinking behavior and socio-economic characteristics of the drinking group. Drinking varies a great deal with respect to the types of schools, the religious affiliations of students, the family background and economic status, national origin, and other variables. The patterns of drinking are somewhat similar to adult patterns of alcoholic consumption. A large percentage of the students who drink started drinking before they went to college. If parents drink, about nine out of ten of their sons and over eight out of ten of their daughters drink on occasion. On the other hand, if parents are abstainers, only half of the sons and less than a fifth of the daughters drink. When the family income is large, a much greater proportion of the children drink than in the families with low income. Thus, the customs and attitudes of young persons with regard to drinking are largely conditioned by the practices, customs, and attitudes of their families, socio-economic groups, and the community.[7]

Our concern here is chiefly with the type of drinking that involves violation of law. The *Uniform Crime Reports* (Vol. XXIV, No. 2, 1954, p. 110) indicate that during 1953 the 1,174 cities with over 2,500 population reported 774,096 arrests for drunkenness, of a total of 1,791,160 arrests made in these cities. Only 4,595 of those arrested for drunkenness were under 18, and 17,488 were 18, 19, and 20 years old. An examination of local police records does not show extensive arrests of juveniles for drunkenness. That rate of arrest increases with age. Since arrests of juveniles are usually made in only extreme cases of drunkenness, and if other offenses are associated with drinking and may be used as ground for arrest instead of the drunkenness, it is obvious that the statistics do not give a true picture of the problem. Juvenile court judges, police and sheriff officers, probation workers, and others who deal with juveniles who get into trouble know that drinking is a greater factor in delinquency than the statistics indicate.[8] Driving while intoxicated, which includes driving or operating any motor vehicle while drunk or under the influence of liquor or narcotics, is more prevalent than reports of traffic violations indicate, and many juveniles are involved in such offenses. The purchase of liquor by minors is an offense for which both the purchaser and the seller are liable.

Most juvenile offenders who have been apprehended for violations of liquor laws are mild or moderate consumers of intoxicants, although they may get drunk. Few teen-agers are alcoholics, for it takes several years to become a confirmed alcoholic; but occasionally children become chronic drinkers at an early age. The Gluecks [9] relate the case of Henry, whose family was in poor economic circum-

---

[7] Robert Strauss and Sheldon D. Bacon *Drinking in Colleges* (New Haven: Yale University Press, 1953). See Reports of this study in *Science News Letter* (July 26, 1952), 61; and *This Week* (September 23, 1953).

[8] Juvenile court judges have claimed that alcohol is involved in such types of offenses as ungovernableness, running away, and sex violations.

[9] Sheldon and Eleanor Glueck, *Later Criminal Careers* (New York: The Commonwealth Fund, 1937), 181.

stances and who lived in a crowded, tumble-down area of a large manufacturing city. The father and an uncle were both chronic alcoholics. The father was a poor provider, but he was always strict with Henry. When Henry was very young he began to drink, steal, lie, and smoke. He was the leader of a gang. At 14, he left school, drank excessively, and had illicit sex experiences. From the age of 16, he was very much an alcoholic and nothing could deter him from drinking. At 17, he was arrested for burglary and sent to a reformatory. Upon release, he worked for a while, but soon began drinking again. He was arrested several times for drinking and for breaking parole. When in an institution he was a model inmate, but he reverted to drinking as soon as he was released. The psychiatrist summarized the case by stating that Henry could not abstain from the use of alcohol without some restraining influence and that little could be done for him until abstinence was brought about.

The prevalence of drinking by parents and other adults, and also among one or more brothers and/or sisters, with whom children are associated, is a potent factor in their misconduct. Healy and Bronner [10] found that 28.5 per cent of the Chicago cases and 45 per cent of the Boston cases of delinquent children came from homes with alcoholic parents. Drinking was relatively less extensive then as compared with the present consumption of alcohol by adults. The Gluecks [11] found that over six in ten (62.8 per cent) of the fathers of 500 delinquents drank to the point of intoxication, as compared with about four in ten (39.0 per cent) of the fathers of 500 nondelinquents. Nearly a fourth (23.0 per cent) of the delinquents' mothers drank excessively, as contrasted with only 7.0 per cent of the mothers of the nondelinquents. The Gluecks likewise tried to ascertain the extent of excessive drinking in the families of the parents of delinquents. According to their findings,[12] 37.0 per cent of the fathers and 46.8 per cent of the mothers of delinquents, as compared with 31.4 per cent of the fathers and 31.4 per cent of the mothers of nondelinquents, grew up in families among whom one or more members repeatedly drank to the point of intoxication. As regards drunkenness among siblings, 21.4 per cent of the delinquents, compared with only 6.4 per cent of the nondelinquents, had one or more brothers and/or sisters who were known to drink to the point of intoxication.

10 William Healy and Augusta F. Bronner, *Delinquents and Criminals: Their Making and Unmaking* (New York: The Macmillan Co., 1926), 98.

11 Sheldon and Eleanor Glueck, *Unraveling Juvenile Delinquency* (New York: The Commonwealth Fund, 1950), 101-102.

12 *Ibid.*, 98.

Even the milder drinkers among parents or sibling relatives may have a direct or indirect effect on the conduct of children. Children tend to imitate their parents, their older brothers and sisters, and sometimes other adults, and they are inclined to go along with the crowd. They do what they see done in their homes and in their social set. A family in which drunkenness exists produces consequences other than imitation in behavior. Excessive drinking may reduce the family income, most certainly the amount of money available for the family budget, produce excessive conflicts, loss of status, and other consequences, which have effects on the welfare of the children. To see intoxicated persons, especially if they are parents, produces certain psychological effects that cannot easily be measured. Alcoholism tends to dispose of the drinking parents as leaders of the family units. In fact, children are often ashamed of drunken parents.

Use of "Drugs" and Opiate Addiction. Newspapers, magazines, and other sources continuously bring the narcotic problem to the attention of the public, with special emphasis on the spread of the use of "drugs" among juveniles. But there is considerable misunderstanding with respect to the meaning of such terms as "drugs," "opiate or drug addiction," and "narcotics." The public likewise has a misconception regarding the extent of the use of narcotics by juveniles. The use of narcotics is a serious problem, not only because of its increase, but because of the effects of opiate addiction and habituation, and the difficulties of treating the patients sufficiently to cure the habit and prevent its spread.

Lindesmith[13] says that when such terms as "drugs," "drug addict," and "narcotics" are used, they refer only to opiate drugs and to opiate addiction. Marijuana (sometimes spelled marihuana) and cocaine are excluded, for they are not opiates and their effects are not comparable to the effects of opiates. However, since they are included in antinarcotic legislation they are included in the statistics of narcotic offenders.

The Expert Committee on Drugs Liable to Produce Addiction, of the World Health Organization of the United Nations, defines drug addiction as

. . . a state of periodic or chronic intoxication detrimental to the individual and to society, produced by the repeated consumption of a drug (natural or synthetic). Its characteristics include: (1) an overpower-

---

[13] Alfred R. Lindesmith, *Opiate Addiction* (Bloomington, Indiana: Principia Press, Inc., 1947), 6. For an extensive glossary of addict's argot and selected bibliography, see pp. 211-232.

ing desire or need (compulsion) to continue taking the drug and to obtain it by any means; (2) a tendency to increase the dose; (3) a psychic
(psychological) and, sometimes, a physical dependence on the effects of
the drug.[14]

Isbell divides the drugs that are addicting under two main classes:
(1) stimulants and (2) depressants.

. . . The stimulants regarded as addicting include cocaine, amphetamine
(Benzedrine), and mescaline. The depressants include morphine and all
its derivatives (heroin, Dilaudid, codeine, dihydrocodeinone, and meto-
pon); the synthetic analgesics—methadone and meperidine (Demerol);
all hypnotics and sedatives (chloral, paraldehyde, bromides, barbiturates,
marihauna, and alcohol).[15]

Isbell thinks that, statistically, alcohol is the most important of all
addicting drugs. He says further that addiction is caused chiefly by
human weakness, not by the drug, and is a symptom of personality
maladjustment rather than a disease in its own right. Usually, people who become addicted are pleasure-seeking (hedonistic), psychoneurotic, and emotionally unstable individuals. Some are more
susceptible to addiction than others. Lindesmith [16] differentiates
between addiction and habituation. Habituation applies primarily
to the nonpsychological aspects of addiction. It is merely a physical
adaptation, whereas in addiction the psychological elements (craving
or desire, emotional factors) accompanying the physiological conditions, and they are more or less independent of their biological
origin.

The narcotics that currently seem to cause the major problems
among juveniles are: heroin, marijuana, and the barbiturates.
Opium, morphine, and cocaine are used also, and they have been
problems for some time, but during recent years they have not
created addicts at the rate of the new menace.

It is not exactly known how extensive opiate addiction is, for
only the arrest records give us a clue regarding changes in the extent
of addiction or use; but accumulating evidence of a rapid increase
in the use of habit-forming drugs by young people has brought sud-

---

14 World Health Organization, *Technical Report Series*, 1950, 21:6.1-6.4. Compare
M. J. Pescor, "The Problem of Narcotic Drug Addiction," *The Journal of Criminal
Law, Criminology, and Police Science*, Vol. 43, No. 4 (November-December, 1952),
471-481; and Harris Isbell, "Meeting a Growing Menace—Drug Addiction," *The Merck
Report*, July, 1951. Dr. Isbell is head of the only laboratory in the world exclusively
devoted to the study of drug addiction—The Research Branch, United States Public
Health Service Hospital, Lexington, Kentucky. For a concise statement of "drug addiction," see Vernon C. Branham and Samuel B. Kutash, Editors, *Encyclopedia of Criminology* (New York: Philosophical Library, 1949), 130.

15 Harris Isbell, *ibid.*, p. 1 of reprint.

16 Alfred R. Lindesmith, *op. cit.*, Chapter III.

den public recognition of the problem. The Federal Bureau of Narcotics has reported increases of arrests, from slightly over 2,000 in 1946 to 6,136 in 1950. The California Youth Authority reported that for the first nine months of 1951, of the total of 2,143 youths admitted to custody of the Authority, 224 of these youths admitted use of narcotics.[17] Using local statistics to indicate a possible trend in a rapidly growing area, we may cite the increase of juvenile narcotic arrests in Los Angeles, as reported by the Police Department.[18] From 1940 to 1943 the number of arrests and petitions filed amounted to only a few each year. The arrests per 100,000 population ranged from only .1 to .9; whereas since the war the range has been from 3.5 to 10.9. It should be added that the Police Department has recently greatly increased the personnel of the Narcotics Division of the Detection Bureau with a view to checking the increase of the consumption of narcotics among both juveniles and adults.

The treatment of any type of drug addiction is difficult. Favorable results cannot be expected unless treatment is continued over a period of months; and the patients should be institutionalized, for the treatment at home by a physician or a psychiatrist is seldom satisfactory. There are only two such institutions operated by the United States Health Service (Lexington, Kentucky, and Fort Worth, Texas), and they accept only those persons addicted to opiates, cocaine, or marijuana, but cannot admit individuals addicted only to barbiturates, Benzedrine, alcohol, or bromides. The treatment involves both the withdrawal of drugs and rehabilitative measures. The addicts usually must be treated also for psychiatric disorders. At the Lexington hospital, 18 per cent of the patients admitted in 1950 were under 21 years of age, as compared with only 3 per cent in 1946. About 40 per cent of the patients in this hospital were repeaters.

Attempts to control the consumption of narcotics include treatment of those already addicted, prosecution of those who engage in the narcotic traffic, and preventive education. No one method of control can be successful, and the combined methods of treatment

---

[17] Justin K. Fuller, "A Review of Some Significant Phases of the Addiction Problem," *California Youth Authority Quarterly*, Vol. 5, No. 3 (Fall, 1952), 16-19. Roma K. McNickle, "Drug Addiction," *Editorial Research Reports* (March 28, 1951), 221 f., has estimated that there are 50,000 drug addicts in the United States, as compared with 750,000 chronic alcoholics. Compare Arthur K. Berliner, "The Drug Addict—Criminal or Victim?" *Focus*, Vol. 33, No. 3 (May, 1954), 78-85. For annual reports, see United States Bureau of Narcotics, *Traffic in Opium and Other Dangerous Drugs*. (Washington, D. C.: U. S. Government Printing Office).

[18] Cf. *Youth and Narcotics*, a bulletin published by the Los Angeles Police Department, 1952, and revised in 1953.

and prevention have been only partially successful. The addict experiences an overpowering impulse to continue taking the drug and to obtain it by any means. As addiction progresses, he takes more frequent doses and larger amounts. The withdrawal distress is so severe that few have the will power to break the habit, even though the majority of them desire to stop using drugs. Most of the drugs are so costly and profitable to sell that the drug peddlers risk being detected in order to continue their trade. Although the arrest and punishment of the drug peddlers are necessary parts of the process of control, most police officers do not believe that law enforcement is the final answer to the dope problem. Rehabilitation is chiefly a community responsibility, as is the problem of prevention. Even though drug addiction may have its major roots in human weakness, it may have its beginnings in unhappy homes or family tensions, in the lack of parental training or control, in cultural conflicts and social disorganization in the neighborhood, and in a variety of other social as well as personal conditions.

Opiate addiction has lasting consequences and is exceedingly difficult to stop, chiefly because of the withdrawal distress, as Lindesmith points out. The smoking of marijuana cigarettes sometimes has immediate effects, however, that may lead to serious delinquencies. Juveniles often start with marijuana, then they want something more potent, and this leads to the use of opiates, such as heroin, one of the most dangerous habit-producing drugs. Before they realize it, they have become addicts. However, not all persons who use opiates become addicted. Some do not develop the strong craving, or desire. They do not possess the psychological weaknesses that accompany the process of addiction.

Bad habits, whether excessive drinking, opiate addiction or habituation, or excessive use of tobacco, are usually hard to break. Well-established habits have a persistence that seems to compel individuals to repeat the acts. But a habit is not merely the repetition of a certain type of act, for running through the repeated activities is a tendency to act that way. This tendency or proclivity to act in a certain way is conditioned by the impulses, tastes, wishes, and other phases of the organism. The whole organism may become geared into the activity. This is particularly true of habits that vitally affect both the biological and psychological phases of personality, and may be re-enforced social customs and pressures, as is true of the use of alcoholic beverages, narcotics, and tobacco.

Sex Behavior and Deviations. Few phases of human behavior are so fraught with the possibility of emotional conflict, social condemnation, personality disorganization, and disease as sex deviations from the mores and laws of society. Throughout history, sex behavior has been a source of concern, and most societies have had some taboos or other means of social control. The Jewish-Christian sexual philosophy and the English-American sex laws are largely built around the early Hebrew interpretations and attitudes, which emphasized the ascetic approach to sex. The Roman cults and the beliefs of the early church leaders set the pattern of sex control. In sharp contrast is the hedonistic doctrine that sexual activity is justifiable for its own immediate and pleasurable return. The new morality and the greater freedom of the sexes have released to some extent the older forms of control, and at the same time have opened the door wider for illict sex relations. Sex urges and tendencies are strong and normally tend to result in behavior contrary to the mores of society.

Few subjects pertaining to or related to the problem of delinquency have been more investigated than the problem of sex deviations, especially as the problem has manifested itself among the young. Sociologists, psychologists, physicians, psychiatrists, social workers, journalists, play writers, reformers, and many others have been interested in the study of sex problems or the part that sex plays in human society.

The study of the sexual behavior of males by Kinsey, Pomeroy, and Martin, commonly known as the Kinsey Report,[19] has received the great amount of notoriety during recent years, and no study has been subjected to more severe criticism from the point of view of research methodology and the findings. The investigators claim that 12,000 persons contributed case histories to the study. Actually, only 5300 histories of males were used in the main tabulations. A rather high standard of research is indicated in the report; but the investigators apparently were unable to live up to it, for many discrepancies in methodology are observable. The interview technique was relied upon as the chief instrument of research, which, though carefully applied, is open to criticism, chiefly because of the possibility of biased or inaccurate replies, especially since many of the questions called for confessions of a very personal nature. Furthermore, many of the persons interviewed were atypical individuals rather than representative of a cross section of the population. Nevertheless, the major findings may be used as indications of sexual behavior among

---

19 Alfred C. Kinsey, Wardell B. Pomeroy, and Clyde E. Martin, *Sexual Behavior in the Human Male* (Philadelphia: W. B. Saunders Co., 1948). Compare *Sexual Behavior in the Human Female* (1953). Paul H. Gebhard is joint author (with Kinsey, Pomeroy, and Martin) of the second volume.

some males. Only a few facts pertain to delinquency, although many forms of sexual behavior are violations of law.

The study pertained to the factors affecting sexual outlet (marital status, age, social and economic levels, stability of sexual patterns, rural-urban and religious background), the sources of sexual outlet (masturbation, nocturnal emissions, heterosexual petting, premarital intercourse, marital intercourse, extramarital intercourse, intercourse with prostitutes, homosexual outlet, and animal contact), and some of the consequences of sexual behavior. Not all of the sexual outlets of children and of adults are abnormal. It is not necessary for our purpose to review all of the aspects of the study in order to point out the possible relations of the findings to juvenile delinquency.

The early heterosexual play begins with the preadolescent age, but the maximum frequencies (total outlet) occur in the late teens, after which they tend to drop gradually but steadily well into old age. Masturbation is chiefly a phenomenon of younger and unmarried groups, for the highest incidence lies between 16 and 20 years of age, when 88 per cent are involved.[20] Individuals differ tremendously in the frequency of masturbation. Petting is also very common among the young, for about 88 per cent of the total male population have petting experience prior to marriage.[21] It is pre-eminently a practice of the high school and college levels. Such practice is not new with the younger generation, but excesses are more common now than they were among the older generations when they were young.

Premarital intercourse is a form of sexual behavior that has become a source of great concern. It is far more common than most people surmise. The highest incidence of premarital intercourse apparently comes in the late teens, where nearly three fourths (70.5 per cent) of the total population is involved, according to Kinsey's study.[22] The average of the single males that engage in heterosexual intercourse drops from 70.5 per cent to 51.3 per cent between the ages of 16 and 50. The 16- to 20-year-old group has not only the highest percentage of individuals that engage in such practice but also the highest frequency, with a mean of 1.32 per week.[23] The premarital intercourse may be had either with companions or with prostitutes. For the younger males, between 16 and 20, prostitution provides outlets for only 4 per cent of the population as a whole,

---

20 *Ibid.,* 238.
21 *Ibid.,* 243.
22 *Ibid.,* 249.
23 *Ibid.,* 250.

and for about 11 per cent of those who have premarital intercourse. The older males, especially those in the lower educational and economic levels, who are not yet married turn to prostitutes more often than do the younger ones, but the larger share still turn to non-prostitutes.

The age of first intercourse is affected by the age of adolescence. For instance, of the boys whose adolescence begins at the age of 11, about 1.7 per cent have intercourse at 11, and the percentage increases year by year, with 15.0 per cent at 15 and 37.2 per cent at 18, after which the rate of increase is affected by the proportion that are married. If adolescence starts at 12 or later, intercourse also starts later and the ratios are lower than among those who reach the adolescent period early. In general, boys who mature early are the ones who most often turn to masturbation and to premarital sociosexual contacts. They engage in both heterosexual and homosexual relations more frequently than do boys who mature later.

In order to appraise fully the sexual behavior of both the young and the older males, the biologic, psychologic, and sociologic factors must be taken into consideration, for these factors tend to operate simultaneously and concomitantly in influencing conduct, and no one factor functions in isolation. There is no single pattern, but scores of patterns, depending upon differentiating conditions. The frequencies of total sexual outlets vary somewhat with educational and economic levels, but they differ not so much as the frequencies of the several sources of outlet, especially the tabooed forms of sexual behavior.

Pre-marital intercourse, whatever its source, is more abundant in the grade school and high school levels, and less common at the college level. Even in the period between adolescence and 15 the active incidence includes nearly half (48 per cent and 43 per cent) of the lower educational groups, but only 10 per cent of the boys who will ultimately go to college. In the later teens, 85 per cent of the grade school group and 75 per cent of the high school group are having pre-marital intercourse, while the figure for the college group is still only 42 per cent. In later years the differentials are not so great but, compared with the grade school group, it is still only about two-thirds as many males who have such intercourse.

The frequency figures show still greater differences between educational levels. In the age period between 16 and 20, the grade school group has 7 times as much pre-marital coitus as the college group.[24]

It should be noted further that the college-bred males who have some premarital intercourse have it less frequently than do any other group. Those in the lower educational levels and in the semi-

---

[24] *Ibid.*, 347. Used by permission of W. B. Saunders Company.

skilled or unskilled occupational groups have the highest frequencies; and if the parents belong to the same educational and occupational levels, the sex offenses of the young seem to become accentuated. However, the sexual history of the individual accords more with the sexual pattern of the social group into which he ultimately moves than with the social group to which the parents belong, although sexual patterns are acquired fairly early in life.

Variations in rural-urban and religious backgrounds have effects on sex behavior. Kinsey's study indicates that in most age groups and at all educational levels, more of the city boys and fewer of the rural boys are involved in premarital intercourse. This is also true of homosexual practices. Considering the frequencies of total sexual outlet, the sexually least active are the Orthodox Jews, the devout Catholics, and the active Protestants (in the order mentioned), whereas the sexually most active individuals are the nonchurchgoing Catholics, the inactive Protestants, and the inactive Jewish group. Within any particular social level, the differences between the most active and the least devout members of each of these religious groups are very much less than they are between the different social levels. In each of the educational levels it is the religiously devout group that has the least premarital intercourse. The nondevout groups have the highest incidence of homosexual behavior.[25] According to these findings, the church exerts a profound influence on sex mores and tends to control sexual behavior. Its influence extends to the nondevout individuals, especially through the mores of society. No social level accepts the whole of the original Judaeo-Christian code, but sex taboos in modern society, especially in the Western Hemisphere, are derived chiefly from some part of the religious philosophy. These are, of course, conflicts between the religious codes and the patterns of sexual behavior.

It is not necessary for our purpose to discuss marital and extramarital sexual intercourse and similar forms of sex behavior that pertain chiefly to adults, although the behavior of adults has a great influence upon the young. Premarital sex intercourse has been singled out as one of the major problems of the younger generation, although other forms of sex behavior may cause serious problems and be closely related to sex offenses.

Some studies show even higher rates of premarital sex relations and related forms of sex behavior than are shown in the study cited previously. Hohman and Schaffner [26] studied 4600 unmarried men

---

25 *Ibid.*, chapters XII and XIII, especially pp. 455, 477-79.
26 Leslie B. Hohman and Bertram Schaffner, "The Sex Lives of Unmarried Men," *American Journal of Sociology*, Vol. LII (May, 1947), 501-508.

between the ages of 21 and 28 (men inducted into the United States Army during the summer and fall of 1941 in accordance with the Selective Service Act) regarding virginity rates, age of first sex relations, masturbation rates, and incidence of homosexuality. The sex histories were correlated with education, economic status, and religious affiliation. Of the white single men (4100), only 20 per cent were virgins. The virginity rate tended to increase with the length of education, increased in a less degree with higher economic status, was highest in the Protestant group (27.1 per cent), slightly lower in the Catholic group (19.1 per cent), and lowest among the Jews interviewed (15.9 per cent). Of the nonvirginal men, 71 per cent claimed that they had sex relations with nice (marriageable) girls. By the age of fifteen 21.3 per cent, by the age of eighteen 63 per cent, and by the age of twenty-one 92.8 per cent of all unmarried nonvirginal men had had their first sexual intercourse. Of the Negro group (500 men), the virginity rate was lower than that of the whites.

Of the white nonvirgins 90 per cent, and of the virgins 87 per cent, admitted masturbation, but the percentage of homosexuality in the group was much smaller than previous investigations had reported. Only 15 of the 4100 whites, or 0.36 per cent, were rejected on the ground of homosexuality, but the army doctors and psychiatrists may have rejected only the most serious cases. Studies of prison groups show higher rates. A homosexual is one who feels an amorous desire for one of his own sex. He may otherwise be normal in intelligence, or he may be feeble-minded or have psychotic and neurotic tendencies. Autoeroticism (masturbation) is commonly practiced during adolescent and later years. Such practices are generally condemned because of the supposed dire consequences, but reports of recent medical investigations do not justify such conclusions. Any ill effects, unless practiced to excess, are mental rather than physical, chiefly because of the sense of guilt that may be associated with it. Carried to excess, such practices may tend to reduce the normal desire for marriage, as it indicates a state of emotional immaturity.

A number of cases of sexual perverts are found among delinquents. Too strong emotional ties between a parent and a child of the same sex, living apart from members of the opposite sex, and association of a migratory boy with homosexual men may prevent a child from attaining heterosexual maturity. Some homosexuals are aggressive and try to seek other homosexuals, while others respond only when urged. Homosexual habits interfere with normal adjustments in marriage.

Although sex offenses are common among juveniles, the extreme cases of habituation are fortunately less common. Girls seem to present more serious difficulties than boys. The law enforcement agencies must deal with the more extreme cases, some of which are difficult to reform. Hartwell [27] cites the case of Clair, who was only 7 years old when first taken to the clinic. His mother had died when he was four, and he and a brother had lived in two different unsupervised homes. He had received plenty of food and clothing, but little attention and affection. Clair was reported as being untruthful, easily repentant, affectionate, interested in boyish activities, sly, revengeful, daring, and fond of adventure. His delinquencies were of the type that go with unsupervised street life of a tenement district. He was a disturbing element in the home, the school, and the settlement house. Although but 7 years old, he was a leader of several serious affairs. Hartwell states that in all his experience he had never known another child of Clair's age with such extensive sex experience and such complete emotional response to it. He and his brother had learned sex habits from older boys in their foster home, and homosexual relations had continued uninterruptedly between the brothers for two years. Clair later became involved with a large gang of street delinquents and was taught all kinds of perverse sex practices by the older girls. While this is an extreme case, it reveals how the very young can be influenced in their sex knowledge and behavior by older companions and can become grave problems.

Venereal disease is one of the consequences of illicit sex relations, especially with prostitutes, but fortunately this condition is less common among juveniles than among adults. The two forms of venereal disease are syphilis and gonorrhea. Syphilis is a contagious and epidemic kind of disease and is regarded as the most vicious because it invades the blood stream, the tissues, the nervous system, and the bones. It often gives rise to other ailments.

Sex behavior is related to delinquency in a number of ways. Illicit sex relations (adultery) are considered a crime. Rape is a serious crime. Then there are the lesser immoralities and unconventional forms of behavior. Sex is related to other forms of crime, such as prostitution and criminal gangsterism. Then, too, certain crimes are rooted in sex frustration and related phenomena.

The *Uniform Crime Reports* list rape as one of the major offenses. In 1953 a total of 17,900 offenses of this type were reported by the law enforcing agencies.[28] This category includes forcible

---

27 Samuel W. Hartwell, *Fifty-five Bad Boys* (Alfred A. Knopf, 1940), 264.

28 *Uniform Crime Reports* (Washington, D. C.: United States Government Printing Office, 1954), Vol. XXIV, No. 2 (Annual Bulletin for 1953), 70.

rape, statutory rape (no force used—victims under age of consent), assault to rape, and attempted rape. More detail statistics are given (p. 110) for 1174 cities over 2500 in population. While these cities reported 1,191,160 of the total of 2,159,080 (estimated) arrests, both rural and urban, in the United States during 1953, they reported only 7151 cases of rape, but 20,345 cases of prostitution and commercialized vice and 14,341 other sex offenses.

California [29] has been making sexual deviation studies since 1950, under the auspices of the Department of Mental Hygiene. The State Legislature passed the California Sexual Deviation Research Act in 1950 to provide funds for the project. Many of the data pertain to adult offenders, but some information has been obtained concerning juvenile sex offenders. In the report published in 1953, based on data tabulated thus far, it is estimated that about 1550 alleged sex offenders were disposed of in California superior courts, and 1150 were convicted during the calendar year 1951, most of whom were men. Sex offenders comprise nearly one tenth of all superior court dispositions and represent about 11 cases per 100,000 population. While rape and crimes against children accounted for the majority of superior court sex offense cases, more than half of all sex crime convictions were for misdemeanor charges, for it is estimated that the annual sex misdemeanor convictions in California inferior courts number about 3400 annually. It must be recognized that the reported sex crime convictions represent minimum figures for sex crimes actually disposed of in the courts and that sex offenders prosecuted in courts provide no accurate measure of the total incidences of sex acts performed contrary to law. Based on reports from 19 of the 58 counties of the state, the Research and Statistical Department of the California Youth Authority has estimated that 2500 boys and girls concentrated largely in the age period 13-18 years are charged each year with sexual misconduct. These are only

29 Report of Karl M. Bowman, Medical Superintendent of the Langley Porter Clinic, *Sexual Deviation Research*, March, 1952, printed by the Assembly of the State of California; and *California Sexual Deviation Research*, January, 1953, by Karl M. Bowman, Frank F. Tallman (Director, Department of Mental Hygiene), and staff, also printed by the Assembly. Compare A. R. Mangus, "Sexual Deviation Research in California," *Sociology and Social Research*, Vol. 37, No. 3 (January-February, 1953), 175-181. Dr. Mangus of Ohio State University was on leave to serve as Research Sociologist for the Langley Porter Clinic of the California State Department of Mental Hygiene and was head of the research staff which prepared the data reported in the above mentioned references. For articles on sex deviation and sex offenders, see *Federal Probation*, Vol. 14, No. 3 (September, 1950). The entire issue is devoted to this problem. Compare Richard L. Jenkins, "The Making of a Sex Offender," *Focus*, Vol. 30, No. 5 (September, 1951).

a part of the data gathered, but they indicate the seriousness of the problem.

Juvenile sex offenses are likely to be associated with alcoholic intoxication or the use of narcotics, gang pressures, petting parties, certain forms of commercial amusements, and a variety of other activities that tend to stimulate the sex urge and to lessen moral controls. Many of them are maladjusted individuals, but, with few exceptions, they are not the "sex maniacs," "degenerates," and "sexual psychopaths" that newspapers may lead the public to believe. The general public has but a vague idea of what the sexual criminal is like. Few know about the meaning and extent of sexual crimes. Actually, it is doubtful if there has been a sex wave, except, perhaps, during and shortly after a war, which generally favors a certain degree of moral looseness. Nevertheless, sexual deviation is a serious problem in modern society and must be dealt with in that manner.

MALADJUSTMENT AND THE READJUSTMENT PROCESS

Other types of behavior traits and habits could be cited to indicate the lack of character training or the breakdown of moral control. Many of the victims of their own habits are maladjusted individuals. There are, of course, maladjusted children who are not deviants in their behavior, at least not in an extreme sense.

The maladjustment and the readjustment processes may go on simultaneously. The forces of disintegration operate in a situation in which unsatisfactory conditions exist; but at the same time the individual, either by his own effort or as the result of assistance received, makes adjustments of one kind or another, sometimes accomplishing fairly complete adjustments in later life. The cases of *The Jack-Roller: The Natural History of a Delinquency Career,* and *Brothers in Crime,* by Clifford R. Shaw and Henry D. McKay, which will be reviewed in the following chapter, illustrate this fact.

The process of adjustment is not merely an individual affair, nor is the maladjustment of an individual exclusively a personality problem. As Kingsley Davis [30] has pointed out, from the standpoint of the individual, the adolescent problem is how each youth can adjust satisfactorily to the social norms. From a societal standpoint. it is how the norms themselves may be changed so as to ease this adjustment and to achieve the maximum use of the adolescent group. The

---

[30] "Adolescence and the Social Structure," *The Annals of the American Academy of Political and Social Science,* Vol. 236 (November, 1948), 8-16. Compare "The Child and the Social Structure," *Journal of Educational Sociology,* Vol. 14 (December, 1940), 217-229.

adolescent period is sometimes characterized as a period of irresponsibility. During this time, adult control is sometimes repudiated. Social maturity lags behind physical and mental maturity. In most social systems the child acquires the rudiments of culture informally. The school system provides the more formal aspects of education. But young people sometimes lack the practical knowledge and the experience to meet concrete situations that they must negotiate in order to get along in society. Cohen [31] points out that the transition from youth to maturity is at best a difficult stage. The child looks to parents, teachers, spiritual leaders, and others in the community for guidance, but he does not always get it. Thus, he becomes confused and uncertain when he faces difficult situations.

Maladjusted Children. Many of the personality factors thus far discussed result in maladjustments. They are the conditions of maladjustment. In order to describe certain personality conditions, we have already referred to environmental influences. Individual factors are not separable from environmental deviation pressures. A deviation pressure is anything in the environment that blocks adjustment or turns an individual into antisocial directions. It usually means a deviation from folkways (customs), mores (traditions), laws, or established institutions. The code-building process begins with the folkways; when sanctioned and enforced, folkways become mores and laws. A deviation pressure is a breakdown in this series of controls.

Children may be physically and mentally normal, and might ordinarily be adjusted emotionally, but because of unfortunate circumstances become maladjusted. Ordinarily, one could say that a person is adjusted when all of the personality traits enumerated earlier in the chapter are fully developed, according to his age, and the several aspects of the personality are well integrated. However, because of abnormal dependency, neglect, abuse, mistreatment, and similar conditions, it is impossible for some children, although otherwise normal, to become adjusted. Underprivileged children, as we shall see later, may go through life with handicaps that they are not able to overcome.

The child's personal characteristics are largely the result of early influences within the home, the school, the play group, and the neighborhood. Many of his habits and attitudes are established early in life. This gives him a direction of life from which in later years he seldom deviates. "Train the child in the way he shall go,

---

[31] Frank J. Cohen (Edited by Hermine I. Hopper), *Children in Trouble: An Experiment in Institutional Child Care* (New York: W. W. Norton & Co., Inc., 1952).

and when he gets old he will not depart from it" is a proverb of great merit—although it is possible to readjust some persons at almost any age.

Children guilty of law violation under a certain age, as was pointed out in the earlier chapters, are usually not classed as delinquent, but as health, dependency, or neglected cases. They constitute problems of welfare rather than of delinquency. The methods of dealing with these cases will be discussed in connection with the treatment process. The line of demarcation between the delinquents and those who are neglected, abused, and underprivileged is not rigid. It is difficult to distinguish between those who have sinned and those who have been sinned against. Usually both factors are present.[32]

As Carr has pointed out, children live in an adult world. No child is born a delinquent. Citing cases of the handicapped boy, the overrestricted girl, the child in a deviant home, the victim of sibling rivalry, and the young gangster, Carr asks, Who is delinquent? Is it the individual, or the parents, or the gang, or the community? It is difficult to say who is the real delinquent in a given situation.

Regardless of the causes of delinquency, the central problem in any case is the delinquent himself. The objective features of the environment, like broken homes, bad companionship, and community conditions, contribute heavily to delinquency; but in order to deal with the offender properly and efficiently, we must understand the person who committed the act and know why he gives in to temptations or to impulses. Behavior is always an affair of stimulus and response between the person and his environment.

What types of delinquencies are committed? What are the physical and mental conditions of the delinquent? Is the emotional life of the delinquent maladjusted? What elements of the ideational life are connected with the delinquent behavior? Is his personality well integrated or are there great deficiencies? How about his character? These are some of the questions that pertain to problems of ascertaining why certain children misbehave and others do not.

Since personality includes the behavior tendencies of the individual, it is important to understand the motivating influences. The dynamic aspects of personality include aggressiveness or passivity, restlessness or listlessness, energy or lethargy, perseverance or the lack of it, gregariousness or solitariness, likableness or repulsiveness, lovingness or mischievousness, ill temper or even temper, and many

---

32 See Samuel W. Hartwell, *Fifty-five Bad Boys, op. cit.*, especially cases like Ralph and Herbert, 60 and 136; also Lowell J. Carr, *Delinquency Control* (New York: Harper & Brothers, 1950), Chapters VI, VII, and VIII.

other contrasting qualities. The character traits of a person are significant, although a person's character is not wholly good or bad. The delinquent may be dishonest in certain ways, but otherwise truthful and square. He may have only a few or many character weaknesses. His mental capacities and abnormalities may be tied up with his character.

As stated in the previous chapter, much stress has recently been laid upon the fact that there is among the delinquents an undue proportion of mental defectives. Few cases of extreme mental diseases or disorders are found, but some of the most difficult problems of delinquent behavior are presented by children who have abnormal personalities. Knowledge that can be gained from intensive case studies of the delinquent's habits is very important. Habits must be interpreted in the light of the customary practices of a group and in relation to the child's own feelings about them. A child may have a sense of guilt and develop an inferiority complex regarding his behavior, or he may justify his acts or be indifferent in regard to his responsibility for them. Habits must be evaluated in terms of the whole personality and the successive social situations in which a child has experience. In the present chapter we have noted, in particular, certain physical habits, as drinking, use of drugs, and various types of sex practices. Habits are an important part of personality, notably of character, but they are not necessarily in and of themselves the chief factors in explaining delinquent behavior. Some individuals with certain habits may be delinquent, whereas others with similar habits may not—unless the habits themselves constitute delinquencies.

This makes the situation exceedingly complicated, but these baffling personality factors must be recognized in dealing with the difficult problem of causation. No matter how much delinquency is the result of the delinquent's contact with his environment, personality factors also must be dealt with.

Maturation and Readjustments in Conduct. Some of the delinquents are able to make adjustments, especially later in life, and cease their criminal behavior. What happens to youngsters who go through the correctional mill, juvenile courts, probation, reformatories, special schools, prisons, parole? As they grow older, what proportion become law abiding, instead of continuing criminal careers?

Fortunately, for the first time we have answers to some of the questions regarding readjustments of juvenile delinquents as they grow up. The Gluecks [33] made most comprehensive and painstaking studies of a thousand juvenile delinquents, and then attempted the most difficult job, in follow-up studies, of following their careers for a period of fifteen years, from their early juvenile court experience, at an average age of 14, through the years of growing up to an average age of 29. Skillful investigators studied the public records and social agency data regarding these youths, and by talking with them, their relatives, and others obtained significant data about them, their employment, their families, and their way of life.

Some of the data presented regarding the characteristics of these delinquents will be used in subsequent chapters dealing with environmental influences, because much of the material deals with social conditioning factors. The study will be referred to again in connection with the discussions of the treatment process, inasmuch as the Gluecks were primarily interested in the effectiveness of the social treatment of delinquents. A number of their conclusions are significant also from the point of view of personality readjustment.

The most important conclusions of their study are: (1) "with the passing of the years there was a diminution in the number of youths who continued to be offenders" (by the age of 29 almost 40 per cent had ceased to be offenders), and "even among those who continued to commit crimes, significant improvements occurred" (the proportion of serious offenders dropped from 75.6 per cent to 47.8 per cent during the fifteen-year period); (2) "the physical and mental changes in the natural process of maturation offer the chief explanation of this improvement in conduct with the passing of years"; (3) comparison of the reformed with the nonreformed revealed that "the former were endowed with a better heredity and enjoyed a more wholesome early environment than the men who continued to commit crimes"; and (4) that, on the basis of the findings, a prediction table was evolved that should enable investigators to determine the probable behavior of different types of offenders.[34]

It is apparent from this study that a considerable number of delinquents discontinue their practices as they mature. Although their explanations (2 and 3) may be questioned, it seems that those endowed with favorable personality traits and more wholesome environmental influences have a better chance of becoming readjusted to normal life than those who are not so favorably situated.

---

[33] Sheldon and Eleanor Glueck, *Later Criminal Careers* (1937); *Juvenile Delinquents Grown Up* (1940); *Criminal Careers in Retrospect* (1943); and *After-Conduct of Discharged Offenders* (1945). These first three were published by The Commonwealth Fund (New York), and the last by The Macmillan Company (London).

[34] *Juvenile Delinquents Grown Up, op. cit.*, 264-266. Used by permission of Commonwealth Fund.

DIFFERENTIAL ASSOCIATION AND PERSONALITY TRAITS

The material presented in this chapter has indicated the importance of character development and training, which is chiefly a learning process, as contrasted with some of the biological and psychological factors discussed in the previous chapter, which are partly the result of heredity. To be sure, even the hereditary factors can to some extent be modified by training and experience. The development of a well-adjusted personality, or the readjustment process after personality has become maladjusted, is likewise chiefly a matter of education and training. The way the personality matures and the kind of character a person develops depend somewhat upon the kinds of associations and contacts a person has.

In the succeeding six chapters, the various environmental influences will be considered, especially the deviant pressures of homes, companionship groups, community institutions, population and cultural factors, economic and physical environmental conditions, and other phases of the social situations affecting the lives of delinquents. In this connection it should be remembered that the individual and the group are not two separate entities, but two aspects of human life. Although the individual himself commits the acts of misconduct, much of delinquency is the result of the individual's contacts with his environment. The dynamic sources of difficulty, then, are to be found not in the personality of the individual or in his environment, but in the way the personality and environmental factors interact.

In this connection, it is appropriate to consider the well-known "differential association" theory of criminology as formulated by Sutherland.[35] According to this theory, crime rates are fundamentally the expression of differential group association and influences, involving the entire learning process. Since his theory emphasizes group contacts and the learning process, it involves both personality and environmental aspects. Sutherland has stated his thesis in nine propositions, as follows:

1. Criminal behavior is learned. . . . 2. Criminal behavior is learned in interaction with other persons in a process of communication. . . . 3. The principal part of the learning of criminal behavior occurs within intimate personal groups. . . . 4. When criminal behavior is learned, the learning includes (a) techniques of committing the crime, which are sometimes very complicated, sometimes very simple; (b) the specific direction of motives, drives, rationalizations, and attitudes. . . . 5. The speci-

---

35 Edwin H. Sutherland, *Principles of Criminology* (New York: J. B. Lippincott Co., 1947), 6-7.

fic direction of motives and drives is learned from definitions of the legal codes as favorable or unfavorable. . . . 6. A person becomes delinquent because of an excess of definitions favorable to violation of law over definitions unfavorable to violation of law. . . . 7. Differential associations may vary in frequency, duration, priority, and intensity. . . . 8. The process of learning criminal behavior by association with criminal and anticriminal patterns involves all of the mechanisms that are involved in any other learning. . . . 9. While criminal behavior is an expression of general needs and values, it is not explained by those general needs and values since non-criminal behavior is an expression of the same needs and values.[36]

Sutherland recognizes that either lawful or delinquent behavior may develop in early childhood and persist throughout life. Delinquency may have its roots deep in the "life experience of the person," as well as in the immediate "personal-situation complex," for the tendencies and inhibitions of a person at the moment are largely the product of his early history.

This theory of crime rates explains much of delinquent behavior. As Cressey [37] has pointed out, the general proposition that criminality is learned is now generally accepted by criminologists, but he feels that the details of the theory have not been sufficiently subjected to empirical research. He questions, in particular, the idea that criminality and noncriminality depend upon a ratio of contacts with criminal and anticriminal behavior patterns. Such contacts cannot be precisely identified and weighted. One cannot observe the associations of a child during his lifetime, not even over an extended period of time.

Attributing crime to a mathematical ratio of exposure to criminal norms makes it difficult to explain why some individuals engage in criminal activities and others do not. Individuals may be extensively exposed to criminal norms, yet they do not become delinquent. Others, with a minimum of contacts with criminal norms and with criminals develop delinquency patterns or on occasion commit acts of law violation. In a way, a person selects his associates and adopts behavior norms before they affect his behavior. The selective environment produces various effects.

Sutherland neglected or minimized the psychogenic trait component and other personality factors discussed in the previous chapter. By indirection, some of these personality factors are included in his contention that the acquiring of criminal tendencies involves

---

36 *Loc. cit.* Used by permission of J. B. Lippincott Company.

37 Donald R. Cressey, "Application and Verification of the Differential Association Theory," *The Journal of Criminal Law, Criminology, and Police Science,* Vol. 43, No. 1 (May-June, 1952), 43-52.

the entire learning process. The importance of training, as well as contacts with noncriminal norms, is implicit in the theory.

The environment of delinquents is complex, involving many variables, as will be indicated in the subsequent chapters.

QUESTIONS AND PROJECTS

For Class Discussion and Research

1. Compare the psychological and sociological interpretations of personality.

2. What is a habit? An attitude? A behavior pattern? How does a habit differ from an attitude or a wish?

3. What is meant by "character development"? How are moral judgments formed? What are the main character-building agencies in the community?

4. Make a study of drinking in a teen-age group. How extensive is drinking? Why do they drink? Has drinking in the group led to delinquent behavior?

5. What factors have contributed to the increase of drinking during the past two decades? List the chief problems of excessive drinking. Define alcoholism.

6. Show the relation between drinking and the culture of society. What are the effects of alcohol on society? On individuals?

7. Study the national systems of liquor control. Outline some basic principles of liquor control. What are the most effective methods of temperance education?

8. What are the chief problems associated with drug addiction?

9. Make a list of sex offenses as defined by law. What are the main problems associated with sex deviations?

10. What are the main determinants of sex delinquencies?

11. Discuss the relative importance of personality disorganization and social maladjustments in relation to problem children?

12. Discuss the pros and cons of Sutherland's differential association theory of crime.

13. Discuss character education in relation to problem children.

14. Discuss character education in relation to the maladjustment child.

15. Discuss maturation as a factor in the development of personal control of conduct.

SELECTED REFERENCES

AICHHORN, AUGUST, *Wayward Youth* (New York: The Viking Press, 1935).

BOSSARD, JAMES H. S., *The Sociology of Child Development* (New York: Harper & Brothers, 1948 and 1954).

DEWEY, RICHARD, AND W. J. HUMBER, *The Development of Human Behavior* (New York: The Macmillan Co., 1951).

DOSHAY, LEWIS J., AND GEORGE W. HENRY, *The Boy Sex Offender and His Later Career* (New York: Grune and Stratton, 1943).

ELLIOTT, MABEL A., AND FRANCIS E. MERRILL, *Social Disorganization* (New York: Harper & Brothers, 1950), Chapters III-IX.

GOLDBERG, JACOB H. AND ROSAMOND W., *Girls in City Streets* (New York: American Social Hygiene Association, 1935).

HAVIGHURST, ROBERT J., AND HILDA TABA, *Adolescent Character and Personality* (New York: John Wiley & Sons, Inc., 1949).

KINSEY, ALFRED C., WARDELL B. POMEROY, AND CLYDE E. MARTIN, *Sexual Behavior in the Human Male* (Philadelphia: W. B. Saunders Co., 1948), and *Sexual Behavior in the Human Female*, 1953.

KLUCKHOHN, CLYDE, AND HENRY A. MURPHY (Editors), *Personality, Society, and Culture* (New York: Alfred A. Knopf, Inc., 1948).

LINDESMITH, ALFRED R., *Opiate Addiction* (Bloomington, Indiana: Principia Press, Inc., 1947).

McCARTHY, RAYMOND G., AND EDGAR M. DOUGLASS, *Alcohol and Social Responsibility: A New Educational Approach* (New York: Thomas Y. Crowell Co., 1949).

McKINNEY, FRED, *The Psychology of Personal Adjustment* (New York: John Wiley & Sons, Inc., 1949).

NEUMEYER, MARTIN H., *Social Problems and the Changing Society* (New York: D. Van Nostrand Co., Inc., 1953), Chapter VI.

PATRICK, CLARENCE H., *Alcohol, Culture, and Society* (Durham, North Carolina: Duke University Press, 1952).

SUTHERLAND, EDWIN H., *Principles of Criminology* (New York: J. B. Lippincott Co., 1947), Chapters I, XII and XIII.

THOMAS, W. I., *The Unadjusted Girl* (Boston: Little, Brown and Co., 1923).

WORLD HEALTH ORGANIZATION, *Technical Report Series*, 1950. Report on drugs liable to produce addiction.

YOUNG, KIMBALL, *Personality and Problems of Adjustment* (New York: Appleton-Century-Crofts, Inc., 1952).

VI

HOMES AND FAMILY CONDITIONS

The family is one of the basic social institutions and it is the outstanding primary group. It is potentially the most effective agency of social control. A normal family has long been regarded as the best insurance against delinquency. Contrariwise, a family that is broken by divorce, desertion, separation, or death, or that functions inadequately as a social unit, is handicapped in carrying on its responsibilities toward the children.

The basic functions of the family are those of reproduction and the physical care of children; the informal education and training of these children, including the transmission of culture, especially moral and religious ideals and standards, and practical knowledge; the provision of opportunities for affection, fellowship, and development of socialized personalities; the exercising of control and protection; and the economic functions of making a living and supplying the basic necessities of life. It is also a status-fixing and status-maintaining institution, giving the individual members a sense of worth and importance.

A family at its best is structurally complete (not broken); the members are in reasonable good health; they constitute a united household, living in a dwelling that is sanitary, well kept, mechanically convenient, and artistically satisfying; family life is intellectually stimulating, and the home atmosphere is morally wholesome and spiritually inspiring; financially the family group is relatively secure, with sufficient income to maintain a desirable standard of living; the members recognize responsibilities to one another and to the community; and the relationship in the home is based on affection, good will, mutual service, and loyalty. The normal family provides the basic needs of the members. Good health has reference to the absence of both physical ailment and mental or emotional inadequacy or disorder. Racial homogeneity, cultural unity, moral conformity, and functional adequacy are essential phases of a unified and cooperative family.

Functionally, a normal home meets the basic needs of individual members. It likewise contributes immeasurably to the development of healthy, well-adjusted, and usefully functioning personalities. Such a home encourages growth, confidence, frankness, respect for personal worth, and an ability to face reality. It provides an emotionally healthy atmosphere. The warm, continuous relationship with his (or her) mother or a mother substitute is very important during a child's early years. Children deprived of their mothers, with no living substitutes, may be retarded in the growth of personality and in their social and adaptive behavior. Affectionless children often suffer personality disturbances and disorders that are not overcome by later family and community experiences.

The condition of the family and what goes on in family life are of great importance to a growing child. The life organization and character of the person take their first and often permanent form under the impress of family life and culture heritage. The family is the first great training school in behavior or in misbehavior, depending upon the type of family life in which a child is reared. It is the chief socializing agent, but it may produce antisocial traits. The child tends to acquire certain moral and social qualities as taught and exemplified in the family. The effectiveness of the training in the home depends upon the character and the ability of the parents, the type of social relationship and moral atmosphere in the home, and the prevailing standards of the community and cultural group of which the family is a part. The family introduces the child to varied life situations. As soon as a child has free motion and begins to act, parents begin to define situations for him by their constant injunctions "be good," "don't do that," and many others.

The socialization process that goes on in the family, especially if the family unit is integrated and functions efficiently, is a significant aspect of the child's training and experience. Early socialization of children (attitude-formation, habit-development, and the establishment of moral judgments) has long been emphasized in sociological and social psychological literature. Socialization implies that individuals become an integral part of a group, recognizing this relationship, and play an active part in collective behavior. Some would add that a highly socialized person has a sense of moral obligation in playing an active part in group life. He recognizes that he has a social responsibility to perform. In a broad sense, socialization means a process of identification whereby the person develops a feeling of belonging.

Family life today still has a great deal of stability. In spite of the changing conditions, there are more family units now than ever before in our history. According to the 1950 census, using the new definitions of "family" and "household," [1] there were 42,500,000 households in 1950, of which 38,788,000 were family units. Both have increased by more than two million since that time. By family is meant a "group of two or more persons related by blood, marriage, or adoption and residing together," whereas a household includes "all persons (without regard to relationship) who occupy a house, an apartment or other group of rooms, or a room, that constitutes a dwelling unit."

The typical American family is commonly thought of as consisting of parents and their own children, living in a separate household. While 35 per cent of the households are of this type, 12 per cent consist of married couples only (either they never had children or the children are married or have died), 27 per cent are of either of the above types plus the addition of relatives or roomers, and about 13 per cent have a subfamily group living with the main family. The rest (about 13 per cent) consist of household groups but they are not complete family units, although some of them are classified as families. In spite of the variety of households and family units, the American family has a great deal of vitality.

What goes on in the family and the degree to which the family satisfies needs are to a great extent the conditioning factors that give

---

[1] Bureau of the Census, *Current Population Reports*, Series P-20, No. 33, February 12, 1951, and Series P-20, No. 38, April 29, 1952. Compare Ernest W. Burgess and Harvey J. Locke, *The Family: From Institution to Companionship* (New York: American Book Co., 1945 and 1953).

direction to a child's life. The family may influence delinquency in innumerable ways. Direct effects of broken homes are most easily discernible, but delinquency may be caused also by conflicting situations, early emotional tensions, failure to provide proper control and protection, failure to socialize the child and to provide sympathetic and understanding confidential relationship, injuring the status in the community, and serving as an agency of criminalistic behavior.

Various methods have been used to measure the effectiveness or failure of the family. According to Sutherland,[2] four main methods have been used to measure the importance of the home as a factor in delinquency. The score card method, illustrated by the Whittier scale, which allowed a maximum score of 5 points on each of the following items: necessity, neatness, size, parental condition, and parental supervision. Out of a possible total of 25, the median score of 162 homes of delinquents was 14, while that of 50 nondelinquents in the control group was 22. Another method was worked out by Miss Fernald to grade homes on the basis of economic status, moral standards, and parental supervision, the distribution of rating ranging from "very poor" to "very good," with three intermediate positions. Healy and others have attempted to measure the effects of homes by the case study method. The Gluecks and others have attempted to show the correlation between delinquency and one or several variables. None of these methods, as Sutherland concludes, have resulted in definite conclusions regarding the extent of the home's importance as a cause of delinquency.

Various objective conditions of delinquent homes have been observed, as the kinds of broken homes, the extent of criminalistic behavior in the home, housing, sanitation, poverty, parental supervision or the lack of it, uncongeniality, conflicts, and the like. These studies have yielded some results, but it is frequently difficult to show the degree of correlation between delinquency and any one of the several factors observed.

Before proceeding with the possible correlation between conditions of the home and delinquency, it is advisable to indicate the major forms of broken homes and the factors that make for an inadequate home.

---

2 Edwin H. Sutherland, *Principles of Criminology* (New York: J. B. Lippincott Co., 1947), 154-158.

THE BROKEN HOME

Family Disorganization and Structural Incompleteness. In its broadest sense, family disorganization means a breakdown of unity, loyalty, consensus, and the normal function for the family unit; but, in a more restricted sense, a broken home is one in which the marriage relationship has been severed by separation, annulment, divorce, desertion, death, or by prolonged absence of one or the other spouse. In other words, the family is structurally incomplete.

The present-day American family scene is marked by many disrupted homes. Although desertion is fairly common, which is the willful and prolonged absence of one spouse, usually without the consent of the other spouse, no other phase of family disorganization has attracted the attention of thoughtful students of modern society as has divorce, which is the most outstanding symptom of the breakdown of the American home.

In 1946, 610,000 divorces were granted in the United States, which was more than twice the number (264,000) granted in 1940, and nearly four times the number (160,380) in 1932. The rate per 1000 population increased from 1.8 in 1932 to 4.3 in 1946. In 1947 the total dropped to 450,000, and the total each year has been declining. In 1951, about 371,000 divorces were granted. In comparison with the record divorce peak of 1946, the rate of 2.4 divorces per 1000 population in 1951 was about 44 per cent lower. Taking a long-range view of the situation, divorces have been steadily on the increase during the past seventy-five years, with occasional decreases during depression and postwar years. Divorces are more common in cities than in rural areas. The largest number of divorces for any five-year period in married life is granted during the first five years. More than half of the broken homes are childless, and approximately three fourths of all divorces are obtained by the wives. Cruelty, desertion, and adultery are the three most important legal grounds used in the order mentioned, although it is generally believed that the real underlying causes include incompatibility, historical movements like individualism and romanticism, industrialism and urbanism, the immediate economic and cultural conditions of our society, the changed attitudes and mores with regard to marriage and divorce, and the lessening of legal and other forms of social control.

Separation precedes divorce, but also separation often takes place without divorce. It is an agreement between husband and wife to live separately. Separation may be permanent or temporary.

Eventually, all families are dissolved by death, unless they have already been broken by divorce, desertion, or separation. Death may remove any member of the family. During the early years of married life, a young couple may lose the parents, and sometimes a child, but fortunately the death rate is not very high among the young and during middle age. If death comes, it is likely to produce an immediate crisis. Long illness preceding death, financial loss due to sickness and death in the home, and the necessity of readjustment of family life may bear down heavily upon the family unit. Eventually adjustments are made, either to loneliness or to a new family unit.

Illegitimate Parenthood and Unwanted Children. Illegitimacy is a baffling problem. Although it is not known exactly how many children are born out of wedlock, it is estimated that about 4 per cent of all children born in the United States each year are born out of wedlock, and that the rate has increased nearly threefold during the last three decades. The designation "illegitimate child" is an unfortunate one, for it stigmatizes and handicaps a child rather than the parents. The community attitude toward illegitimate children makes it very difficult for them to live a normal life and to receive proper treatment. Besides being classed as illegitimate children, many are further handicapped in that the mothers may be too young to rear children, or may be characterized by any one or several of the following: have low intelligence, lack training, belong to low income and occupation groups, come from broken homes, have low moral standards, and lack means of livelihood.

A large number of the illegitimates start life with the handicaps of abnormal birth, a heritage of mental subnormality, the records of parental immorality and crime, and the lack of normal home atmosphere. When mothers try to keep these children, they have to assume the role of both parents. This is not a home in the real sense of the term. Many illegitimates are placed in foster homes; but it is difficult to find good foster homes for them. Besides the circumstances of their birth and the abnormal home life, if any, they are stigmatized and frequently ostracized by society. They may be rated as misfits.

The growing sense of resentment that normally accompanies such an experience, coupled with personality handicaps, often drives a child to antisocial behavior.

Quasi-broken Homes. During World War II homes were disrupted by the millions of men and women under arms. For the most part, it was the young men who were taken from the home and deprived of their home life, but fathers and mothers also went into the armed services or into defense industries away from home. This meant a great strain, and those who were left at home suffered from lonesomeness and anxiety. Both marriage and the birth rates increased during the war, but unfortunately the divorce rate increased also. Many families were uprooted by migration. Life in boom-towns, with overcrowded housing, excessive mobility, inadequate services of social institutions, health and other problems, was difficult, to say the least.

The problem of family adjustment projected itself into the post-war era. Securing new jobs, acute housing shortages, adjustments in the family after long absences from home, and similar problems have confronted the family since the war.

The extensive employment of mothers during the war was considered as one of the contributing factors to the increase of delinquency, especially of girls. Mothers in war plants were blamed for some of the delinquency of the time. Young children were often left to shift for themselves, and they did not receive needed attention and supervision during critical periods. Older children had to assume the burden of household duties, and younger children were left to the streets. With the father on a night shift, and mother on a day shift, or both on night shifts, children were often on the "street shift." With both parents working, and with older boys and girls either in the armed services or employed, the family as a functional unity was disrupted.

Tired parents often are nervous, irritable, and quick to abuse the children or quarrel among themselves. Parents working overtime have neither the time nor the energy to take care of a home properly. Defective discipline, lack of supervision, and dissatisfaction with home routine life, especially if accompanied with a loss of the sense of parental responsibility, produce unhappy homes.

Increased income, as we shall see later, may have both positive and negative effects on the family. It enables the family to purchase more of the necessities and luxuries of life; but, with more money on hand, members of the family are inclined to spend less time at home and spend more time and money in the pursuit of commercialized amusements. Poverty, on the other hand, produces many economic and accompanying hardships, but may keep the family closer together.

Even though the family may not be broken or disrupted physically, and the family as a unit is still complete, it may, nevertheless, be broken through emotional disturbances and insecurity, the breakdown of social status, and the reduction of its functions. Through dissension and conflict, the physically unbroken home may be socially and psychologically broken. Conversely, the physically broken home, as by death, may be socially and psychologically unbroken, provided the remaining members of the family carry on as a close family unit.

Institutional and Foster Home Children. The first White House Conference on Child Care, in 1909, recommended, among other things, that every child should have a home or the nearest substitute for it. The natural home should be preserved, through public aid if necessary. If this is not possible, a child should be placed in a foster home. If institutionalization is required, the institution should have an atmosphere as near homelike as is possible. Still, about 250,000 children are in child-care institutions in the United States. Institutional care is especially necessary for the physically and mentally handicapped, but far too many normal children are provided for in institutions because no homes are found for them.

It is not possible to measure the effects of institutionalization on children, for usually such children go through unfortunate experiences before they are sent to institutions. A number of studies have shown disproportionately high rates of delinquency among institutionalized children. Even if institutionalization does not produce delinquent tendencies, children brought up in institutions often present problems of control. The normal patterns of self-inhibition are sometimes undeveloped, personalities are distorted, and more incidences of aggressive and uncontrolled actions are likely to occur, especially if such children face difficult social situations.[3]

Foster home care is better than institutionalization, but the emotional experiences in the transition from the natural to the foster home and neglect or abuse prior to placement may have lasting effects. Deming[4] calls attention to the fact that an apparently promising placement sometimes fails because the experiences that aroused emotions in the child in the natural home are still active and continue to disturb him after placement in a foster home.

Broken Homes and Delinquency Rates. It is commonly believed that broken homes contribute considerably to the delinquency of children. Many studies have revealed the extent of broken homes

---

[3] Cf. Leon J. Yarrow, "When a Child Is Deprived of Mothering," *The Child,* Vol. 17, No. 5 (January, 1953), 84-85.

[4] Julia Deming, "Foster Home and Group Placement," *The American Journal of Orthopsychiatry,* X (July, 1940), 586-94.

in the groups studied. Sutherland,[5] in citing various studies, states that juvenile court cases show that from 30 to 60 per cent, or an average of about 40 per cent, of the children handled by courts have come from broken homes, but he concludes that broken homes are less important as causal factors than was previously believed. Delinquency is less likely to result from homes broken by death than from those broken by desertion, divorce, annulment, and separation.

The concept "broken homes" does not have a universal connotation. In the study of delinquency, most investigators have defined the term rather broadly, including all homes broken by divorce, separation, desertion, annulment, death of either father or mother, or both, and those involving remarriages after homes are broken. The re-established families are not always included in this category. Families with stepparents or foster parents have had the experience of a break in the structure, but the re-established family units may be highly integrated. Those who include quasi-broken homes under the category of family disorganization, in addition to actual breaks in homes, find a higher correlation between broken home conditions and delinquency.

The statistics of the relationship between broken homes and delinquency would be more meaningful if we knew the extent of broken homes in the general population. In order to make valid comparisons, it is necessary to have a control as well as an experimental group. These groups should be matched for age, sex, race, economic status, social class, living conditions, and other variables. This is precisely the difficulty, for controls should compare favorably with the delinquents in basic elements; otherwise the differences in the social frames of reference present difficulties in making valid comparisons. Furthermore, care must be exercised in selecting the delinquents. Cases must be analyzed in terms of the seriousness and types of offenses—whether they are first offenders or recidivists, general run-of-the-mill court cases or institutionalized cases—and the areas in which the individuals live. For instance, the more serious cases, especially if there is little hope of adjusting the family situations, are more likely to be filed on and institutionalized than the less serious cases. The fact that broken homes loom up more extensively in the more difficult cases is in itself significant. Then,

---

5 *Op. cit.*, 158-160. The percentages differ somewhat for boys and girls. H. Ashley Weeks, "Male and Female Broken Home Rates by Types of Offenses," *The American Sociological Review*, Vol. 5, No. 4 (August, 1940), 601-609, found 68.1 per cent of the girls who appeared before the Spokane County Juvenile Court came from broken homes as compared with 44.9 per cent of the boys, and the rates varied even more for certain types of offenses.

too, the kinds of broken homes and the process of family disorganization preceding actual breaks must be taken into consideration.

Shaw and McKay studied 7275 boys from broken homes. They used a sample of 1675 delinquent boys appearing in the Cook County Juvenile Court in 1929 with a like number of boys, matched for age, race, and nationality, from 29 Chicago public schools. They found that 42.5 per cent of the delinquent boys and 36.1 per cent of the nondelinquent (school) boys came from broken homes, the difference expressed in ratio being 1.18 to 1.0. The incidence of broken homes varied by racial and nationality groups, from 16.3 per cent for Jewish children to 46 per cent for Negro children. The older the children are, the greater the percentage of boys that come from broken homes, the range being from 26.2 at the age of ten to 38.9 at the age of sixteen.[6]

Although Shaw and McKay found that the difference between the rates in the delinquent and the control groups furnished an inadequate basis for the conclusion that the broken home is an important factor in delinquency, they point out that this does not mean that the family is of no significance in behavior problems. The actual separation of parents, divorce or desertion, may not be so important in the life of the child as the tensions and emotional conflicts which resulted in the breakdown of family relationships.

A British study, that of Carr-Saunders, Manheim, and Rhodes,[7] reports a relatively high percentage of delinquents from homes of normal structure. Their summary of cases revealed that 68 per cent of 1953 delinquents and 80 per cent of 1970 controls came from homes in which husband and wife were living in the same house with their children (with the addition of relatives or nonrelatives in some homes). The controls were provided by picking boys of the same ages and from the same schools to match the delinquents. Although the difference is not very marked, the findings indicate a degree of association between delinquency and families of abnormal structure. The structurally normal homes were divided into those where the home atmosphere was normal and where it was not. The investi-

---

[6] See Clifford R. Shaw and Henry D. McKay, "Social Factors in Juvenile Delinquency," *Report on the Causes of Crime*, No. 13, Vol. II, National Commission on Law Observance and Enforcement (1932), Part IV, especially pp. 273-284. Compare William C. Kvaraceus, *Juvenile Delinquency and the School* (New York: World Book Co., 1945), 72-74. Kvaraceus found that one third of the children dealt with by the Passaic Children's Bureau came from broken homes. The proportion of girls from broken homes was 42.5 per cent and of the boys it was 30 per cent. He suggests that homes broken by death should be differentiated from those broken by divorce, desertion, and separation.

[7] A. M. Carr-Saunders, Hermann Mannheim, and E. C. Rhodes, *Young Offenders* (New York: The Macmillan Co., 1944). See especially, Conclusions.

gators arrived at the conclusion that the chance of a delinquent coming from a home with an abnormal atmosphere was three or four times as great as the chance of a delinquent coming from a home with a normal atmosphere.

Merrill[8] studied 300 delinquents who were consecutive juvenile court cases and compared them with a similar number of nondelinquents, matched for age, sex, and home neighborhood with respect to several environmental factors that constituted the social frames of reference. Information was obtained regarding the structure of the home, the economic status and parental occupations, home relationships and family controls, recreations, companionships, and the use of leisure time. There were about four times as many boys as girls in the experimental group, and the average age was 15 years. About five years later, information was obtained regarding the after-treatment adjustment of 100 delinquents and 100 controls. It was found that 50.7 per cent of the delinquents and 26.7 per cent of the controls came from broken homes (divorced, divorced and remarried, separated, deserted, mother dead, father dead, both dead, father dead but mother remarried, mother dead but father remarried).

In the delinquent group there were more families in which both parents were foreign born than in the nondelinquent group. The home atmosphere is difficult to measure, but by using the Bell Adjustment Inventory, it was found that 15 per cent of the delinquents and 4.3 per cent of the controls came from very unsatisfactory homes; whereas only 3.8 per cent of the delinquents and 14.4 per cent of the controls came from excellent homes. The case histories and interviews indicated that a much larger proportion of the homes of delinquents had poor discipline and poor affection than was true of the controls. The controls showed better attitudes toward home and greater fondness for parents. From a study of the number of siblings and their respective positions in the families of 100 delinquents and 100 controls, the author concludes that the delinquent boys came from larger families and more of them were brothers of delinquent siblings than was true of the controls. Of 286 homes of delinquents, 11.5 per cent were in comfortable economic circumstances, 65.8 per cent were in the economically marginal group, and 22.7 per cent were in the dependent class. Of 295 controls, 31.5 per cent had a comfortable economic status, 51.2 per cent were marginal, and 17.3 per cent were dependent. Fewer of the parents of the delinquents than of the controls were in the professional, semiprofessional, cleri-

---

[8] Maud A. Merrill, *Problems of Child Delinquency* (New York: Houghton Mifflin Co., 1947), 64-70.

cal, and skilled occupations, and considerably more were in the unskilled and semiskilled jobs.

Besides differences in home and family conditions, delinquents lacked resources for satisfactory recreational outlets at home and in the community. In checking the clubs and other organizations the boys in both groups had ever belonged to, it was found that 45 per cent of the delinquent boys had never belonged to any clubs, whereas this was true of only 23 per cent of the control boys. A larger proportion of delinquents than of controls attended movies. The delinquents had poorer placements in school, less satisfactory conduct records and attitudes toward school, and slightly lower I.Q.'s, and they quit school earlier. A number of other comparisons were made, most of which indicated that the delinquents were less favorably situated than were the controls. While the controls were fairly well matched with the juvenile court cases for age, sex, and home neighborhood, many significant differences existed, indicating the difficulties of getting a comparable control group.

The Gluecks[9] made a fairly elaborate study of the home conditions, the setting and quality of family life, and the degree of stability or instability of the families of 500 delinquents and 500 nondelinquents. In the life span of the boys from birth to the time of the inclusion in the study, 302 (60.4 per cent) of the delinquents as compared with only 171 (34.2 per cent) of the nondelinquents had experienced broken homes (Table XI-8, p. 122). Of the children who experienced breaks in family life, 56.3 per cent of the delinquents and 46.7 per cent of the nondelinquents experienced the first break before they were 5 years old; and 28.1 per cent of the former and 21.0 per cent of the latter experienced the breaks 5 to 9 years of age, inclusively (Table XI-9, p. 122). The types of breaks, in the order of frequency, were: one or both parents deserted the boy, death of a parent, temporary separation of parents, permanent separation of parents, a prolonged absence of a parent because of delinquency, parents never married and soon abandoned boy, and prolonged absence of a parent because of illness. The nondelinquents experienced the same types of breaks, except more of them experienced breaks because of death of a parent, permanent separation or divorce of parents, and prolonged absence of a parent because of illness, and fewer for the other reasons mentioned (Table XI-10, p. 123).

It is important to note that broken homes are not isolated phenomena. The Gluecks found that even though both of the groups

9 Cf. Sheldon and Eleanor Glueck, *Unraveling Juvenile Delinquency* (New York: The Commonwealth Fund, 1950), Chapters VIII-XI. Compare *Delinquents in the Making: Paths to Prevention* (New York: Harper & Brothers, 1952), Chapters IV-VI.

(experimental and control) lived in the under-privileged areas, more of the families of the delinquents than the families of the nondelinquents lived in blighted slum tenement areas, they moved more frequently, paid lower rents, had fewer modern conveniences and sanitary conditions, their homes were furnished more poorly and lacked cleanliness, more of them were dependent, more of the breadearners were unskilled and low-paid workers, and they suffered from other wants. Only 11.7 per cent of the delinquents as compared with 27.2 per cent of the nondelinquents lived in "good" houses; whereas over a third (33.9 per cent) of the former and less than a fifth (19.8 per cent) of the latter lived in "poor" houses, which leaves about the same number living in "fair" houses.

Other differences noted were that more of the families of the delinquents than of the control group had persons with physical, mental, and emotional handicaps, drunkenness and criminality; fewer had adequate schooling and could meet financial and economic stress, many of whom lacked the ability to plan and manage finances; more homes lacked cultural refinement, and the families lacked pride, self-respect, and ambition; the conduct standards were lower, and the children tended to persistently misbehave over a longer period of time; the conjugal relations of parents were poorer, with less supervision and more dominance of parents over their children; and there was less cohesion in the family. On the other hand, the two groups of families did not differ much in birth places of mothers and fathers, except that slightly more of the parents of the delinquents were either both foreign born or both native born, and fewer had mixed parents; but the differences were not very great. As indicated in Chapter IV, the Gluecks used the items of parental discipline, supervision, affection, and the cohesiveness within the family as the main categories for their prediction score.

MALADJUSTED AND INADEQUATE HOMES

A home may not be broken and yet be very inadequate because of certain conditions of maladjustment. Family disorganization is a process, and the disrupting factors that lead to a broken home may have more telling effects on children than the actual break. This is particularly true in cases of divorce, annulment, desertion, and separation. Furthermore, even though the home may not be broken, the family may be in a mild or a serious state of disintegration because of a variety of conditions. A child may be able to overcome one or a few disrupting factors and influences emanating from the family; but when confronted with a number of such conditions, especially if the disruption is serious, some form of deviant behavior is likely to occur. So, whether the home is broken or structurally complete, it is necessary to take into consideration unsatisfactory home conditions in order to appraise properly the effects of the home on children's behavior. Quasi-broken or poorly adjusted homes are not conducive to the proper training of the young. Among the various conditions of maladjustment may be noted the inadequate functioning of the home even though it otherwise may be a fairly normal family, inadequate discipline and control, certain physical and psychological abnormalities, mixed parentage and divergent standards of conduct, dissension and conflict, and various other elements of inadequacy.

Functional Inadequacy. The close relationship between the structure and functions of the family or of a given society has been recognized for a long time, but the intricacies of this relationship have not been fully comprehended. Various interacting elements and variables must be noted; but, simply stated, the structure of the family affects its functions, and, conversely, the functions tend to affect its structure. In a dynamic society, such as the modern social order, both the structure and the functions of groups are continuously changing, whether slowly or rapidly, and group life is disrupted by the processes of disorganization and disintegration. Difficulties are likely to arise when the balance and unity of a group are upset.

Earlier in this chapter the basic functions of the family and the elements of a more or less ideal or well-adjusted family were noted. The changing conditions of modern society have made inroads into the traditional functions of the family. To be sure, a large proportion of the families are still performing the basic functions to a greater or lesser extent, but in other families the fundamental needs of children are not met because the family is either incapable or too maladjusted to perform the functions necessary to meet these needs and wants. The lack of the rudiments of practical education, including moral and religious training, may be an even greater handicap. Studies have shown that children derive most of their practical knowledge of everyday living, and the training in ethical living, from their parents. It has been found that the concepts of right and wrong come chiefly from parents and playmates, and to a lesser extent from teachers and other adult leaders. The family is still unexcelled in matters of affection, love, response, enjoyable companionship, and wholesome informal recreation; but it is evident that in some homes these functions remain unperformed. Instead, children experience the opposite reactions. The family is regarded as one of the chief socializing agents in society. Children learn how to live with others, first in the home, then in the play and school groups. A maladjusted home is likely to produce antisocial tendencies and disorganized personalities. The presence of loosely integrated or maladjusted families, particularly in urban areas, and the decline of sociopsychological functions are evidences of disintegration of family influence.

Possibly the greatest changes in the family have occurred in its economic, protective and controlling, and status-fixing functions. Some families suffer not only because of inadequate income, but because they do not know how to manage their meager income. Consequently, children suffer from inadequate food, clothing, and shelter.

The warm relationship between a child and his parents is of great significance in developing a wholesome set of ideals and in satisfying the wish for response. Love is essential for a child. If he is not loved and feels that he is not wanted, or if the emotional identification with the parents is disrupted, the growing child may seek substitute satisfactions in companionship or he may pass through a period of grave insecurity, frustration, and resentment, even hatred. It is in this type of situation that a child may turn to gang associations and other undesirable types of companionships. The feeling of loneliness and of being treated ruthlessly produces mental and emotional conflicts which may predispose a child to most any sort of adventure or delinquency that seems to provide a way out of an unsatisfactory situation. It must be remembered that not all children who are unloved and frustrated become delinquent. Some find substitute satisfactions in other groups and situations. On the other hand, some children do not seem to lack affectional relationship with their parents and yet they seem to be frustrated. Overprotectiveness, especially by the mother, is sometimes stressed as a possible cause of delinquency or of neuroticism in children. The children's affection for the parents, or the lack of it, must be noted also, for parent-child relationship is a two-way process. Likewise, the affectional relationship of the brothers and sisters for a boy (or a girl) is important. A child who is not a favorite or who is regarded as a "black sheep" in the family may feel deep resentment and emotional stress.

Inadequate Discipline and Control. Defective discipline or control in the home is generally recognized as a contributing factor to misconduct. Most training of the young involves elements of trial and error, but defective discipline is more common among delinquents than among nondelinquents. Burt[10] found defective disci-

---

[10] Cyril Burt, *The Young Delinquent* (New York: D. Appleton and Co., 1925), 92-95.

pline five times as often with delinquents as with nondelinquents, and the coefficient of association soared to .55. Twenty-five per cent of the cases showed weak, ineffective discipline, whereas 10 per cent showed overstrictness. Healy and Bronner [11] found that 40 per cent of 4,000 cases of delinquents in Chicago and Boston came from homes in which there was a definite lack of effective discipline. The discipline was too strict, too lax, unjust, or too inconsistent.

The Gluecks in their earlier studies found unsound discipline as one of the major sources of difficulty. In their later study,[12] they noted the disciplinary attitudes and methods of control by the mother and the father in both groups (delinquents and nondelinquents), but they do not indicate specifically how they obtained the statistical data.

In the delinquent group, 95.8 per cent of the mothers and 94.3 per cent of the fathers were too lax, overstrict, or erratic in their discipline, and very few of them were firm but kindly in their disciplinary practices. In the nondelinquent group, 65.6 per cent of the mothers and 55.5 per cent of the fathers were firm but kindly in their discipline, giving the boys the feeling that whatever control was imposed was based on fairness. More mothers and fathers of delinquents than of nondelinquents were lax in their disciplinary practices, but the mothers were more lax than the fathers. Very few of the mothers of either group were overstrict (harsh, demanding, unreasoning) with the boys; but over a fourth of the fathers of delinquents and nearly a tenth of the fathers of nondelinquents were too strict. Over two fifths of the fathers and over a third of the mothers of delinquents were erratic in handling their sons, swinging from overstrictness to laxity, without any consistency. These findings indicate that the parents of delinquents use worse methods than the parents of nondelinquents in dealing with their sons. Furthermore, they resorted more to physical punishment, deprivation of privileges, threatening and scolding, and less to reasoning, than the parents of nondelinquents.

Overindulgence and coddling may produce antisocial traits, as do overstrictness and severity. Lack of cooperation between parents or differences in their methods of control confuse the child. Frightening children may prove a dangerous way of affecting control.

---

[11] William Healy and Agusta F. Bronner, *Delinquents and Criminals: Their Making and Unmaking* (New York: The Macmillan Co., 1926), 125.

[12] *Unraveling Juvenile Delinquency, op. cit.,* pp. 131-133, especially Table XI-22, "Parents' Discipline of Boy," and Table XI-23, "Methods of Control of Boy by Parents." Compare their summary in *Delinquents in the Making: Paths to Prevention* (New York: Harper & Brothers, 1952), 65-67.

Nagging tends to alienate them from the home. Favoritism and injustices may lead to the loss of respect for parents, and not infrequently to grudges against them or against the more favored brothers and sisters. Even though there may not be evidences of overt dissension, difficulties of discipline, injustices in matters of treatment, and frequent complaining by the parents have unfavorable effects on children. Sometimes they are bored with frequent discussions of the hard day's work, employer-employee difficulties, hard times, ill health, and other complaints. Home life that is dull and uninteresting makes the street or the gang all the more enticing.

Punishment of the parents of delinquents has been advocated, and in some cases achieves desired results; but some juvenile court judges are of the opinion that to punish parents accomplishes little for the children themselves.

Physical and Psychological Abnormalities of Parents. In Chapter IV the possible effects of physical and psychological abnormalities of juveniles in relation to their conduct were described. Similar abnormalities of parents may affect the children in various ways. Even though the individuals involved in offenses may be otherwise quite normal, abnormality in the family provides the possibility of misconduct or neuroticism. It is a well-known fact that a great deal of sickness or physical disability on the part of any member of a family is a handicap. It tends to interfere with the normal functioning of the family group. Feeble-mindedness and psychological disorders are even more potent forces of disruption. Much feeble-mindedness is inherited, hence it is in the family. Even dull normal parents find it difficult to provide the best kind of environment for their children. Mental disorders, emotional instabilities and disturbances, and abnormal habits of the parents are more likely to affect children adversely than the biologically inherited elements.

A number of investigators have pointed out the possible effects of the shortcomings of parents on their offsprings. Hirsch [13] found the following conditions and habits among parents (one or both) of 2,000 juvenile delinquents, with percentages of such conditions as given: emotional instability (56.35), alcoholism (41.45), sexual promiscuity (25.25), financial dependence (15.45), criminal records (12.7), feeble-mindedness (11.), psychoses (8.35), syphilis (7.3), psychopathy (3.93), constitutional inferiors (2.9), epilepsy (1.), with only 19.7 per cent of families in which both parents were fully normal. This seems to be an array of abnormal parental conditions.

---

13 Nathaniel D. M. Hirsch, *Dynamic Causes of Juvenile Crime* (Cambridge: Sci-Art Publishers, 1937), 97.

Mixed or Immigrant Parentage and Divergent Standards. Special problems of training and discipline appear in the homes of mixed parents with divergent cultural backgrounds, or if the standards of the home differ greatly from those found in the community. There is a greater incidence of delinquency among American-born children of immigrant parents or mixed parents (one foreign born and the other American born) than among children of American-born parents. As was indicated in Chapter II, the rates of delinquency are higher in Negro and other minority groups than in the majority group. Shaw and McKay[14] attempted to correlate the rates of delinquency with the percentage of foreign-born and Negro heads of families. Wide variations were found between the rates in the classes where the percentage of foreign-born and Negro heads of families was high and in those where it was low. However, they observed considerable mobility and changes in population composition by areas, while the variation in rates remained about the same. Some areas seem to have high delinquency rates regardless of the types of people living in them and the changes in population over a period of time. This made it difficult to determine the degree of association between rates of delinquency and the proportion of children with foreign-born, mixed, or Negro parentage. Other factors apparently played important roles also.

Studies of correctional or reformatory institutional cases have revealed that a larger percentage of the inmates were native born of foreign or mixed parentage than were found in the general population. The cultural conflicts and divergent standards to which these individuals were subjected have been given as the major factors in their delinquency. But other deviant conditions have been noted also, notably the lower economic status of many of these families, living in slum and blighted areas, poorer houses, discrimination against them, lower education status and less interest in education, larger families, and more adult crime. The limited institutional facilities in such areas make it difficult to provide corrective measures to offset the disorganizing forces.

In *The Polish Peasant in Europe and America,* by W. I. Thomas and Florian Znaniecki, are descriptions of the breakdown of controls after the Polish peasants had migrated to American cities. In the old world, their lives were controlled chiefly by their families, the church, and the local community. In America all these controls were relaxed, and sometimes there was considerable breakdown of controls. The

---

14 Clifford R. Shaw and Henry D. McKay, *Juvenile Delinquency in Urban Areas* (Chicago: University of Chicago Press, 1942), 147 ff.

family became disintegrated, the church lost some of its influence, and the community as a unified group hardly existed.

The conflicts of cultural patterns in mixed homes often are serious matters even though they may not lead to delinquency. When parents have widely different backgrounds, such as foreign and American born, Jew and Gentile, Catholic and Protestant, religious and nonreligious, rural and urban, they do not provide uniform and consistent standards and codes of conduct for children to live by; and as a consequence children are subjected to divided loyalty, confused definitions of situations, and emotional tensions.

Dissension, Conflict, and Family Tension. Constant quarreling and nagging, serious dissension and conflict do not necessarily produce broken homes, but they may produce social crises and disorganization in the home. A social crisis arises when existing rules of behavior break down, or the organization and functions of the family unit are disturbed so greatly that the members cannot meet the basic needs satisfactorily. In a broad sense, family disorganization means the breakdown of consensus and loyalty, often resulting in the loss of family consciousness and the development of the attitude of detachment.

Dissension occurs when members of the family cannot reach workable unity. The failure to make adjustment and to effect accommodation to changing conditions may go back to previous difficulties. Families may go on for years in a mild state of disorganization, or the process of disintegration may come to a crisis quickly. The first years of marriage sometimes are stormy ones, especially if incompatible elements exist. This is the period when the children are young and impressionable.

There are no statistics to indicate the exact extent of the influence of social conflict and dissension on conduct, but the case studies of delinquents are full of references to the conflicting and divergent forces that operated in certain situations. In relatively simple and homogeneous societies, youth experiences few conflicts and uncertainties, especially as compared with the conflicting situations faced by boys and girls in modern society. The controls are relatively uniform, and the elders have ready-made definitions for many of the situations that youth faces. But this is not the case in a dynamic, rapidly changing, and urbanized society. Here considerable confusion of values exists. Conflicts of values are especially prevalent in areas or homes in which divergent systems of ideals and standard of conduct prevail, but they may also grow out of the complexity of social conditions. The difficulties arise when the behavior situations are so complex that neither the individual nor his family can supply definitions adequate for action. Parents often do not know what to tell their children when they come to them with their problems. Sometimes the children's ideas of what is right and proper differ greatly from the standards set by their parents or the traditions that parents may wish to enforce.

Abrahamson [15] found that there was much more family tension in the families of 100 offenders than in the homes of 100 nonoffenders. Ofttimes tension was not overtly evident but existed as a strong undercurrent, which colored the behavior of family members. One case is cited in which the parents thought that they had successfully buried their inner loathing for each other and that their hatred for each other was not noticed by the children, but their 8-year-old daughter sensed it and was greatly affected by the tensional situation. She became a nuisance at school, played truant often, wrote obscene words in the girls' room, and played pranks around school. The psychiatric examination disclosed that she reacted severely to an unhappy home situation, felt rejected, and was hostile and depressed. The Rorshach and other psychological tests applied to some of the families who submitted to them revealed a high incidence of psychomatic disorders among offenders and their families. Much of the rebellion of the children was caused by the emotional shock of being rejected, the feeling of insecurity and unrest growing out of bickerings and quarrels, and in some cases by the feeling of being overprotected and not having enough independence. Outside factors, such as coming from low economic strata of society, economic want, and other inadequacies, intensified the tensional situation in the home.

Davis,[16] in attempting to answer the broader question regarding the extraordinary amount of parent-adolescent conflict in contemporary Western civilization, concludes that such conflict results from the interaction of certain universals of parent-child relation and certain variables of values in our culture. Three universals stand out, namely: (1) the basic age or birth-cycle differential between parent and child, which means that they are always at a different stage of development; (2) the decelerating rate of socialization with advancing age; and (3) the resulting differences of the two generations on the physiological, psychological, and sociological planes. Parental authority is affected by conflicting and competing norms, the lack of

---

15 David Abrahamson, "Family Tension, Basic Cause of Criminal Behavior," *Journal of Criminal Law and Criminology*, Vol. 40 (September-October, 1949), 330-343.

16 Kingsley Davis, "The Sociology of Parent-Child Conflict," *The American Sociological Review*, Vol. 5, No. 4 (August, 1940), 523-535.

explicit institutionalization of steps in authority, its concentration within the small family unit, open competition for socio-economic position, and sex tension. Conflict between parent and child is conditioned by certain variables in modern society, such as the rapid rate of social change, the complexity of social structure, the degree of integration in the culture, and the velocity of movement within the structure and its relation to the cultural values.

Other Elements of Inadequate Homes. The matters of drunkenness, drug addiction, and vice were discussed in the previous chapter; and economic insecurity and inadequacy, poor housing and overcrowding, and poor neighborhood surroundings will be discussed in subsequent chapters. However, it must be recalled that these conditions are chiefly family problems and that they have direct or indirect effects on members of the family.

Alcoholism in one or both parents is a constantly recurring factor in the family situation of the children appearing in juvenile courts. The influences of alcoholic parents on home life are both physical and psychological. Such a condition may be the reason for poverty, cruelty, quarreling, home irritation, lack of parental control, immodesty and obscenity, sex immorality, and other consequences. Alcoholism of the mother has a more disastrous effect on children than has alcoholism of the father. Repeaters and serious offenders seem to show the effects of alcoholism in the home more extensively than do others.

Prostitution in the home is especially productive of evil consequences. Parents guilty of immorality and loose living have a baneful influence. Children may acquire sex habits early in life and be led to a life of immorality as a consequence of the example of parents. Investigators and case workers have come across many families where sexual malpractices have been inculcated by parents, and where sex misbehavior of children was either condoned or directly stimulated by parental misbehavior.

The prevalence of criminal behavior by adults in a home has an untoward effect on children. Criminal patterns of parents are imitated by their children. Stealing and petty pilfering are sometimes condoned or encouraged by parents to provide desired articles. The lack of law observance will be noted later, a condition often prevalent in homes.

Economic insecurity, poverty, poor housing, overcrowding, and other material defects of the home are potent factors in shaping the lives of children. These factors are so important that a special chapter (Chapter X) will be devoted to them. Lack of proper diet or of sufficient and proper clothes, insufficient pocket money, lack of toys, and inadequate personal property may lead to delinquency to make up for these deficiencies.

J. Edgar Hoover,[17] Director of the Federal Bureau of Investigation, indicates seven "bad influences" of parents and tells how they may ruin their children. (1) Neglect is mentioned first. A 13-year-old boy led a group of boys in burglarizing and burning a bowling alley. What was back of the crime? Both parents worked, and George worked at the bowling alley until after midnight. Parents paid little attention to George. He would come home when he pleased, sleep late, prepare his own breakfast, spend much time at a soda fountain or playing a slot machine, and attended school when he pleased. (2) Broken homes victimize many children. John's story is typical. John, a teen-age boy, was arrested for stealing a truck and driving it across a state line. His parents had separated before he could crawl. He was left with anyone available while his father worked. He shifted for himself most of the time, with little guidance and supervision. He began to cheat, lie, and steal. Belatedly alarmed, the father resorted to harsh words and whippings, with little understanding of John's problem. (3) Unhappy homes, marked by incompatibility, produce a state of mental turmoil and contribute to the emotional instability of children, often creating a rebellious attitude. The case of Bill is cited as an example of such a victim. Although being of above-average intelligence and a natural leader, he had been implicated in a number of burglaries and robberies by the time he was 14. His mother blamed his youthful associates; his father blamed city officials for allowing cheap amusements to cater to boys. The father worked from 12 to 13 hours a day, drank to extreme, and was more interested in his bar friends than his family. The wife nagged him and accused him of unfaithfulness. The parents lost complete control over Bill. (4) Parents set bad examples for children and show a lack of responsibility to their dependents. A teen-age girl from a wealthy home confessed to burglarizing eight apartments in a fashionable area of a city. She could not invite playmates to her home because of the intoxication of the mother, who sometimes came to the boarding school in so intoxicated a condition that she was unable to talk coherently. The unhappy girl wanted to go to Mexico City. The father refused to let her go unless accompanied by her mother. Determined to leave home, she tried to finance her trip by burglarizing the apartments of friends. (5) Lack of discipline and (6) doting parents are held responsible for many delinquencies of children.

17 *This Week*, Magazine Section, *Los Angeles Times*, April 20, 1944.

Jimmy's home was comfortable, his father provided a good living, his mother was devout, but the discipline was lacking. He was permitted to quit school because he did not like the teacher, could take the father's car when he wanted to, at an early age became intimate with girls, and was guilty of many boyish pranks. Some parents pamper their children and, if they are guilty of delinquencies, stand up for them and excuse their lawlessness.

Hoover mentions outside influences as the seventh (7) group of factors that contribute to delinquency, including certain types of movies, radio programs, crime books, and dangerous literature.

In a survey of boy life in Los Angeles, Bogardus [18] found that a large number of parents were failing in the training of boys and girls because of such conditions as uncontrolled temper, inflexible attitude and the inability to adjust their thinking to changed conditions, lack of supervision, nagging, unjust treatment, oversolicitousness, "split" homes, immoral conditions in homes, improper sex education, being too busy to bother, and allowing children too many privileges or not giving them opportunities (underprivileged children). Immigrant parents fail particularly in that they are not able to make adjustments to the conditions of living in American cities, and consequently fail to guide and supervise children properly. Children in boarding and rooming houses, small apartments, and other undesirable living quarters likewise are handicapped.

Running Away from Home. Children who face some of the difficulties indicated in this chapter thus far sometimes resort to an escape from the intolerable situation. Running away from home seems to them a way out, the child often not realizing that this is regarded as a form of misconduct, and, if it becomes habitual, he is subject to official action. To consider running away as a habit is not doing justice to the total problem, for the social influences surrounding the child are usually more obvious and more important than personality disintegration.

Armstrong [19] made a study of why boys desert their homes. This study deals especially with the problem of causation. The 660 runaway boys of the study had been arraigned in the Children's Court of New York City by parents and others who charged that the children had left their homes. Two small groups of boys were held for delinquencies other than deserting their homes, including 70 cases

---

[18] Emory S. Bogardus, *The City Boy and His Problems* (Los Angeles: Rotary Club of Los Angeles, 1926), Chapter II.

[19] Clairette P. Armstrong, *660 Runaway Boys* (Boston: Richard G. Badger, 1932).

of "unlawful entry" and 60 cases who were "incorrigible, ungovernable, habitually disobedient and beyond the control of parents."

The runaways on the average were younger than the delinquent boys; the average I.Q. of 78 made the group slightly superior to the other groups in intelligence; only a fifth were of white American parentage, as compared with nearly half of the incorrigibles who were of American stock; less than half were graded according to ability to progress in school, as compared with over half of the incorrigibles and unlawful entry groups; they came from families among whom the lowest economic levels were more prevalent than the higher; more than half had disrupted families, a much higher proportion than was found among unselected school children or in other delinquent groups; they came from larger families than the other groups; they lived in overcrowded houses; and family pathologies (alcoholism, immorality, psychoses, psychoneuroses, illness, and criminality) were extensively present. The boys themselves suffered more than the other groups from nervous habits and physical defects, and they had a larger incidence of orphanage or institutional experience. All but 9 per cent had concomitant charges or complaints against them and 36 per cent were recidivists. Strange as it may seem, the majority of the runaways offended alone, although they sometimes joined others in their wanderings. Seventy per cent reported that they had deserted because they had trouble at home, 37 per cent because of some trouble in school.

Armstrong presents other data to show that "family maladjustments are the general cause of a boy deserting his home and the school plays a conspicuous role in stimulating this reaction." [20] In other words, the runaway is the victim of the situation. The various factors, personal and social, act singly or concomitantly in the individual runaway. He runs away from unpleasant environmental conditions; but once having formed the habit, it becomes abnormal when persisted in to the exclusion of socially desirable forms of behavior. In substance, it becomes a personality problem. Many runaways suffer from emotional instability or from thwarted wishes.

Many of the runaways from home are also truants from school, although the relationship between the two factors has not been clearly established. Once running away and truancy habits are established, they easily lead to other delinquency habits.

---

20 *Ibid.*, 192.

DELINQUENTS AND NONDELINQUENTS IN THE SAME FAMILIES

Not all children in broken or inadequate homes become delinquent, and some delinquents come from relatively normal homes. Children may be rejected, spoiled, mistreated, and feel frustrated, inadequate, and revengeful, but some find expression for their conflict in ways that are not legally forbidden. The unhappy child, however, especially if he lives in a community in which antisocial attitudes and behavior prevail and in which the pattern of crime is traditional, is more susceptible to delinquency than a child in a happier situation.[21]

When children observe the attitudes and behavior patterns of crime of their parents or of other adults, or are driven from the home by unpleasant experiences, or if the home fails to train them to deal with social situations in a law-abiding manner, or if habits of disobedience are formed in the home, and if these conditions are accompanied by tensions and emotional disturbances, one can normally expect misconduct; but it does not always happen. It might be expected that, if one child becomes delinquent in a home in which the above described conditions prevail, all children in that home would naturally become delinquent also; but this does not necessarily follow.

Studies have been made of the relation of order of birth and sibling position to delinquency. Sletto[22] compared 1145 delinquents in Minneapolis with an equal number of school children matched for age, sex, and sibling position. He concluded that the order of birth, when taken in connection with the sex distribution of siblings, is statistically significant in juvenile delinquency. Older brothers have a greater delinquency rate than have younger brothers, and older sisters than younger sisters, in comparison with school children of the same age, sex, and sibling position. The delinquency ratio is higher for girls who have only brothers than it is for girls who have sisters but no brothers. Apparently girls with no sibs of the same sex tend to approach the delinquency standards of the brothers. But a boy with no sisters does not show an analogous behavior tendency. The ratios for both boys and girls are higher when elder siblings are of the same sex and younger siblings are of the opposite sex than when the reverse is true. The explanation of the differences in delinquency ratios for children in various sibling positions may lie in the

---

[21] *Understanding Juvenile Delinquency,* United States Children's Bureau, Publication 300 (1943), 12.

[22] Raymond F. Sletto, "Sibling Position and Juvenile Delinquency," *American Journal of Sociology,* XXXIX (March, 1934), 657-669.

roles that children play in family life. The order of birth and the relation to other siblings may have significance, but one must reckon with other factors. The younger children of the home may change because of the death of a parent, a change in economic status, changing habits of parents, a difference in affection given the various children, and many other factors. Sometimes delinquency is more or less accidental. No two children live in identical environments. Not even twins have the same environment. Many objective and subjective variations occur in homes, some of which have subtle influences. For instance, the "black sheep" in the family does not live in the same kind of situation that the other children are privileged to have.

A number of studies deal with the possible relation between delinquency and the "only child," or the first child, or the number of children in the family, but the various investigators have come to different conclusions.[23] The only child and the child in the large family are supposed to be prone to delinquency, but such conclusions have not been verified sufficiently to be conclusive.

One of the most exhaustive studies of delinquents and nondelinquents in the same families was made by Healy and Bronner.[24] The family, rather than the individual delinquent, was regarded as the unit of study and treatment. A total of 133 families was studied, with 153 delinquents and 145 nondelinquents. Of the delinquents, 143 were accepted for treatment, of whom 105 were paired with 105 nondelinquents used as controls, and 38 were studied without controls.

The incidences of personality attributes of the parents in the 133 families, in terms of percentages, are as follows: proportion of both parents with little or no education, 36; both parents dull or subnormal mentally, 10; both parents average or above in intelligence, 50; parents with court record, 20; parents heavily alcoholic, 26; father's interests (aside from alcoholism) poor or vicious, 12; father's interest good, 24; and mothers working after marriage, 49. In addition, certain attributes in which parents differed were noted, including personality liabilities (fathers 36, mothers 32), poor ethical standards (fathers 21, mothers 15), poor emotional control (fathers 28, mothers 30), and abnormal personality, neurotic or psychotic (fathers 10, mothers 11). Except for the item "No outstanding personality liabilities" (fathers 46, mothers 52), few parents had superior qualities, high ethical standards, or satisfactory social relations

---

23 See Edwin H. Sutherland, *op. cit.,* 166-169.

24 William Healy and Augusta F. Bronner, *New Light on Delinquency and Its Treatment* (New Haven: Yale University Press, 1936). The entire book should be consulted, especially chapters II-IX.

outside the home and place of work. Furthermore, only 22 per cent of the parents recognized and attempted to meet the problem by much corporal punishment, and in 34 per cent of the homes at least one parent attempted to understand the problem but was unable to cope with it. The others either were unaware of the problem (12 per cent) or refused to recognize the problem as serious (32 per cent). Other data regarding these families reveal certain background conditions.[25]

Many of the circumstances and attitudes of the parents, and the delinquents themselves, are provocative of delinquency. But why are these delinquents and nondelinquents in the same families? From the wealth of material presented regarding the 105 delinquents paired with an equal number of nondelinquents, used as a control group, including 8 pairs of twins, one may draw certain conclusions.[26]

A comparison of the objective data regarding the personality traits of the two groups shows certain differences. There was no great difference in age distribution, except that the delinquent group had more eldest children and fewer youngest. While 92 of the delinquents as compared with 81 of the controls were boys, a more detailed comparison did not reveal significant differences in sex factors. Biologically, the two groups presented marked similarities. The developmental history of the children brought forth some remarkable contrasts, with 170 deviations for the delinquents as compared with 74 for the controls, and with the following items showing more than 50 per cent difference: much worry of mother during pregnancy, very sickly pregnancy, fussy babyhood, difficult toilet habit-training, much underweight in early childhood, many or severe illnesses and severe head injuries. Only 44 of the delinquents were in distinctly good health as compared with 75 in the control group. Personality deviations, especially neurosis and early psychosis, showed up especially among delinquents, with at least 25 definitely diagnosed incidences, and 8 probable cases among the delinquents, as contrasted with only 2 cases in the control group. In addition, the delinquents had more peculiar habits, such as food idiosyncrasies, sleep disturbances, nail biting, thumb sucking, and other nervous mannerisms, also enuresis. Surprisingly, the mental age levels of the two groups proved to be only slightly contrasting, but the school records of the delinquents were far worse than those of the controls, with a much

25 *Ibid.*, especially pp. 34-35, for general statistical summary of 133 families, and Chapter IV for summary of characteristics of 153 delinquents.

26 *Ibid.*, Chapters V-IX give the concrete comparisons of personalities, favorable and inimical family situations, a special analysis of the 8 twins, comparisons of emotional experiences, and the meaningfulness of delinquency for the individual.

higher incidence of nonattendance and truancy and a lower scholarship record. Not all of the delinquents were poor students, but at least 40 per cent of them expressed marked dislike for school in general and 13 per cent had a marked dislike for some teacher. Hyperactivity, overrestlessness, extreme physical aggressiveness, and great impulsiveness were recorded in 46 delinquents, and none in the control group. The delinquents also were more gregarious, exhibited fewer attendance-submissive tendencies, displayed emotional moods, expresssed feelings of inadequacy or inferiority, showed fewer ethical sensibilities, daydreamed more extensively, showed less interest in church or Sunday school. More registered club connections, but attendance was irregular and interest of short duration; and more interest was shown in active sports, reading, and movie attendance.

Nineteen of the 105 delinquents lived in apparently favorable situations. Of these, 14 showed marked personality or psychophysical deviations, and nearly every one had emotional attitudes favorable to delinquency tendencies. By way of contrast, 75 nondelinquents coming from inimical circumstances, all of whom had at least one delinquent sibling, had fewer negative qualities. It seems from this that children with positive personality characteristics are more able to meet inimical family situations and social environmental pressures without becoming delinquent.

Using the 8 pairs of twins, all nonidentical, and all boys except one girl control, ranging from 6 to 17 years of age, Healy and Bronner (Chapter VII) hoped to find some combinations or spot patterns that characterize delinquents and not controls; but, except for the combination of abnormal personality, coupled with deeply felt thwartings and dissatisfaction and inimical family situations, which were found in a few cases, no clear-cut composite of factors that prognosticate delinquency was found. The detail case analysis revealed merely individual conditions that tended to make a difference in behavior.

The authors lay great stress on the comparative emotional experiences of the two groups. No less than 91 per cent of the delinquents were unhappy or discontented in their life circumstances and extremely disturbed over emotion-producing situations and experiences, whereas only 13 per cent of the controls had such inner stresses. One may criticize the authors' emphasis on personality problems, especially emotional disturbances, as the chief conditioning factors in delinquent behavior, but no studies of families in which both delinquents and nondelinquents have occurred have been more carefully conducted.

CASE STUDIES OF BROKEN OR MALADJUSTED HOMES AND
DELINQUENCY

Many cases of the effects of broken or inadequate homes on
delinquency could be cited. Nearly all of the Judge Baker Foundation *Case Studies* could be given to show the influence of home life
on the children studied. The most outstanding cases of the effects
of homes, gangs, and community factors are those described by
Clifford R. Shaw.[27] These case studies will be reviewed briefly here,
because they are outstanding examples of the effects of disorganized
homes; but they also illustrate the effects of gang life, poverty and
slum living, and a variety of other factors. These are also good
examples of unwise and inadequate treatment of offenders.

The Jack-Roller (1930), the first of a series of detailed case studies
of young male delinquents, using the "boy's own story" material,
illustrates clearly the effects of the home on Stanley's behavior. It
presents a microscopic view of one case, with over 200 pages devoted
to the details of the case, including Stanley's own story and appraisal
of his condition. Stanley's story reveals his point of view, the social
and cultural situations to which he was responsive, and his life. The
personal attitudes and interests, feelings and complexes, moral strug-
gles and successes, ideals and philosophies, mental conflicts and social
antagonisms, prejudices, rationalizations, and many other factors of
the inner life of an individual are revealed in the story.

The history of Stanley's behavior as shown in the official record,
from the time he was 6 years and 5 months old until he was 17 years
and 8 months old, includes 38 items of arrests, pick-ups, probation,
placing in institutions, and parole from institutions, for such offenses
as burglary, "jack-rolling," running away and sleeping away from
home, and many others. During this time he had 33 jobs and attended school very irregularly.

Stanley lived in three different areas of the city, all more or less
slum areas, with considerable crime and delinquency, gang activities,
poverty, physical deterioration, and many other undesirable influences. Still, it seemed that the chief cause of his trouble was the
home, which was characterized by disorganization, poverty and want,
heavy drinking and abusive conduct on the part of the father, and

---

27 *The Jack-Roller: A Delinquent Boy's Own Story* (1930); The *Natural History of
a Delinquent Career* (1931); and in collaboration with Henry D. McKay and James F.
McDonald, *Brothers in Crime* (1938), all publications of University of Chicago Press.
Compare the case study of Nick in "Social Factors in Juvenile Delinquency," No. 13,
Vol. II, *Report on the Causes of Crime* (1931).

mistreatment by his stepmother. Stating his philosophy, Stanley says:

> To start out in life, everyone has his chances—some good and some very bad. Some are born with fortunes, beautiful homes, good and educated parents; while others are born in ignorance, poverty, and crime. In other words, fate begins to guide our lives before we are born and continues to do so throughout life. My start was handicapped by a no-good, ignorant, and selfish stepmother, who thought only of herself and her own children. . . . My life was filled with sorrow and misery. The cause was my stepmother, who nagged me, beat me, insulted me, and drove me out of my own home. My mother died when I was four years old, so I never knew a real mother's affection. My father remarried when I was five years of age. The stepmother was a rawboned woman, devoid of features as well as emotions. She was of Polish stock. (p. 47)

This Polish woman had apparently forced herself upon Stanley's father. She was decidedly favorable to her own children. The father thought of them, as well as his own, as just kids who had to be provided for but not to be loved. The children, however, did not have enough to eat. Altogether there were fifteen children, including those by previous marriages.

As soon as Stanley was old enough, he took to the street. He had two chums: William, a stepbrother, who had Stanley in the palm of his hand, and Tony, a lad of the street. William had a particularly bad influence on Stanley, for he taught him to steal. The three boys roamed around a great deal. It was William who planned the stealing and, while Stanley would take goods in the market, he would stand guard. The stepmother endorsed stealing, provided they brought some of the goods home: but when they did, she sometimes would whip them, take the goods, and then would tell them to run away again. Once away from home, the other runaways were easy. The idea of freedom appealed to him.

Shaw gives a long recital of Stanley's experiences in correctional institutions, which the boy hated, from the earliest experience in the "Baby Bondhouse" (Juvenile Detention Home) to St. Charles School for Boys and the Illinois State Reformatory at Pontiac. Between periods of institutionalization, Stanley roamed the streets. The lure of the underworld was too much for him. Once, after being released from Pontiac, he felt that he was nothing but an outcast, for even the "jail-bird" who was released with him deserted him. This was a terrible blow to his pride. But he found a pal, and the old sights affected him again. After orgies of drinking, sex episodes, and crime, Stanley hit the road, which ended in Omaha when the police gave him the opportunity to be released if he left town. He went back to Chicago, to his pals, to the "main stem" of hoboes. After further violations of law, arrests, and institutional experiences, the case was referred to the Illinois Institute of Juvenile Research for intensive study.

After a careful analysis of the case, Shaw concludes:

. . . The case presents a picture of the origin and gradual formation of a delinquent-behavior trend as it emerged in the process of interaction between the individual and the social and cultural situation in which he lived. Through his personal contacts with experienced delinquents in the underworld life of West Madison Street and in various correctional institutions to which he was successively committed, Stanley's delinquent behavior became increasingly serious, and his wishes and ambitions became more clearly defined in terms of the social values of the adult criminal world. By the time of his release from the House of Correction, it was clear that he definitely identified himself with the adult criminal group. (p. 164)

Can one imagine a tougher case to handle than Stanley, after such a long career as a delinquent? Yet Mr. Shaw tackled the job of trying to do something for and with Stanley. It is not necessary to review here the methods of procedure used; the personal guidance, the securing of jobs and vocational training, the association with a different class of young people, and finding a new home for him; but it seems that Mrs. Smith, who took him into her home, provided the chief influence in his rehabilitation program. Stanley liked her from the start, and he also liked her children. It was a modest home, but it had a warmth and kindness that he had never experienced before. The contrast between this home and his own home and the prison life from which he had just emerged bewildered him. He felt out of place. It was a new world for him. He had nothing to talk about, except crime and prisons, and to talk about them would be out of place. He finally told Mrs. Smith that he was unfit to live in her home, but she was "full of sympathy and understanding," patted him gently on the shoulder, and gave him a cheering word which worked wonders with his spirit. He felt that after all there were good people in the world, and with persons like Mrs. Smith and Mr. Shaw to help him, life was worth living. He finally made good in his work, married a girl he loved, and became a respectable citizen. His marriage was one of the most powerful factors in his rehabilitation, according to Shaw. Four years after release from the "House of Correction," he was settled in a home of his own, with his wife, and a son in whom his hopes and plans for the future were all tied up. The story is closed with the statement that five years had passed without a single recurrence of delinquency.

The Natural History of a Delinquent Career (1931), by Shaw, is a sequel to *The Jack-Roller* and represents a similar case, except that it had a different ending, although Sidney was eventually rehabilitated. No one apparently intercepted the process that led, step by step, to serious offenses and to imprisonment. It is the story of a young male recidivist, Sidney Blotzman, who, by the age of 16 years and 8 months, had been arrested and sent to institutions a number of times. Sidney was a leader of a notorious gang, called the "Moron" gang by newspapers. Their major offense was rape. The publicity of the case produced a strong attitude of public vengeance and indignation. These boys lived in a delinquency area, from which more than 15 per cent of the males 10 to 21 years of age living in the vicinity were apprehended as alleged delinquents each year.

The Blotzman family background was marked by poverty, drunkenness, domestic discord, and desertion. Sidney's parents were born in Poland of Jewish descent. Sidney's father had served a year's jail sentence for nonsupport, was drunk frequently, and worked infrequently. He took a rather hostile attitude toward Sidney.

Sidney's life, he confessed, was pointless and haphazard. He miserably misunderstood life and bungled critical situations. His emotions were largely those of hate and bitterness. Not having money to spend, he and his chums began to take things from stores. These adventures provided "joyous occasions," which led to more serious offenses. The institutional treatment, and his reaction to it, presents a picture similar to the one presented in Stanley's story. When he received his final sentence, he was in a trance. Death was preferable to a life sentence in an institution. He hoped for a miracle to happen, but it didn't. The only hopeful sign in the prison was that the new commanding officer and his assistant were beginning to introduce humane methods of treatment.

Brothers in Crime (1938), also by Shaw, in collaboration with Henry D. McKay and James F. McDonald, with chapters by Harold B. Hanson and Ernest W. Burgess, is a sequel to the previous case studies, but this case involves five brothers—John, Edward, James, Michael, and Carl Martin (fictitious names)—all of whom had criminal records. John, who was 35 when the study was made, is described as friendly, sociable, carefree, easygoing, and indifferent. He had been committing delinquencies and crimes since the age of 11—but not for the last ten years—with 23 items of offense, commitments, or releases, including begging, petty stealing, truancy, escape, dependency petitions, and the like. He remained unmarried. Edward, age 33, was married, had one child, was industrious, ambitious, and shrewd. He had committed no offenses for eight years, but prior to that, for eighteen years, 64 items are noted, as truancy, begging, petty stealing, and burglary. Begging appears most frequently in the record. James, 29, was also married and had one child. He, too, was shrewd, alert, aggressive, industrious, ambitious, and affable. He had been apprehended and arrested 20 times, appeared in court 13 times, and served 2 periods of confinement in correctional institutions. During the thirteen years of delinquency, 71 items are noted in the record. Michael, age 26, tall, attractive, bright, alert, and full of energy, started his delinquencies at the age of 4, with 57 items noted during the twenty-two years of delinquency record. Carl, the youngest, age 25, and unmarried, resided with the mother. He was more stolid and reserved than his older brothers. He started his delinquency career at the age of 3 in company with the older brothers. He was arrested 14 times, was in court 16 times, served 6 periods of confinement, and had a total of 28 items noted.

The delinquency careers of the five brothers started in about the same manner, with begging and petty stealing, and led to more serious offenses, but they followed somewhat different courses. John and Edward continued to engage in burglary, James and Carl became more involved in the larceny of automobiles, and Michael in armed robbery. In the case of each, the specific kind of delinquency engaged in conformed to the type of criminality current among other offenders with whom each brother was associated (p. 94).

The family resided in a slum and crime zone, near the Chicago River. A great deal of unemployment, poverty, and economic dependency existed. The confusion and wide diversity of norms and standards of behavior were even more significant than economic want and physical deterioration of the area. Neither the family nor the community exercised much positive control. The companions of the Martin brothers were for the most part bad. The social isolation of the brothers from conventional neighborhood institutions added to the difficulties.

With each of the five brothers, the social factors were much more important than personality traits in influencing their behavior, a fact which seems to refute somewhat the major conclusions by Healy and Bronner in their study of delinquents and nondelinquents in the same families. The delinquencies in these cases seem to have been the more-or-less direct outcome of the poverty-stricken condition of an immigrant family in a neighborhood of boys' gangs and criminal traditions, and of the lack of uniform standards and modes of control, so concludes E. W. Burgess in discussing the personality traits and environmental background of the cases. The personality and social factors, of course, were intertwined in these cases, as in most instances.

The fact that John, Edward, James, and Carl made good upon their last release from institutions was probably due to such factors as the development of favorable attitudes toward reformation, the intelligent assistance given them, and the matter of "maturation."

These cases give a more complete picture of the influences that shape behavior, including the inner life of the delinquents as revealed by their own stories, than can be obtained by a statistical study of the observable items in a large number of less detailed case records. A combination of thoroughgoing case studies and broad statistical summations of items involved in delinquency situations gives a more accurate appraisal of the effects of home conditions on delinquency.

The attitude of teen-agers toward their parents or other adults and their concept of their reaction is naïve, but the feeling behind it is nevertheless sincere, as is illustrated in the case of Jean.[28] When she was 15 the court commitment designated her as a delinquent. She had defied adults and their rules, had gone her own way, angry and defiant, running away from home, spending nights out at dubious places, stealing now and then, and recklessly inviting trouble from strange men. When her mother objected, she exploded and screamed that she would do just as she pleased. Her behavior had frightened the adults around her, and the court put a stop to her dangerous activities by placing her in an institution. The community saw Jean at best as a nuisance, at worst as a menace, but those who were aware of the conditions that surrounded her life knew that there were reasons for her conduct. She was an illegitimate child, was reared by an aunt, who, she was told, was her mother. She knew her own mother as a "cousin," who was scorned by the family because she was an alcoholic, a prostitute, and a hopeless failure. While the aunt tried to do her duty by Jean, she really did not want her and resented the irresponsibility of Jean's mother. The reaction of the aunt toward Jean ranged from rejection to indulgence, which did not make for good discipline.

The important element in this case is how all this looked to Jean. Ever since she could remember there was something wrong about her, something that made her different from other children, and that for some reason made her a burden to someone. She felt that she was unwanted, had no place of her own, and consequently she had

---

28 Cf. Leontine R. Young, "Delinquency from the Child's Viewpoint," *Focus,* Vol. 30, No. 3 (May, 1951), 69-74.

no sense of security. She concluded that she was just so bad that nobody loved her. When she discovered that the aunt was not her mother, why should she obey her? Outwardly she was cocky, defiant, tough, and indifferent; inwardly she was frightened and confused. She needed kindness, love, and consideration. Fortunately, in the institution she met for the first time adults who were concerned with protecting, not punishing, her. Wary of the attitudes and reactions of the leaders, she tested the staff by defiance. When the staff refused to regard her as a menace, although they held firmly to the demand which precipitated the explosion, Jean began voluntarily to give up some of her destructiveness. She became ashamed of her temper. It took a long while for her to change her attitude and behavior, and she did not achieve complete realization of her goals, but in the end she became a useful and self-respecting person.

There is no substitute for the type of home described earlier in this chapter; but when it becomes structurally disorganized or fails to perform its basic functions, foster home or institutional care may be necessary to provide a child with more adequate living and training. Broken and maladjusted homes are potentially, if not actually, the sources of trouble and frequently lead to deviant behavior.

QUESTIONS AND PROJECTS

For Class Discussion and Research

1. Indicate the characteristics of a stable and well-adjusted family.

2. List the major family problems of the modern era, especially from the point of view of the rearing and training of children.

3. What are the difficulties involved in measuring the relationship between broken homes and delinquency? On the basis of the best available studies, what conclusions may be drawn with respect to the relative effects of broken homes on the conduct of children?

4. When is a home maladjusted, though structurally complete?

5. Discuss the subject of discipline versus permissiveness in training children. What are the evidences of inadequate or unwise discipline?

6. Analyze case histories of delinquents to determine the possible relationship of family life to the conduct of children. See Judge Baker Foundation *Case Studies,* and the more extensive cases described by Shaw and McKay.

7. Study a selected case of a delinquent, giving as complete a report as you can of the conditioning factors, noting particularly the family situation.

8. Why do certain families produce delinquents while others do not? How would you explain the presence of delinquents and nondelinquents in the same families?

9. Devise a method of research to ascertain the extent of the family factors that are correlated with delinquent behavior. Differential marital and family relationships of parents of delinquents and nondelinquents could be singled out for special study.

10. Devise a method of research for the comparison of delinquents from relatively well-adjusted homes.

11. Family tensions and children's behavior problems.

12. Effects of physical and mental abnormalities in families on children's conduct.

13. Mixed marriages and children's behavior problems.

14. Parental responsibility for the deviant behavior of their children.

15. Causes and conditions of children running away from home.

SELECTED REFERENCES

ARMSTRONG, CLAIRETTE, *660 Runaway Boys* (Boston: Richard G. Badger, 1932).

CARR-SAUNDERS, A. M., HERMANN MANHEIM, AND E. C. RHODES, *Young Offenders: An Inquiry into Juvenile Delinquency* (Cambridge: University Press; and New York: The Macmillan Co., 1944).

GLUECK, SHELDON AND ELEANOR, *Unraveling Juvenile Delinquency* (New York: The Commonwealth Fund, 1950), and *Delinquents in the Making* (New York: Harper & Brothers, 1952).

JUDGE BAKER FOUNDATION, *Case Studies,* Series 1, Cases 1 to 20, 1922-1923.

MERRILL, MAUD A., *Problems of Child Delinquency* (New York: Houghton Mifflin Co., 1947).

SHAW, CLIFFORD R., *The Jack-Roller* (Chicago: University of Chicago Press, 1930).

———, *The Natural History of a Delinquency Career* (Chicago: University of Chicago Press, 1931).

———, HENRY D. McKAY, AND JAMES F. McDONALD, *Brothers in Crime* (Chicago: University of Chicago Press, 1938).

SHULMAN, HARRY M., "The Family and Juvenile Delinquency," *The Annals of the American Academy of Political and Social Science,* Vol. 261 (January, 1949), 21-31.

SULLENGER, THOMAS EARL, *Social Determinants in Juvenile Delinquency* (Columbia, Missouri: University of Missouri Press, 1929).

VII

COMPANIONSHIP AND JUVENILE GANGS

Aside from the family, the most effective of all stimuli comes from playmates and companions outside the home. Companionship exists in the home, but in this chapter the emphasis will be on associations and companionships with people outside the family circle. Individual friends, chums, pals, cliques, and other intimate associates have a great influence in shaping the lives of boys and girls.

ASSOCIATIONS AND COMPANIONSHIPS

The Place of Chums in a Child's Life. Nearly all children have their playmates and intimate friends and companions. Rare is the child who does not particularly care for this type of association. During certain periods of a child's life, often the playmates mean more to him than does his family. Chums influence each other in

191

many ways. The choice of a friend may either make or break a person. One of the great concerns of parents is the kind of friends their children have, for the playmates may have wholesome effects on them or they may be the source of much trouble.

Ever since Charles Horton Cooley [1] called attention to the importance of primary groups, sociologists and many others have analyzed their meaning and indicated their significance. According to Cooley, primary groups are characterized by intimate face-to-face association and cooperation, involving the sort of sympathy and mutual identification for which "we" is the most appropriate expression, and they give the individual his earliest and completest experience in social unity. The family, the play-group, and the neighborhood or community are the most important spheres of this intimate association and cooperation. Life in the primary groups gives rise to the major social ideals and ideas of life. Experience in these groups likewise re-enforces the larger systems of idealism, such as Christianity and democracy.

Children's play life is a give-and-take affair. They stimulate one another, cooperate in common enterprises, and in the process of intimate interaction the social nature and ideals of individuals are formed. In the companionship groups one can discern a oneness and fusion of personality. There are a mutual identification and a "we-feeling" not to be found in the larger relationships. One seldom finds greater loyalty, friendliness, and *esprit de corp* than in the intimate companionship groups. To be sure, the unity of the primary group is not one of mere harmony and cooperation. It is usually a differentiated unity, admitting of self-assertion, wishes, special interests, and various appropriate passions; but these differentiated motives are socialized by sympathy and good will and are brought under the discipline of a common spirit. Jealousies, excessive competition, and conflict may disintegrate companionship groups. It is not uncommon to observe children playing harmoniously together for awhile and then engage in violent quarreling and even open combat. Sometimes the conflicts take place among several companionship groups or between groups of children and adults, such as parents and various adult groups in the community.

Shaw and McKay [2] cite the case of Nick, a 14-year-old boy, who was having trouble with his parents and with the law. Nick and a gang of boys in the neighborhood had gotten into difficulties be-

---

[1] *Social Organization* (New York: Charles Scribner's Sons, 1909), Part I.

[2] Clifford R. Shaw and Henry D. McKay, "Social Factors in Juvenile Delinquency," *Report on the Causes of Crime*, No. 13, Vol. II; National Commission on Law Observance and Enforcement, 1932, 4-20.

cause they wanted to play all the time. Nick's mother stated in court that the boy did not work, that he wanted to play all the time, and that he made faces at and "cussed" everybody. In the family interview, the father added that they had ten "kids," pointing to the children who were standing in the room, but that Nick caused lots of trouble, that he ran away, stole, fought, and wanted to play more than work. The married daughter complained that Nick was lazy, stubborn, and that he would not work.

Nick admitted that he was an enthusiastic participant in the activities of a group of boys in the neighborhood. It was found that the group's interests and activities on the whole were wholesome. Nearly all of the boys in this group attended school regularly, and only one had a record of delinquency. Their chief interests were in various types of athletics, especially baseball. As Nick put it, "I started to play with the guys around my home. These guys are my best friends. We like to play ball the most. We always play ball. Gee, I like to pitch and I like to catch." Then he proceeded to say that they played other games also, that they read the sports section of newspapers, and that they had lots of fun together.

The immigrant parents could not understand this interest in play and in his chums, so they punished him severely for his activities, which drove him farther away from home. It was clear that they had very little understanding and appreciation of Nick's problems and the kind of social world in which he lived. To the boy, the chief interest was not in the home or in the work that the parents wanted him to do, but in his chums and the play activities of the group.

As one peruses the case record of delinquents, one is impressed with the place of intimate "pals" in their lives. It is in the intimate association with their friends that they sometimes acquire antisocial tendencies. In many of the Judge Baker Foundation *Case Studies* the problems of pals and intimate associates loom up largely. Tillie (Case Study 9, Series 1) got along fine until her chums gave her information about sex life and created in her an undesirable attitude toward sex when she was only 12 years old. Later, when she contacted a sailor, with whom she lived for several days, she became a sex delinquent. In the case of Emily (Case Study 15, Series 1), the negative influence of her companions came at a critical time, when she was only 10 years old. Her curiosity about sex was aroused while going with a crowd at school. This group was composed of both boys and girls. After the first "thrill" of sex experience, they met often for a period of time. John Long (Case Study 13, Series 1) belonged to a group of six boys, who were together constantly—going to school, at and after school, and at night. Their adventures eventually led them to delinquency. In the beginning John did not like to "crook," but the others would say, "Come on, Jackie," and he did not like to hang back. He did not "crook" alone. Filipa Nopola (Case Study 18, Series 1), at 12, began associating with girls of another family, considered bad by Filipa's parents, who tried to dissuade her, then punished her, but to no avail. She was so attached to her chums that, even though it led to shoplifting and other delinquent activities, she went along with the leaders of the group.

Types of Associates and Playmates. It is evident that the types of associates have a considerable bearing on a child's behavior. If the playmates are of the type that exert wholesome influences, the contacts are likely to be constructive and wholesome. If the contacts are of the opposite type, the results are likely to be accordingly. It is difficult to classify the associates, for they may range from the best to the worst types.

Sutherland's theory of differential association, described in Chapter V, has application here. Individuals may have associations both with criminals and with noncriminals, but, if the predominant contacts are with criminal patterns, they are likely to go in that direction. Any person is likely to assimilate the surrounding culture unless other patterns are in conflict. Some associations, of course, have no bearing on crime and can be said to be neutral in influence in regard to behavior that comes under the heading of criminal. Much of a person's life has no relation to law observance or law violation.

The associations with both criminal and anticriminal patterns may vary in frequency, duration, priority, and intensity, according to Sutherland. The learning of criminal behavior is not restricted to the process of imitation, for other factors may play a part in the process leading to crime. Sometimes juveniles follow gang leadership, which may be largely a matter of imitation, or group stimulation, but at other times there is no evidence of direct imitation. Nevertheless, the types of associations a child has, especially during the formative years, give him a direction of life and lead to patterns of behavior that may have lasting consequences.

THE PRESTIGE STRUCTURE AND SOCIAL STRATIFICATION OF THE COMMUNITY

The stratification of the population is not new. History is replete with examples of social classes, amounting to a caste system in some countries. Ethnic groups are not the only devisive forces in the community, for the social class system may exist in otherwise relatively homogeneous areas. In pioneer American territories, such as the early Colonial settlements and the later frontier regions, the conditions of living and the liberating forces that operated in the new world tended to reduce class barriers. Marriage became more and more independent of economic considerations, social gradation, parental restraint, and community control. The scarcity of women and the devotion and heroism of pioneer women, the softening influence of isolation, and the growth of the democratic spirit furthered the equality of women and men, even though it took a long time to achieve women suffrage and complete political franchise. The social changes that worked to the elevation of women and undermined arbitrary sex distinctions; that equalized the relationships between parents and children, husbands and wives, and employers and employees; and the forces that promoted political and religious freedom generally tended to level class barriers of all kinds. Not all classes were equalized, especially in the southern states; but the ideals of freedom, equality, and self-government affected every phase of life. In time, social division and class differences, other than on the ethnic basis, began to develop.

The flexible nature of our class system and the democratic relations that exist in many important aspects of social life make it difficult to identify fixed classes of people. During recent years a number of investigators, chiefly sociologists, have analyzed the prestige structure of various communities. Among the best-known studies are those by the Lynds, Warner and associates, and Hollingshead. The cross-sectional study of Middletown emphasizes social change and cultural conflicts, as the title and subtitle indicate.[3] However, this so-called typical American city revealed several more or less distinct classes of people, ranging from the wealthy X family of the business class to the homes of the working class and the Negro community.

The best-known studies of social classes in America were made by W. Lloyd Warner and collaborators.[4] The publications, known

[3] Robert S. and Helen M. Lynd, *Middletown in Transition: A Study in Cultural Conflicts* (New York: Harcourt, Brace and Co., 1937). Compare their earlier report, *Middletown* (1929).

[4] Cf. W. Lloyd Warner and Paul S. Lunt, *The Social Life of a Modern Community*, Vol. I (1941), and *The Social System of a Modern Community*, Vol. II (1942); W. Lloyd Warner and Leo Srole, *The Social System of American Ethnic Groups*, Vol. III (1945); and W. Lloyd Warner and J. O. Low, *The Social System of a Factory*, Vol. IV (1947), published by Yale University Press. For description of the research techniques used in measuring social class and the class positions of individuals, see W. Lloyd Warner, Marchia Meeker, and Kenneth Ealls, *Social Class in America* (Chicago: Social Science Associates, Inc., 1949).

as the Yankee City Series, reveal the extent of the class system in an eastern manufacturing city and the class positions of the families and individuals in such a system. This community has ethnic divisions, but the major phase of the study has dealt with the prestige structure which is indicative of social stratification in modern society. Warner and his colleagues identified three main classes (upper, middle, and lower), each of which is subdivided into upper and lower groups. The families and individuals in the community tend to fall into a hierarchy of social status classes. Among the factors that differentiate groups into classes are the matters of socio-economic position or leadership, the sources of wealth, the amount of education, occupational levels, and living conditions. The attitudes of the people toward various groups of families tend to accentuate the stratification of the population.[5]

Adolescent Behavior and the Social Structure of the Community. The most important study of the relation of adolescent behavior to the class system was made by August B. Hollingshead.[6] This Middle Western Corn Belt community (Elmtown, as it is called in the study) is in many ways a typical American community. The basic thesis used is: "The social behavior of adolescents appears to be related functionally to the positions their families occupy in the social structure of the community."[7] The field study involved the analysis of 735 adolescents in 535 different families. The 735 adolescents consisted of 369 boys and 366 girls, ranging in ages from 13 to 19, and all were native-born whites, of whom 96 per cent were born in the Middle West, and the parents were predominantly Middle Westerners. Thus, the class system is not complicated by ethnic difference. In order to ascertain the prestige structure, Hollingshead used more than 100 items in the interview, which were finally grouped under (a) the way the families live, (b) their income and possessions, (c) their participation in community affairs, and (d) the

---

5 For an analysis of the social configuration of American families, see Ruth Shonle Cavan, *The American Family* (New York: Thomas Y. Crowell Co., 1953), Part II.

6 Cf. *Elmtown's Youth: The Impact of Social Classes on Adolescents* (New York: John Wiley and Sons, Inc., 1949). The writer is indebted to this source for the material on how the social system of a community tends to control the social behavior of high-school-age adolescents reared in it. Compare Hollingshead's article, "Selected Characteristics of Classes in a Middle Western Community," *American Sociological Review*, Vol. 12, No. 4 (August, 1947). Compare Kingsley Davis, "Adolescence and the Social Structure," *Annals of the Academy of Political and Social Science*, Vol. 236 (November, 1944), 8-16; and "The Child and the Social Structure," *Journal of Educational Sociology*, Vol. 14 (December, 1940), 217-229.

7 *Ibid.*, 9.

prestige and standing of these families in the community as appraised by the adult observers.

The community consisted of approximately 10,000 people (in 1941), including the farm and nonfarm families in the rural hinterland; and the population has been almost exclusively white, with only one Negro family and a few Orientals and Mexicans. Nevertheless, an elaborate social prestige structure existed, which organized Elmtowners' daily activities. The five main classes are: (1) the upper group in which wealth and lineage combined through economic, legal, and family systems to provide stability from one generation to another; (2) the group in which families achieved their position chiefly through their own efforts and which provided much of the civic leadership; (3) the middle class, which occupied a pivotal position between the extremes of the prestige structure, with fairly substantial incomes, houses, and active participation in institutional activities, but not quite so well educated as those in the upper classes; (4) the working class, which was aware of the inferior prestige position in comparison with the higher classes, with less money and education; and (5) the lowest-ranking stations in the prestige structure, almost totally isolated from organized community activities. This prestige structure affected the entire community, but the functional relationship of this system to the behavior of high school boys and girls is the main concern of the study.

Cliques and Peer Groups. From the point of view of antisocial behavior, the clique system and the indulgence of tabooed pleasures are of special importance. As many leaders and adolescents expressed it, the town was full of little cliques. A clique comes into existence when two or more persons are together a great deal. The members plan to be together in order to do things together, and there is a mutual exchange of ideas. Hollingshead studied 259 cliques (106 school, 120 recreational, and 33 institutional). Who chums with whom is important. Most of the clique relations are with equals, but some go across one or two class lines. The clique ties are very close, for the "best" friends are found in these intimate groups. Also, the reputation in the community depends somewhat upon the clique relationships. From a reputational point of view, these groups range from the "elite" or the "good kids" to the "grubby" gang.

One of the most revealing evidences of the influence of the prestige structure of the community is found in the dating patterns of the adolescents.[8] Most of the boys and girls of Elmtown dated

---

[8] *Ibid.*, Figure IV, p. 231.

within their own class, and if they dated outside of their class they dated with persons usually not more than one class removed from their own. 'The clique and class relationships affected also their religious affiliation, jobs and ideas of jobs, recreation, school participation, sex and marriage, and nearly all other phases of their existence; and the clique relationship, in turn, was affected by the families they belonged to and the positions of these families in the class system of the community.

A peer group tends to take up the child where the family's influence ends, even though the family status and influence condition the choices of peer group relationships. According to Bossard,

. . . a peer in the common social sense of the word is a person whom one meets on terms of approximate equality, a companion or fellow. For the child, a peer, negatively considered, is a non-adult, a non-parent, a non-teacher; on the positive side, it means another child, relatively of the same age, in certain instances of the same sex, with whom he can associate on terms of equal status, at least as far as his elders are concerned. It is important that this dual nature of the peer group concept be recognized, for the peer group is more than an association of equals whose concern is with each other; it is, in a certain very specific sense, also a grouping in which the adult is assigned the status of alien and the purpose of which is to maintain that status.[9]

While the play group, the clique, and the gang are the chief small, intimate, and influential groups outside the family, peer group relationships extend to more formally organized groups as well. These groups often constitute the dominant social media for satisfying fundamental wishes and needs of children. The wishes for response, security, new experience, and recognition often go unsatisfied in the home or in the larger community relationships. So juveniles turn to their peer groups for the satisfaction of their felt needs. As Bossard has pointed out, since these peer groups satisfy social needs, their development follows the character of the need. The peer groups are important agencies in controlling the behavior of its members.

Deviant Behavior of Adolescents in a Stratified Society. The indulgence in tabooed activities is of special importance from the point of view of antisocial behavior. According to the attitudes of the people of Elmtown, some activities are generally approved (reading good books, going to church functions, Boy Scout membership),

---

9 James H. S. Bossard, *The Sociology of Child Development* (New York: Harper & Brothers, 1954), 523-524. Used by permission of publisher. Chapter XXIII deals with "The Role of the Peer Groups," with special emphasis on the play group, the clique, and the gang.

others depend to some extent upon the viewpoint of the individual (bowling, roller skating, attending movies, dancing), while smoking, drinking, gambling, and sex play come under the heading of forbidden pleasures. Participation in tabooed activities is carefully masked and not generally admitted. The boys and girls who smoke know where to smoke. Boys may smoke in the pool hall, in the hangout, in a private car, on the street after dark, on dates, and out of town; but girls must be more careful or they will "lose caste." Gambling is mainly a male activity, and it is concentrated disproportionately among the boys in classes II and III. Elmtowners have one public bar for each 525 inhabitants, but drinking by boys and girls is generally tabooed. Only 39 per cent of the boys and 19 per cent of the girls admitted that they drank alcohol in some form during the school year, usually away from home, church, and school.

The out-of-school youth produced more problems, not only from the point of view of truancy, school failure, and the like, but in their leisure-hour activities. The withdrawee's leisure hours revolve around the clique and the date. Off the job, the out-of-school youth, the boys particularly, spend much of the time in aimless activities, except that they are in search of excitement. This aimless activity goes on night after night. Boys get into their cars and drive from one place to another, searching for excitement and girls. The hangout is the place where the clique meets. Both the high school and the withdrawee groups of classes IV and V congregate in the "disreputable joints." Their adventures may begin at the hangout, but the nightly search for excitement may include speeding, drinking, picking up girls, gambling, and sometimes fights.

The pleasure-bent youths of Elmtown violated the mores of the community, if not the laws of society, almost every night. Boys got into trouble more extensively than girls, and the withdrawee groups had a much higher delinquency rate than the school group. Based on court records, the combined delinquency rate of the boys in classes III through V was 9 per 1000; whereas the withdrawee group in the same classes had a rate of 165 per 1000. Apparently, only one high school girl (in class IV) was charged with an offense; but the withdrawee girls had a rate of 104 per 1000. Most of the delinquencies were concomitant with clique activity or sex play.

GANGS AND STREET CORNER SOCIETIES

Play groups and gangs are spontaneously formed and may be perfectly normal. They exist to satisfy basic wishes and needs, and provide opportunities for friendship and response, recognition, adventure, and security or protection.

Characteristics of Gangs and Street Corner Societies. Thrasher's [10] study of gangs and Whyte's [11] study of street corner societies have given close-up views of the chief characteristics of the various boys' groups and societies one may find in a modern city.

Thrasher studied 1313 gangs with approximately 25,000 members. His major conclusion is that gangs are found in geographically and socially interstitial areas of the city, the areas between the more normal communities. The Chicago gang empire is divided into three main ganglands—"North Side Jungles," "West Side Wilderness," and "South Side Badlands."

Gangs arise chiefly from spontaneous play groups, which are gangs in embryo. The members develop a "we" feeling and start the process of ganging. Later, as they come in conflict with other gangs, and sometimes with police authorities and irate citizens, they may become more solidified. Natural leaders arise within the groups as they are formed. Gangs represent efforts of the boys to form a society for themselves.

Thrasher maintains that no two gangs are exactly alike, although a general classification is possible. Some are of the diffused type and never grow beyond the rudimentary stage. Their solidarity is not lasting, and the loyalties of the members cannot be counted on too far. The solidified type, in which a high degree of loyalty exists, is the antithesis of the diffused type. The members may be together for a long while with a minimum of friction. The conventional type is like an athletic club. Some gangs have elements of secrecy, such as passwords, secret meetings, initiations, rituals, and codes. Then there are the criminal gangs, having degenerated into predatory and various other forms of delinquent behavior.

The gang age, according to Thrasher, is chiefly from early adolescence to adulthood, although boys' gangs sometimes graduate into adult racketeering and criminal groups, as Whyte has pointed out. Although most of the gangs are composed of boys, girls may form gangs also, and some groups are mixed or there may be alliances between boys' and girls' groups. Gangs are not peculiar to any racial or nationality group, for many are mixed groups; but in Chicago the

---

10 Frederic M. Thrasher, *The Gang* (Chicago: University of Chicago Press, 1927 and 1936).

11 William Foote Whyte, *Street Corner Society* (Chicago: University of Chicago Press, 1943).

Polish, Italian, Irish, Negro, and Jewish gangs outnumber others of single nationality or culture complexion.

Whyte analyzes the gang structure in what he calls "street corner societies." Doc and his boys and Chick and his clubs are described in detail. These street corner groups are together frequently, and they form a structure or pattern of relationships. Doc had his associates, Mike and Danny, who in turn were superior to Nutsy, and Nutsy was superior to Frank, Joe, and Alec. Then there were Angelo, Fred, and Lou, who recognized Danny and Doc as their leaders, and Long John was Mike's friend. These represented the lines of influence. Over a period of time the alignment changed, with some members less frequently present, new ones added, and the relative status changed. Other groups formed similar structures but functioned on different levels.

Three social levels were represented in the Nortons and the Italian Community Club; with the corner boys at the bottom, the college boys at the top, and between them the intermediaries. Within the community were groups of racketeers and politicians, the graduates of corner societies.

The corner-gang structure arises out of the habitual association of the members over a long period of time. The nuclei of most gangs can be traced back to early boyhood, when living close together provided the first opportunities for social contacts. School years modified the original pattern somewhat, but I know of no corner gangs which arose through classroom or school-playground association. The gangs grew up on the corner and remained there with remarkable persistence from early boyhood until the members reached their late twenties or early thirties.[12]

Home plays a very small role in the life of these corner boys. Except to eat and to sleep, or in case of sickness, the boys are rarely at home, and they seldom mention their homes. The family names are seldom mentioned, for most of the boys are known by their nicknames. Even the married men seem to be more interested in the corner gang than in their homes. The boys usually meet regularly, and life on the corner proceeds within narrowly prescribed channels. Out of the continuous interaction, a system of mutual obligations, social status, and activities arises.

The leader occupies an important place, for he is the focal point of organization and activities. He acts when the situation calls for it. The followers look to him for decisions, advice, encouragement, and direction. He, in turn, must hold their confidence by being able, fair minded, generous in spending money, and skillful in handling

---

12 *Ibid.*, 255.

critical situations. He has to deal with the individuals and mobilize the group.

As Thrasher points out,[13] social patterns and controls develop in gangs which regulate the conduct of the members, some of which are demoralizing. Most adolescent gangs have an intimate knowledge of the underworld. The informal education of the streets is often more influential than that which the boys receive elsewhere. The gang has its own universe of discourse, the jargon of the underworld. Corporate behavior requires cooperation, *esprit de corps,* morale, and loyalty. The structure of the gang grows out of the interaction within the gang and through its activities. Status in the gang is achieved through personality traits, activities, and accomplishments. The nicknames usually grow out of personality characteristics.

Sheer physical activities, such as roughhouse, movement from place to place, playing games and gambling, sports and predatory activities, appeal to gang boys. Cheap movies, dime novels, wandering to picturesque places, gang warfare, and almost any function that offers excitement and adventure are specially appealing.

The Gang and Delinquency. Boys, and girls too, seldom commit delinquencies alone. They usually engage in such activities in association with others. The strong influence exerted by the corner gang leads to group activities. As Thrasher has pointed out, the undirected gang demoralizes its members. It aids in making out of them chronic truants and delinquents who eventually may become finished criminals. The demoralizing process may begin with the boys' entrance into the gang or even earlier, and it continues progressively as the boy grows older. The boy may start as a truant, then commit minor delinquencies, followed by more serious offenses and reckless daredevil activities; and, if the process is not checked, he develops into a seasoned gangster or a professional criminal. His training may be interrupted by periodic institutionalization, but upon release he returns to the old gang haunts and the repetition of delinquency. The gang life tends to invite truancy and to facilitate delinquency. Of the 1313 gangs studied by Thrasher, 652 probably had demoralizing influence, 609 may or may not have had such influence, and only 52 had no demoralizing effects. Most of the latter were regarded as wholesome groups. Of the 652 whose influence was demoralizing, 530 were reported definitely as delinqent or criminal gangs.[14] But Thrasher did not advance the thesis that the gang is a

---

13 *Op. cit.,* Chapters XIV-XVIII.
14 *Ibid.,* 386.

direct "cause" of crime. Rather, it is more accurate to say that the gang is an important contributing factor that facilitates the commission of offenses and greatly extends its spread and range. Its demoralizing influence on its members and the opportunity that it provides for the dissemination of information regarding the techniques of crime, and the excitement created by gang activities, all tend to promote criminal behavior.

Taft [15] points out that juvenile gangs may influence members to commit delinquencies by developing attitudes of conflict with the community and with the agencies of social control, by teaching a general hoodlum pattern of destructiveness, and by teaching the techniques of crime. More important than the teaching of techniques is the gang's code, the caste system that emphasizes bigger and better crimes, the hero worship of the "Big Shot" who is bold and successful, and the enmity for the police. The gang is a medium of contact between beginners and the more experienced delinquents, and also professional gangs and adult criminals. The order is usually from the play group to the imitation of gang heroes, and finally to professional gangs. The gang encourages continuance of crime by welcoming the members just out of institutions, and stimulates crime through its own organization.

Shaw and McKay [16] also found that most juvenile offenses are committed by groups of boys, few by individuals alone. Out of 5480 offenders, 81.8 per cent had committed their offenses in company with others. Stealing was particularly a group phenomenon, for 89 per cent of those charged with theft had had companions. Similar findings have been reported by the Gluecks, Healy and Bronner, Puffer, and others.

Chambers,[17] who studied gangs in New York, thinks that the significance of gang conflict is deeper than mere juvenile delinquency. He indicates the ferociousness of the modern city gang as evidenced in the types of weapons they use today in comparison with the less vicious ones previously associated with kid gangs. Also, the bloody warfare that goes on between groups and the serious nature of the offenses indulged in by gangs show the change that has taken place. He suggests that gangs are symptoms of deep-seated social and economic disturbances brought about by unemployment, slums, and racial discrimination.

The Pachuco or "Zoot Suit" gangs are good illustrations of

---

15 Donald R. Taft, *Criminology* (New York: The Macmillan Co., 1942), 42.
16 *Op. cit.*, 195.
17 Bradford Chambers, "The Juvenile Gangs of New York," *The American Mercury* (April, 1946), 480-486.

groups arising out of a situation in which race discrimination, economic want, and cultural conflicts exist. The word "Pachuco" is probably derived from a Mexican colloquial designation of former residents of El Paso, Texas, who had migrated elsewhere, principally to Los Angeles. It came into popular use to designate boys and young adults, also some girls, of Mexican and Spanish ancestry. The term "Zoot Suit" applies to the way they were dressed.

The groups were especially discernible by their dress and personal appearance. Draped trousers with narrow cuffs constituted the distinctive style of dress. On formal occasions, and later for street dress, finger-length coats were used. The combination of draped trousers, long coats, and peculiarly combed long hair gave them the notorious designation of "Zoot Suit" gangs. The girls, though fewer in number, became a part of these groups. They wore skirts reaching just above the knees, with sweaters or blouses, and short bobby socks. Their black hair was worn long, over shoulder length, combed into a high pompadour over the forehead. Exaggerated use of cosmetics was another characteristic of the girls.

The group was distinctly clannish, often belligerent in the face of real or fancied slights and discriminations by other groups. The attitudes were chiefly antisocial, partly as a defense mechanism. They used "Pachuco talk," a form of speech characteristic of the group, consisting chiefly of Spanish expressions. Spanish was preferred to English.

Although the feeling of group solidarity existed, the Zoot Suiters were not organized in gangs in a strict sense. The neighborhood groups were loosely organized, the members were highly individualistic, and they resented attempts at control. The conflicts with the outside world, the rivalry among individual groups, and occasional feuds and assaults produced a certain amount of group solidarity, at least on occasion, although many individuals who imitated Zoot Suiters had no connection with any group.

General rowdiness and disturbance, excessive use of tobacco and alcohol, and a certain amount of sex delinquency between boys and girls in the neighborhood were the chief symptoms of maladjustment. But the majority of the group did not engage in delinquent activities that might bring them to the attention of law enforcement officers.

Psychologically, their behavior patterns were characteristic responses of individuals who feel the need of doing something to compensate for a sense of inferiority. Their language, a mixture of Spanish and English, and the lack of knowledge of the conventions of the larger society made them extremely self-conscious. Ignorance and discomfiture brought out responses that were both surly and uncouth, even when no disrespect was intended. Injustices and discriminations made them feel that they were set apart. So they took pride in being called Mexicans, insisted on speaking the Spanish language, clung to the folkways of the group, and above all clung to a mode of dress that definitely distinguished them from the majority group. They challenged anyone who insulted them and had an almost pathological fear of being called cowards.

The Zoot Suit riots in Los Angeles during the early part of the war attracted nation-wide and even international attention and challenged local authorities with the situation. But there was little understanding of the nature of the problem. The conflict between rival groups, not all of them were Zoot Suiters, subsided shortly after the situation was thoroughly analyzed, the rival forces were brought under control, and a program of constructive activities was carried on in the area.

Many illustrations of the effects of gangs on individual members could be given. The cases of *The Jack-Roller, The National History of a Delinquent Career,* and *Brothers in Crime* by Clifford R. Shaw and associates, cited in the previous chapter, all illustrate the effects of gangs as well as the influence of the home and of community conditions. According to Stanley, when he was out of money, and he felt that he could not enjoy life without "dough," his buddy, being an old "jack-roller," suggested "jack-rolling" as a way out of the dilemma. So they started to put the strong arm on drunks. It was bloody work, but they felt that necessity demanded it, for they had to live. They used various schemes to entice men into a room to rob them. One day his partner failed him, so Stanley lost his nerve, for he needed someone to be with him. He was too cowardly to rob and to steal alone. As he put it, "a companion made me brave and gave me a sense of security. I couldn't to save my soul steal a dime alone." [18]

Sidney Blotzman (*The Natural History of a Delinquent Career*) tells a similar story of how he was led to steal. He was playing in front of his house when a boy by the name of Joseph came along. Sidney liked Joseph quite a bit. When they went into a fruit store, located about a block from home, Joseph took some fruit, which the two boys consumed in an alley. Sidney did not realize at first that this was stealing, for he considered it quite an adventure. This, however, led to later adventures and to more extensive gang activities.

---

[18] Clifford R. Shaw, *The Jack-Roller* (Chicago: University of Chicago Press, 1930), 85-86.

During Sidney's career as a delinquent, he was involved with members of three distinct delinquent groups. His early delinquencies grew out of the influences of his playmates. Later the family moved into another neighborhood, and Sidney became associated with a second delinquent group. When the family moved into the third area, Sidney was brought into contact with the younger members of an adult criminal group. The official record shows that he committed most of his delinquencies in association with others in delinquent groups. They were his companions.

The gang may provide the adolescent boy with definite patterns of behavior for the entire gamut of criminal disorganization. The general pattern of behavior of gang members includes such objectionable personal habits as vulgarity, obscenity, profanity, alcoholism, drug addiction, gambling, and sordid aspects of sex behavior. Through the gang the child learns criminal practices and techniques. The code of the corner boy requires that he must help a friend when he can and refrain from doing anything to harm him, but a different code is applied to outsiders. The security of the street corner gang acts as a buffer between the individual and society. The residents of slums and of immigrant communities feel especially the need for someone or a group to act in their interest and to defend them. Crime may be regarded by them as normal behavior under certain conditions, as a defense against what gang members regard as external encroachment.

Juveniles and adults alike may resort to gangster tactics and racketeering, political corruption, and similar devices to gain advantages in an organized society that is considered as hostile to them. The gang leaders map the deals and plan the procedures. Loyalty to the gang compels the members to conform. Every boy knows the importance of the gang. The individual who attempts to throw off his background and get away from the gang influences loses the support of the group.

The relationship between gang life and delinquency and crime applies chiefly to cities. Clinard [19] found in his study of the rural offender that almost two thirds of the farm boys had not been associated with groups of boys who stole; and, if restricted to serious thefts, 86.7 per cent had had no previous association. Very little about gang behavior appears in the life histories of rural offenders. More often, if they have accomplices, crimes are committed with one or two companions rather than gangs.

---

[19] Marshall B. Clinard, "Rural Criminal Offenders," *The American Journal of Sociology,* Vol. 50, No. 1 (July, 1944), 38-45.

COMMUNITY PATTERNS AND JUVENILE GANGS

Juvenile gangs are closely related to the patterns of conduct and disorganized conditions in the community. Although gangs are in conflict with the larger society in which they exist, they are nevertheless an integral part of the social world in which they thrive and from which they receive their chief stimulus.

The Presence of Adult Criminals. There is no question but that adults exert a tremendous influence on the youth with whom they associate. Adult criminals selfishly exploit the willing apprentices for their own purposes, while the young ones zealously seek their instruction and follow the practices of the sinister art of crime. Success and experience are respected by the young disciples, and they make the most of their associations with their "superiors." For this reason, association with older delinquents and adult offenders is especially harmful.

Older criminals seldom feel the need for justifying their relationship with younger people, regardless of the nature of that relationship. The philosophy of the hardened criminal is one of cynicism and bitterness, and he is not bound by the conventions of society.

White-collar crime includes embezzlement and fraud and a host of minor violations of law that are practiced, but the perpetrators are seldom brought to justice. Some of the white-collar offenses are not crimes in the strictly legal sense, for the parties concerned have been able to prevent legislation declaring them illegal. But many such forms of behavior are detrimental to society.[20] Criminals, observing such conduct, either justify their own acts or do not even regard them as crimes.

Society is full of conflicts and contradictions that the young person fails to understand. Our customs, traditions, and laws tend to lag behind other phases of the environment. When no satisfactory definitions of situations are given, some juveniles are inclined to take the path that seems most likely to satisfy their interest.

There is a rather high correlation between the rates of adult crime and juvenile delinquency in urban areas, as has been pointed out by Shaw and McKay, Healy and Bronner, and others. Some-

---

[20] See Edwin H. Sutherland, *White Collar Crime* (New York: The Dryden Press, 1949). Compare "White Collar Criminality," *American Sociological Review,* V (February, 1940), 1-12; "Crime and Business," *Annals of the American Academy of Political and Social Science,* CXVII (September, 1941), 112-18; "Is 'White Collar Crime' Crime?" *American Sociological Review,* X (April, 1945), 132-139.

times the rate of juvenile misconduct is almost identical with the rate of adult offenses.

The Spirit of Delinquency. The objective characteristics of delinquency areas, as we shall indicate later, are not the only deviant pressures that affect youth. Sometimes the traditions, standards, and moral sentiments that characterize the neighborhood have a more powerful influence in shaping the lives of children. These more intangible factors have been called the "spirit of the delinquency." The moral atmosphere of the area is reflected early in the conduct of children. Children consciously or unconsciously absorb the conceptions of right and wrong that are prevalent in the adult world. If there is much talk of law violation, and hostile attitudes are expressed toward law and law enforcement, especially if there is a breakdown of the customary rules of behavior, children quite naturally follow in the footsteps of adult offenders. It is sometimes considered the thing to do. Delinquency represents a sort of adjustment to the traditions, behavior standards, and expectations of the neighborhood. In substance, delinquency becomes a part of the tradition of the neighborhood.

The delinquency traditions of an area are transmitted through the companionship group. The close association of its members, the influence of the leader, and the moral atmosphere of the gang have a compelling influence. The young members readily acquire the delinquency code of the gang. The corner gang serves as a medium through which the newly initiated members gain familiarity with the attitudes, standards, and code of the leaders of the group and with the traditions of the gang itself. Delinquent groups, like all social groups, develop their own patterns of conduct, by which the leaders seek to control and regulate the behavior of its members. The gang not infrequently inflicts punishment upon those who violate the rules of conduct, but, more likely, the members are so under the spell of the gang and its leaders that few dare to violate its codes. Disloyalty to the gang and violations of its sacred codes are considered greater offenses than the violations of law. It is sometimes the in-group versus the out-group. Law and order sometimes have no meaning to the youngsters. They simply do what the others do. They absorb the delinquency tradition of the area.

Once delinquency and crime have become common in an area, and the spirit of delinquency has been thoroughly established, misconduct tends to persist even though the population changes from one nationality or culture group to another. The relative rates of delinquency in the various areas of the city tend to remain the same over a long period of time, unless radical changes are made in the system of controls and new forms of activities are provided for the youngster. It is possible to reduce the rate of delinquency, but to do so requires more than changes in the external aspect of the community. The thinking of the people must be changed.

Wartime Conditions and Delinquency. It was noted in Chapter III that the statistics of wartime (World War II) and postwar trends are on a somewhat shaky basis. The wartime increases may have been overly publicized. Nevertheless, war creates new conditions and accentuates old conditions that affect juvenile conduct in one way or another. The rise in delinquency was noticeable, especially in the urban centers where the population grew rapidly, mobility was extensive, and community life became disorganized. Parents and children alike had difficulty in adjusting themselves to the new situation.

With adult members of the family in the armed services or in war industries, and with less time and energy on the part of the adults who stayed at home to supervise their children, the younger ones were left to their own devices much of the time. Naturally they sought companionship in the neighborhood. The necessity of making new contacts, often with strange boys and girls, and the lack of the old forms of control provided the atmosphere for adventure and new forms of activities. The uprooted families had not established firm anchorage in the community. The spirit of restlessness, anxiety, excitement, and the emotional tensions growing out of war provided an abnormal stimulation. In a way, the young constituted a lost generation. The war diverted the attention of adults to the national task of securing a victory, which left the children to their own devices. It must not be assumed that the conditions of war produced an entirely new batch of offenders, but it did create conditions favorable to delinquency.

In war-camp communities were found uncounted numbers of young people, many of them young girls who went to these centers to see their boy friends. Many unattached women swarmed around these camps also. They were drawn to the camp area in search of adventure. Some had been emotionally starved, lonesome, and frustrated at home. So they moved to the camp communities to escape the past, blindly caring little for the uncertain future, anxious to live in the present. They existed in an upset world. Some lasting new friendships were formed in these centers; but many a frustrated person, lonely and away from home, contacted undesirable persons. Being away from home and community restraints, and controls, many yielded to the temptations of the situation, often finding themselves violating the law.

Summarizing the relation of gangs and companionship to delinquency, it should be noted that the corner gangs and the intimate friends exert a most powerful influence on boys and girls. The factors underlying ganging are exceedingly complex. As Thrasher [21] has so ably put it, "such underlying conditions as inadequate family life, poverty, deteriorated neighborhood, and ineffective religion, education, and recreation must be considered together as a situation complex which forms the matrix of gang development." One cannot adequately control the situation without dealing with all factors, for they are closely interwoven. In an individual case, several of the factors usually interact to create the situation and the opportunity for entrance into the gang and for participating in gang activities. Furthermore, the control of ganging is difficult, because the members of gangs enjoy unusual freedom of action unhampered by the usual restrictions found in normal communities. Their play is usually spontaneous; and the delinquency area furnishes them a realm of adventure unexcelled in the more orderly sections of the city, for there is no dearth of excitement in this kind of disorganized environment. This free and wild life constitutes a great obstacle in attacking the gang problem, for it is difficult to provide an adequate substitute program. When the underlying conditions are accentuated by wartime atmosphere, the problem of control becomes immeasurably more difficult. Even otherwise normal boys and girls may be drawn into gang life by the exigencies of war.

QUESTIONS AND PROJECTS

For Class Discussion and Research

1. If American society is stratified into social classes, and members of the lower classes do not date and mate with members of the upper classes, is our social system undemocratic?

2. If adolescent boys and girls form cliques on the basis of socially stratified groups in the community, what problems for the underprivileged are created?

3. Discuss the influence of playmates on conduct of children.

4. What are the chief characteristics of ganglands? In what parts of a city are gangs likely to be found?

5. Describe the composition, organization, social relationships, and structure of gangs and street corner societies.

---

21 *Op. cit.*, 491.

6. In describing the life in gangs, what are the chief gang activities?
7. What controls are exercised in gangs?
8. What are the chief problems created by gangs?
9. Describe the process whereby gang life may lead to delinquency.
10. Why is it difficult to control gangs?
11. Discuss criminal gangs.

SELECTED REFERENCES

BOGARDUS, EMORY S., *The City Boy and His Problems: A Survey of Boy Life in Los Angeles* (Rotary Club of Los Angeles, 1926).

BURROUGHS, HARRY E., *Boys in Men's Shoes* (New York: The Macmillan Co., 1944).

FURFEY, PAUL H., *The Gang Age: A Study of the Preadolescent Boy and His Recreational Needs* (New York: The Macmillan Co., 1926).

HOLLINGSHEAD, AUGUST B., *Elmtown's Youth* (New York: John Wiley & Sons, Inc., 1949).

MINEHAN, THOMAS, *Boy and Girl Tramps of America* (New York: Farrar and Rinehart, 1934).

SHAW, CLIFFORD R., AND HENRY D. McKAY, "Social Factors in Juvenile Delinquency," *Report on the Causes of Crime,* No. 13, Vol. II, National Commission on Law Observance and Enforcement, 1931.

SUTHERLAND, EDWIN H., *White Collar Crime* (New York: The Dryden Press, 1949).

THRASHER, FREDERIC M., *The Gang. A Study of 1,313 Gangs in Chicago* (Chicago: The University of Chicago Press, 1927 and 1936).

TUNIS, JOHN R., *All-American.* (New York: Harcourt, Brace and Company, 1942).

WHYTE, WILLIAM FOOTE, *Street Corner Societies: The Social Structure of an Italian Slum* (Chicago: The University of Chicago Press, 1943).

VIII

INFLUENCE OF COMMUNITY INSTITUTIONS AND AGENCIES

Personality factors, home conditions, and associations with playmates in intimate groups, such as gangs and cliques, are primary elements in the etiology of delinquency. But delinquent behavior is not the product exclusively of personality maladjustment or contacts with family members and companions. It is linked also with community factors and conditions of the larger social world. Of the environmental influences that may shape the behavior of a child, community institutions and agencies, population and cultural differentiation, economic and physical environmental conditions, and law enforcement and observance often are of vital importance. The over-all society and culture whose standards are reflected in the family, the gang or play group, and the immediate community or neighborhood may have a decisive influence in some forms of conduct. Certain economic, political, and cultural elements in the larger society may seem far removed from the immediate environment in which children live, yet they may be responsible for a chain of consequences and pressures that have an important bearing on a given form of deviant behavior.

The community, especially if it is somewhat disorganized, is a source of deviant behavior. The conditioning factors of delinquency that have their roots in the community are usually numerous, and they frequently occur concomitantly in a situation; but their relative effects are not easily measurable. To deal with the primary and secondary influences of the community and of the larger society requires a broader perspective than the analysis of personality, family, and gang factors.

COMMUNITY FACTORS

The relationship between delinquency or crime and the community is a total relationship and not a partial one. It involves institutions and agencies, social conditions, and a series of selective influences. Within the total complex, certain factors may be more dynamic than others.[1]

The Community and Its Institutions and Agencies. Communities differ widely in size and function, but they always have one common characteristic. The attribute that distinguishes a community—whether it be a rural neighborhood, a small town or city, a large city or metropolitan area, a region or even a larger territory —is the fact that it comprises an aggregation of people inhabiting a contiguous geographic area, functioning together in the chief concerns of life, with common centers of interests and activities, and with similar behavior patterns. As a primary group, it refers chiefly to a locality grouping of people, with personal contacts and more intimate relationships. As a secondary group, it is characterized by wider and often more impersonal relationships, the people being less closely bound together, often with smaller subunits within the larger territory. The community, therefore, whether small or large, has reference to a group of persons living in a contiguous geographic area and sharing interests and activities.[2]

The community is made up of social institutions and agencies that constitute its chief structure. They arise in response to needs.

[1] Compare Frank Tannenbaum, *Crime and the Community* (New York: Columbia University Press, 1951). This book was originally published by Ginn & Co., 1938.
[2] Compare *Dictionary of Sociology,* edited by Henry Pratt Fairchild (New York: Philosophical Library, 1944).

There is great ambiguity in the literature on institutions as to the exact meaning. This confusion is partly the result of the variation in sizes, organizational setup, functions, and influences. In a broad sense institutions are sets of organized human relationships that are purposely established by the will of the people. They grow out of the folkways and mores of society. From the point of view of the basic functions that they perform, institutions may be broadly classified as: (1) domestic (family, foster home, children's home); (2) educational (school, library, museum); (3) religious (church, synagogue, temple); (4) recreational (playground, park, theater, dance hall, athletic club); (5) economic-business, industrial, financial, transportation (store, factory, bank, railroad system); (6) governmental (court, post office, legislative body); (7) social welfare (social centers, welfare organizations); and (8) health (hospitals, clinic, health department). Sometimes the term "institution" is applied to service clubs, women's organizations, art, law, science, property, and the like. Institutions overlap in functions. Some are diffused types and others are more appropriately called "agencies."

The concept "social institution" is not clearly defined in the literature on the subject, and there is no agreement as to its exact meaning. The differences in the classification of types of institutions stem in part from the confusion of the meaning of the term and the obvious divergencies in the structural and functional aspects of the different kinds of institutions and organizations in modern society.

The interrelationship of the institutions or agencies of a community must be recognized, for no organization functions independently and separately. The degree of integration of the community depends somewhat upon the relative functioning and integration of the institutions and agencies. The community, however, is not a static entity; it is an ongoing affair, always changing. It is dynamic in character and teeming with life. It is the changing aspect of community life that often results in the breakdown of the effective functioning of the organized phases of society.

Relative Influence of Secondary or Indirect Community Factors.
Before proceeding with the analysis of the possible effects of community factors, one must keep in mind that some of them are of a secondary or indirect nature. Newspapers, comic books, radio and television, motion pictures, and other media of mass communication and entertainment undoubtedly have effects on the behavior of juveniles, but their relative influence has not been adequately measured. A realistic appraisal of these and other media of influence indicates that, although there are cases in which they may be important, on

the whole the effects may be more indirect than direct. They may intensify and aggravate already existing tendencies.

The acquistion of behavior norms, both conventional and deviant, is primarily through intimate associations and other personal influences, rather than through the agencies of mass impression. However, the mass media of social stimulation are carriers of cultural patterns and behavior norms, and as such must be recognized. The world of secondary relationships can by no means be eliminated as an area of influence in shaping conduct, but the possible effects have not been fully ascertained.[3]

In view of the limited knowledge concerning the actual effects of certain institutions and agencies on conventional or deviant behavior, dogmatic assertions or conclusions should be avoided. One can find statements ranging all the way from the view that the secondary influences are almost nil, or very limited, to the assertions that they have a far-reaching and all-pervasive impact on conduct. In reviewing the possible effects of certain recreational agencies, as well as some of the other community institutions, the author does not pretend that the types of studies cited present adequate proof one way or another of the positive or negative effects that may emanate from them. For purposes of analysis, the recreation and amusement agencies are singled out for special consideration; which is followed by a brief summary of the ways in which institutions like schools, churches, and youth serving agencies may fail to prevent delinquency in some instances or may even contribute to antisocial behavior if they function inadequately. That they may fail in reaching the delinquents or predelinquents, and thus not be able to prevent deviant behavior, does not mean that their influence in general is not constructive. The basic institutions of the community are the chief preventive agencies, as will be indicated in Part Three. It is not necessary for our purpose to review the possible influences of all kinds of community institutions and agencies, for some have only remote relationships to delinquency.

RECREATION, AMUSEMENTS, AND MASS COMMUNICATION

It is generally believed that uncontrolled and harmful amusements, especially if commercialized, have certain detrimental effects; but before we consider some of the most popular forms of com-

---

[3] Cf. Marshall B. Clinard, "Secondary Community Influences and Juvenile Delinquency," *The Annals of the American Academy of Political and Social Science,* Vol. 261 (January, 1949), 42-54. Compare Charles E. King. "Community Factors in Juvenile Delinquency," *Sociology and Social Research,* Vol. 39 (September-October, 1954), 18-21.

mercial recreation, the broader aspects of the relationship of recrea tion to delinquency need to be analyzed.

Recreation and Delinquency. It is generally assumed that wholesome recreation tends to prevent delinquency, whereas unwholesome and harmful amusements lead to misconduct. The most comprehensive study of the relationship between recreation and delinquency was made in Chicago for the Chicago Recreation Commission under the auspices of its Committee on Recreation and Juvenile Delinquency, of which Ernest W. Burgess was chairman.[4] Spurred on by the fact that during 1939 the Chicago Police Department investigated 11,549 complaints of delinquency of boys and girls under the age of 18, and the fact that petitions were filed with the courts for 1542 of these, it was decided to make a special study of the relationships between recreation and delinquency. Four so-called "delinquency areas" and one control area were selected to determine the extent of participation of delinquent children in recreation and the variation in the activity preferences of delinquent and nondelinquent children. A threefold classification of the children was made—official and unofficial delinquents and nondelinquents. Each child who appeared in a supervised recreation center was carefully checked.

During the period of observation, 15,217 boys from 10 to 17 years of age and 7939 girls of the same age group participated in supervised recreation, including 1262 official and 536 unofficial delinquents. A total of 1,281,853 hours was spent in supervised recreation by the boys and girls. Although this figure appears large, only about a fourth of the boys and girls spent, on the average, an hour a week in supervised recreation. The recreation agencies were fairly successful in contacting the boy population, although the proportion of participation ranged from 95.5 per cent in the control area to 63.2 per cent in the worst delinquency area. During any one season of the year, less than half of the year's total was represented. The delinquent boys had a considerably lower participation record than the nondelinquents. The boys and girls of the five areas, delinquents and nondelinquents alike, were regular movie goers and ardent radio listeners, spending about twice as much time in the movies as in supervised recreation. Delinquents attended motion pictures more frequently than the nondelinquents.

The boys under 14 participated in supervised recreation more

---

[4] *Recreation and Delinquency:* A Study of Five Selected Chicago Communities, Ethel Shanas, Director, with the collaboration of Catherine E. Dunning (Chicago: University of Chicago Press, 1942).

extensively than the older boys, and the boys participated more extensively than the girls. Delinquent boys spent less time than the nondelinquents in supervised recreation; and, when they attended, they usually concentrated chiefly on two types of activities—the game room and active competitive sports. The game room is usually the least supervised. In the high delinquency areas, most children limited their attendance to only one of four types of recreation agencies studied. Delinquent boys have a tendency to travel from one recreation center to another.

A special analysis of the boys who committed delinquent acts during the period of the study revealed that those who attended recreation agencies committed fewer delinquencies than those who did not attend them. Nearly two thirds of the delinquent acts were committed by boys who had no previous delinquency records. Of the nondelinquents studied, only 1.7 per cent of those who participated in supervised recreation became delinquent during the period, whereas 5.1 per cent of those who did not participate became delinquent. "The proportion of nondelinquents not in recreation who became delinquent was three times as high as the rate for non-delinquents in recreation." [5]

The program of delinquency prevention through organized recreation will be discussed in a later chapter. It should be noted here that recreation is only one factor in a broad program of delinquency control. Besides an effective program of community recreation, it is necessary to control commercial amusements, as we shall see later, enlarge the circle of wholesome companions, provide more home recreation, strengthen group work agencies and other community institutions, and improve methods of treatment. In other words, no preventive program can be effective unless the roots of delinquency are ascertained and combated by united action.

Constructive leisure time interests for children are at best meager, and the facilities for desirable recreation are limited. The inadequacy of recreation facilities and programs in communities may be considered as a condition of delinquency.[6]

There is a general belief that certain commercial amusements are factors in the causation of juvenile delinquency. Included in the category of harmful commercial recreation agencies are certain

---

[5] *Ibid.*, 241.

[6] The most comprehensive study of recreation in a large city was made in Chicago during the depression years under the joint sponsorship of the Chicago Recreation Commission and Northwestern University, with the aid of the Works Progress Administration, National Youth Administration, and Illinos Emergency Relief Commission *Chicago Recreation Survey*, volumes I-V (1937-1940), Arthur J. Todd, Editor.

types of movies and theaters, radio and television programs, dance halls, liquor establishments selling liquor to minors, commercial sports, salacious and obscene literature, comics and cartoons, and other reading material. Studies by Thurston, Sullenger, the Gluecks, and others have demonstrated that delinquents often get into trouble when they have too much spare time on their hands and are in search of something to do. Sullenger claims that more than half the delinquents studied in Omaha got into trouble while in search of recreation, and the Gluecks concluded from their study of 1000 delinquent boys that approximately 9 out of 10 spent their leisure harmfully.

Notwithstanding the seemingly obvious relationship between the uses of leisure and delinquency, it is difficult to prove the exact correlation between certain types of amusements and delinquent behavior. The influence of any amusement depends upon the individuals participating, the circumstances, and often the accompanying factors. It is necessary, therefore, that we be wary in attributing causal relationships between these agencies and behavior. It is safer to consider such influences as additional factors in the larger over-all pattern of the child who deviates from normal forms of behavior and of the social milieu in which such behavior takes place.

While certain forms of amusements may have harmful effects on some people, the influences are by no means uniform. Many who participate in relatively harmful amusement do not become delinquent. It must also be remembered that people select their amusements before these forms of recreation affect them. For instance, those who are criminally inclined or who have engaged extensively in delinquent behavior may select crime pictures. Such pictures may give added stimuli, but the chief causal factors in their delinquencies have already affected them.

Not all movies, radio and television programs, dance halls, comics, and the like, are harmful. Although commercial amusements are promoted for economic gain and constitute profit-making activities in the field of recreation, they have rendered a service by providing a great variety of pleasurable leisure activities. Measured in terms of the number of persons participating, commercial enterprises reach more people and exert a far greater influence than community forms of recreation. Recreation for which people pay large sums of money represents a dynamic clue to existing interests.

For purposes of illustration and of analysis, we may single out a number of highly commercialized forms of recreation to indicate the possible effects of commercial amusements on delinquency.

Movies and Theaters. The most comprehensive study of movies and children was made under the sponsorship of the Payne Fund, Inc., during the early 1930's. A vast amount of information was gathered and analyzed, showing the effects of movies on sleep, emotional responses, attitudes, conduct, and delinquent behavior. A series of thirteen monographs, the results of the studies, made under the general supervision of W. W. Charters, were published.[7] The bulk of the reports deals with the relation of motion pictures to moral standards, social attitudes, and conduct. This is particularly true of the studies of Peters, Peterson and Thurstone, Shuttleworth and May, Blumer and Hauser, Cressey and Thrasher.

The reports are too voluminous to summarize here, but a few pertinent facts may be gleaned from the studies that dealt most directly with movies and crime. In 115 pictures on the screens at that time, 406 crimes were actually committed, 43 were attempted, and many of the characters were far from models of human conduct. Too long a procession of crimes, illicit enterprises, misdemeanors, and techniques of delinquency presented in the movies should leave a certain deposit of impressions on the minds of juveniles. Blumer and Hauser [8] endeavored to find out to what extent the usual run of boys and girls is made more tolerant of crime and criminals by pictures dealing with these subjects, and to what extent delinquents are affected by certain pictures. They drew the conclusion that not only did high school boys and girls often express sympathy for criminals, or become less critical of them, but also crime became more attractive to the boys and girls. More than half the truant and problem boys examined indicated that pictures dealing with gangsters and gun-play stirred in them a desire to make money easily. The spirit of bravado, boldness, and toughness appealed to them. Some spent considerable time daydreaming about crooks and crime pictures.

While only 10 per cent of 368 male criminals studied believed that motion pictures had had some effects upon their career, 49 per cent of 110 inmates in a penal institution indicated that movies gave them a desire to carry a gun, 28 per cent thought that movies gave them the desire to practice holdups, and from 12 to 21 per cent felt that movies taught them ways of stealing, ways to fool the police, and plans for holdup. Not all yielded to the suggestions. Indirect in-

---

[7] See popular summary by Henry S. Forman, *Our Movie-Made Children* (New York: The Macmillan Co., 1933), and the research summary by W. W. Charters, *Motion Picture and Youth* (New York: The Macmillan Co., 1933). Cf. Martin H. and Esther S. Neumeyer, *Leisure and Recreation* (New York: A. S. Barnes & Co., 1939), Chapter XII on "Commercial Recreation."

[8] Herbert Blumer and Philip M. Hauser, *Movies, Delinquency, and Crime* (New York: The Macmillan Co., 1933), especially 35-37, 72, 111.

fluences may be greater than direct effects. Of 252 delinquent girls, mainly 14 to 16 years old, 25 per cent stated that they had engaged in sexual relations with men following the arousing of sex impulses by a passionate love picture; 41 per cent thought that movies had led them to wild parties, 38 per cent to live a wild and fast life, and 33 per cent to run away from home. More than half of these girls had stayed away from school to attend movies. Cases are presented to show how pictures directly or indirectly affect the conduct of the youngsters studied. Very few confessed that pictures had a chastening effect.

These findings, and others showing various kinds of influences on conduct, are a serious indictment of crime pictures and those showing sex suggestive material. The reports, especially Forman's summary volume, attracted widespread attention and had considerable influence in shaping public opinion regarding movies. This was bound to produce critical appraisals of the studies. Adler and Moley [9] maintained that some of the investigators, particularly Blumer, Hauser, Peters, and Dale, confused the scientific, moral, and political questions, and that they did not stick to the facts. This was especially true of the studies showing the negative effects of movies. The study by May and Shuttleworth (*Social Conduct and Attitudes of Movie Fans*) is cited as more scientific. They undertook to determine the net effect of the general run of motion pictures, by selecting from 7000 school children the 10 per cent of the total who reported most frequent attendance and the 10 per cent who went the least. The 1400 cases finally selected were equated for such factors as age, sex, school grade, socio-economic status, intelligence, and nationality of parents; and they were tested regarding their attitudes on a large number of subjects. It was found that no significant difference existed in the conduct of about 90 per cent of the movie goers and nongoers alike.

While the criticisms of Adler and Moley have certain merit, it must be remembered that they had certain biased attitudes in their appraisal of the results of the studies. The fact that Moley wrote the book "at the suggestion of the representative of the motion picture industry" may have had some influence on his attitude.

What has been said about movies can be stated with equal validity about various theaters other than motion picture shows, although the latter are by far more popular. Burlesque, vaudeville, and similar shows are regarded as having harmful effects. Even though

---

9 Mortimer J. Adler, *Art and Prudence* (New York: Longmans, Green & Co., 1937), and the more simplified analysis by Raymond Moley, *Are We Movie Made?* (New York: Macy-Masins, 1938).

the extreme forms of these are forbidden by certain city ordinances, police have found it difficult to control them. Children tend to find their way into such places, even though some cater to men only.

It is not possible to arrive at an unqualified conclusion with respect to the social impact of the mass media of communication and entertainment. The fact that millions of people are reached by these media would lead one to believe that their influence is considerable and that the emphasis on crime and violence has influenced some to engage in activities that are in violation to laws and ordinances. It must be recognized that mass media have a differential effect on juvenile behavior, depending on a number of factors, such as the background and experience of the children involved, their personalities and training, and the competing influences of the moment.

Newspapers, Comic Books, and Other Reading Material. American newspapers and periodicals have been severely criticized for their part in crime and delinquency. Taft [10] has pointed out that newspapers may be responsible for increasing crime by teaching the technique of crime; by making crime seem common, attractive, even exciting, and unduly profitable; by adding prestige to criminals and stimulating sympathy or hero worship for criminals; by appealing to the lower impulses and by sensationalism; by reflecting crime-producing elements in our culture; by making the escape from justice seem easy or by failing to stress the punishment for crime; by ridiculing the machinery of justice; by conducting "trials by newspapers"; or by advocating types of treatment that would increase crime. Sutherland [11] enumerates the charges made against newspapers—namely, that they promote crime by constant advertising and glorifying of it, by interference with justice through "trial by newspapers," by producing a public panic regarding crime that makes sober procedure impossible, by interfering with the right of innocent individuals to decent privacy, and by becoming agencies of corruption, as by employing children under morally injurious conditions.

Newspapers maintain that by giving to the public information regarding crime they contribute to the control of it. Sometimes, such publicity arouses public opinion. But the constant presentation of crime news to the public, especially by what is known as "yellow journalism," makes the process of justice difficult and creates an undue interest in criminals and criminal behavior.

---

10 Donald R. Taft, *Criminology* (New York: The Macmillan Co., 1942), 200-207.
11 Edwin H. Sutherland, *Principles of Criminology* (New York: J. B. Lippincott Co., 1947), 184-185.

Holmes [12] has called attention to epidemics of crime growing out of undue publicity given to individual cases, such as the Hickman case. A reporter applied the name "Purple Gang" to a relatively unimportant Detroit group, which enhanced the reputation of this gang and resulted in other gangs taking the same title. Newspapers make crime and gangsterism too colorful.

Today there are approximately 2000 daily newspapers in the United States with about 52,000,000 papers sold daily; and the Sunday newspaper editions total nearly 43,000,000 copies. The circulation of periodicals, magazines, and various special types of papers runs into the millions. Add to these the publications of books and pamphlets, and one can get an idea of the extent of reading in America. If only a fraction of the various kinds of publications was to deal with crime news, detective stories, and the like, the total impression would be immeasurable. The constant repetition of these items makes the impression more substantial than is true of movies, which portray the story in one picture, usually with an ending involving some type of justice, or at least the apprehension of the criminal. Children know that the pictures are not true stories, but newspaper crime stories are portrayals of what actually happened.

Obscene, sex suggestive, and suggested sadism material, usually known as salacious literature, and also horror and related literature have usually been condemned. The objectionable features in salacious literature can be found in the story content, the advertisements, and the illustrations. The authors, editors, artists, publishers, and distributors of such literature claim that they are producing what the people want. That there is a market for this literature is evidenced by the extent of sales. When young people have access to such reading material, and most of them can get it if they want to, the consequences are sometimes far-reaching.

Boys in a junior high school of a western city were cutting classes and losing out in their studies, and a few were already showing signs of becoming behavior problem cases. The vice principal, hunting for boys who were absent from classes, paused between two rows of lockers in the boys' locker room. Hushed voices told that there was something mysterious going on. The boys were perusing salacious magazines, which one of the boys had acquired and stored in his locker. Of more than thirty boys in another school who were reading this type of material, nearly all were failing in their school subjects and many were maladjusted at school. They had become

---

12 Joseph R. Holmes, "Crime and the Press," *Journal of Criminal Law and Criminology*, XX (August 1929), 258. See other articles on the same subject in other issues of this journal.

easy prey to the distributors of salacious literature and quietly had passed on these wares to other pupils. These incidents and a subsequent investigation of the extent and possible influence of salacious material in the area led to the successful prosecution of the leading wholesale and retail distributors.

Comic books, as well as the comics in newspapers and magazines, flood the market and penetrate to nearly every home of the nation. Although most of the comic books are small and cheap, it is estimated that from 70 to 100 million copies are sold in America every month. It is estimated that nearly one half of the population reads comics. The percentage of reading of comics among juveniles is even higher. Catherine M. Wolf and Marjorie Fiske [13] have pointed out that there are three types of comics: (1) those of the Walt Disney "funny animal" type; (2) adventure, crime, and mystery comics of the Superman kind; and (3) educational or the classic kind. Children pass through stages of reading, following the three types of comics mentioned above. Some comic readers are fans, others are moderate readers, and only a few are indifferent or hostile to comics. The fan is not merely an excessive reader; he is a qualitative reader as well. Maladjusted, neurotic, and psychotic children are likely to be excessive readers of comics. When children were asked if their parents objected to the reading of comics, the majority said that they did not; and of those who said that their parents objected, approximately 90 per cent disregarded the objection.

Objections have been voiced against crime, gangsterism, "blood and thunder" mystery, and similar types of comics. The effects of reading comics depend upon the types of readers. For the fans, comic reading becomes possessive. The interest, cultural background, and degree of adjustment to reality of the reader have a bearing on both the choice of comics and their effects.

Both delinquents and nondelinquents read comics; but a pilot study made by Thomas Ford Hoult [14] revealed that the delinquents (235 boys and girls in a juvenile hall) read comics more extensively than a like number of nondelinquents (the control group, matched for age, sex, grade in school, and the like) and they showed consid-

---

[13] "Children Talk About Comics," in *Communication Research,* edited by Paul F. Lazarsfeld and Frank N. Stanton (New York: Harper & Brothers, 1948-1949). For studies of social and psychological influences of comic books on children, consult educational and related journals, such as the *Journal of Educational Sociology, National Education Association Journal, School Review, Social Education, National Parent Teacher,* and *Parents' Magazine.*

[14] "Comic Books and Juvenile Delinquency," *Sociology and Social Research,* Vol. 33, No. 4 (March-April, 1949), 279-284.

erably greater interests in the comics that are often classified as harmful and objectionable.

Mystery, detective, and certain art magazines, and a variety of other publications if they play up crime or sex scenes, may have deleterious effects, especially if the readers possess an abnormal interest in these subjects. However, there is a difference of opinion among law enforcement officials, case workers, child counselors, and others in regard to the extent of the effects of lurid crime stories on conduct. Some feel that children are particularly vulnerable to the impact of excessive reading of crime stories, especially if they already possess antisocial tendencies, while others are not so sure about the total impact of children's reading.

Radio and Television Programs. Rosel H. Hyde, Chairman of the Federal Communications Commission, in an address before the National Association of Radio and Television Broadcasters in Los Angeles on April 30, 1953, reported that there were 2557 AM and 741 FM radio stations, and 433 television broadcasting stations, making a total of 3731 stations in the United States that broadcast to the public. It is estimated that there were over 105,000,000 radio receivers (including those with FM receiver attachments), and more than 26,000,000 television receivers in the United States in 1953. Today, it can be said that a radio receiver is a standard equipment in the American home, and a television receiver is rapidly becoming so in the areas where television reception is good.[15]

Realizing the significance of radio and television as media of communication and their potential and actual impact upon listeners, radio-television audience studies have been made. The chief reason for such studies is to measure the possible effectiveness of advertising. In spite of the various kinds of audience measurements and studies of listeners' interests, the social impact of either radio or television programs upon individual listeners or upon society has not been fully measured. It is generally believed that the influence is far reaching. A number of studies have dealt with special aspects of this problem. For instance, Edward C. McDonagh [16] and

---

15 According to Arthur C. Nielsen, "Radio Audience in 1953," *1954 Broadcasting-Telecasting Yearbook,* approximately 98.1 per cent of American homes now have radios and the average home has the radio on over two and a half hours a day. Prior to the advent of television, average daily listening exceeded four hours a day. Families with television receivers may devote more time to television viewing than to radio listening.

16 "Television and the Family," *Sociology and Social Research,* Vol. 35 (November-December, 1950), 113-122. Compare Dallas W. Smythe, *New Haven Television, May 15-21, 1952* (Gregory Hall, Urbana, Illinois: National Association of Educational Broadcasters, 1953).

associates attempted to measure certain effects of television on the family. By means of interviews, a group of families with television sets was compared with a nontelevision group. It was found, among other things, that the television families listened less to radio, did less reading, spent less time in movies, and spent less time in driving for pleasure or participating in sports than the nontelevision families. Such objective forms and changes in behavior can be observed. But how do broadcasts affect the attitudes and behavior of persons? What is the impact upon the mores and standards of society?

It is estimated that American children spent about as much time during the week listening to radio broadcasts or viewing television programs as they do in the classroom. What do these broadcasts do to these children? A goodly number of the broadcasts have wholesome effects, but some are alleged to have deleterious effects. Crime and horror programs have been objected to because it is believed that they have bad effects on listeners. Opinion surveys seem to indicate that many of the experts who respond to the questionnaires are of the opinion that certain programs are bad. For instance, the *National Parent-Teacher* (January, 1948) reported a study of the opinions of 314 persons (148 pediatricians, 22 sociologists, 72 neuropsychiatrists, and 72 psychologists) regarding radio crime and thriller programs. Ninety per cent of them believed that radio crime programs have a detrimental psychological effect on children, and 93 per cent believed that radio thriller shows and programs ending in suspense affect the health of the children who listen. When asked whether the effect on health was good or bad, 97 per cent thought that it was bad. Furthermore, 81 per cent felt that present-day radio programs contribute to children's delinquency or antisocial behavior. It is obvious from the way the questions were asked that a large percentage of the respondents would state that crime and thriller programs are bad, for some of the types of programs indicated probably have detrimental effects. It is doubtful if any of the respondents had ever gone to the trouble to make a study of the actual effects of these types of programs. Opinion studies of this type have little value in determining the exact impact of any medium of communication and entertainment.

Dance Halls and Commercial Sports. Places of commercial amusement may become centers of various kinds of problems if not properly controlled. Many kinds of commercialized forms of recreation have become sources of difficulties, but unsupervised dance halls and various types of sport centers are usually considered places where problems may occur, especially if there is a lack of adequate supervision. This is true in part because they are popular and it is difficult to control large crowds.

Social dancing is very popular today. Variations of the fox trot, the waltz, and the modern Tango, Rumba, La Conga, and a variety of jitterbug dances are fashionable. Each generation seems to have its specialties in dancing. The popularity of social dancing is due to many factors, such as the simplicity of movements and the ability to dance with a reasonable degree of skill, the adaptability to various occasions and situations, the opportunity afforded for social contacts, commercial promotion, and the relative absence of other forms of recreation. Dancing is conducted in many places. The commercial dance halls attract large numbers of people. The popularity of dancing attests its value as a means of enjoyment and sociability.

Commercial dance halls, such as dance palaces and pavilions, the dine and dance places, roadhouses and pleasure-boat types, and the taxi-dance halls, are the centers of most of the problems of control, although difficulties may arise in almost any place that is without proper safeguards.

The taxi-dance hall is one of the newest of all commercial dance halls. The girls are employed to dance with the patrons on a ticket-a-dance basis. The taxi-dancer is in the game for all that she can get out of it. Hence, exploitation is uppermost. She uses her sex appeal as an aid in her occupation. All types of patrons are served. Because of the peculiar problems connected with the institution, cities have found it necessary to add special clauses to the dance hall ordinances designed to control this type of dance place. But the chief controls come from the management and the taxi-dancers themselves, chiefly in their own interest.

The problems of controlling commercial dance halls are numerous. Municipal and county dance hall ordinances are the usual legislative controls. Such ordinances pertain to the licensing of halls and the posting of said licenses and regulations, minimum age of admittance, conditions under which minors may attend, closing hours, Sunday regulation, lighting and ventilation of premises, conduct of dancers and types of dancing that are tabooed, and the means and methods of enforcement. The difficulties of enforcement are numerous. In the larger cities, police departments have special dance hall details, whose job it is to enforce the law. The best results are obtained when the proprietors and managers of public (commercial) dance halls cooperate with the police in maintaining order and in enforcing the dance hall ordinance. Municipal dance halls, or dance places operated on a nonprofit basis by civic-minded groups, are usually the most wholesome places in which to dance. A constructive program of community control involves not only the regulation of commercial dance halls, but the provision of places in which people may dance in accordance with the best standards and with adequate supervision.

Many sports have become highly commercialized. Baseball, football, bowling, horse racing, ice or roller skating, boxing, wrestling, pool and billiard, and a variety of others are widely supported sports that have become commercialized because of their popularity. Among these, bowling is one of the most popular indoor sports.

It is not necessary to enumerate the problems associated with the various types of commercial amusements. If properly controlled and supervised, commercial amusements are assets in a community and provide a wide variety of recreation for large segments of the population. If not controlled, they can become sources of trouble. Solomon [17] contends that the low-grade amusements are the types that cause the chief difficulty from the point of view of delinquency. Low grade of entertainment or low standards, indifference or incompetence of managers, and a lack of supervision and control open the way for difficulties in behavior. The situation is especially deleterious when juveniles are able to obtain liquor or drugs in or near these places. Drinking or the use of drugs may be an accompanying activity, especially after attending shows, dances, and other types of commercial amusements.

It is not all a matter of management and control, for certain types of people who patronize such places cause much of the trouble. Amusement centers are the mecca for all kinds of men and women with diverse purposes. Unscrupulous adults mingle with minors and prey upon them. Some commercial centers are used as recruiting places for houses of prostitution and vice dens. Loneliness and the lack of emotional satisfaction elsewhere drive individuals to seek this type of association. The innocent and naïve, in their desperation, become victims of all kinds of exploitation. Lacking proper facilities for meeting and entertaining boy friends, young girls, in particular, are often the victims of unscrupulous exploiters.

SCHOOLS, CHURCHES, AND YOUTH-SERVING AGENCIES

It is not the function of this section to discuss the problems connected with our schools, churches, and youth serving agencies. Their place in society is well established. They are recognized as

17 Ben Solomon, *Juvenile Delinquency: Practical Prevention* (Peekskill, New York: Youth Service, Inc., 1947).

some of the most constructive institutions and agencies in society. Their influence in preventing delinquency will be indicated in Part Three.

Apart from the home, the major responsibility for the training of children and young people rests with these institutions and organizations. Many functions formerly performed by the family have been transferred to community institutions. Formal education is now considered the major responsibility of schools, and religious education is the major responsibility of churches. Neither, of course, can properly perform their designated functions without the co-operation of the home. We usually think of them as constructive agencies, and that is what they are; but, when they fail to perform their designated functions, they may become, by virtue of their negligence, contributors to delinquency.

It should be noted at the outset that by far the majority of those who go to school, attend churches, and are a part of groups work and community recreation agencies have a wholesome experience. That some individuals turn out to be antisocial in their behavior is not necessarily due to neglect on the part of community institu-tions. No matter how effective community institutions may be in the performance of their functions, they cannot be expected to over-come all the undesirable influences of home and community condi-tions, personality defects, and gangs.

Unsatisfactory School Experience and Maladjusted Juveniles. The American system of education has developed rapidly and is one of the finest in the world. The school enrollment during the past half century has increased from slightly over 15 million in 1900 to almost 30 million by mid-century. Approximately a million persons are engaged in teaching and school administrative work. The total annual expenditure for public school education is about 5 billion dollars, and the cost is rising each year. It is not the purpose here to evaluate the school system or to describe its problems. Of the millions of children who have gone through our school system, most of them have acquired practical and useful education, and the school experience was satisfactory. But there are some problem areas. Some children have unsatisfactory school experience, or they are decidedly maladjusted in school. They may be maladjusted indi-viduals, and the problems which they create in school are simply a part of the general problem of maladjustment. Sometimes the seri-ous behavior difficulties begin at school.

The school is an important agency, together with other agencies, to help adjust individuals to society so that they may build up self-respect, self-confidence, and a successful orientation to life. To accomplish these and other purposes, many services are performed in the classroom by the teachers or by special facilities provided by schools. Schools must be prepared to deal with problem children, have special classes and schools for certain types of problem cases, and provide counseling and other services to meet the special needs of some children.[18]

The Gluecks,[19] in comparing 500 delinquent boys with 500 nondelinquent boys, found considerable differences in these groups of boys in their school status, retardation, subject preferences, scholarship and achievement, attitude toward school, relation to schoolmates, maladaptive behavior, and truancy. It was found that the delinquents drop out of school about one year earlier than the nondelinquents; they attend more schools, which is indicative of greater mobility of the families of delinquents; they repeat more grades, consequently are more retarded; more than twice as many delinquents were placed in special classes; they dislike such subjects as arithmetic, English, languages, and social studies, but prefer manual arts subjects; and they have poorer scholarship achievement records. The slower progress in school, poorer scholarship, fewer preferences and more dislikes, and the greater scatter of achievement all point to the greater antipathy for school on the part of the delinquents. Not being able or willing to learn as readily as the nondelinquents, they feel inferior, resent restrictions, and in general lack interest. The delinquents are also more vague about academic and vocational ambitions, and they do not get along very well with their schoolmates.

The Gluecks found that the delinquents showed marked maladaptive behavior in school at an earlier age. For instance, almost a third of the delinquents as compared with only a twelfth of the nondelinquents misbehaved before they were 8 years old. Altogether, 478 of the 500 delinquents as compared with only 86 of the nondelinquents persistently or seriously misconducted themselves at school, including such forms of behavior as truancy, stealing, mischievousness, disobedience, defiance, stubbornness, lying, smoking, and sexual deviation. So, despite similarity of age and general intelligence, and the time at which they entered school, the delin-

---

18 Cf. Edward H. Stulken, "Schools and the Delinquency Problem," *The Journal of Criminal Law, Criminology, and Police Science,* Vol. 43, No. 5 (January-February, 1953).

19 Sheldon and Eleanor Glueck, *Unraveling Juvenile Delinquency* (New York: The Commonwealth Fund, 1950), Chapter XII, "The Boy in School."

quents were markedly more retarded in school and misbehaved more extensively than did the nondelinquents.

Kvaraceus [20] calls attention to the frustrating experiences in schools. Delinquents or predelinquents are often enmeshed in unwholesome, unsatisfactory, unhappy, and frustrating situations. More than half of the children referred to the Passaic (New Jersey) Children's Bureau came from a span of grades 6 to 10, inclusive. Almost all of them had repeated one or more grades, girls repeating more grades than boys. Almost without exception they had received low grades. Thus, scholastic failure or near failure characterized most of the juvenile offenders. One third had been truant before being referred to the Bureau for some misdemeanor. Two thirds expressed a marked dislike for school or for some person connected with the school, and one fifth had unsatisfactory social adjustments. About three fourths had moved and had transferred from one school to another at least once. A large proportion had left school as soon as they reached the "leaving age" of 16. Most of them did not go beyond the junior high school. Kvaraceus concludes that the extremely frustrating situations either preceded or accompanied undesirable behavior, all of which indicates that the school plays an active part in shaping the reaction patterns of children. For many maladjusted and potentially delinquent children, going to school often is just another frustrating and unhappy experience.

It is possible to discover symptoms of behavior problems fairly early in a child's life. Wickman's [21] study of children's behavior problems as rated by teachers and mental hygienists indicates that behavior problems can be observed, even though the observers do not agree with respect to the seriousness of the problems. Teachers tend to list traits that are serious from a disciplinary standpoint and in terms of moral taboos. The fifty traits are listed in the following order, from the most serious to the least significant: heterosexual activity, stealing, masturbation, obscene notes and talk, untruthfulness, truancy, impertinence and defiance, cruelty and bullying,

---

20 William C. Kvaraceus, *Juvenile Delinquency and the School* (New York: World Book Co., 1945).

21 E. K. Wickman, *Children's Behavior and Teachers' Attitudes* (1928). See résumé of the comparative ratings of the relative seriousness of 50 common behavior problems of children as given by teachers and mental hygienists, as obtained by Wickman, in Paul H. Landis, *Social Policies in the Making* (Boston: D. C. Heath and Co., 1952), 174-175. For a series of papers on delinquency and the schools by well-known authorities, see Nelson B. Henry, Editor, *Juvenile Delinquency and the Schools.* The Forty-Seventh Yearbook of the National Society for the Study of Education (Chicago: University of Chicago Press, 1948). For an intensive study of schools as related to delinquency, see Esther Grace Nolan, *School Factors Related to Delinquency* (Doctor of Education dissertation, University of Southern California, Los Angeles, June, 1950).

cheating, destroying school material, disobedience, unreliableness, temper tantrums, lack of interest in work, profanity, impudence and rudeness, laziness, smoking, enuresis, nervousness, disorderliness in class, unhappy and depressed, easily discouraged, selfishness, carelessness in work, inattention, quarrelsomeness, suggestible, resentfulness, tardiness, physical coward, stubbornness, domineering, slovenly in appearance, sullenness, fearfulness, suspiciousness, thoughtlessness, attracting attention, unsocialness, dreaminess, imaginative lying, interrupting, inquisitiveness, overcritical of others, tattling, whispering, sensitiveness, restlessness, and shyness. The mental hygienists considered traits of special importance in terms of the long-range effect on personality development; hence their selection of the above-mentioned items was in a somewhat different order.

Teachers and school officials are in a special position to detect behavior disorders. The retarded or failing students need attention; otherwise they drop out prematurely and create various other problems. When children are adequately dealt with during the early stages of maladjustment, the problems can be more easily solved than later in the process. The problems encountered are numerous, for personality conditions and environmental pressures sometimes make it difficult for schools to overcome their detrimental effects. Furthermore, schools are not always equipped to deal with problem cases. The curriculum is sometimes not adjusted to the needs and interests of pupils, teachers are inadequately trained for the job, buildings and equipment are meager, classrooms are overcrowded, and many schools are not equipped to deal with special types of maladjusted children, including the behavior problem cases.

It is difficult to correlate the relationship between school experience and delinquency. Investigations of delinquents have revealed that many of them have had unfortunate experiences at school and many of them dislike going to school. Since nearly every child in America, except the few who are incapable of doing so, goes through a public or private school, the school has a special responsibility to create a wholesome atmosphere and a constructive program of education. Deviations from normal behavior should be observed by teachers and school administrators, especially by the counselors, and the school system should provide the child with corrective influences that lead to normal social participation.

Truancy and Out-of-School Youth. By far the majority of school pupils attend school regularly. After an extensive study of the problem of nonattendance, especially the children involved in serious truancy, the Citizens' Committee of New York City [22] concluded that most children eligible for school attendance seem to go to school when well and their parents seem to want their children to go to school and cooperate in assuring attendance. Over a period of nearly a half century (1900-1901 to 1947-1948), the attendance rate in the New York Schools (public and private) ranged from 85.7 per cent (the lowest point) in 1903-1904 to 93.3 during the 1929-1930 school year (the highest point). During thirty years the attendance rate was over 90 per cent of the enrollment. In spite of "attendance pressure" on the part of school personnel during some of the years, attendance rates have fluctuated somewhat but have changed relatively little in actual percentages since 1900. The constant expansion of an attendance bureau did not seem to reduce the nonattendance rate a great deal. This may be accounted for in part by the fact that the majority of the absentees are either ill or absent for other legal reasons.

The chief problem of absences from school is the relatively small percentage of pupils who are excessively and illegally absent, commonly known as truants. The term "truancy" is usually not regarded as synonymous with "running away," but is used to describe prolonged absence from school with the knowledge and sometimes consent of parents or guardians.[23] Truancy *per se* may not be a serious problem, but it frequently is a part of a series of difficulties. The process may start with some form of personal or social maladjustment, unsatisfactory school experience, early misbehavior at school, and occasional absences from school; which is followed by more serious truancy and misconduct. If the process is not stopped, the child's violations of law will bring him to the attention of law enforcement agencies, and a repetition of offenses will require juvenile court action and probation supervision. The Gluecks found that truancy was the most frequent sign of maladjustment among the delinquents who misbehaved in school and that misbehavior among delinquents starts earlier than among nondelinquents, and occurs more frequently.

Many studies have been made of truancy and the literature on the subject is voluminous, yet few investigators have concentrated their efforts to discover causes. Attempts to learn from the available

---

22 *Children Absent from School,* a report and a program by the Citizens' Committee on Children of New York City, Inc., 1949.

23 The *California Education Code* (State of California, 1949, Article 12, Section 16834) defines a truant as "any child between the ages of 8 and 15 (inclusive) who has been absent from school without valid cause more than three days or tardy more than three days." If a child has been reported as truant three or more times, he is regarded as an "habitual truant."

data the causes of unlawful absences from school have been for the most part unsuccessful, for studies have not dealt with etiological factors, except in a very general way. Those who have been concerned with causation have emphasized school conditions as responsible for much of truancy. That the school plays a conspicuous part in the process is evident, but there are also other basic factors that must not be overlooked. Studies have revealed such unsatisfactory school situations, which may have a bearing on truancy, as overcrowded conditions in some schools, with too large classes; excessive distance from school, as in rural areas; the lack of understanding of the needs of children or the lack of attention given to the problem cases, and the counterpart, the lack of interest in school or dislike for certain teachers or subjects on the part of pupils; an inflexible curriculum, with insufficient courses for those interested mainly in practical and applied rather than the more academic subjects; fear of punishment because of tardiness, misconduct, or failure; embarrassment because of shoddy or ill-fitting clothes; and frustrations growing out of low marks, repetition of grades, and inability to keep up with their classmates.

Comparative studies of truants and nontruants are more likely to reveal differential factors, both personal and environmental, of the two groups. Charles J. Browning and Vernon A. Snowbarger have recently made such studies.[24] Browning made a comparative study of two delinquent groups (62 auto thieves and 57 truants, all wards of the Los Angeles Juvenile Court) and a control group (58 perfect attenders in school). The purpose of the study was to differentiate two subgroups of delinquents and a nondelinquent group. These groups were matched for age, sex (all boys), school, grade, race and cultural factors (all boys had American-born parents). Data for comparing these groups were obtained from court records, school records, and home interviews. Each boy was given the California Test of Personality; the mother completed a marital adjustment, family solidarity, and father participation scale; and the interviewer, with the aid of the parents, completed a socio-economic status scale and a schedule of items identifying each family in detail. Among the many items of findings, it was discovered that the perfect attenders had significantly better scores than the delinquent groups on most variables of family life and personality, and that the

---

24 Charles J. Browning, "Differential Social Relationship and Personality Factors of Parents and Boys in Two Delinquent Groups and One Nondelinquent Group," Ph.D. Dissertation, University of Southern California, 1954; Vernon A. Snowbarger, "Factors Associated with Truancy among Boys in Selected Junior High Schools of Los Angeles County," Ph.D. Dissertation, University of Southern California, 1954.

truant group was the least favored. The null hypothesis could be rejected at the one per cent level in most comparisons of the truancy group with the perfect attenders, but frequently only at the 5 per cent level when comparing the auto theft group with the perfect attenders. The truants experience significantly less favorable situations or had significantly lower scores in such matters as: frequency of broken homes, education of parents, number of parents employed, socio-economic status, marital adjustment of parents, father participation in family life, family solidarity, sibling position, family relations, school relations, mental maturity, reading and arithmetic achievement, personal and social adjustment. Snowbarger compared 90 truants with 90 nontruants, matched for sex, school attended, school grade placement, and ethnic background. He used the California Test of Personality and a family interview schedule to obtain the data. The California Test of Personality as applied to the junior high school pupils revealed that the mean score was significantly higher for nontruants than for truants in all three sections—personal adjustment, social adjustment, and in total life adjustment. The nontruants rated the marital adjustment of their parents significantly higher than did the nontruants, and they also had a considerably better school, family, and community adjustment record. The truants attended more schools, had lower I.Q.'s, lower average grade, lower achievement in reading and arithmetic, poorer citizenship rating by teachers, more conflicts with teachers, less interest in school subjects, fewer friends among classmates, held fewer school offices, and had a greater desire to quit school. At home, they experienced more conflicts, less affection between members of the family, less companionship with parents, less cooperation and enjoyment as a family group, more of them ran away from home, and there was less mother-son attachment. In the community, the truants were less adjusted, attended church less frequently, more of them lived in the "zone in transition," associated more with law violators, and did not regard their neighborhood very highly. Significant differences were found between truants and nontruants on certain general characteristics, such as housing, mobility, employment and income, and broken homes.

The out-of-school adolescents constitute in many ways a special problem group, as was pointed out in the preceding chapter. This group has left school and taken employment for the most part, even though some may be out of school only temporarily. In some states all juveniles under a specified age, if they are physically and mentally fit and otherwise not exempted, must attend school for a specified number of hours per week even though otherwise permanently employed. Since there are many reasons for dropping out of school, it is difficult to generalize about the adolescents who do not attend school.

A. B. Hollingshead [25] made a special study of the adolescents who had dropped out of school. Of the 345 young people who had stopped attending, 240 were in class V (the lowest group), 129 in class IV, only 12 in class III, and none in classes I and II. Hollingshead maintains that the relationship of the class structure to school attendance or nonattendance is a two-way affair. On the one hand, the class and family to which the child belongs furnish him with certain beliefs about the school system and condition his attitude toward going to school. On the other hand, the school system, including the teachers and administrators, and Elmtowners in general provided pupils in the several classes with differential attitudes toward the school system. In analyzing the withdrawal process, Hollingshead studied not only the relationship of withdrawees to their class system, but such factors as sex, grade completed, seasonal factors, family conditions, the withdrawee's school record, and his own reasons for leaving school. The three most common explanations given by them for leaving school were: (1) economic need, (2) peer isolation and discrimination, and (3) mistreatment by teachers. Economic need does not necessarily mean that the family is in dire financial want, but boys, in particular, desire to own automobiles and to have other luxuries.

The policies of modern schools toward truants and out-of-school youth have changed from one of coercion, punishment, and institutionalization of the more serious cases to one of understanding the child and dealing with the underlying difficulties. The old-fashioned truant officers have been replaced by well-trained and sympathetic officers, visiting teachers, clinical psychologists, and psychiatrists. They use the case-study instead of the legalistic approach, studying the child in the light of his own background. It is recognized that any attempt to study nonattendance is difficult and that progress has been slow in improving the methods of treatment. Preventive programs are scarcely underway. [26]

---

[25] *Elmtown's Youth* (New York: John Wiley & Sons, 1949), Part IV. See especially the statistics of class position in relation to the continuance in or dropping out of school, p. 330. See previous chapter for discussion of the class system in relation to companionship, cliques, and dating.

[26] For brief summaries of the nonattendance problem and methods of treatment, consult Walter S. Monroe, "School Attendance," *Encyclopedia of Educational Research* (New York: The Macmillan Co., 1941); Florence Poole, "School Social Services," *Social Work Year Book of 1954,* Russell H. Kurtz, Editor (New York: American Association of Social Workers, 1954), 463-470; Ralph B. Winn, Editor, *The Encyclopedia of Child Guidance* (New York: Philosophical Library, 1943), 438-439; and recent issues of edu-

Lack or Inadequacy of Religious Instruction and Experience. There is considerable difference of opinion of the relation of religion and church attendance to the prevention of delinquency. No positive conclusions may be drawn with respect to the correlation of religion with delinquency, because of few authentic studies on this subject. When religious ideals are firmly believed in and religious observances are adherred to, they can be effective means of controlling human behavior.

According to the 1953 edition of the *Yearbook of American Churches,* the annual reference work published by the National Council of Churches, 251 religious bodies had a total of 92,277,129 members, representing 59 per cent of the population of Continental United States, as compared with only 36 per cent membership in 1900. It is not known how many people attend church services and other activities, but the 1953 report indicates that 231 religious bodies reported Sunday or Sabbath School enrollment of 32,638,879 persons in 257,318 schools. The enrollment in weekday religious classes and parochial schools is not given. These statistics indicate the extent to which churches are reaching the people.

The number of delinquents that belong to churches and attend church schools or other activities is not known. The few studies that have reported the relation of delinquents to churches show a wide variation in membership and attendance. Institutionalized cases show a much lower church affiliation than the cases handled by police authorities, and recidivists have a lower church affiliation rate than first offenders. Studies of reformatory inmates have indicated that most of them had only nominal relation with churches and church organizations, and few attended regularly prior to their placement in institutions. The Gluecks, in their study of *500 Criminal Careers* (1930, pp. 131-132), found only 8.5 per cent of their reformatory men attending church regularly before commitment, 88.5 per cent were irregular in attendance, and 3 per cent reported that they were nonchurchgoers. When a prison population claims extensive church connections, it is obvious that some fake their statements. The church is a positive force in the lives of many people, but when juveniles have only a nominal affiliation with church organizations or do not attend church functions, religion cannot easily exert a positive influence in their lives, except through the mores and standards of society that receive their support from religious institutions and individuals.

Several investigators, who have analyzed clinical cases or juve-

---

cational journals. For a journalistic story of the role of a female "hookey cop," see Florence McGehee, *Please Excuse Johnny* (New York: The Macmillan Co., 1952).

niles who come into contact with the police and other law enforcing agencies, have indicated that a much larger proportion of them have attended churches than is usually assumed. Many of these are first offenders and not all of them have been in serious difficulties.

Kvaraceus [27] studied 761 delinquents composed of 563 boys and 198 girls, referred to the Passaic (New Jersey) Children's Bureau during the preceding five-year period. Of these, 67.59 per cent were Catholics, 22.58 per cent were Protestants, and 1.99 per cent were Jews. With few exceptions, these boys and girls claimed some type of church connection. In 594 cases information was available as to the extent to which they actually attended church. Of these, 54.21 per cent claimed that they attended church regularly, 20.37 per cent were irregular in attendance, and 25.43 per cent never attended. Very slight differences between boys and girls were noted in church attendance. It must be remembered that these statistics are based on what they claimed and that the study covered a wide range of cases. Furthermore, in a highly urbanized area, especially in slums and blighted regions, the rate of delinquency would be relatively high despite the efforts made by churches to reach the underprivileged children. Churches located in these areas are likely to have higher proportions of delinquents among their constituents than those in the better residential areas. Otherwise, no one religious group is disproportionately represented in the delinquency population.

William W. Wattenberg [28] reports a study of 2,137 boys who were interviewed on complaint by the Detroit police in 1946. Among the various questions asked, the police officers inquired about the frequency of church attendance, if any. The responses, in terms of percentages, were as follows: regular 43.56, occasional 25.54, seldom 15.86, never 14.15, and not stated .89. Of the original group, 672 got into trouble again in 1947. The church attendance of nonrepeaters, in terms of percentages, were: regular 46.2, occasional 24.8, seldom 14.2, never 13.8, and not stated 1.0. The corresponding percentages of repeaters were: 37.8; 27.1; 19.5; 14.9; and not stated .07. An effort was made to ascertain the relationships between church attendance, character of neighborhood, and intactness of homes of the boys interviewed. While it was not possible to untangle the interlocking patterns of these variables, a consider-

27 William C. Kvaraceus, "Delinquent Behavior and Church Attendance," *Sociology and Social Research,* Vol. XXVIII (March-April, 1944), 284-289; see also *Juvenile Delinquency and the School* (1945), *op. cit.,* Chapter X, "The Community and Character Education."

28 "Church Attendance and Juvenile Misconduct," *Sociology and Social Research,* Vol. XXXIV (January-February, 1950), 195-202.

able proportion of the boys came from broken homes and poor neighborhoods, which seems to indicate that factors apart from church attendance or nonattendance have a considerable bearing on the behavior of juveniles. It may be assumed that when low church attendance is associated with broken homes, poor neighborhoods, and other undesirable factors, delinquency is likely to be higher than in the relatively normal areas in which church attendance is fairly regular.

When boys and girls who have already gotten into difficulties are questioned by police or court officials regarding their church connections or membership in youth serving agencies, some may claim active participation when actually they have had only occasional contacts. If the replies to questions regarding church attendance are not verified by the churches in which they claim affiliation, the data may not give an accurate account of their participation in church activities. The same is true of claims of membership in youth serving agencies on the part of delinquents.

Failure of Youth-Serving Agencies to Reach Delinquents. Youth-serving agencies have reached millions of boys and girls and young people. According to M. M. Chambers,[29] the Boy Scouts of America, Girl Scouts, Camp Fire Girls, Boys' Clubs of America, 4-H Clubs, Future Farmers of America, Young Men's Christian Association, Young Women's Christian Association, International Society of Christian Endeavor, Methodist Youth Fellowship, Catholic Mission Crusade, Sodality of Our Lady, and National Jewish Welfare Board alone had nearly fourteen million members in 1945-1946, and the American Junior Red Cross had a membership of nearly twenty million. Not all of these are juveniles, but there are many other types of youth-serving agencies not listed. These organizations try to enrich the lives of the members, to develop personality and character, and to help juveniles make adjustment to life situations. It is not their primary function to deal with delinquents or to prevent delinquency, although that is frequently mentioned as one of the purposes. During recent years efforts have been made in some of the larger cities to provide special leadership and organizational opportunities for the children in the under-privileged areas. Considerable sums of money have been earmarked for this purpose by community chest and other fund raising organizations, and public agencies have made a special effort to reach the people

---

29 *Youth Serving Agencies: National Nongovernmental Associations* (Washington, D. C.: American Council on Education, third edition, 1948). Compare *Social Work Year Book. 1954* (New York: American Association of Social Workers, 1954).

in the underprivileged regions. In some cities, the police department, and other law enforcing agencies have set up special programs to reach the potential delinquents. Yet, in spite of all of the various efforts to reach the delinquents or the predelinquents, many of them remain untouched by these agencies.

The study on recreation and delinquency by the Chicago Recreation Commission, mentioned earlier in the chapter, revealed that the official delinquents in all areas studied did not participate so extensively as the nondelinquents in supervised recreation. The range of participation in recreation by delinquent boys in the five areas was from 34.8 to 61 per cent; whereas the proportion of the nondelinquent boys who participated ranged from 63.2 to 95.5 per cent. As stated previously, when delinquents did go to centers of supervised recreation, they usually concentrated on the games room or participated in active sports. They tended to select activities that have little supervision and usually went to only one type of recreation agency, although they sometimes traveled a considerable distance to get to the desired place. The delinquents go to commercial amusements more extensively than to centers of supervised recreation. It is evident from this study that the recreation and youth-serving agencies did not reach a large proportion of the delinquents. This is one of the problems of organized recreation and group work.

In summary, the community has a responsibility for the conduct of its young people. By neglecting to provide adequate community institutions to meet the needs of youth, the public may be responsible for misconduct through negligence. Inadequate provision of community recreation through public and semipublic agencies, and the inadequate functioning of schools and churches, may be the occasion for youth to seek enjoyment and amusement elsewhere. Commercial recreation concerns have capitalized upon the leisure and pleasure interests of youth and to some extent have abused the opportunity afforded them. The exploitation of pleasure is especially prevalent in places where social controls are lacking or inadequate to meet the situation.

It must be recognized that the correlations between community institutions and delinquency involve elements of conjecture. Little proof has so far been established of the influence exerted by either the inadequate functioning of generally recognized constructive institutions or the negative effects of uncontrolled commercial amusements. The criteria of measurement and the methods of research are beset with many difficulties. Further research is needed to ascertain more exact correlations between the various recreation activities and conduct.

QUESTIONS AND PROJECTS

For Class Discussion and Research

1. Compare rural and urban communities as to integration and social controls.

2. Study a selected community from the point of view of the institutional provisions for the youth.

3. In what ways is an inadequate program of community recreation for the young a cause of delinquency?

4. What problems of community recreation are revealed by the Chicago study of *Recreation and Delinquency?*

5. Does participation in supervised recreation tend to reduce delinquency?

6. What are the special values of an intensive program of group work agencies in providing programs on the primary group basis?

7. How may the lack of interest in supervised recreation be overcome?

8. What aspects of the school program may create frustration situations for the pupils? Discuss unsatisfactory school situations in relation to maladjustment of children.

9. Enumerate the types of behavior that may lead to truancy if not adjusted. Enumerate the causes of truancy from school.

10. Discuss truancy as a symptom of maladjustment.

11. Discuss problems of the out-of-school youth.

12. Discuss children's behavior problems in schools.

13. In what ways does the lack of religious and moral training affect the behavior of a child?

14. Make a comparative study of the religious affiliation of delinquents and nondelinquents.

15. Discuss commercial amusements in relation to children's behavior.

16. Are criminals movie made?

17. Analyze a community from the point of view of possible harmful amusement centers. By what standards can amusements be judged to determine their positive or negative effects?

18. Discuss recreation therapy for problem children.

19. Suggest ways of controlling commercial amusements to prevent them from contributing to delinquency.

SELECTED REFERENCES

BLUMER, HERBERT, AND PHILIP M. HAUSER, *Movies, Delinquency, and Crime* (New York: The Macmillan Co., 1933).

CARR, LOWELL J., *Delinquency Control* (New York: Harper & Brothers, 1951), Parts II-V.

CLINARD, MARSHALL B., "Secondary Community Influences and Juvenile Delinquency," *Annals of the Academy of Political and Social Science,* Vol. 261 (January, 1949), 42-54.

FORMAN, HENRY J., *Our Movie Made Children* (New York: The Macmillan Co., 1933).

HOLLINGSHEAD, A. B., *Elmtown's Youth* (New York: John Wiley & Sons, Inc., 1949), Part IV.

KVARACEUS, WILLIAM C., *Juvenile Delinquency and the School* (New York: World Book Co., 1945).

LANDIS, PAUL H., *Social Policies in the Making.* A Dynamic View of Social Problems (New York: D. C. Heath and Co., 1952).

McKAY, HENRY D., "The Neighborhood and Child Conduct," *Annals, ibid.,* 32-41.

NEUMEYER, MARTIN H. AND ESTHER S., *Leisure and Recreation* (New York: A. S. Barnes and Co., 1936 and 1949).

SHANAS, ETHEL, Director, with collaboration of Catherine E. Dunning, *Recreation and Delinquency* (Chicago: Chicago Recreation Commission, 1942).

Social Work Year Book, 1954 (New York: American Association of Social Workers, 1954).

SOLOMON, BEN, *Juvenile Delinquency: Practical Prevention* (Peekskill, New York: Youth Service, Inc., 1947).

STROUP, HERBERT H., *Community Welfare Organization* (New York: Harper & Brothers, 1952).

TANNENBAUM, FRANK, *Crime and the Community* (New York: Columbia University Press, 1951).

TEETERS, NEGLEY K., AND JOHN O. REINEMANN, *The Challenge of Delinquency* (New York: Prentice-Hall, Inc., 1950).

TODD, ARTHUR J., Editor, *Chicago Recreation Survey* (Chicago Recreation Commission, 1937-1940), Volumes I-V.

WRENN, C. GILBERT, AND D. L. HARLEY, *Time On Their Hands.* A Report on Leisure, Recreation, and Young People (Washington, D. C.: American Council on Education, 1941).

IX

POPULATION FACTORS AND CULTURAL DIFFERENCES

Population problems are numerous and have far-reaching effects. The growth and decline of groups, differential birth and death rates, composition and distribution (age, sex, race, nationality), social stratification and division, migration and social mobility of the population, and the effects of these on society are sources of various kinds of social problems. Closely associated with population factors are the cultural differences and conflicts of groups of people.

The population of the United States more than doubled during the first half of the present century. The total population was 150,697,361 in 1950, a density of 50.7 per square mile of land area; and, according to the estimates of the Bureau of the Census (August 10, 1953), it has exceeded the 160,000,000 mark and will probably be close to 175,000,000 by 1960. During the first three decades of the present century, the growth of the population was accentuated by the influx of 18,546,306 immigrants. During the last two decades only 1,563,470 came. Immigration, of course, is always partly offset by emigration. Nevertheless, we still had 10,147,000 foreign-born whites in 1950, as compared with 11,419,198 in 1940, a reduction of 11.1 per cent. Besides the volume of immigration during the early part of the present century, the composition of the immigrant group changed considerably in terms of national origins. Increasingly, the new immigrants came from southern and eastern Europe with markedly different cultural background than was true of the earlier immigrants. The differences in ethnic and cultural backgrounds made it difficult to assimilate large segments of the new immigrants. Hence, cultural conflicts and segregation occurred in many places. During recent years many of the immigrants have stemmed from world upheaval areas. The refugee problem has become world wide in scope and intensity, and the United States will increasingly become the mecca of dispossessed groups.

The increasing birth rate has added considerably to the growth of the population since 1940. The total number of births per year has exceeded three and a half million during the postwar years and the birth rate per 1,000 population has ranged from 24 to 27. On the other hand, the death rate, especially the infant mortality rate, has been declining. The child population under 10 years of age increased by more than eight million from 1940 to 1950, representing an increase from 16.1 to 19.6 per cent of the total population. It is evident that the adolescent population will increase considerably during the 1950's, also later if the birth rate continues to remain high.

Another important change in the population during recent years has been the excessive mobility of the people. Modern migration movements have far surpassed all known movements of past ages. The internal migration has resulted in several shifts in the population. At the beginning of the present century, the United States was still largely rural. In 1950, 64.0 per cent of the population lived in cities, using the new definition of urban, or 58.9 per cent according to the previous definition. Furthermore, the 168 standard metropolitan areas had 84,500,680 inhabitants, or more than half the population of Continental United States. The twelve most highly urbanized areas (each 1,000,000 or more inhabitants) had a combined population of 37,817,068, or about one fourth of the total population. The West Coast, the Southwest, Florida, and a few Eastern and Northcentral states have experienced the most rapid growth of population since 1940. These highly urbanized areas, with excessive mobility of the population, have experienced the greatest amount of social change and disorganization.[1]

The population changes have affected all phases of life. The

---

[1] For further details of population changes, see the author's book on *Social Problems and the Changing Society* (1953), Chapters III-V.

implications of these changes from the point of view of delinquency have not been fully explored. For convenience, the conflicting and overlapping population and cultural factors that may condition delinquency are discussed under age and sex factors; race, nationality, and other elements producing heterogeneity of the population; the problem of minority groups, especially those growing out of segregation and discrimination; social mobility and transiency, and the changing composition of the population; the succession of culture groups and culture conflicts; and the broader conflicts between the delinquents and the community.

POPULATION FACTORS

Age, sex, race, and similar population factors can hardly be considered as direct causes of delinquency. But if population factors are accompanied by deviant environmental pressures and influences, they may condition the incidence of delinquency. The composition of the delinquent population was discussed in connection with the extent and distribution of delinquency (Chapter II), wherein lies its chief significance. It is not necessary to repeat the data here, except to call attention to the fact that, in the interplay between a person and the environment, the age and sex of the individual, as well as the race and nationality background, constitute conditions that affect conduct. If there is a mixed population in the community, with a variety of heterogeneous elements, the situation becomes more complicated. Mobility and transiency create conditions of instability and bring about changes in the composition of the population of the area.

The changes in the population, and the accompanying economic and social changes, often bring about a disruption of the established folkways and mores and, frequently, a disintegration of social institutions. When the transitions are rapid and thoroughgoing, society loses its control over individuals. Social disorganization and personal disintegration may follow. Excessive immigration or internal migration disturbs the patterns of behavior and the agencies or means of social control.

In a relatively stable situation, the people tend to conform in their behavior to the folkways, mores, laws, beliefs, and standards of their society. Individual differentiation, of course, produces differences in conduct, as was indicated in the earlier chapters. Individuals differ in many respects, and their responses to situations vary considerably. But when there are culture conflicts and a confusion of mores occurs, deviations are likely to be extensive.

The United States is full of minority or subculture groups. As people move from one group to another, even on the same cultural or economic plane, they encounter different standards of conduct. They sometimes have great difficulty in becoming reconciled and adjusted to these standards. Consequently, both personal and social conflicts ensue. Although children and young people more quickly than adults adjust themselves to changing conditions, they are apt to become victims of the confused and disorganized situation. Delinquency is more prevalent in such areas than in the more stable communities.

Age and Sex as Conditioning Factors. The juvenile court statistics and the reports of arrests *(Uniform Crime Reports)* show that the peak period of law violation from the point of view of age ranges from the early adolescent period to young adulthood and the ratio of boys' cases to girls' cases ranges from 4 to one of juvenile court cases to approximately 10 to one of the arrest cases. It is evident from the best available statistics that in so far as known delinquents (official and unofficial cases) are concerned, the problem of law violation is fundamentally one of adolescent boys. (See Chapter II).

Although the juvenile courts handle only the age group specified by law as coming under their jurisdiction, and there is a considerable variation by states as to the minimum and maximum age levels, the courts reporting to the Children's Bureau have repeatedly indicated that the adolescent age is the chief period of deviant behavior.

Using the total number of offenders in the different age brackets does not give a true picture of the relative extent of delinquency in an age group, since the statistics are not correlated with the age distribution of the population. Sellin[2] has called attention to the fact that if we consider the proportion of youth in the adolescent age group, the participation of this group in the total offenses dealt with by police and judicial agents seems relatively small. However, this report was published in 1940 when more than twelve million individuals were in the age bracket from 15 to 19 inclusive, the largest group in any five-year age period. Since that time the population pyramid has changed considerably. In 1950, there were fewer than eleven million individuals in this age group, a reduction of 13 per cent since 1940, chiefly because of the relatively low birth rate during the depression period. The high birth rate since 1940 will greatly increase the relative proportion of adolescents, probably 40 to 50 per cent during the decade ending in 1960.

---

[2] Thorsten Sellin, *The Criminality of Youth* (Philadelphia: American Law Institute, 1940), 67-68.

Juvenile offenses must likewise be interpreted with respect to the types of laws that apply to them and the methods of handling cases. In addition to the laws that apply to all age groups, there is a variety of federal, state, and local laws that apply to juveniles only. This tends to increase the possibility of law violation. On the other hand, since many of the juvenile offenders, especially the very young and some first offenders, are handled informally and not reported in delinquency statistics, the official reports do not account for all cases of law violation by juveniles. Various studies of the ages of first offenders have been made to determine when children commit their first offenses. Even though the results of these studies are not uniform, it is obvious that deviant behavior begins much earlier than the official statistics of delinquency indicate.[3]

There is no particular age, more than any other age, in which certain biological or psychological conditions predispose individuals to delinquency, although puberty has been regarded as a period during which certain somatic and mental disturbances stealthily make their appearance. Closely related to the disorders of puberty are the growth crises that occur a little later. However, unless these are accompanied by deviant social reactions and conditions, they are not likely to cause serious disturbances in conduct. Delinquency increases with age, but after awhile the process of maturation tends to reduce the incidence of crime, according to the Gluecks. The fact that criminality reaches a peak during later adolescence and the early twenties has been explained in a variety of ways, none of which seems entirely satisfactory. Undoubtedly many factors contribute to the lessening of offenses after a certain age. With advancing age, individuals mature, frustrations tend to decrease, and better adjustments are made to deviant environmental conditions.

The period of youth represents a transition between the coming of biological manhood and the achievement of social maturity. When the growing physical strength, energy, and as yet ill-defined strivings and ambitions demand expression, and when inadequately inner or social controls have been established, youth may not always follow the socially approved channels.

The number of youths involved in assaults, and other forms of violence against persons, embezzlement and fraud, violations of narcotic drug laws, liquor law violations, drunkenness and drunken driving, organized vice, sex offenses other than rape, disorderly conduct, vagrancy, and gambling appears to be relatively small. On the other hand, youthful offenders are extensively involved in larceny,

---

3 Cf. Hans Von Hentig, *Crime: Causes and Conditions* (New York: McGraw-Hill Book Co., 1947), Chapter VI, "Age and Crime."

auto theft, robbery, burglary, receiving stolen property, and carrying dangerous weapons. There seems to be a progression in types of offenses as boys grow older, starting with minor offenses, then larceny, auto theft, and burglary, to robbery, carrying or possessing deadly weapons, rape and other sex offenses, sometimes forgery and counterfeiting; and, if the process is not checked, young adults may engage in assault, homicide, embezzlement and fraud, and similar crimes. The process may be arrested, however, and individuals may cease to commit crimes, or they may tend to commit fewer crimes as they grow older.

The difference in the male and female rates of crime is more difficult to explain. The statistics of crime may present an exaggerated picture; but, with the exception of such offenses as prostitution and soliciting, males have higher rates of crime than is true of females in nearly all categories of crime. Among the juveniles, girls have a higher rate of sex offenses, but boys lead in all other categories of delinquency. Girls also have fairly high rates in such categories as being ungovernable, running away, and truancy; but, in proportion to boys, fewer are involved in such offenses. Boys far exceed the girls in offenses against property (stealing, auto theft), acts of carelessness or mischief, and traffic violations.

There seems to be nothing inherent in the male that perforce predetermines his misconduct, although some writers have emphasized that the male has stronger desires, is more pugnacious, has greater strength, and is more active than the female. The environmental influences and conditions of living of males and females differ considerably. As Von Hentig[4] has pointed out, sex includes social status as well as personality conditions. Among adults, far more males than females are gainfully employed and face more economic burdens; whereas many females live in the protective isolation of household work. Males are more migratory, face more hazards, are given fewer preferences in nearly every stage of judicial procedure, and face other difficulties not encountered to the same degree by the females. These conditions, however, have been changing during recent years. The differences that still exist apply chiefly to adults rather than to children. Yet girls are more protected and restricted in their conduct than are boys, and they have fewer opportunities of law violations. These differences in conditions of living and social control, however, do not offer a full explanation of the sex differences in crime. More scientific studies are needed before definite conclusions can be reached.

---

4 *Ibid.,* Chapter V, "Sex and Crime."

Race, Nationality, and Heterogeneity of the Population. By race is usually meant a division of mankind possessing more or less uniform and constant traits transmitted by descent. As such, the continuity is largely of a physical type, such as features and color, carrying over inherited uniformities. However, during recent years race is increasingly being thought of as a biosocial group. Skin color and markedly different physical features are not sufficiently accurate bases of anthropologic grouping, but in crime statistics the common classification is white, Negro, and other non-whites. Nationality has reference chiefly to those of a common national origin, with emphasis on cultural rather than physical traits, although some nationality groups have fairly distinct physical characteristics. However, most nationality groups in America are mixed, both culturally and biologically, and the racial and nationality types overlap considerably. The Negro group is composed of people ranging from very dark to almost white mulattoes. The Mexican group, although classified as white, is composed of several racial strains. Some of the Mexicans and other Latin-American people are of mixed Spanish and Indian descent. In local crime statistics the Mexican, Mexican-Americans, and other Latin-American or Spanish-speaking groups are frequently lumped together.

According to Bonger,[5] there is very little authentic material on race and crime. In general, the available material is superficial. One of the difficulties in ascertaining the relationship between racial factors and crime rates is that race is intertwined with many other elements. The traditions and conditions of living of a particular group have much to do with their law-abiding or criminal tendencies.

The relative crime statistics of whites, Negroes, Indians, Chinese, and other races, as compiled by the Federal Bureau of Investigation *(Uniform Crime Reports),* and similar data compiled by the Children's Bureau, were presented in Chapter II. The arrests statistics pertain largely to adults, and the juvenile court data are somewhat limited in scope. But according to these reports, more than a fourth of all fingerprints sent to the Federal Bureau of Investigation are those of nonwhite groups, although only about a tenth of the total population is nonwhite, chiefly Negro. The percentage of child population in these groups is slightly higher. The proportion of nonwhites referred to juvenile courts is more than a fifth of the total, and nearly a third of the children in institutions are non-whites.

---

[5] William A. Bonger, *Race and Crime* (New York: Columbia University Press, 1943), 18. Translated from the Dutch by Margaret M. Hordyk.

Arthur L. Wood[6] summarizes computations of comparative crime statistics of majority and minority groups, but the data pertain chiefly to adults and were compiled for the most part during the depression years. The commitment rates of male felons per 100,000 males 15 years old and over were: 144 for the total, 117 for the whites, and 447 for the Negroes. The "old" immigrants who came from northern and western Europe had a lower rate than the "new" immigrants who came from the southern and eastern parts of Europe.[7]

The American Negro is by far the largest racial minority group and in many ways the most typically American in culture and background. In 1950, the Negro population was 14,890,000, which was 9.9 per cent of the total population. In 1953, a total of 1,791 cities over 2,500 in population reported 481,095 arrests of Negroes, or 26.9 per cent of the total number arrested in these cities.[8] It seems that ever since criminal statistics have been compiled, Negroes have registered a higher criminality rate than have white. This has been true in nearly every age group and in the various categories of crime. Various conclusions have been drawn as to the reasons for the relatively high rate of crime. Some have alleged that this group possesses certain inherent personality traits which lead to crime, but this claim has largely been refuted. The opposite broad theory that the crime rate is the result of the kind of environment in which a group lives has greater validity. Such factors as segregation and discrimination, cultural conflicts and hostile treatment, low economic and social status, inadequate education and training, the traditions of the group, and the reactions of individuals to these conditions explain a large part of the relatively high rate of crime. Unfortunately, few studies have delved into the possible underlying causes of Negro crime.

The Houston, Texas, and the Baltimore, Maryland, studies have

---

[6] "Minority-Group Criminality and Cultural Integration," *The Journal of Criminal Law and Criminology,* Vol. 37 (March-April, 1947), 498-510.

[7] Cf. Donald R. Taft, "Nationality and Crime," *American Sociological Review,* Vol. I, No. 5 (October, 1936), 724-736.

[8] *Uniform Crime Reports,* 1953 Annual Bulletin, Vol. XXIV, No. 2 (Washington, D. C.: United States Government Printing Office, 1954), 114. The relatively high percentage of arrests of Negroes may be due in part to difference in treatment of Negroes by law enforcement agencies. Compare Sidney Axelrad, "Negro and White Male Institutionalized Delinquents," *The American Journal of Sociology,* Vol. LVII (May, 1952), 569-574. While Axelrad limited his study to 300 institutionalized cases (179 Negroes and 121 white children), he found that "Negro children are committed younger, for less serious offenses, with fewer previous court appearances, and with less prior institutionalization." (p. 574). He also found that Negro children came from more unstable homes with more family pathologies.

revealed that the crime rates of both Negroes and whites vary by regions in a city and that the rates can be correlated with the socio-economic conditions of the areas.[9] The detailed analysis of the ecological distribution of delinquency in Houston revealed that while Negro children have a higher rate of delinquency than white children for the city as a whole, the rates vary by sections of the city in accordance with the density of the Negro population. In the four census tracts where the Negro group constituted over 90 per cent of the total population, the delinquency rate was 21.8; whereas, in thirty census tracts in which Negroes constituted less than 10 per cent of the total, the rate was 49.7. The rates in the other tracts were between these extremes, varying in accordance with the proportion of Negroes in each region.

In the Baltimore study, sponsored by the Maryland State Commission on Juvenile Delinquency, it was found that the delinquency rate (number of cases per 1,000 population in the age group from 6 to 17) ranged from 14.58 in Zone I to 3.65 in Zone IV, after which there was a slight increase, according to Lander *(ibid.,* p. 25). Furthermore, in areas where the Negro group was less than 50 per cent of the total population, any increase in the number of Negroes lead to a corresponding increase in delinquency; but when the Negro population exceeded the 50 per cent mark, any further increase in the proportion of Negro population did not lead to a corresponding increase in the percentage of delinquency. The Baltimore study, as well as the Houston study, seems to indicate that the higher the proportion of Negroes in a community the lower the rate of delinquency in the Negro group.

If these studies indicate the pattern of distribution of cases of Negro delinquency in cities, especially in southern areas, what factors produce the differences in rates? No complete explanation is offered. There is no practical answer. It is possible that in the predominantly Negro areas some cases of offenses are not reported because of the treatment given them by the police and in the courts, and there may be less police control. But, according to the Negro leaders in Houston who were asked by the Research Bureau to interpret the data, there probably are more fundamental reasons for the differential rates of Negro delinquency in the various areas of

---

[9] Cf. *Social Statistics: The Houston Delinquent in His Community Setting,* Research Bureau, Council of Social Agencies, Vol. II, No. 1 (June, 1945); Bernard Lander, *Towards an Understanding of Juvenile Delinquency* (New York: Columbia University Press, 1954); Earl R. Moses, "Differentials in Crime Rates between Negroes and Whites, Based on Comparisons of Four Socio-Economically Equated Areas," *American Sociological Review,* Vol. 12 (August, 1947), 411-420. See Chapter II for statistical summaries of these studies.

the city. In the Negro areas, there are greater race consciousness and pride, more group support and morale, and better community institutions and organizations to meet the needs of youth. Negroes living in the white areas lack group support and social control; they are subjected to greater discrimination, and hence race conflicts and tensions are more intense; the conditions of living are poorer, and they have worse housing. As a consequence, the Negro youth are more rebellious than white youth, and there are more incentives to commit offenses.

The basic data of the studies indicate certain typical patterns of distribution of delinquency and underlying conditions, similar to those in other cities. Delinquency is concentrated mainly near the center of the city, with the central business district and the areas more or less surrounding it, known as the "interstitional" or transitional zones, having the highest rates. The transitional zones are characterized by such factors as low economic and educational status of the people, poor housing, high rates of tuberculosis and venereal disease, mental illnesses, extensive truancy, personal and family disorganization, and relatively high adult crime rates. It is apparent that delinquency does not exist in isolation, but is deeply rooted in community life. Since racial and nationality minorities are often forced to live in the "interstitional" areas, the conditions that produce delinquency are more prevalent in such groups than among people living in the better residential areas. This is particularly true in southern cities where segregation is more prevalent than in northern cities, but we lack comparative studies to show the difference. Frazier,[10] who made an intensive study of Negro family life in Chicago, has indicated that Negroes furnish a disproportionate number of cases of delinquency in most cities for which statistics are available, and he cites studies made in northern as well as in southern cities. But the Chicago study revealed that Negro delinquency rates vary by zones. The first, second, and third zones (from the heart of the city) have higher rates than the outer zones, corresponding to the variations in rates of delinquency for the city as a whole and also of adult crime. Furthermore, the variations in rates of delinquency showed the same trend as found in the case of dependency, desertions, illegitimacy, and other indexes of family and social disorganization.

These studies indicate that despite the preponderance of Negro delinquency in urban areas, one must beware of imputing any causal significance to race per se. There is no necessary direct concomitance between the presence of Negroes in an area and the delinquency

---

[10] E. Franklin Frazier, *The Negro Family in Chicago* (Chicago: University of Chicago Press, 1932).

rate of that section of the city. The fact that Negro delinquency rates vary widely by areas seems to indicate a difference in behavior patterns that are not the direct result of race.

Not all racial minorities have high delinquency rates. The Asians, for instance, have relatively low rates. In 1953, only 144 Japanese and 407 Chinese arrests were reported by 1,174 urban areas to the Federal Bureau of Investigation.[11] The studies of Asians (Japanese, Chinese, Filipinos) have revealed that their crime rates are considerably lower than is true of the whites in the same areas.[12] This is in spite of the fact that these groups are not highly assimilated into our culture. They represent small minorities that have experienced considerable discrimination and isolation, and they usually do not live in the better residential areas. Yet they have been traditionally law-abiding people, with strong family ties and controls. Their relative isolation and the communality within the group seem to favor social controls. During recent years certain groups have shown increases in delinquency rates. The second and third generation Japanese (Nisei and Sansei) have begun to acquire delinquency traits, especially in the groups of the Pacific Coast area that were uprooted during the war.

The North American Indian population has more extensive crime rates. According to the 1953 *Uniform Crime Reports,* from 1,174 cities of more than 2,500 in population, 32,084 Indians were arrested. Their chief offense is drunkenness, for which 23,753 were arrested.

The publications of the National Commission on Law Observance and Enforcement (especially No. 10, *Crime and the Foreign Born,* 1931) have shown that foreign-born groups do not necessarily have a worse criminal record than native-born people. Certainly, immigrants are not inherently worse than native-born Americans. When one considers their lack of knowledge of our laws and mores, the discrimination against them in certain quarters, the adverse living conditions in immigrant colonies in our cities, the economic struggle, and the slow process of assimilation of those with cultural backgrounds that differ markedly from ours, it is surprising that the crime rates are not higher. An important factor in the differential crime rates of the several nationality groups is the strength and con-

11 *Uniform Crime Reports,* 1953 Annual Bulletin, *op. cit.,* 114.

12 Cf. Norman S. Hayner, "Social Factors in Oriental Crime," *American Journal of Sociology,* Vol. 43, No. 6 (May, 1938), 908-919; compare "Delinquency Areas in Puget Sound Region," *American Journal of Sociology,* Vol. 39, No. 3 (November, 1933), 314-328.

sistency of the traditions which they have assimilated in their home country.

The relatively high delinquency rates of some of the second and third generation groups is quite another matter. The descendants of foreign-born parents are cultural hybrids. The parents sometimes endeavor to maintain the old-world mores and folkways and to enforce them upon their children. The children, on the other hand, have contacts with American groups in schools, on playgrounds, and in the neighborhood. Here they acquire knowledge of different standards and ways of living. The results of this type of situation will be indicated later in this chapter.

Even though it is difficult to obtain authentic comparative statistics of the delinquency rates of nationality groups, the studies of Mexican-American youth indicate that they are more delinquent than the native Anglo-Saxon youth. People who live in the Southwest and Pacific Coast areas are familiar with the problem of delinquency of the Mexican-Americans. This group is composed chiefly of the children of Mexican immigrants, but in the statistics of law enforcing agencies are included a variety of others, such as those who were born in Mexico or in other Latin-American countries. In 1950, there were approximately 3,500,000 Spanish-speaking people in the United States, the majority of whom were of Mexican extraction. About nine tenths of the Mexican and Mexican-American people live in five states—Texas, Arizona, California, New Mexico, and Colorado. According to the tabulation of the Bureau of the Census, Los Angeles County alone had 285,986 persons with Spanish surnames which constituted 6.9 per cent of the population of the county. The Mexican peon workers, eager to better their economic condition, have come into this country in large numbers, some of them illegally, known as "wetbacks." Since they are poorly equipped to adjust to the American communities because of language difficulties, low education and economic status, sometimes superstitious religious views, and ignorance of our customs and laws, they encounter difficulties, experience conflicts and disorganization, and often irritate our law enforcing officers. Those who know them well respect their cultural background, their artistic ability, and their eagerness to make a living in the new environment.

The behavior problems vary considerably in different Mexican and Mexican-American groups. Some groups, especially those with better education and occupations, who can live in a better community, show no evidence of extensive delinquency; whereas others, especially if segregated in slum and blighted areas, have relatively high delinquency rates. The fact that there are more Mexican-American children in correctional and detention institutions, in proportion to the number of juveniles in this group, is not necessarily an indication of excessive delinquency, for sometimes it is necessary to institutionalize them because of their condition of dependency. Nevertheless, the second and third generation Mexican boys and girls are distinct social problems in the communities in which they live. The leaders in these areas, who know the problems, recognize that they exist mainly because of the lack of education and training, low economic status, and poor living conditions of the people. Gangs in such communities are difficult to control, as the pachuco and "Zoot Suit" groups have indicated.[13]

Minority Group Problems: Segregation and Discrimination.[14] While minorities include more than racial and nationality groups, the term is usually applied to Negroes, the foreign born, Mexican-Americans, Jews, Asians, and others who are sufficiently different from the majority of people by color, features, language, customs, or culture-patterns (including any combination of these factors) to be regarded as separate types. America's strength and weakness lie in the diversity of American people and their cultural heritage. Immigrants have come from all over the world, and they have brought their respective cultures with them; but our chief roots are in the civilizations of central and western Europe, especially England, France, and Germany, with strains of culture from Spain, Scandinavia, and the Low Countries. Least like our own are the cultures of eastern and southern Europe, and of Asia and Africa. The latter

---

[13] See discussion in Chapter VII. Compare Ruth Tuck, *Not With the First: Mexican-American in a Southwest City* (New York: Harcourt, Brace and Co., 1946).

[14] For discussions of ethnic and other minority group problems, consult Brewton Berry, *Race Relations: The Interaction of Ethnic and Racial Groups* (New York: Houghton Mifflin Co., 1951); Francis J. Brown and Joseph S. Roucek, *One America: The History, Contributions, and Present Problems of Our Racial and National Minorities* (New York: Prentice-Hall, Inc., 1945 and 1952); Maurice R. Davie, *Negroes in American Society* (New York: McGraw-Hill Book Co., Inc., 1950); Henry Pratt Fairchild, *Race and Nationality: As Factors in American Life* (New York: The Ronald Press Co., 1947); Edward C. McDonagh and Eugene Richard, *Ethnic Relations* (New York: Appleton-Century-Crofts, 1953); Charles F. Marden, *Minorities in American Society* (New York: American Book Co., 1952); Gunnar Myrdal, *The American Dilemma: The Negro Problem in Modern Democracy* (New York: Harper & Brothers, 1944, 2 vols.); Robert Ezra Park, *Race and Culture* (Glencoe, Illinois: The Free Press, 1950, edited by Everett C. Hughes, Charles S. Johnson, Jitsuichi Masuoka, Robert Redfield, and Louis Wirth); Arnold M. Rose, Editor, *Race Prejudice and Discrimination: Readings in Intergroup Relations in the United States* (New York: Alfred A. Knopf, Inc., 1948); R. A. Schermerhorn, *These, Our People: Minorities in American Culture* (New York: D. C. Heath and Co., 1949); and George E. Simpson and J. Milton Yinger, *Racial and Cultural Minorities: An Analysis of Prejudice and Discrimination* (New York: Harper & Brothers, 1953).

immigrants, because of their diverse culture and biological strains, have not become fully assimilated into our culture.

Race prejudice and discrimination against minority groups, and the injustices that grow out of them, are the most conspicuous aspects of American "race" problems. The Negro group is not only the largest of the minorities, but the center of interracial tension. As Myrdal [15] puts it, the Negro problem is in the heart of America, for it is here that interracial tension has its focus. Our dilemma is that we have an American creed that stresses liberty and equality, but in practice we fall far short of the ideal, especially in regard to equal opportunities for Negroes. We have developed a color caste. The rank order of discrimination, from the greatest to the least, as manifested in the attitudes of whites, is as follows: intermarriage and sex intercourse; behavior in personal relations, as eating and dancing together; use of public facilities, as schools, churches and means of conveyance; political disfranchisement; discrimination in courts, by police, and by other public servants; and discrimination in securing property, credit, jobs, and welfare services. The degree of Negro resistance to these discriminations is the reverse in order, except for the first, which is as much opposed by Negroes as by whites.

Race tensions tend to come to a focus when the equilibrium between majority and minority groups is upset, as when a minority group suddenly increases in size and importance. The Chicago and Detroit race riots may be cited as examples of this type of situation, for the rapid influx of Negroes from the South, their entrance into various occupations and positions formerly held by whites, and the expansions of segregated "black belts" constituted some of the major background conditions of these outbreaks.

Segregation varies in intensity according to locality, numbers, and degree of prejudice inherent in the mores of the dominant group. It is not strictly an urban phenomenon, for no matter how small the place, there is usually a "shanty town" or similar isolated areas. Minority groups are segregated by the force of public opinion and are punished by severe social pressure if they dare to encroach upon the domains of the favored class. Such prejudices and segregation result in the formation of conflicting groups and factions. Children reared in segregated areas tend to develop an antisocial attitude toward the society that makes them outsiders. Segregation frustrates basic desires and tends to stimulate aggressiveness.

Rose [16] classifies discriminations into four groups: (1) economic

---

[15] *Op. cit.*, Chapter I, and elaborations in subsequent chapters.

[16] Arnold M. Rose, Editor, *Race Prejudice and Discrimination: Readings in Intergroup Relations in the United States*, *op. cit.*, Part II.

discrimination, which prevents members of minority groups from earning an adequate living or in getting other material benefits; (2) legal discrimination, including restrictive legislation and misapplication of existing laws or violation of legal protective devices; (3) political discrimination, such as voting restrictions, restriction of citizenship, and preventing minority group members from securing and holding offices or employment; and (4) social discrimination, which means putting up barriers between people to obtain advantages for one's own group, and which in turn works to the disadvantage of others. The range of action against minorities is all the way from debarring or physical exclusion to subtle remarks designed to differentiate people.

The inequalities in educational and employment opportunities, the lack of status in the community, and the treatment accorded minority groups, including the treatment of offenders, place them at a disadvantage and increase the resentment against such discrimination. The minority groups have increasingly become more aggressive and less submissive. This trend was accentuated by World War II and the industrial opportunities afforded by the demand for labor.

It is difficult to ascertain how extensively segregation and discrimination have affected delinquency, but it is generally believed that these conditions are increasingly becoming factors in the delinquency rates of minorities. Children in segregated groups are no longer ready victims of threats and discriminations because of their race or social position. They feel that they have rights and begin early to demand them. Submission has given way to aggression, and some have come in conflict with the law in their attempt to break through arbitrary cleavages.

It may be concluded that individuals of any given race or nationality are congenitally neither more nor less prone to criminality than are those of any other group. But some evidence has been accumulated to show that race or nationality, as a factor in conditioning social and economic status and well-being, may play an important part in this respect. Segregation, discrimination, poverty, lack of education, excessive mobility, poor housing, and overcrowding are factors in producing a condition of criminality in certain groups.

There are various ways of dealing with the problems of minority groups. To allow conflicts and discriminations to go on without concerted efforts to alleviate the situation is an unsatisfactory way of meeting the problem. More constructive methods are needed to achieve better intergroup relations.

It is essential that groups cooperate and adjust their differences.

One of the first steps in the process of cooperative enterprise is to adjust conflicting elements and to unify divergent groups and interests. Accommodation is the process that brings about a conscious adjustment of conflict through consideration of the difficulties involved and through mutual acceptance of a possible solution of the problem. Assimilation goes deeper, for it implies a fusion in which persons and groups acquire common sentiments, attitudes, values, and mores by sharing experiences and incorporating them in a common cultural life. The process of integrating diverse groups into some sort of unity is a difficult one and the desired or ideal objectives are never fully achieved.

Mobility and Transiency; and the Changing Composition of the Population. An important trend in migration in the United States has been the accelerated movement of the people from rural to urban areas. The proportion of people living in cities of 2500 and over increased from about one third in 1900 to nearly two thirds in 1950. The metropolitan areas, especially along the deep waters, have been the chief centers of growth.

The urbanization process has affected all groups, but young people have experienced considerable disorganization. Persons who migrate to cities from the relatively simple rural life often experience the same type of culture shocks as immigrants who move from one country to another. Even rural communities have felt the impact of the urbanization process. A number of studies were made of rural youth during the depression years, showing the problems faced by them, as well as by those who migrated to cities.

Immigrants in large numbers have made the transition not only from one country to another but from rural communities in Europe to crowded cities in America. Peasant farmers from Poland, Russia, and Italy, constituting the bulk of immigrants who came during the first three decades of the present century, found that there was no room for them in rural America, so they migrated to already crowded tenement sections of highly industrialized cities. Thus cities became the centers of minority groups and of diverse cultures. About a third of the population is composed of foreign-born citizens, their first generation descendants, and alien people who are legally here. Most of them live in cities.

Besides the migration to cities, the United States has experienced an even greater mobility of people from city to city and from community to community. It is not possible to ascertain the volume of mobility. During the past decade nearly all means of transportation have been overtaxed. The transiency of the population is particularly noticeable in the poorer economic zones of the city. Some schools in such areas register over 50 per cent turnover of pupils each year. The pupils in city schools have lived on the average in at least two communities.

Mobility does not necessarily result in delinquency, for many children of mobile families make adjustments to the new communities without becoming disorganized. However, the necessity of making extensive adjustments to a new neighborhood, differences in standards of conduct or the breakdown of controls, lessening of home spirit and unity, wanderlust, and many other conditions of excessive mobility and transiency tend to increase delinquency among the young. The reports of the Children's Bureau have indicated that the greatest increases in delinquency have occurred in the urban areas of most rapid growth of population, whereas decreases occurred in some of the areas of stationary or decreasing population. It is, of course, expected that delinquency will follow population trends, but many regions of population growth have experienced increases in delinquency out of proportion to the growth of the juvenile population, which is the truer index. Ample cases could be cited to indicate that personal disorganization accompanies an abrupt change in the social milieu.

It is exceedingly difficult to correlate mobility and transiency with rates of delinquency. Sullenger [17] found a relatively high correlation between mobility and delinquency before the depression. According to his studies, 38 per cent of the delinquent families in Omaha, Nebraska, and 53.3 per cent in Columbia, Missouri, were mobile families. Mobility has become accentuated since that time, especially during and since World War II. Migrations to areas of military camps and war industries accelerated greatly after 1940. In San Diego County, California, the total population increased from 289,348 in 1940 to 508,000 (estimated) in 1946, a percentage increase of 75.5. A large proportion of the increase was due to the influx of adults. It is estimated that the juvenile population increased only 18 per cent during that period, but the delinquency petitions filed in the juvenile court increased 35.21 per cent and the nondelinquency petitions increased 241.94 per cent. The increases were far more marked during the first two years of this period than during subsequent years. The San Diego (City) Police Department made an effort to segregate the local juveniles from the transients. From 1940-41 to 1942-43, arrests of local juveniles increased 24.5 per cent and arrests of transients, though fewer in number, increased 400 per

---

17 Thomas Earl Sullenger, *Social Determinants in Juvenile Delinquency* (Omaha, Nebraska: Douglas Printing Co., 1929), 62.

cent.[18] It must be remembered that these statistics cover entire cities (or counties), with no breakdown of data by areas within the cities. The local areas of cities show different rates of increases or decreases.

Shaw and McKay [19] studied the relationship between increase and decrease of population in the cities of Chicago, Philadelphia, greater Boston, Cincinnati, greater Cleveland, and others. Comparisons were made of the increases and decreases of the population and of delinquency by areas. It was noted that the areas of decreasing population almost completely surrounded the central business districts of these cities, and that practically all of the areas of rapid increase were near the periphery. Although the increase or decrease of population and rates of delinquents, by square-mile areas, did not exhibit an exact linear relationship, on the whole the areas of decreasing population showed increases in delinquency, and the areas of increasing population showed decreasing delinquency rates. However, in the areas where the population increased more than 70 per cent, no corresponding drop in delinquency was observable; but up to a point the rates in delinquency varied inversely with the increase or decline of the population. It should be recalled that the areas of decreasing population are those marked by such factors as physical deterioration, high percentage of families on relief, little home ownership, high proportion of Negroes and foreign born, and other factors closely associated with the incidence of delinquency, whereas the growing areas near the periphery are the better residential districts, which are more highly integrated, with fewer delinquency-provoking conditions. It is apparent that mobility and transiency are associated frequently with other factors, some of which are closely linked with the incidence of delinquency. The classes of people that move in or move out of an area also have a bearing on the changes in the rates of delinquency. However, mobility affects various groups in different ways.

CULTURAL DIFFERENCES

The Negroes, the foreign born and their immediate descendants, and the transients tend to concentrate in the areas of high rates of delinquency, but there is not necessarily a direct causal relationship between these groups and the delinquency condition. The relatively higher rates found among the children of Negroes as com-

---

18 *The Coordinator*, Vol. III, No. 7 (September-October, 1942).

19 Clifford R. Shaw and Henry D. McKay, *Juvenile Delinquency and Urban Areas* (Chicago: University of Chicago Press, 1942), 27-31, 137-139, 198-202, 235-236, 251-253, 272-274.

pared with those of whites, and the children of foreign-born parents as compared with those of older immigrants may be attributed to the different types of communities in which they live and the degree of cultural change and conflicts in these areas. No racial, national, or nativity group exhibits uniform rates of delinquency in all parts of a city. Within the same area, the foreign born and the natives, the recent immigrant nationalities and the older immigrants, and other groups may have similar rates of delinquency. Boys and girls brought to courts are not necessarily delinquent because their parents happen to be Negro, foreign born, or mixed, but rather because of other aspects of the total situation in which they live. The inability of parents to train, guide, and control their children properly is an important matter, of course; and this condition apparently is prevalent in the minority groups, especially if people move a great deal and families are uprooted from the customary community relationship and controls.

In a society that is relatively stable, the folkways, mores, laws, institutions, and the machinery of government function with such success that serious deviations from established norms are rare. An integrated culture produces a unified effect. Minor departures from customary ways of behavior can be dealt with by informal means of control. As Margaret Mead [20] has pointed out, adolescents in relatively primitive (preliterate) societies may experience some conflicts, yet for the most part they are subjected to uniform controls, more so than in the more complex modern societies. We still have some relatively isolated communities in the United States [21] that are able to maintain a degree of continuity and unity even though they have become somewhat modernized and changes have occurred. In such regions the continuity of folkways and mores contributes to the stability and effectiveness of social control. There may be many unrecognized and unsolved problems, and society may be quite stagnant.

The larger and more complex societies do not possess the same structural-functional unity that can be found in the smaller and more integrated groups.[22] All groups have some degree of integra-

[20] *Coming of Age in Samoa* (New York: William Morrow & Co., 1928, and reprint by The New American Library of World Literature, Inc., 1949). Compare Robert Redfield, *The Folk Culture of Yucatan* (Chicago: University of Chicago Press, 1941). See summary of these and other studies of folk societies by Robert E. L. Faris, *Social Disorganization* (New York: The Ronald Press Co., 1949), 7-14.

[21] Cf. Lloyd Allen Cook and Elaine Forsyth Cook, *Community Backgrounds of Education* (New York: McGraw-Hill Book Co., Inc., 1939); and *A Sociological Approach to Education*, 1950.

[22] Cf. Robert K. Merton, *Social Theory and Social Structure: Toward a Codification of Theory and Research* (Glencoe, Illinois: The Free Press, 1949), 28 ff. Compare Talcott Parsons, *The Social System* (Glencoe, Illinois: The Free Press, 1951), and

tion, but not all of them have a high degree of integration. Social usages and mores may be functional for some groups and dysfunctional for others in the same society. When the concept "functional unity" is transferred from the realm of small preliterate groups or from simple rural communities to the realm of large, complex, and highly differentiated modern societies, such as the metropolitan areas of America, it becomes less useful. In a dynamic society both the structures and functions of groups are continuously changing and group life is disrupted by the succession of culture groups, excessive conflicts, and social disorganization.

As Ing [23] has pointed out, cultural differences play an important part in the dynamics of juvenile behavior and must be recognized among the interlocking causes of juvenile delinquency. A study of alleged juvenile delinquents referred to the Honolulu juvenile court in 1950, analyzed on the basis of the racial breakdown by offenses (both sexes), revealed that the part-Hawaiian youngsters led other racial groups in both major and minor delinquencies; the Japanese youth led in traffic offenses; and the Korean, Hawaiian, and Puerto Rican delinquents were at the bottom of the list. No attempt was made to compare the various racial groups and offenses in terms of population ratios, because the 1950 United States census report was not complete. However, the classification and statistics of ethnic groups, as compiled by the Honolulu Bureau of Vital Statistics, indicate that there were fewer part-Hawaiians than Caucasians and only a little over a third as many as Japanese, yet they had committed nearly twice the number of offenses committed by the Caucasians and a few more than the Japanese.

Succession of Culture Groups and Culture Conflicts in Relation to Delinquency. When one culture group succeeds another, the social controls tend to break down. The movement of immigrant groups from the areas of the first immigrant settlement to the areas of the second and third settlement, and the succession of nationalities in the areas adjacent to the center of the city are matters of great significance, when considered in relation to the process of city growth and the distribution of juvenile delinquents. Attracted by employment opportunities, accessibility to employment, and low rents, the newer immigrants settle in the areas adjacent to industry and business, force out the older immigrants, and later in turn give way to

Talcott Parsons and Edward A. Shils, Editors, *Toward a General Theory of Action* (Cambridge, Massachusetts: Harvard University Press, 1951).

[23] Walter Ing, "Cultural Factors and Juvenile Delinquency in Hawaii," *Focus*, Vol. 30, No. 5 (September, 1951), 141-143.

still newer immigrant groups. It is in these changing and deteriorated areas that immigrants and their children must make adjustments to the new world.

Upon arrival in the city, an immigrant group tends to settle in
a very compact community near the industrial areas adjacent to the
center of the city. After some years, the group tends to move outward to some new district, giving up many European traditions and
habits of life. This is known as the area of second settlement. As
individual members of these immigrant communities become more
fully assimilated, they tend to move away from their particular communities into cosmopolitan American residential areas. The successive stages of movement represent progressive stages of assimilation.
The process, however, is not without disorganization.

In some areas both the native whites and the immigrant groups
are replaced by Negroes. In contrast to the increasing dispersion
of European immigrant groups, the Negroes have tended to become
highly concentrated in one or a few areas. Scattered Negro groups
live in predominantly white areas, but during recent years the Negro
population has become more diffused and scattered in some urban
areas. Culture conflicts and social disintegration accompany the
succession of these various types of groups. Migration into a region
of diverse groups produces a variety of patterns of behavior.

Culture heterogeneity has reached its epitome in the United
States. Immigrants have brought their culture traits with them. The
commingling of people in America has provided the occasion for
extensive culture fusion.

Until people migrated extensively and modern means of communication greatly extended the range of contacts, the impact of
the controlling forces in society resulted in considerable uniformity
of behavior and conformity to the established mores. The recent
shifting of population has thrown people of varied cultures into
contact with one another. Conflicts have inevitably resulted from
such contacts.

Sellin[24] has summarized the main studies of the relation of culture conflicts to crime. In addition to the theoretical considerations,
Sellin has pointed out projects for research in this field, which, if
pursued, would undoubtedly add greatly to our knowledge of the
influences exerted by culture conflicts on human conduct. Statistical
studies of such conflicts have not yielded significant returns. The
more intensive studies of racial and nationality groups have revealed

---

[24] Thorsten Sellin, *Culture Conflicts and Crime* (New York: Social Science Research
Council, 1938), 67 ff.

the importance of culture conflicts. It is here that the conflicts of conduct norms are very extensive.

If the conduct norms are inconsistent in a group, or if several groups possess inconsistent norms, members of these groups invariably reflect such group attitudes. Hence, culture conflict may be viewed as a conflict of conduct norms or as mental conflict.

Delinquency apparently is more prevalent in the areas of racial and language frontiers, on the boundary or in interstitial areas, where two or more groups with diverse cultures come in close contact. In the interiors of these groups, as in areas where nearly all the inhabitants are Negroes or of one nationality, the rates are lower. Conflicts are bound to be most intense along the margins of cultural areas. The children of immigrants are frequently the chief victims of such conflicts. The behavior problems of these children are greater when the difference between the culture of their parents and the prevailing American culture is great. The wider the divergence between children's culture background and the American standards, the greater the adjustment problem. When a child finds a fundamental conflict between the culture of his playmates and that of his parents, he is apt to choose the playmates' standards. The old-world mores, which are so meaningful to the parents, seem contemptible to the child whose playmates ridicule them. Most people prefer the approval of their group to that of the elders. The relatively high rate of delinquency among children of foreign-born or mixed parents can be traced in part to the breakdown of parental control and the consequent failure in training and disciplining the growing child. Counter tendencies in the community are relatively more influential.

Sutherland presents a more comprehensive theory of criminology than is involved in the culture approach to the subject, but he recognizes the importance of culture patterns in shaping conduct.[25] Criminal behavior is learned by association with criminal patterns. The process by which a particular person comes to engage in criminal behavior involves a number of factors; but it is chiefly a matter of learning, which takes place for the most part in intimate primary groups. This learning process includes both the techniques of crime and the direction of motivation, and involves all the mechanisms of learning, not merely imitation. Children come in contact with both criminal and anticriminal patterns. When the prevailing definitions of the situation are favorable to law violation, criminal behavior is more likely to be the result than one in which anticriminal patterns

---

[25] Edwin H. Sutherland, *Principles of Criminology* (New York: J. B. Lippincott Co., 1947).

prevail. Differential associations with criminal and anticriminal behavior patterns may vary in frequency, duration, and intensity.

It seems evident that delinquency is likely to be more extensive in areas in which the prevailing patterns are favorable to crime than in the more stabilized communities in which law observance is stressed and in which there is a strong opposition to crime. When the prevalence of definitions favorable to crime is accompanied with considerable social disorganization, the crime rate is likely to be high.

Pauline V. Young [26] has called attention to the importance of culture contacts and conflicts in the causation of delinquency, based on the study of Molokans in Los Angeles. The Molokans, a religious sect, arrived from Russia in 1905, settled in the heart of the city, and tried to maintain a communal existence, with the Sobranie (assembly of the people) as the center of religious activities. They tried to perpetuate Molokan traditions and the "brotherhood." However, their relations with the outer world produced many problems. The cultural hybrid situation resulted in conflicts and in the disintegration of social control within the group. Juvenile delinquency became one of the social problems.

Although the statistics of juvenile delinquency in the group are now out of date, for the Molokan community has changed considerably since the study was made, they indicate how extensive deviant behavior may become in a situation of conflict between the behavior norms of a sectarian group and the larger urban society.[27] Deviant behavior among the older Molokans, except for drunkenness, rarely brought them into conflict with American law, but the situation was quite different among the younger ones, especially among the boys. The younger generation apparently felt no special necessity of preserving the uniqueness of the religious sect and was somewhat critical toward the traditions of the "brotherhood." Conflicts between the older and the younger generations pertained to nearly every phase of life. Although extreme cases of personal disorganization were rare, deviations from communal standard were extensive. But the seriousness of the delinquency problem apparently had a more or less direct relation to the extent and nature of the contacts which the Molokan boys had with the social world outside of their

---

26 *Pilgrims of Russian-Town* (Chicago: University of Chicago Press, 1932).

27 See especially Table 3. "Behavior Record of 175 Boys, Members of 108 Molokan Families" (Los Angeles Metropolitan Area only). Of the 275 boys, 181 had court records. The highest rate of delinquency was in the age group 9-19, in which group 155, or 78.3 per cent, appeared in the Juvenile Court within a period of two years. The girls in the Molokan families committed fewer offenses than the boys, for only 24 girls were involved in offenses.

own families and the sectarian group. After a careful examination of the possible factors involved in the situation, Dr. Young concludes that

. . . such factors as (1) race, (2) nationality, (3) economic status, (4) broken homes, (5) dependency, (6) physical condition, (7) mentality, (8) temperamental traits, (9) psychosis, (10) adolescence, and (11) genetic factors have failed to explain the differences in social behavior of the Molokan delinquent and nondelinquent groups. They can, however, be clearly differentiated in terms of cultural contacts. The evidence points in this study to a direct relationship between the extent of contact with urban life and the extent of delinquency in this group.[28]

Conflicts Between the Delinquents and the Community. The culture and other conflicts to which children of foreign-born parents are subject are often more intense than are the conflicts faced by other children. However, nearly all children and young people have some difficulties in making adjustments to community demands. Tannenbaum [29] points out that conflicts between the young delinquents and the community may be due to two opposing definitions of the situation. The delinquent defines it in terms of play, adventure, excitement, interest, mischief, and fun. This may include breaking windows, annoying people, and climbing over roofs or fences —all in the interest of play and excitement. To the community these forms of activities are a nuisance, and constitute delinquencies, demanding control, admonition, punishment, and suppression. The public not only considers these acts as evil but sooner or later regards the individuals as evil. The individual who habitually does bad things has become a bad person. The delinquent may also change his attitude toward the community and his relation to it. Slowly a sense of grievance and injustice develops. He feels that he is unduly mistreated and punished. Eventually he tends to identify himself with the gang, the delinquent group, with whose members he shares his activities and fate. The relationship of the gang to the community is frequently strained and conflicting.

There is a more or less direct relationship between conditions existing in the local communities and the rates of delinquents.[30] Areas with high rates have culture, social, and economic conditions that differentiate them from communities with low rates. Certain delinquency-producing conditions seem to be inherent in certain

---

[28] *Ibid.*, 210-211. Used by permission of the University of Chicago Press.

[29] Frank Tannenbaum, *Crime and the Community* (New York: Columbia University Press, 1951).

[30] Compare Clifford R. Shaw and Henry D. McKay, *Juvenile Delinquency and Urban Areas* (1942), *op. cit.,* especially Chapter XX for summary.

localities, especially those in the urban zones in transition. Communities differ greatly in social values, norms, and attitudes.

In the delinquency-producing areas, children encounter competing and often conflicting systems of values. The culture impact is not unified and integrated. There are few common definitions of situations. The delinquent's immediate social world is his gang. The gang sets the pattern, provides the stimulus, defines the situation, and offers the rewards or administers the punishment. It also provides protection and loyally supports its members. The community at large is remote and offers few of the compensations derived from the intimate associations in gangs and street-corner groups. A gap exists between this intimate group and the outside world. Friction between youth and the older persons in the community is inevitable, for they tend to live in different worlds.

The intensity of the conflict between the younger and the older generations varies by areas and with time. When the dominant traditions of a community are conventional, and the conventional norms are embodied in the homes, schools, churches, and other institutions and agencies, and there is a minimum of social disorganization, it can be expected that the conflicts will be less tense than in areas of disintegration and confusion of culture. In communities occupied by Orientals in which the solidarity of Old-World culture patterns and institutions have been preserved, the control of children is still sufficiently effective to keep delinquency rates at a relatively low level.

The real factor in the conflict of children with a community comes particularly from that section of the population which is most likely to complain, according to Porterfield.[31] This hypothesis is supported by 1500 cases of children whose accusers in a juvenile court could be identified. Parents, school officials, and others register complaints. Parents give many reasons why they issue complaints, as disobedience and incorrigibility. Children are rejected by their parents, but parents too have problems.

The community, as we shall see later, can be a unit of operation in meeting the needs of youth and in bringing about readjustments. An integrated and constructive community program can be helpful in readjusting behavior problem cases and in preventing delinquency.

---

31 Austin L. Porterfield, *Youth in Trouble: Studies of Delinquency and Despair* (Fort Worth: The Leo Potishman Foundation, 1946), 15.

QUESTIONS AND PROJECTS

For Class Discussion and Research

1. In what age categories do most of the delinquents appear? Why is there a concentration of cases in certain age brackets?

2. What is the sex ratio of delinquency? Why do boys commit more delinquencies than do girls?

3. Differentiate between race and nationality. Criticize the classification of delinquents as white, Negro and Mexican.

4. What are the difficulties involved in getting adequate statistics of the distribution and extent of delinquency among racial groups?

5. Discuss race and nationality factors in delinquency.

6. Discuss the problems of Negro delinquents.

7. Why is Negro delinquency relatively high? How would you explain the lower rate of delinquency among Negroes in the predominantly Negro areas than in the areas that have few Negroes?

8. Enumerate the problems faced by minority groups. Make a comparative study of delinquency rates of majority and minority groups.

9. Study the process of segregation. What factors contribute to the formation of a "black belt," "Little Mexico," and other segregated groups?

10. Analyze crime and deviant behavior among the foreign born. Why is the delinquency rate relatively low among the foreign born?

11. Explain the conditions of second- and third-generation children that may lead to delinquency.

12. How has urbanization affected the growth of delinquency?

13. Show the possible relation of excessive mobility to forms of misconduct. Correlate mobility rates with crime rates.

14. Correlate the succession of culture groups with antisocial behavior.

15. Analyze the explanation that culture conflicts are basic factors in juvenile misconduct.

16. In what ways do conflicts arise between juveniles and the community?

17. Discuss the cultural implications of children's behavior.

SELECTED REFERENCES

BONGER, WILLIAM A., *Race and Crime* (New York: University Press, 1943).

RESEARCH BUREAU, Council of Social Agencies, *Social Statistics: The Houston Delinquent in His Community Setting*, Vol. II, No. 1 (June, 1945). Pamphlet.

SELLIN, THORSTEN, *The Criminality of Youth* (Philadelphia: American Law Institute, 1940).

————, *Culture Conflict and Crime* (New York: Social Science Research Council, 1938).

SHAW, CLIFFORD R., AND HENRY D. McKAY, *Juvenile Delinquency and Urban Areas* (Chicago: University of Chicago Press, 1942).

TANNENBAUM, FRANK, *Crime and the Community* (New York: Columbia University Press, 1951).

TEETERS, NEGLEY K., AND JOHN O. REINEMANN, *The Challenge of Delinquency* (New York: Prentice-Hall, Inc., 1950).

VEDDER, CLYDE B., SAMUEL KOENIG, AND ROBERT E. CLARK, *Criminology: A Book of Readings* (New York: The Dryden Press, 1953).

VON HENTIG, HANS, *Crime: Causes and Conditions* (New York: McGraw-Hill Book Co., Inc., 1947).

YOUNG, PAULINE V., *The Pilgrims of Russian-Town* (Chicago: University of Chicago Press, 1932).

X

ECONOMIC, ECOLOGICAL, AND PHYSICAL ENVIRONMENTAL FACTORS

The bearing of economic conditions and physical environmental factors on delinquency and crime cannot be definitely established. Although many delinquents come from poor homes and live precarious lives, yet millions of poor people have not become offenders. Neither poverty nor prosperity per se may be the cause of crime. Even in slum and blighted neighborhoods where poverty is rampant and wretched housing conditions exist, only a fraction of the children become delinquent. Yet poverty and want, poor housing, unemployment, child labor, mothers working, street trades, invasion of industry and business in a residential area, urban blight, and related conditions, individually or collectively, have significance for the conduct of people who are affected by them.

The economic factor looms large in the American culture. As the Lynds have pointed out,

One's job is the watershed down which the rest of one's life tends to flow in Middletown. Who one is, whom one knows, how one lives, what one aspires to be,—these and many other urgent realities of living are patterned for one by what one does to get a living and the amount of living this allows one to buy.[1]

The measure of success or failure is largely in terms of income, wealth, and the standard of living one may be able to maintain. Our culture has a materialistic aspect.

The pursuit of dollars may lead to crooked roads. Much of our crime is committed in the interest of money. Offenses against property are common. A highly competitive society often leads to exploitation. Economic considerations may be involved in many kinds of offenses. Individuals who are starving or who have other wants, those who are idle through lack of employment, the recipients of relief who feel that society owes them a living, those who have a sense of inferiority because of business failure or unemployment and the inability to "keep up with the Joneses," those who are forced to live in slums and blighted areas—people living under these and many other similar conditions are subject to antisocial conduct. Housing and the type of neighborhood in which people live are closely related to the economic and social status of the family.

ECONOMIC CONDITIONS AND DELINQUENCY

The early studies of the relation of economic conditions to crime and delinquency were somewhat inadequate because of faulty methods of study. Gillin points out that six methods have been used during recent times to measure more adequately this relationship. These are:

(1) Comparison of seasonal fluctuations with crime rates, usually measured by convictions; (2) study of the trade cycle in connection with convictions; (3) research on the economic status of committed persons; (4) investigation of the occupational distribution of criminals; (5) study of early employment and juvenile delinquency; (6) study of professional criminals.[2]

Most of these types of studies pertain to adult crime rather than to juvenile delinquency. They represent efforts to correlate changes and other aspects of economic conditions with crime rates.

Seasonal variation and cyclical changes in delinquency were discussed in Chapter III in connection with the consideration of trends in rates of law violations. As was pointed out, several studies have indicated that the increases and decreases of cases in monthly pe-

---

[1] Robert S. and Helen M. Lynd, *Middletown in Transition* (New York: Harcourt, Brace and Company, 1937), 119-120. Used by permission of publisher.

[2] John L. Gillin, *Criminology and Penology* (New York: D. Appleton-Century Co., 1945), 134. Used by permission of publisher.

riods tend to follow a seasonal pattern; but there is no uniformity of trends, except that most of the studies cited show a decline in delinquency during the summer months, especially during the early part of the summer season. A number of studies have been made of business cycles in relation to delinquency. Here, again, there is no agreement of the findings, but the studies by Bogen in Los Angeles and those in Michigan and Pennsylvania (reported by Carr) indicate fairly clearly that delinquency rates tend to follow the business cycle. However, their findings are somewhat contradicted by the studies in Ohio by Reed, in New York by Maller, and in Pennsylvania by Reinemann. Few of the studies cover a sufficiently long period of time to indicate long-range trends. In order to make valid comparisons, the same types of cases, methods of research, and periods of time should be used in all the studies.

Adult crime apparently does not follow the same pattern as delinquency. Fairly reliable data have been assembled to show that crime rates rise in periods of depression and unemployment, and equally convincing statistics have been presented to show that crime goes up in time of economic prosperity. Few recent studies to show these possible relationships have been made.

If juvenile court petitions follow the business cycle, as Bogen and Carr have found, does this mean that changes in economic conditions, as occasioned by cyclical changes, produce corresponding changes in delinquency? Economic depressions, while creating extensive poverty and dependency, apparently have a deterrent effect on juvenile delinquency, but not necessarily on adult crime. Changes in family solidarity, mode of living, law enforcement procedures, community controls, and constructive welfare programs may account for the decline of delinquency during depression periods. Conversely, economic prosperity may stimulate delinquency. Do these explanations (although some are hypotheses) imply that poverty and dependency are not such important factors in delinquency causation as was supposed?

Poverty and Dependency as Conditions of Delinquency. Poverty is regarded by many as one of the great social problems of society, but it is not so extensive in the United States as in most countries of the world. The relatively high standard of living makes the deviation more obvious. Poverty is usually thought of as a condition of living in which a person and the family, because of either inadequate income or unwise expenditure of the available income, are unable to maintain a minimum standard of living. That is, they cannot provide for the physical necessities of life, and conse-

quently they are not able to function usefully according to the standards of society of which they are a part. Dependency is of two kinds,
natural and abnormal. The latter means that people are so poor
that they must be supported in part or in full by public or private
agencies, or by individuals other than their natural supporters. It
is difficult to measure the extent of poverty and dependency, for the
standard of living is constantly changing, the purchasing power of
the spendable income varies from time to time, and until the last
few decades there were no available statistics that could give one
even an approximation of the extent of problem.

As a background for an analysis of the possible relation between
the levels of income and delinquency, the contrast between income,
also dependency, during the depression years and the years following the depression may be made. The National Resources Committee[3] made an extensive study of family income during the year
1935-1936. Approximately 14 per cent of the families received less
than $500 during the year; 42 received less than $1000; 65 per cent
received under $1500; leaving only 35 per cent receiving more than
the minimum standard of living. When the incomes of all families
were added together, the aggregate amounts received by the different income groups varied even more than the percentages of families
in the groups; and the distribution of income of single individuals
showed an even greater disparity, both in aggregate income and in
percentage of persons in the different income levels, than the distribution of family incomes. The depression period produced the
greatest disparity of income levels and the largest percentage of dependency cases in our nation's history. In 1934, approximately
28,000,000 people, or slightly under 20 per cent of the total population, derived income from public assistance and work projects. During the first decade (1933 through 1942) of extensive government
participation in public aid to the needy, the total public expenditures for various types of assistance amounted to nearly 25 billion
dollars.[4]

According to the 1950 census,[5] the average (median) income in
1949 of 49,580,000 income units (families and unrelated individ-

---

3 Cf. *Consumer Income in the United States* (Washington, D. C.: Government Printing Office, 1938).

4 *Social Security Bulletin*, Vol. 6, No. 2 (February, 1943).

5 "Employment and Income in the United States," *Preliminary Reports: 1950
Census of Population* (Bureau of the Census, U. S. Department of Commerce, April 11,
1951), 4, 34-36. The December 2, 1951, reports indicate the distribution of family income levels in 1949 for four geographic regions and for ten selected states. The 1953
estimates of average family income range from $3500 to $3700 per year, ranging from
over $4000 in cities to slightly over $2000 for farm families.

uals) in the United States was $2599. The median income of 38,-
788,000 families was $3068, ranging from $2248 in the South to
$3435 in the West. The median income of 3,237,000 nonwhite
families was only $1426; and over five and a half million families of
all classes reported incomes under $1000 a year. But the average
family (or individual) was in a better financial position than during
the prewar era. Still about 10,000,000 individuals, including 2,000,-
000 veterans, were receiving all, or a substantial part, of their income from welfare, social security or veterans' service programs.
However, some of them were beneficiaries of social insurance programs rather than recipients of noncontributory public assistance.
The income of families and individuals has steadily increased since
the 1950 census was taken. Because of the extensive employment,
higher income, and more substantial public assistance for the needy,
fewer families and individuals are actually suffering because of lack
of the bare necessities of life. Still, delinquency is more extensive
now than it was during the depression years. This does not mean
that poverty is no longer a factor in delinquency, but it seems to
indicate that delinquency is relatively extensive during an era of
prosperity.

· Another factor to note is that the majority of poor families do
not produce children with antisocial tendencies, even though they
may suffer from want. Thousands of poor people evidence great
moral stamina and honesty. They are law-abiding citizens and they
inculcate law observance in their children. This seems to indicate
that poverty per se is not an inevitable cause of delinquency. Nevertheless, whether during an era of depression or during prosperous
years, the highest rates of delinquency are found in the regions of
greatest poverty. Contrariwise, the lowest rates of delinquency are
in the better residential areas in which there is practically no poverty. ·

Of the many studies that have included data with respect to the
economic conditions of delinquents, only a few need to be mentioned to indicate the general emphasis. Burt [6] contended that 19
per cent of the delinquent children studied came from very poor
homes, whereas only 8 per cent of the total population of London
belonged in this category; 37 per cent came from moderately poor
homes, as compared with 22 per cent of the population in this class.
In short, over half of the total volume of delinquency in London
was from poor or very poor families. Burt concludes, however, that
poverty alone does not necessarily produce delinquency. Although

---

[6] Cyril Burt, *The Young Delinquent* (London: University of London, 1938), 68-69.

the majority of the delinquents were needy, the majority of the needy were not delinquent.

William Healy [7] has stressed individual factors as causes of delinquency and consequently has minimized the influence of poverty. In his earlier study he recognized that poverty played a major or minor part in some cases. In the later studies with his co-worker, Augusta F. Bronner, he used a scale of standards similar to that developed by Burt. Only 5 per cent of the delinquents (in their 1926 study) came from destitute families, but 22 per cent were classified as belonging to the poverty class. Nevertheless, they remind the reader of the fact that this means that 73 per cent of the delinquents came from normal or better than normal homes. In their 1936 study, they likewise minimize poverty as a basic cause, but they state that unsatisfactory human relations may flow from destitution and poverty. Poverty-stricken homes and neighborhoods are drab places in which to live and to rear children. Inadequacy, frustration, and emotional insecurity that may accompany poverty play a real part in delinquency. The eradication of poverty would not eliminate misconduct, for other factors would still be present. However, removing the consequences of poverty undoubtedly aids in reducing the amount of delinquency.

The Gluecks, in their earlier studies, classified between a fourth and a fifth of their cases in the dependent class, and they found that a much larger proportion were in marginal economic circumstances. In their latest study,[8] in which they used a control group, they found that 28.6 per cent of the families of the 500 delinquents were in the dependent class, 66.4 per cent were classed as marginal, and only 5 per cent lived in comfortable circumstances. The economic conditions of the 500 nondelinquents, in terms of corresponding percentages, were as follows: 12.0, 76.0, and 12.0.[9] Furthermore, 23.6 per cent of the families of the delinquents derived their income entirely from sources other than from legitimate earnings, the earnings of those who wholly or partially supported themselves were much less than the earnings in the nondelinquency group, and a larger percentage of the fathers (breadearners) of the delinquents were in the unskilled or semiskilled worker classes.

---

[7] *The Individual Delinquent* (Boston: Little, Brown & Co., 1915); and with Augusta F. Bronner, *Delinquents and Criminals: Their Making and Unmaking* (New York: The Macmillan Co., 1926), and *New Light on Delinquency and Its Treatment* (New Haven: Yale University Press, 1936).

[8] Sheldon and Eleanor Glueck, *Unraveling Juvenile Delinquency* (New York: The Commonwealth Fund, 1950), 84-88.

[9] See Table VIII-10, *ibid.*, 84.

Maud A. Merrill,[10] in a comparative study of 300 juvenile court cases and 300 in a control group (nondelinquents), found that about two thirds of the delinquents came from the economically marginal group, as against only half of the nondelinquents, and that there were fewer comfortable homes in the delinquent group and more economically dependent families. The author recognizes that poverty and low social status are important only in relation to what they mean to the individual.

The comparative studies in which the investigators have used control groups give a more accurate index of the relation of poverty and dependency to delinquency than the studies in which no controls are used. In the Gluecks' study, the controls were matched for a number of items, including the type of neighborhood in which they lived. Both the delinquents and the nondelinquents lived in blighted and underprivileged areas.

The relation of juvenile behavior to the class system was discussed in Chapter VII, in which connection Hollingshead's *Elmtown's Youth* was used as the chief source of the data. Warner and Lunt [11] correlated the percentages of arrests with the proportions of the population in the six classes in the community. The lower-lower class had 64.69 per cent of all arrests, whereas the population in this class was 25.22 per cent of the total. All other classes had lower percentages of arrests than the percentages of the population in the classes. The official and unofficial delinquents coming from the poor and marginal homes living in the lower classes, as compared with the delinquents coming from families in better economic circumstances, may not give a true picture of the actual differential rates, for the economic and social status of a family sometimes makes a difference in the treatment procedure. Even if law enforcement agencies endeavor to be impartial in dealing with delinquents, owing to poverty or family disorganization, action must be taken, sometimes requiring the removal of juveniles from their homes for treatment and protective purposes; whereas in the more normal homes in the better residential areas the families can provide corrective treatment.

The Employment Situation and Occupational Maladjustment in Relation to Delinquency. The employment situation has fluctuated a great deal during the past quarter of a century. Following

---

10 *Problems of Child Delinquency* (New York: Houghton Mifflin Co., 1947), 76-88.
11 W. Lloyd Warner and Paul S. Lunt, *The Social Life of a Modern Community* (New Haven: Yale University Press, 1941), 376. A study of a New England industrial town.

extensive employment during the 1920's, civilian employment reached the lowest ebb in 1932 and 1933, when about 15,000,000 people of the slightly more than 48,000,000 in the labor force were unemployed. Even in 1940, when the civilian labor force was 52,-511,499, a total of 7,623,416 were classified as unemployed, although about a third of these were on various types of public work projects. By 1950, only about 2,773,603 of the 58,998,943 in the civilian labor force 14 years old and over were unemployed. During 1952 this total dropped to 1,700,000, even though the labor force had increased to 61,293,000.[12]

Unemployment is admittedly a perplexing social problem. No segment of the population is immune from the consequences of this condition. Although unemployment is usually widely distributed among age, sex, occupational, and racial or nationality groups, it is more extensive in the minority groups and the unskilled occupational classes. Of the 5,355,000 nonwhites in the labor force in 1950, 492,000 were unemployed, which was nearly twice the ratio of unemployment in the white group.

The relation of unemployment to delinquency has not been fully measured. It is difficult to isolate this variable from related conditions of disorganization. The causes of unemployment are numerous and not easily discernible. Personality weaknesses and disorganization, family disruptions, business cycles and changes, the effects of technological developments, and a variety of social or cultural factors have a bearing on unemployment. That unemployment has disorganizing effects cannot be doubted, but much of the disorganization may stem from the causes that produce the problem.

The external effects of unemployment are well known. With lessened income, families must change their mode of living: cut down their expenses, move to less desirable houses, omit luxuries, and in the end may have to go on relief. But the psychological and social effects are also apparent. Frustration, the thwarting of ambition, the breakdown of family and personal morale, and the lowering of social status sometimes have disastrous effects. At any rate, the children of the unemployed do not have the opportunities for education, personal achievements, and social participation that they would have if the families could be adequately supported.[13]

---

12 Source: "Employment and Income in the United States," *Preliminary Reports: 1950 Census of the Population, op. cit.,* 19-20; and report released July 19, 1953. See also *Statistical Abstract of the United States, 1953* (Seventy-fourth edition), Bureau of the Census (U. S. Government Printing Office, 1953).

13 For reports of the effects of unemployment and economic depression on family life, consult Ruth S. Cavan and Katherine N. Ranck, *The Family and the Depression* (Chicago: University of Chicago Press, 1938); R. C. Angell, *The Family Encounters the*

The employment of women, especially the mothers of small children, has been regarded as an important factor in the lessening of family control. The occupational history of American women shows gains in the number of women gainfully employed and an increase in the types of occupations open to them. In 1900 only 5,144,461 women 14 years old and over were gainfully employed. By 1950 the total was 15,326,000, and in 1951 it was 17,326,000.[14] Since 1951 the employment of women has exceeded the twenty million mark. The significant change during the war and postwar period is that more married women are gainfully employed than single women. In fact, the number of working wives in 1952 was 10,400,000, which topped the peak wartime figure by about 2,000,000.

The employment of mothers has been regarded as a problem. It is difficult to generalize with reference to the positive and negative effects of such employment. In many instances, the added income makes it possible for the families to live better and to provide more adequately the material necessities of their children. On the other hand, when mothers are away from their homes, especially where there are young children, the members of the family do not receive adequate care and supervision. During World War II this became such a problem that the War Manpower Commission issued a directive to employment agencies to the effect that mothers with small children should not be gainfully employed until after all other sources of labor supply had been fully utilized. Yet, in spite of every effort made to keep them at home with their children, the number of working mothers increased rapidly. During more normal times, a considerable number of working mothers come from low-income groups. A much larger proportion of mothers in the low-wage brackets are gainfully employed than in the groups in which the husbands have adequate incomes.

Neglected and unsupervised children of the economically insecure are the source of a large share of the social misfits who come to the attention of law enforcement agencies and who eventually become the inmates of correctional institutions. A considerable number of the mothers in these homes are employed. Kvaraceus [15] found that, of 761 cases handled by the Passaic (New Jersey) Children's Bureau, the mothers of 25 per cent of the white boys and 44 per cent of the Negro youth were gainfully employed, generally as

---

Depression (New York: Charles Scribner's Sons, 1930); and W. L. Morgan, *The Family Meets the Depression* (Minneapolis: University of Minnesota Press, 1939).

[14] Source: Bureau of the Census, Decennial Reports, *Current Population Reports, Labor Force,* July 6, 1951, gives the total for February 19, 1951.

[15] William C. Kvaraceus, *Juvenile Delinquency and the School* (New York: World Book Co., 1945), 90.

factory operatives, domestic servants, and clerks. He compares these percentages with the study made by the Child Care Committee of Working Mothers of School Children, which discovered that only 17.8 per cent of the mothers in the study were employed. The Gluecks [16] found in their earlier study of one thousand institutionalized delinquents that the mothers were employed over four times as frequently as the mothers in the country generally. Daughters seem to be affected more than sons by working mothers. When mothers are away from home, the basic functions of the family cannot be adequately performed, the children do not get sufficient supervision and guidance, and they may feel unwanted or neglected because the mothers are too preoccupied with occupational and household duties.

Child labor, including employment of older boys and girls, is regarded by many as a serious problem. The 1950 census reports that 3,783,000 of the 12,876,000 in the age group 14-19, or 30.7 per cent, were in the civilian labor force. Of these, 89.8 per cent were gainfully employed. Probably one sixth of the 14- and 15-year-old children were in gainful employment. A much larger number of children and young people have been gainfully employed since the beginning of World War II than during the depression years, and the wages of youthful workers have been relatively high. It is generally agreed that the employment of children involves certain hazards. The work may be harmful and morally unwholesome; and many of the employed children do not attend school, which may handicap them in future years. Of all the minors working in factories inspected between 1943 and 1948 under the child labor provision of the Fair Standards Act, 10 per cent were illegally employed, of whom 85 per cent were under 16 years of age.

The employment of children, especially in street trades and in certain types of industries, endangers their morals and physical health, lessens the opportunity of education and adequate vocational preparation, curtails future earnings and opportunities for employment, and may ultimately lead to antisocial behavior. Our industrial order has exacted a heavy toll from innocent childhood. Certain occupations and industries involve special possibilities of exploitation. Canning industries, certain forms of agricultural employment, mining, and dangerous industrial occupations are potentially harmful to youth.

Child labor in the form of street trades is usually considered as being more closely associated with delinquency than any other kind

---

16 Sheldon and Eleanor Glueck, *One Thousand Juvenile Delinquents* (Cambridge: Harvard University Press, 1934), 71.

of work. This is particularly true of boys who sell the early morn-
ing editions of newspapers to the after-theater crowd and to cus-
tomers of night clubs and taverns, or who deliver papers in areas of
unusual social hazards. It is not the street trade itself that makes
boys go wrong. Rather, it is the condition under which the work
is done. Delinquency among juveniles engaged in street trades has
been from three to ten times as great as among nonworking youth
and those otherwise employed. Studies made of boys committed to
correctional institutions indicate that from 60 to 70 per cent of the
delinquents had been employed in street trades. Child peddlers,
bootblacks, junk collectors, magazine sellers, and newsboys constitute by far the largest number of street workers. Most of the street
workers are school boys, many of whom work outside school hours.

The type of industries and business establishments near a child's
home largely determines his early employment. Farm boys and girls
work on the farm or in the orchard. Such work is wholesome, unless
it interferes with a child's education. However, exploitation of
child labor occurs in rural areas, as in truck-farming regions, fruit-
growing areas, and in the rural South. But, it is in industrial centers
that one finds the greatest exploitation of child labor.

A great deal has been done to prevent delinquency of boys and
girls engaged in certain types of occupations. Many of the large
newspaper concerns have special organizations and projects for the
newsboys. One of the most outstanding examples of services for
newsboys has been the work done by the Burroughs Newsboys Foundation in Boston and its affiliated Agassiz Village in Maine.[17] Mr.
Burroughs, who himself was a Russian immigrant newsboy in
Boston during the early part of the century and who later became
a successful attorney, established this foundation to help newsboys.
In his account of the work of the institution, he presents a warm,
sympathetic, and intensely interesting account of the experiences of
newsboys and their problems. He thinks that the needs of newsboys
can best be met through wise counseling, by providing educational
opportunities and wholesome recreation for them, and in some cases
by giving economic aid.

The children of migratory workers are sometimes the most
neglected. Migrant workers are a part of the constant movement of
people. The underlying reasons for migratory labor are many. The
economic pressures that dislodge workers include unemployment or
the inability to find suitable work, inadequate income, shifts in employment, undesirable working or living conditions, and a variety

---

[17] Cf. Harry E. Burroughs, *Boys in Men's Shoes* (New York: The Macmillan Co.,
1944).

of personal or family conditions. Not all displaced workers become migrants and not all migrants are job hunters, but migration of workers has been stepped up at a rapid rate. It is estimated that 10,700,000 civilians, or 7.7 per cent of the total population, changed their places of residence (one half moved from one state to another) during the first year following V-J Day (August 14, 1945).[18]

The chief victims in the families of migratory workers are the children. They not only are robbed of normal home life and wholesome community relations but are handicapped in that they attend school irregularly, are subject to labor exploitation, face health and moral hazards, and suffer from other disorganizing conditions. Moving from place to place makes them feel insecure. It is in this kind of situation that antisocial tendencies are likely to develop, and there are insufficient controls to regulate conduct.

Low income and employment conditions are some of the economic factors that are likely to affect juvenile behavior. In summarizing the relationship of economic factors, especially low income, to juvenile delinquency, Burgess[19] discusses the main points under three questions. Who is a delinquent? How is low income related to juvenile delinquency? Would an adequate income for existing low income families reduce juvenile delinquency?

When studies are made of the relationship between income and delinquency, usually only official cases are used, not the cases of all the boys and girls who have committed acts of delinquency. Official delinquents are those who have been arrested, brought into court, put on probation or parole or placed in correctional institutions. Most of them have committed more or less serious offenses. These studies have shown that juvenile delinquency is highly correlated with all the indexes of low income and with other social problems resulting from poverty. However, low income is seldom a single direct cause. It can become an underlying and basic condition, but it is usually related to such factors as poor housing, slum neighborhoods, the prevalence of gangs, and the lack of community organization. An adequate minimum income would probably be a significant factor in the prevention of the more serious types of offenses, for the rise of income would permit families to move from high delinquency to nondelinquency areas. The assumption that a

---

18 Source: Bureau of the Census, *Postwar Migration and Its Causes in the United States, August, 1945, to October, 1946* (Current Population Reports: Population Characteristics, Series P-20, No. 3, 1947).

19 Ernest W. Burgess, "The Economic Factor in Juvenile Delinquency," *The Journal of Criminal Law, Criminology, and Police Practice*, Vol. 43, No. 1 (May-June, 1952), 29-42.

stable and adequate income, if accompanied by improvement in family life and in neighborhood conditions, is a significant influence in reducing delinquency has considerable merit, provided we recognize that low income in many instances is merely a symptom and not a fundamental cause. In such cases it is necessary to pry beyond the surface economic conditions and examine the roots of the difficulty.

PHYSICAL ENVIRONMENT

Historians, geographers, and sociologists have noted the influence of the physical environment on human society. Only a few subscribe to the theory that the physical setting is a direct cause of crime. Efforts have been made to measure the effects on conduct of such items as geography, climate, and location. ⟨The physical environment is very complex, including geographic and geologic factors, plant and animal life, microorganisms, and the physicosocial creations of man. The influence of any one or a combination of these factors on conduct is for the most part indirect, and it is difficult to correlate them with social problems. Some social problems may be more or less directly affected by the immediate physical environment, whereas others are only remotely influenced by the physical setting.⟩

The proponents of the geographic school have endeavored to discover some correlations between such factors as geographic levels, climate, weather conditions, and seasonal factors and crime rates.[20] Their findings are not conclusive, and most of the studies were confined to adult crime, not to delinquency. Seasonal variations in delinquency were noted earlier in this chapter.

A number of studies of delinquency have stressed the importance of the conditions of the physical environment that are physicosocial, such as slum and blighted conditions, poor housing, the invasion of industry and business into a residential area, and the accompanying social conditions. Those who have stressed the physical environmental conditions of crime vaguely anticipated what the human ecologists have endeavored to do, except that they did not define environment very sharply and they did not use statistical and cartographic methods that are distinctive of the ecological approach. The ecological locations of slums and blighted areas, poor houses, and other conditions of the physical setting are significant from the point of view of delinquency areas.

---

[20] For a review of the geographic approach to crime, see: John L. Gillin, *Criminology and Penology, op. cit.,* Chapter V.

Slums and Blighted Areas. Slums are usually thought of as areas in which dwellings or other buildings are dilapidated, obsolescent, poorly arranged, lacking proper ventilation and light, unsanitary and unhealthful, and in other ways detrimental to the health, safety, comfort, and morals of the inhabitants thereof. It is chiefly a residential area in which the houses and conditions of life are of a wretched character, making it unfit for human habitation. Certainly, it is not a desirable place in which to rear children. Such areas are usually overcrowded, as well as unsanitary and undesirable.

A blighted residential area is one that is on the downgrade. Although it is beginning to show some slum traits, it is not yet a slum. The community is becoming an economic and social liability. The taxes do not pay for the public liability. First a barely noticeable deterioration sets in and then progresses gradually through stages, until the whole region becomes a slum.[21]

The physical condition is only a part of a slum or a blighted area. Culture patterns discernible in them are of the slum type. Regardless of the stage in the slum cycle, these areas are inhabited by certain classes of people, predominantly the poor, the population is changing and usually is declining as business moves into the territory, the home exhibit slum patterns, institutions show signs of deterioration, certain undesirable agencies operate in the neighborhood, and social problems are widespread. Crime and juvenile delinquency are especially noticeable in such areas. The picture of the slum is always disheartening. It represents a cultural lag in society.

As Shulman[22] has pointed out, a slum is not merely a mass of physically deteriorated buildings. It represents a culture pattern, consisting of a way of living and thinking. Not all of those living in slums are slum people or have slum ways. Yet, if a city wishes to eliminate the slum, it is necessary to deal with the people and their way of living as well as to improve the buildings. This is fundamentally an educational process.

Zorbaugh[23] characterizes the slum as a distinctive area of disintegration and disorganization. Business is encroaching upon the area, property is becoming dilapidated, and a transient population inhabits the overcrowded houses. It is an area of freedom, individualism, and anonymity. Aside from a few marooned families, a large

---

21 See Mabel L. Walker, *Urban Blight and Slums* (Cambridge: Harvard University Press, 1938), especially Part I.

22 Harry M. Shulman, *Slums of New York* (New York: Albert and Charles Boni, Inc., 1938).

23 Harvey W. Zorbaugh, *The Gold Coast and the Slum* (Chicago: University of Chicago Press, 1929), Chapter VII.

part of the population consists of transients, including hoboes, criminals, prostitutes, and the down-and-out. A mixture of immigrants and their descendants occupy the territory. Accordingly, as Zorbaugh has pointed out, a slum is characterized not only by mean streets and ramshackled buildings, but by certain types of submerged humanity. The cheap rooming houses and tenements are occupied by economic or social failures. Broken homes, desolating poverty, and human derelicts are found everywhere. The tenements are full of people speaking foreign tongues and with the earmarks of alien cultures. The cheap rooming places are occupied by human wreckage. The records of the families and individuals tell the tragic stories of economic failures, physical illness and handicaps, drink, dope, gambling, prostitution, and a loss of grip on life. This is a sordid picture, yet one can hardly exaggerate the conditions of the worst slums in our large cities.

Slums and blighted areas provide breeding places for crime. Experienced criminals find shelter there, often transmitting the techniques of crime to younger people. The less stable population is permitted to concentrate in such regions. There are few wholesome facilities for recreation, but undesirable influences are apparent everywhere. Thus, the environment of slums is physically and morally unhealthy for growing children. Such background conditions inevitably leave their imprint on the personality of the child. Clearer illustrations of the influence of the neighborhood on crime could hardly be found than in the cases of *The Jack-Roller, The Natural History of a Delinquent Career,* and *Brothers in Crime,* both by Clifford Shaw. The five Martin brothers lived in a neighborhood adjacent to heavy industry; a drab, unattractive, and deteriorated community. Dwellings were old, and many had been condemned for demolition. It was an area of declining population, poverty, unemployment, and economic insecurity.[24]

Poor Housing in Relation to Delinquency. The housing problem has many facets. It is more complex than merely the presence of poor houses in certain areas. It includes housing shortage, financial and construction aspects, government control versus planlessness, and the conditions of blight. In other words, there are quantity and quality aspects, and each in turn is related to other factors. But

---

[24] For an account of the home life and social environment of children in an industrial slum district in England, see Arthur T. Collis and Vera E. Poole, *These Our Children* (Boston: The Beacon Press, 1951). The book gives a sordid picture of the way children live in slums, showing the effects of overcrowding, family disorganization, the suffering of unwanted children, and the life on the streets, including delinquent behavior.

according to the 1937 United States Housing Act, poor housing implies buildings that are dilapidated and overcrowded, have faulty arrangement or design, lack proper lighting and ventilation, are unsanitary and lack sanitary facilities, are unclean, or have any combination of these factors that make them detrimental to the safety, health, and morals of the occupants.

In studying the possible relation of poor housing to delinquency, investigators have used certain indexes, such as the general condition of dilapidation (old, out of repair, unpainted, ramshackle) or lack of sanitation. Some of the home rating scales have included other items.

It is not exactly known how many poor houses there are in America, for our standards are unusually high and there are differences of opinion as to what constitutes a substandard house. If substandard houses mean unsanitary facilities, dilapidation and unsafe conditions of the physical structure, lack of proper heating and lighting, and, in general, unfitness for use, then a relatively small percentage of houses would be so rated; but if houses are rated as substandard when they lack only a few of the items that constitute good houses, then a much larger number of houses could be regarded as falling below the standard. The absence of some of the conditions of good housing may or may not be regarded as evidence of poor quality, depending upon the value-judgment that is applied. Using the term "substandard" broadly, the sample survey of housing made in 1947 [25] classified as substandard 27 per cent of the nonfarm dwellings and 80 per cent of the farm dwellings. However, farmers themselves would probably rate many of the substandard houses as quite desirable.

It is generally believed that poor housing, especially overcrowding, inadequate sanitation, physical dilapidation, and uncleanness are conducive to deviant behavior. Studies by Shaw and McKay and many others have pointed to the fact that a large proportion of the delinquents come from the areas of poorest houses. However, some of these investigators have cautioned against too hasty conclusions regarding the direct influence of poor housing on delinquency rates. Housing, like poverty, is only one of many factors, the relative importance of which has not been fully tested.

In comparing 500 delinquents with 500 nondelinquents living in approximately the same areas, the Gluecks [26] found that despite

---

[25] Cf. *Housing Characteristics of the United States* (Bureau of the Census, April, 1947).

[26] Sheldon and Eleanor Glueck, *Unraveling Juvenile Delinquency, op. cit.,* Chapter VIII.

similarity in the type of housing and the monthly rental per room, the sanitary conditions in the homes of the delinquents were less adequate than in those of the nondelinquents, and they had less adequate furniture, lacked in cleanliness and neatness, and were more overcrowded. Consequently, 33.9 per cent of the homes of the delinquents were rated as poor as compared with 19.8 per cent of the homes of the nondelinquents; whereas only 11.4 per cent of the former were rated as good as compared with 27.2 per cent of the latter.

Various home rating and housing scales have been devised to measure the effects of housing on conduct and family life. One of the earliest of such rating devices was the Whittier Scale for Grading Home Conditions,[27] which resulted from the efforts to classify homes in which delinquents lived previous to their commitment. In this way the "home index" of every boy could be ascertained. The items used in rating homes came under the headings of necessities, neatness, size, parental condition, and supervision of children.

Part of Chapin's [28] "Social Status Scale" deals with the material equipment and cultural expression of the living room and the condition of articles in the living room, including cleanliness, orderliness, conditions of repair of furnishings, and general expression of good taste. This scale could be used for the rating of homes of delinquents and nondelinquents.

The DuVall-Klein Home Rating Scale, devised by Everett W. DuVall and Helen Smith Klein, directors of Child Welfare Clinic of the All Nations Foundation (Los Angeles), was used to measure the homes of 500 underprivileged children.[29] The scale was designed to measure the amount of economic security, type of neighborhood, exterior and interior appearances of the home, equipment and furnishings in the home, the food served and how it is served, sleeping arrangements, the sort of home management, and care of the home. Using the rating scale, a quantitative study was made of each of the

---

27 Cf. J. Harold Williams, *A Guide to the Grading of Homes* (1918), pamphlet published by the Whittier (California) State School, now the Fred C. Nelles School for Boys, originally published as "The Whittier Scale for Grading Home Conditions," *Journal of Delinquency,* Vol. I (November, 1916), 273-286.

28 Cf. F. S. Chapin, *Contemporary American Institutions* (New York: Harper & Brothers, 1935), Chapter XIX; also Louis Guttman, "A Revision of Chapin's Social Status Scale," *American Sociological Review,* Vol. VII (June, 1942), 362-369.

29 See Everett W. DuVall, *A Sociological Study of Five Hundred Underprivileged Children in a Selected Area of Los Angeles,* Doctor of Philosophy dissertation in Sociology, University of Southern California, 1936, and *Relative Influence of Primary Groups on Underprivileged Children* (Los Angeles: University of Southern California Press, 1938), containing portions of the dissertation. This study was made during the existence of the Clinic in the early part of the 1930's.

homes from which the 500 cases were drawn. By using step intervals of five points each, the home ratings ranged from 45 to 181, with an average of 118.06 ± .727. As compared with the theoretical normal curve, the ratings of most of the homes indicated that housing conditions in the area were poor, especially those of the Mexican group, except the homes of the Orientals, which were superior even to those of the American, Negro, and European groups.

Home rating scales, especially those pertaining to housing items, have not been widely applied to a comparative study of the homes of delinquents and nondelinquents, but they possess elements of value if properly applied.

Delinquency Areas and Ecological Correlates. Studies in twenty-one American cities by Shaw and McKay,[30] carried on over a period of twenty years, revealed that the incidence of delinquency is correlated with areas of social disorganization. They used the ecological method in locating the areas of high delinquency and other factors of disorganization. By taking several series of delinquency cases, they correlated their distribution with the juvenile population of the areas of the city (chiefly in Chicago) in order to ascertain the rates of delinquency. The rates were also ascertained on the basis of zones. After they had located the high delinquency areas, an analysis was made of the social conditions prevalent in them. High rates of delinquency were found for the most part in the regions adjacent to industry and commerce, which has been designated as the "zone in transition." [31]

An analysis of the delinquency areas revealed the following types of objective characteristics: (1) physical deterioration, with many old and dilapidated buildings, some of them condemned as unfit for human habitation; (2) economy dependency, with a corresponding variation in the rates of dependency and the rates of delinquency in the five groups of areas studied; (3) increasing and decreasing population, depending upon the extent of the invasion of business and industry into the region; (4) high percentage of foreign and Negro population; (5) succession of cultural groups, with changes in the distribution of racial and nationality groups; (6) disintegration of

---

[30] Clifford R. Shaw and Henry D. McKay, *Juvenile Delinquency in Urban Areas* (Chicago: University of Chicago Press, 1942). Compare "Social Factors in Juvenile Delinquency," *Report on The Causes of Crime*, Vol. II, No. 13 (National Commission on Law Observance and Enforcement, 1931), and *Delinquency Areas* (Chicago: University of Chicago Press, 1930).

[31] Cf. Ernest W. Burgess, "The Growth of the City: An Introduction to a Research Project," in *The City* by Robert E. Park, Ernest W. Burgess, and Robert D. McKenzie (Chicago: University of Chicago Press, 1925).

neighborhood organization; and (7) the greatest concentration and highest rates of adult offenders. Shaw and McKay point out that the rates of delinquency in these high-rate areas remained more or less constant over a period of twenty years even though the population composition changed considerably during this time. They conclude that perhaps more important than the external realities of the area are the traditions, standards, and moral sentiments that characterize the neighborhood life, which is designated the "spirit of delinquency." [32]

A number of authorities have called attention to the inadequacy of the statistical method in ascertaining the exact extent of delinquency and the difficulties involved in making comparative studies of juvenile court and police arrest cases on a regional basis. One of the recent critical analyses of the ecological studies of Shaw and McKay in Chicago was made by Kobrin.[33] He calls attention to the fact that the enumerations of cases of delinquency in the high delinquency areas exhibit a wide range. The appearance in juvenile court shows a higher rate than commitments, and the police complaint cases show a still higher rate. The unduplicated count of police cases over a seven-year period, which was the period used for the analysis of court cases, shows the highest rate of all. Although the proportion of delinquents in these areas is high, this group represents a minority of the age eligible population. He thinks that, since less than one fourth of the boys in the high delinquency areas are brought into the juvenile court, this appears to invalidate the hypothesis that in the disorganized areas of the city delinquency is primarily the product of cultural rather than personality processes. He calls attention to the variability of behavior status and the varieties of conventional and criminal value systems in delinquency areas. Few people would disagree with his contention that these areas are characterized by a dual system of conduct norms, or possibly a range of conflicting values, but one may question the importance attached to the personality or psychological processes in relation to the conflicting value systems. Both personal and social disorganization and the processes underlying them have a bearing on delinquent behavior.

The analysis of social data by ecological methods has thrown new light on many aspects of city life, particularly in the study of delin-

---

[32] See *Report on the Causes of Crime*, Vol. II, *op. cit.*, Chapters III and IV, for an analysis of the objective and subjective aspects of delinquency areas.

[33] Solomon Kobrin, "The Conflict of Values in Delinquency Areas," *American Sociological Review*, Vol. 16, No. 5 (October, 1951), 653-661; and discussion by George B. Vold, 661-662.

quency and crime, economic dependency, population changes, and various forms of social disorganization in the community. More refined methods are needed to get the best results, but even the simpler methods make it possible to locate the focal points of social problems.

Longmoor and Young [34] correlated juvenile delinquency with dependency rates and population movements in Long Beach, California. In order to make direct comparisons of the three groups of data on the spot maps, the median centers and median contour lines were located. The median centers are the central points of geographic concentration for each of the three groups of factors and the median contour lines are the halfway distances between the centers and the peripheries of distribution. The contour lines show the dispersion of cases about the median centers. It was found that transciency of population and juvenile delinquency distribution were closely correlated; but the distribution of relief cases extended in the direction of the cheaper hotels and apartment house areas, in which lived relief clients who had few children. However, the high peaks of both delinquency and public relief cases were found in approximately the same area. The high delinquency area near the center of the city was found to be identical with the zone in transition between the business district and the harbor area.

The Baltimore study [35] represents an analysis of the relation between the social and economic data for census tracts, given in the 1940 United States Census, and the delinquency rates for 1939 to 1942 inclusive. In this study the investigators endeavored to obtain data regarding such matters as the variation of delinquency rates among the different census tracts, the geographic (spatial) distribution of cases (does this confirm the Burgess Concentric Circle Zone and Gradient Hypotheses?), the location of the highest delinquency rates, the correlation between delinquency rates and certain economic and social variables (rent, overcrowding, substandard housing, home ownership, population composition, and education), and various other types of correlations. It is not possible to review here the details of the findings, but the data reveal a preliminary confirmation of the Burgess' concentric zone hypothesis, for the highest rates of delinquency were found in the central zone and the zones surrounding it. (See especially tables I, II, and III, pp. 22-25.)

---

[34] Elsa Schneider Longmoor and Erle Fiske Young, "Ecological Interrelationships of Juvenile Delinquency, Dependency, and Population Movement: A Cartographic Analysis of Data from Long Beach, California," *The American Journal of Sociology*, Vol. 41, No. 5 (March, 1936), 598-610.

[35] Cf. Bernard Lander, *Toward an Understanding of Juvenile Delinquency* (New York: Columbia University Press, 1954).

However, there was no continued and regular decline in rates of delinquency, especially of the Negro group, from the central to the outer zones. Lander concludes that the concentric zone hypothesis, as emphasized in the Chicago study, oversimplifies the spatial distribution of delinquency in Baltimore. It is recognized that the distribution of industry in Baltimore does not conform to the zonal hypothesis used by Burgess and his associates in the study of Chicago and other urban communities. The Baltimore study likewise indicates that while statistical measures show surface associations between delinquency rates and the various variables used for comparative purposes, they do not necessarily suggest fundamental relationships.

One of the fundamental theories of human (social) ecology is that social problems, such as delinquency and poverty, appear in the pattern of concentration and scatter in space. There are underlying reasons for the concentration of social problems in certain areas of the city. The methods of ecologists are to plot on maps the locations of cases, thus enabling one to ascertain the areas and zones in which concentrations of social disorganization occur; and, having located the spatial distribution of cases, especially the areas of high concentration, to analyze the conditions (variables) that are presumably correlated with the problems studied. The difficulties of the ecological methods are obvious. It is quite easily possible to plot distributions of cases and to draw certain inferences from them, but it is difficult to demonstrate correlations between the distribution of cases of a given type of problem and other variables. Furthermore, as in the cases of delinquency and crime, the official registration of cases is not necessarily a true index of the actual prevalence of the problem. Even the correlation of delinquency rates of the distribution of the juvenile population is beset with difficulties.

In summary, it may be stated that economic, physical environmental, and ecological factors have a bearing on delinquency, but the exact relationship between specific conditions and deviant behavior has not always been established. A complete theory of delinquency must be stated in terms of all types, situations and factors, including differential experiences of individuals in these situations. The personality and environmental factors intertwine, and they are complicated by the differences in individual experiences.

It may also be stated that social reformers have been inclined to exaggerate the importance of physical environmental factors as causes of delinquency. Some have assumed that by abolishing undesirable conditions, or by improving them, delinquency could very nearly be wiped out. That slum clearance greatly aids in reducing social disorganization cannot be gainsaid, but by itself it is not sufficient to control a social problem that has many types of causal or conditioning factors.

QUESTIONS AND PROJECTS

For Class Discussion and Research

1. Is it true that the economic factor looms up large in American culture? Give evidences in support of your answer.

2. Test the conclusion of Carr, Bogen, and others that juvenile delinquency follows the business cycle by studying trends in delinquency rates in a selected county and comparing these with the business index.

3. Why does delinquency tend to go down during depression years and rise in times of prosperity?

4. What are the dangers of the employment of mothers and of children?

5. Is poverty a cause of delinquency? How could you test or measure the correlation between poverty or dependency and delinquency?

6. What are the characteristics of slums and blighted areas? Differentiate between slums and blighted areas.

7. What are the objective and subjective characteristics of delinquency areas?

8. What is the relationship of lack of stability or community disintegration and delinquency?

9. Show the relationship between the lack of home ownership or poor housing and delinquency.

10. Why is it important to consider the spirit of the community, its mores and values, in relation to community disorganization in order to gain a more complete picture of the causal factors in delinquency?

11. How are external factors in the community reflected in the life history of the individual, and why is this relationship important in understanding a delinquent and his career?

12. Discuss child labor and delinquency.

13. Discuss ecological factors in relation to delinquency.

SELECTED REFERENCES

Bogen, David, "Juvenile Delinquency and Economic Trend," *American Sociological Review*, IX (April, 1944), 178-184.

Burroughs, Harry E., *Boys in Men's Shoes*. A World of Working Children (New York: The Macmillan Co., 1944).

Carr, Lowell J., *Delinquency Control* (New York: Harper & Brothers, 1950).

ELLIOTT, MABEL A., *Crime in Modern Society* (New York: Harper & Brothers, 1952).

———, AND FRANCIS E. MERRILL, *Social Disorganization* (New York: Harper & Brothers, 1950).

GILLIN, JOHN L., *Criminology and Penology* (New York: D. Appleton-Century Co., 1945).

LANDER, BERNARD, *Towards an Understanding of Juvenile Delinquency* (New York: Columbia University Press, 1954).

SELLIN, THORSTEN, *Research Memorandum on Crime in the Depression* (New York: Social Science Research Council, 1937).

SHAW, CLIFFORD R., AND HENRY D. McKAY, *Juvenile Delinquency and Urban Areas* (Chicago: University of Chicago Press, 1942).

TANNENBAUM, FRANK, *Crime and the Community* (New York: Columbia University Press, 1951).

TEETERS, NEGLEY K., AND JOHN O. REINEMANN, *The Challenge of Delinquency* (New York: Prentice-Hall, Inc., 1950).

XI

Inadequate Controls: Law Observance and Enforcement, and Treatment of Offenders

The conditioning factors discussed thus far are the major underlying sources of deviant behavior. However, any one of these types of factors, or a combination of them, may be present in a given situation without producing deviant behavior or antisocial tendencies. Many people face difficult situations without violating laws, provided they exercise sufficient self-control or society provides adequate safeguards and social controls. In a broad sense, all social problems turn out to be problems of personal and social controls. From the point of view of delinquency, the failure of controls, whether personal or social, may be regarded as a factor in causation.

FAILURE OF PERSONAL AND SOCIAL CONTROLS

On the basis of the analysis of juvenile court cases, Reiss contends that

... delinquency may be defined as the behavior consequent to the failure of personal and social controls to produce behavior in conformity with the norms of the social system to which legal penalties are attached. Personal control may be defined as the ability of the individual to refrain from meeting needs in ways which conflict with the norms and rules of the community. Social controls may be defined as the ability of social groups or institutions to make norms and rules effective.

Delinquency results when there is a relative absence of internalized norms and rules governing behavior in conformity with the norms of the social system to which legal penalties are attached, a breakdown in previously established controls, and/or a relative absence of or conflict in social rules or techniques for enforcing such behavior in social groups or institutions of which the person is a member. Hence delinquency may be seen as a functional consequence of the type of relationship established among the personal and social controls.[1]

The author does not intend this to be a single-cause explanation of delinquency, although his theory represents a special emphasis. His main purpose in making the study was to develop an instrument of research by means of which the outcome of persons on probation could be predicted. The predictors that were evaluated were found in the materials of the official court records of 1110 white juvenile delinquent probationers between the ages 11 and 17, placed on probation by the judges of the Cook County Juvenile Court. From the first 736 case folders, items were selected that were regarded as measures of personal and social controls. The predictors were validated by using a followup sample of 374 cases. This study is mentioned here not for the purpose of evaluating the accuracy and validity of the prediction instrument, but to call attention to the importance of personal and social controls in children's behavior. Failure to develop appropriate controls may lead to delinquency.

Lack of Personal Controls. The development of character and conscience was discussed in Chapter V. Character and conscience

---

[1] Albert J. Reiss, Jr., "Delinquency as the Failure of Personal and Social Controls," *American Sociological Review*, Vol. 16, No. 2 (April, 1951), 197-214; and discussion by Joseph H. Greenberg, 214-216. Used by permission of editor. Paper was read at the annual meeting of the American Sociological Society held in Denver, September 7-9, 1950. The paper is a summary of part of Reiss' doctoral dissertation on "The Accuracy, Efficiency and Validity of a Prediction Instrument," (unpublished Ph.D. Dissertation, Department of Sociology, University of Chicago, 1949). Compare Albert J. Reiss, Jr., "Social Correlates of Psychological Types of Delinquency," *American Sociological Review*, Vol. 17, No. 6 (December, 1952), 710-718.

have reference to a system of attitudes, habits, and forms of action that involve standards of values and the elements of right and wrong in matters of conduct. Children acquire moral values and norms of conduct through experience. It is a learning process.

The major factors in personal controls are the moral ideals and values the children acquire in various situations in which decisions need to be made in matters of conduct. The nondelinquent has developed contradelinquent personal controls. When faced with a situation in which a choice needs to be made between compliance with a norm of the group or his own standard of conduct and a form of conduct that represents a deviation from this norm or standard, the individual refrains from violating the established rule. The delinquent, on the other hand, does not have the appropriate contradelinquent personal controls and hence is likely to yield to a temptation. In fact, he may have developed a system of values that are in opposition to the prevailing mores of society.

The nature and strength of personal controls are an index of the person's definition of a certain type of situation and how he is likely to act when he faces a situation in which a moral decision needs to be made. With strong personal controls, a child is likely to succeed in acting in conformity with the norms of the group and his own conception of what is right in matters of conduct. Even though a child may have relatively weak personal controls, he can still be a conformist provided the group exercises relatively strong controls. But if a person has weak personal controls, accompanied by equally weak societal controls, delinquent behavior is a natural consequence when that person is faced with a critical situation. Thus, personal and social controls are intertwined.

Failure of Primary and Secondary Group Controls. Social control is a "collective term for those processes, planned and unplanned, by which individuals are taught, persuaded, or compelled to conform to the usages and life-values of the group." [2] Some forms of control are informal, natural, spontaneous, and to some extent unconscious. These arise out of the living conditions of primary groups. Other forms of control are more artificial, indirect, and less meaningful, such as those in secondary groups. The agencies and means of control are varied, but from the point of view of the behavior of children they include primarily the folkways and mores (customs and traditions), moral norms and religious ideals, primary institutions and agencies of the community, and the individuals who

2 Cf. Joseph S. Roucek and Associates, *Social Control* (New York: D. Van Nostrand Co., 1947), 3.

exert an influence. Law and the machinery of law enforcement are operative only in certain instances. Public opinion, art, music, symbols, rituals, and the like may likewise become agencies of control.

Most of the controls of children are exercised by primary groups through which the means of control are channeled. Primary groups are those in which there are intimate face-to-face contacts, association, and cooperation, particularly the family, the school, the church, the gang, the play group, and the neighborhood. These groups are fundamental in forming the social nature and ideals of the person. In them one can find a oneness and fusion of personalities. A mutual identification and a "we-feeling" are present that are not to be found in the larger relationships.

The unity of the primary group is not one of mere harmony and love. It is usually a differentiated unity, admitting of self-assertion, wishes, special interests, and various appropriate passions; but these differentiated motives are socialized by cooperation and are brought under the discipline of a common spirit. The primary ideals and values of life, such as those of love, freedom, justice, fair play, honesty, and good will do not come from isolated living or abstract philosophy. They are derived from everyday experience, chiefly in these primary groups.

The child who is reared in the congenial atmosphere of a normal home and has wholesome contacts in the play groups and in the neighborhood develops a system of values in accordance with the prevailing norms of the groups of which he is a part. Primary groups provide special controls and correctives whenever personal controls are not sufficient. They supply the child with nondelinquent or contradelinquent norms, and they employ techniques to make these norms effective.

If the primary groups fail in the training programs to develop nondelinquent norms and standards or if they fail to provide correctives in critical situations, deviant behavior is the expected consequence. An important part of the process of control is the discipline of children. If parents are too strict or too lax or erratic in their discipline, as the Gluecks have pointed out, delinquency is more prevalent in such homes than in those in which the parents are firm but kindly in their discipline. Disorganized or economically dependent homes deprive the members of the family of the physical needs, security, social status, and training necessary for normal living. When families are unable to provide corrective influence or, what is worse, when they actually orient their children toward criminal careers by their own behavior, it can be expected that some of them will become delinquent.

It is generally agreed that children develop and maintain personal controls less readily when reared in a milieu other than such primary groups as the family. Children who live in or have spent considerable time in children's institutions are less likely to develop adequate personal controls. They are usually in an environment that is depersonalized, the relationships are secondary rather than primary, and the behavior patterns do not become deeply rooted.

The larger secondary groups are those that do not necessarily depend on face-to-face contacts and direct personal relations. The members are separated from one another, with their contacts mediated by devices of communication, such as the newspaper, the radio and television, and the motion picture. Hence, the relationships are more impersonal, indirect, casual, and less meaningful. The essence of secondary groups, such as complex urban areas, is the casualness of contacts and the impersonal character of human relationships. Sometimes there is considerable anonymity. Over vast areas of the city people do not know one another. They are "neigh-dwellers" but not real neighbors.

As was pointed out in the preceding chapter, delinquency is more prevalent in some areas than in others. These are largely the zones in transition or the interstitial areas, as Thrasher calls them. These areas exercise little control over the people, either as individuals or as family units. The norms and dominant behavior patterns are sometimes at variance with the mores of the larger society. Lacking unity and consensus, the interstitial zones are relatively ineffective in controlling behavior in accord with nondelinquent rules and norms. Individuals are less apt to accept institutional control and some are hostile to any form of control by constituted law enforcement agencies.

Underlying Processes of Disorganization. Throughout the discussions of conditioning factors, attention has been directed to some of the underlying processes involved, such as segregation and cultural conflicts, social differentiation, personal disintegration and social disorganization. Social and personal controls tend to break down under the pressure of disorganizing forces in society.

By social process is meant the characteristic recurrent social change. Social contact is the first step or stage of social interaction, and social interaction is the all-inclusive social process. The subprocesses can be broadly classified into two groups: (1) the processes of social opposition and disintegration, notably competition, conflict, social differentiation, and segregation; (2) the processes of cooperation and integration, including accommodation, assimilation, socialization, social organization, and social control. Suggestion and imitation are mechanisms of interaction.

The first group constitutes the chief processes involved in causation of delinquency. The competition for status, favors, advantages, and means of making a living may not have disastrous effects, unless competition is keen and verges on conflict. Culture conflicts, conflicts between criminals and the protective agents of society, and many forms of group or personal conflicts are dynamic factors leading to misconduct. Personal frustrations, emotional tensions, and many other forms of inner conflicts tend to disintegrate the person and may lead to psychopathic and other forms of personality conditions back of overt antisocial behavior.

The conflicts between the individual and the community, between the delinquents and law enforcement agencies, and between members of the same gang often have devastating effects. In a way, there is a perpetual warfare between law violators and those entrusted with the job of law enforcement. To gain advantage in this conflict, both criminals and protective officers appropriate the inventions of modern science as far as they are useful to them. It is a process of competitive development of techniques of crime and of protection against crime.

The segregation of minority groups and the stratification of society into classes often not only produce disorganizing conditions in the region or group but also tend to produce rebellion and aggressive opposition to the rules and restrictions imposed by the majority or the upper groups. Segregation of the criminal population by the public is a common practice. Criminals are isolated from the normal society. Sex offenders are ostracized. Those guilty of felonies, notably manslaughter, are put into prisons. Prisoners who are difficult to handle are isolated in solitary cells (in prisons). A person may have status in the underworld, but any individual who is identified with the underworld lives entirely apart from law-abiding society. Even those with peculiar or socially undesirable personality traits find themselves isolated and alone. The processes of social differentiation, segregation, and isolation are present in many situations and are in one way or another related to various forms of misconduct.

The inability to make satisfactory adjustments to social situations or to resolve conflicts by means of accommodation accentuates the difficulty. The treatment process, as we shall see later, is largely a process of adjustments of difficulties and the removal of conditions that cause them. If accommodations can be affected, personality and social conflicts lose their force for disorganization. Assimilation is a more penetrating process than accommodation. It means the fusion of attitudes, ideas, ideals, and culture. As people become identified with the group and recognize a responsibility to others, they are to that extent socialized. A breakdown in these processes opens the way for antisocial tendencies.

When the forces of disintegration are not brought under control, or when the machinery of law enforcement fails to operate efficiently, the situation may get out of hand. A breakdown in either the treatment of offenders or the control of conditioning factors opens the way for increased antisocial behavior.

LACK OF LAW OBSERVANCE

America has probably more laws than most other nations, and Americans are accused quite commonly of having the least respect for law of any people. During the pioneer days, the colonial and frontier communities had few laws, although mores and the pressure of public opinion held people in line. However, rugged individualism found expression in many areas of life. As society became more complex, legal regulations were multiplied. The division of the United States into states, and the states into counties and incorporated cities, and in some states township divisions, greatly increased the laws and legal regulations. As laws increase, it is inevitable that violations increase accordingly. This fact must be noted in comparing present rates of crime with earlier rates. Statistics of crime in terms of total offenses are not a true index of criminality of the population. The increase of the population, as well as the multiplication of laws and the machinery of law enforcement, has a bearing on the number of offenses committed, not to mention the added occasions provided by a complex social order.

Community Attitudes toward Law Observance. The American Creed, if it can be said that there exists such a creed, is a blend of democratic and Christian idealism, with emphasis on liberty, equality, and brotherhood. Furthermore, Americans believe in law and order. These are lofty ideals, yet most Americans are practical people, too, insisting on the application of creeds to everyday living. In practice, however, we often fall far short of the professed ideals. Citizens have been accused of giving lip service to laws and to ideals, and of supporting them heartily as long as they do not interfere with what they want to do individually. For instance, traffic regulations are almost universally acclaimed as necessary for the safety of citizens; yet when traffic violators are caught, they not only resent it but even try to find legitimate or illegitimate ways of avoiding the penalties, often boasting of their ability to "put it over" the traffic officer or the judge of the traffic court. Laws, in the minds of many, are meant for other people, not for themselves, except for their protection. During the war, parents boasted, in the presence of their children, of having obtained extra rationing coupons, or of purchasing commodities on the black market, or of beating the game in other ways. Disrespect for property and persons is evidenced by vandalism and violence which are reported daily in newspapers.

Gillin, in discussing the problem of law enforcement and the public attitude toward it, contends that underlying the inefficiency of the courts is a more fundamental sociological condition,

. . . the lack of unified desire of the people that in all circumstances the law should be enforced. Most laws are not made for ourselves or for our class, but for some one else. We do not want the police in all cases to arrest an offender. We do not want one of our friends to be prosecuted for his crime. Labor-unions do not want to see one of their leaders, nor business men one of their fellows, convicted and sent to jail. Hence when prosecution threatens, we exert whatever influence we have to protect from the law those who are closely tied to us by social and business bonds. These attitudes affect the police and the judges. No amount of fiddle-faddling with the machinery of justice, while it will help, will alter this fundamental sociological condition. It can be altered only by gradually building up in the public—all classes of it—a lively consciousness that law and its machinery is for the protection of the whole society, not only for our particular class, or business, or profession.[3]

When citizens are unwilling to make sacrifices that are required to maintain law and order, and to remove the menace of law violations, law enforcement becomes difficult. Inequality in the application of law confuses the citizens, especially the young. "White-collar crime" may be allowed to go on unhampered, whereas persons guilty of petty offenses are dealt with severely, especially if the offender belongs to a lower economic class or is a member of a minority group.

A considerable share of the unrest and antisocial behavior of preadolescent and adolescent youth has its origin in confusion of controls and the loss of basic standards of behavior. The criteria of what is desirable and what is undesirable have undergone considerable changes during recent years. Each generation normally takes its ideals and standards from the preceding one. Because of the changing conditions and the complexity of modern society, parents

---

3 John L. Gillin, *Criminology and Penology* (New York: D. Appleton-Century Co., 1945), 300.

and the elders of the community no longer occupy the position of respect they once held. Blind obedience to parental demands and community leaders is no longer demanded. Hence, other controls must be substituted, which include devotion to a way of life that is mutually acceptable.

A community can have almost any degree of law observance, provided a considerable number of the people agree that they really want such a state of affairs to exist and through concerted effort enact laws and back up the law enforcement agencies.

The attitude of youth toward law observance and enforcement reflects the community attitude. If there is respect for law, children naturally develop the same attitude. If parents and other adults indulge in minor infractions and wink at similar activities of their friends, children are quick to sense the spirit and often exaggerate the situation.

The Force of Delinquency Traditions. The more objective conditions of a delinquency area can be measured and correlated with delinquency rates. These serve as the basis for making distinctions between areas. Although difficult to measure, a more significant influence is the spirit of delinquency that frequently prevails in the neighborhood. As Shaw and McKay put it, "More important than the external realities of the area are the traditions and moral standards which characterize the neighborhood life." [4] When law violation is prevalent in a community, the criminal tradition is reflected in the conduct of the children. Such influence is especially felt when social disorganization is prevalent and there is a relative absence of social controls.

Delinquency tends to persist in an area not only because of the absence of constructive influences and the inefficiency of preventive measures, but also because lawlessness has become a tradition that is handed down from one generation to another. Criminal patterns persist in slums and blighted areas. Deteriorated regions in cities provide the type of environment in which crime can thrive.

Not only is the delinquency tradition transmitted from one generation to another, but the delinquent groups even have codes of their own, as Thrasher, Whyte, and others have pointed out. These are preserved and transmitted through the medium of social contact within the gang or the unsupervised play groups. As was noted in Chapter VII, a boy's contact with a gang frequently marks

---

[4] Clifford R. Shaw and Henry D. McKay, "Social Factors in Juvenile Delinquency," *Report on The Causes of Crime*, Vol. II, No. 13 (National Commission on Law Observance and Enforcement, 1931), 109.

the beginning of his career in delinquency. Boys in cities seldom commit offenses alone. Mischief making and violations of law usually occur in groups, not by individual boys alone. Groups, with delinquency traditions and knowledge, often become the chief source from which boys derive criminal attitudes and techniques. Many forms of crime require special skills. Gangs are the schools in which specialized techniques are acquired.

Criminal gangs tend to have codes of conduct of their own. These codes are often at variance with the prevailing laws. It is quite all right, according to such codes, to steal or commit other offenses against society, but to squeal on one another is a serious breach of the gang code. The members of a delinquent group not only set up their own standards, but may even inflict severe punishment upon those who violate the gang rules. Loyalty and conformity are rewarded by praise, increased social status, and often in monetary ways. The gang members develop a contemptuous attitude toward a traitor, as indicated by such epithets as "squawker," "rat," and "stool pigeon." To divulge to police the secrets of a gang, or to identify its members, or to "squeal" on an offender is a most serious offense according to gang code. However, members of gangs, if handled skillfully, will reveal secrets of gang activities to police, provided they are assured that the information will be held strictly confidential.

Since the influence of companionship and juvenile gangs was discussed in an earlier chapter, it is not necessary to repeat the description here, except to call attention to the importance of the traditions of the criminal group. The criminal gang is more or less a closed system, and the influence on its members is pervasive. Once in the swing of gang activities and identified with the traditions of the gang, it is very difficult to break away from them. In certain criminal groups "toughness" must be displayed in dealing with the public, especially in dealing with police officers, who represent the public in the matter of law enforcement. The criminal processes of groups explain in part the uniformities of crime.

The Element of Chance and Its Effects on Law Observance.[5] It must be admitted that chance often is an important element in delinquency or in the reformation or maturation of the delinquent. Von Hentig points out that when the complex of causal combinations grows too variform for us to understand, we speak of the ele-

---

[5] See Hans Von Hentig, *Crime: Causes and Conditions* (New York: McGraw-Hill Book Co., Inc., 1947), Chapter XIV.

ment of chance, not as a gambler's chance but as a conspiring force that enters the lives of causal factors.

It is not necessary for our purpose to discuss theories of chance. Some maintain that there is no such thing as chance. We have simply invented the notion of chance or accidental factor to conceal our ignorance of causative trends. There is a widespread belief among criminals that their own offense was due chiefly to a chance factor, that luck was against them, or that, in the process of trial and sentence, justice was against them.[6]

Case records of delinquents, especially if the boys' or girls' own stories are included, are full of references to the element of chance. The fact that they themselves believe that this is true is a significant item to note in the matter of treatment. Of course, chance may operate in the opposite direction to restrain a person from law breaking, but the preventive influence is often not stressed. Clarence Darrow [7] firmly believed that luck and chance are factors that really affect man. The whole journey of life is a matter of luck, and chance is a great element in life. It may be that Darrow simply reflected, more or less unconsciously, the prevailing attitude of criminals. In his defense of alleged criminals, and his wide experience as a criminal lawyer, he saw accidents save one man from conviction, and then again the accidental elements spun a web of circumstantial evidence around another man that led to a prison sentence.

From the point of view of law observance and enforcement, it is important to note the elements of chance and its importance in the minds of lawbreakers. As Von Hentig puts it,

> Treatment by police, courts, parole boards, and penal institutions may be the final cause in the development of a confirmed criminality. Of course, it is by no means the only cause, yet without these errors the life of an offender might have taken a different turn.[8]

It is not only a matter of accidental occurrences in the heredity, environment, or personal experiences of the individual prior to the lawbreaking incident, but the way the alleged delinquent is handled that may condition his future career. The accidental character of many occurrences is overlooked, both in appraising the conditions that led to the offense and in dealing with the offender. It is difficult properly to appraise this element, for chance differs in many ways from other causative factors.

Although it is difficult to control the elements of chance in the

---

6 Cf. Clifford R. Shaw, *The Jack-Roller* (Chicago: University of Chicago Press, 1930), 47.

7 *Crime, Its Causes and Treatment* (1922), 257-258. Cf. Von Hentig, *op. cit.*, 353.

8 *Op. cit.*, 358.

complex of causative factors, they can be minimized in the processes of treatment and reformation. In the administration of justice, fortune must not be allowed to shuffle the cards. Judges, police and probation officers, witnesses, institutional workers, and others who deal with delinquents or report them have a responsibility in not letting human prejudices and emotions interfere with the processes of justice and of reformation.

BREAKDOWN OF THE PROCESS OF LAW ENFORCEMENT AND THE TREATMENT OF OFFENDERS

Any breakdown in the process of law enforcement means an increased opportunity for lawbreaking. Inadequate methods and facilities for the treatment of offenders likewise affect the incidence of delinquency, especially the number of recidivists. Incomplete administration procedures and personnel mean ineffective law enforcement—often miscarriage of justice. With limited facilities, even efficient personnel cannot deal effectively with the problem of delinquency. Since these are items to be discussed in Part Three of this text, it is not necessary to deal with the matter here, except to emphasize the fact that the breakdown of the process of law enforcement and the way offenders are treated may be either a cause of further delinquency or a preventive.

Inadequate or Inefficient Personnel of Law Enforcement Agencies. The operation of justice is a single process working through a number of agencies, involving the machinery and procedures used in apprehension, arrest, detention, trial, treatment, institutionalization, and prevention. The program is composed of many parts and involves various kinds of procedures. The personnel of the different governmental and nongovernmental agencies that deal with offenders is the key to the success or failure of the process of law enforcement. The law enforcement representatives are in a better position than the other agencies to deal effectively with lawbreakers and to discover the harmful influences that contribute to delinquent behavior. Police or sheriff and probation officers have direct contact with offenders and occupy a strategic position to deal directly with the situation. It is, therefore, important that they be adequately trained for the job.

The manner in which the officer handles the child in his first difficulty with police may be the making or breaking of the youngster's future life. For this reason, it is imperative that every officer, from the chief or sheriff down to the newest rookie or deputy, have an understanding of how juveniles should be interviewed and treated.[9]

The beat officer on patrol has many occasions to talk to boys and girls engaged in acts of mischief. He can summarily dispose of many cases by a firm but friendly warning or by discussion of the problems with parents as well as with the offenders. It is common knowledge that a large portion of youthful offenders begin their careers with petty offenses or simply mischief making. If the process is not checked, more serious offenses will be committed later; and as the individual grows older, he becomes a habitual offender. A large percentage of adult criminals begin their careers as juvenile delinquents.

Police officers can best deal with lawbreakers by gaining their confidence instead of arousing antagonism. The manual, designed for the guidance of enforcement officers in dealing with juvenile offenders and in establishing prevention bureaus within the law enforcement agencies, previously referred to, suggests that officers should treat juveniles with consideration, be friendly, be firm, discover the child's problems, try to gain his confidence and respect, and be positive in his attitude. Officers should refrain from using vulgarity or profanity, branding the juvenile as a "liar" or "thief" or "burglar," or losing their tempers. Warnings and notifications should be made with care. The cooperation of parents is very important in dealing with juveniles.

It is difficult to be firm and at the same time be considerate. The personality of the officer is an important qualification. Some of the larger police departments and sheriff offices give prospective employees psychological and personality tests to determine their fitness.

August Vollmer [10] has pointed out that the ability to distinguish between criminals and noncriminals and to handle successfully the various types of cases requires intensive training and considerable experience. Lacking the behavior specialist's ability to detect the causes of delinquency, the policeman may do more harm than good in his attempt to fulfill his official obligations. Although intelligent and well intentioned, if he is uninformed with respect to personality factors and environmental influences he may use the wrong approach. Ability to get the facts quickly, and thus prevent a mis-

---

[9] *Techniques of Law Enforcement in the Treatment of Juveniles and the Prevention of Juvenile Delinquency* (1944), a manual compiled by the National Advisory Police Committee on Social Protection of the Federal Security Agency, approved by The International Association of Chiefs of Police and The National Sheriff's Association.

[10] *The Criminal* (Brooklyn: The Foundation Press, Inc., 1949), Chapter VII on "Law Enforcement Aspects."

carriage of justice, requires able investigators who are skilled in analyzing behavior problems. Anyone who is intimately acquainted with police officers cannot fail to be impressed with the interest, courage, zeal, and ingenuity that they display in doing their work. The policeman's job is not an easy one and the public does not always understand the difficulties that are encountered in enforcing the laws. Unfortunately there are few institutions of higher learning to train officers for juvenile work. The Delinquency Control Institute of the University of Southern California, in cooperation with the law enforcement agencies of the state of California, was established in 1946, after several years of planning, to offer an intensive course of training for juvenile officers. This Institute has established its practical worth in the law enforcement field in many ways, as will be shown in Part Three.

Incompetence of certain officers is far more common than corruption. Politics and political corruption may have a bearing on criminal behavior, especially in dealing with adults. The professional criminal often depends upon connections with politicians. However, political corruption has less effect on the problem of juvenile delinquency than on adult crime. Racketeers may use juveniles and often have a great influence on them; but the business of racketeering is largely an adult game, although racketeering groups may grow out of juvenile groups. Racketeers need to be entrenched with the police in order to have protection, which is the source of corruption.

Whyte [11] has given a vivid picture of the Cornerville racketeers, with a detailed description of the structure of racketeering. He depicts the struggle between Tony Catoldo, the racketeer, and Carlo Tedesco, the corner boy, for control of the Cornerville Social and Athletic Club. This club grew out of a barbershop gang. As the boys grew older, the group began to have political aims. The barbershop clique and the lunchroom clique were loosely joined in the Cornerville S. and D. Club, with Tony as the over-all leader and with members of a racket organization interspersed in both cliques. Whyte depicts the intricate organization of the club and its relation to other groups, the shifting of leadership and membership alliances, the political issues and racketeering activities, and the various crises that occurred as a result of these activities. It is not a problem of lack of organization, but a failure of the Cornerville organization to mesh with the structure of the larger society around it. For a Cornerville man to get ahead, he has to move either in the world

---

11 William Foote Whyte, *Street Corner Society* (Chicago: University of Chicago Press, 1943), Part II.

of business or in the world of the rackets, and have corresponding political alignments, for he cannot move in two worlds at once.

Inadequate Methods and Agencies for Dealing with Delinquents. The methods of dealing with offenders have been improved, as will be indicated in the succeeding chapters. Police practices, probation procedures, and juvenile court methods have all undergone changes and improvements. Yet, in so far as the methods of treatment fall short of the best practice, it can be said that the failure to deal adequately with individual cases is in itself a factor in the incidence of delinquency. This is obvious to anyone who has dealt with delinquents or who has read their case records.

In most communities the institutional facilities for dealing with offenders are too limited and inadequate. The volume of cases cannot be adequately cared for; nor is the quality of service adequate. Overcrowding, insufficient facilities and trained personnel, and defective methods lead to difficulties. Even the best institutions, from detention homes to specialized correctional institutions, may fail because of inherent difficulties in the corrective process.

Correctional institutions have sometimes been labeled "schools of crime." Surveys of such institutions and follow-up studies of released inmates have confirmed this contention in many instances. The boys' own stories, such as *The Jack-Roller* and *The Natural History of a Delinquent Career,* by Clifford R. Shaw, show that the delinquents themselves have considered some of the institutions to which they were sentenced as schools of crime. Here they mingled with crooks of every description. Even in the best institutions, the inmates may carry on a counteradjustice process with varying degrees of success. Juveniles who are held in jails or prisons where they have contacts with adult criminals, or in institutions where the first offenders are housed with seasoned delinquents, find it difficult to overcome the influence of hardened criminals.

These conditions, as well as improved methods of treatment, will be considered in the succeeding chapters. Investigators have found that the percentage of failures of institutional treatment varies considerably in different institutions. Albert Deutsch [12] has given a somewhat journalistic picture of some of the correctional institutions. The Gluecks, Healy and Bronner, and many others have called attention to the failures as well as successes of institutional treatment.

In summarizing the inadequacy of law observance and enforce-

<hr>

[12] *Our Rejected Children* (Boston: Little Brown and Company, 1950).

ment, and the methods of treating delinquents, we must recognize the multiplicity and confusion of laws, the inequality and often unfairness in the application of law, and the attitude of the public toward law enforcement, for they have a bearing on the extent of crime. When the prevailing definitions and attitudes are in opposition to the observance of law, and when individuals are in conflict with law-enforcement agencies, there are always some who follow the prevailing pattern of thought and behavior. The lack of uniform desire of people to enforce law under all circumstances often has far-reaching consequences. When citizens are unwilling to put forth the effort to see to it that law and order are maintained, law enforcement is difficult.

Any breakdown in the law-enforcement process and in handling cases of law violators in correctional and penal institutions may be a factor in furthering crime. Insufficient or incompetent personnel in police, sheriff, probation, court, and prosecuting departments often results in the miscarriage of justice and breeds disrespect for law. Inadequate supervision of probation and parole cases may lead to recidivism. Detention, correction, and penal institutions sometimes fail to modify conduct and to adjust deviants to more normal living. It must be recognized that under most favorable circumstances the correctional process may fail because of the counterforces at work in these institutions. The institutionalized cases are usually recidivists or persons who have committed serious offenses, some of whom have deeply rooted antisocial attitudes. At best, then, law enforcement and correctional procedures are beset with difficulties. Any failure in social control opens the door wider for future law violations.

In Retrospect: Summary and Conclusions

In the introduction to Part Two, a general theoretical frame of reference was outlined for the purpose of orientation before proceeding with the more detailed analysis of the basic factors and conditions of delinquency. It was pointed out, however, that etiological research is beset with difficulties. One cannot always be sure about the cause of any social problem, and delinquency is a complex problem. It is a part of a dynamic social process. The character of this process is conditioned by the personality of the individual, involving both inherited and acquired traits; the social world in which the person lives, including certain physical as well as social environmental factors; and the sequence of events, together with the interplay of various factors and variables that culminate in the delinquent act. It is in the process of interaction between the child and the successive situations in which he lives that misconduct evolves. Basically, delinquency arises in the matrix of personal and social disorganization, growing out of a complex situation in which there is a functional interaction of the various conditions.

Since delinquency appears to be the product of the interaction of many factors and variables, any single cause or explanation must be rejected as unsatisfactory. Delinquency is not an unidimensional phenomenon. In view of the multiplicity of conditions that play a part in the process leading to delinquency, any theory of causation that singles out only a few elements, especially if others are minimized or omitted, is likewise unsatisfactory. The multiple causation theory, without some frame of reference or integration of the varied findings, is admittedly somewhat vague and indefinite. It must be recognized that frequently a number of factors occur together, but simply occurring concomitantly in a situation does not necessarily mean that they are the basic causes of delinquency, for apparent conditions may root in deeper causes. The functional frame of reference appears to be a desirable method of analysis for unraveling the multiplicity of variables and the system of intricate relationships between the factors connected with crime. The difficulty lies in establishing valid correlations between variables.

Even though the conditioning factors are complex and varied, they can be classified under certain broad categories to indicate the groups and types that are significant. A sevenfold classification was used for convenience of analysis. The items do not cover the entire gamut of possible causes, but they call attention to the ramification of the problem. The classification provides a framework for the summarization of available material rather than a system of verified causes. The fact that a chapter is devoted to each group of factors, except the first, does not mean that they are of equal importance. The sequence of items in a general way indicates the order in which they were studied or emphasized. The earlier studies emphasized the individual approach, chiefly biological and psychological factors; whereas the later studies, especially by sociologists, have stressed environmental influences.

Delinquency is not inherited, and the notion that hereditary factors play a major part in deviant behavior is stressed less now than formerly. Studies of cases have revealed certain deviant physical, psychological, and behavior traits of delinquents. Experts do not agree in their appraisal of the relative influence of physical or biological characteristics of delinquents. Some writers have pointed out that biological inferiority, poor health and certain types of diseases, physical handicaps, glandular imbalance, malnutrition, and similar deficiencies are more prevalent among delinquents than among nondelinquents. Others maintain that no significant statistical comparison of the frequency of such defects in the criminal and noncriminal population has been made. Sheldon and the Gluecks have maintained that delinquents are superior rather than inferior in bodily structure.

The psychological factors have received considerable attention. Mental tests have been used in the analysis of thousands of cases. As compared with the theoretical distribution of levels of intelligence, most studies show that a larger proportion of delinquents are in the feeble-minded or dull normal categories than is true of the general population. However, comparative studies of the relative intelligence of offenders and nonoffenders are difficult to make, partly because of the inferiority of testing methods and the types of cases studied. As the composition and administration of intelligence tests improved, fewer of the inmates in institutions have been classed as feeble-minded, although many are in the dull normal class. In certain types of offenses, such as sex offenses and opiate addiction, low intelligence seems to play a more important part than in other types of crime. Low intelligence per se is not a cause of crime, but the difficulties in scholastic achievements, frustrations, low social status, and similar accompanying factors may have a more direct bearing on deviant behavior. Whatever the relationship of mental deficiency to crime, the defective delinquents require special forms of treatment. Mental diseases and functional disorders, minor personality maladjustments and emotional tensions, and various other psychiatric difficulties have received increasing attention during recent years. The various types of psychological disorders are more prevalent among adults than among juveniles, but the beginnings of them often manifest themselves fairly early in childhood. The psychoanalysts have been particularly concerned with the early manifestations of disorders and maladjustments, and the orthopsychiatrists have concerned themselves with the diagnosis and treatment of borderline cases of mental and emotional deviations. Emotional conflicts, disturbances, frustrations, and instabilities are frequently associated with deviant behavior. When dynamic wishes and other motivating tendencies are thwarted by circumstances or by inner repression, antisocial behavior may be the consequence. The acceptance of the idea of deviation is a prelude to misconduct.

One of the most neglected aspects of personality analysis from the point of view of delinquency is that of character traits and their development. Character is an integral part of the total personality and it conditions or determines how a child will act in situations involving choices between right and wrong in matters of conduct. The child learns from experience that certain forms of action are proper and right, and that others are wrong. How the child will act when tempted to deviate from the norms of society depends somewhat upon the type of character training and the strength or weakness of inner controls. When he has developed or learned "definitions" favorable to law violation over the opposite "definitions," deviations from norms are likely to occur. Either lawful or unlawful behavior may develop in early childhood and persist throughout life. To appraise conduct adequately, it is necessary to recognize the early experiences of a person as well as the personal-situation complex of the moment.

Personality factors are important in behavior and should be fully recognized, but not overemphasized. Individual maladjustments and deviations are not separable from environmental conditions and deviant social pressures. Individual and group aspects of disorganization occur together, and the influences are reciprocal. In a disorganized society, personalities tend to become disintegrated and demoralized; whereas in a harmonious and well-adjusted society, personalities are more integrated and stable. Contrariwise, the presence of deficient or maladjusted individuals produces and constitutes social disorganization.

The social variables in the etiology of delinquency are even more complex and varied than the conditions of personality. Family relations, gang associations, institutional influences, heterogeneity and mobility of the population and conflict of cultures, economic and physical environmental conditions, and the subtle sociopsychological influences surrounding juveniles are so varied and changing that no positive conclusions regarding their relative influences can be drawn.

Studies of delinquents have shown that from 30 to 60 per cent, on an average about 40 per cent, of juveniles who are brought into courts or who are handled by other law enforcement agencies come from broken homes. The extent of family disorganization depends somewhat upon the types of cases studied. Statistics of the relationship of broken homes to delinquency are made more meaningful by comparing them with the extent of broken homes in the general population or in control groups. The studies by Merrill and the Gluecks indicate that nearly twice the proportion of delinquents come from broken homes than in the control groups. Quasi-broken homes, poorly adjusted families, inadequate discipline and control, and homes that function inadequately are not conducive to the proper training of the young. Dissension and conflict, physical and mental abnormality, mixed parentage, and other forms of maladjustments and inadequacies often are more detrimental to child welfare than the eventual breakdown of the home. Delinquency often runs in families in which deviant conditions exist. When both delinquents and nondelinquents come from the same homes, the differential behavior is more difficult to explain. The home is generally regarded as one of the most influential institutions in child training, in providing affection and love, and in meeting other basic needs. If it fails in the performance of its functions, it is likely to be the most potent social force in producing antisocial tendencies and forms of behavior.

Nearly all children have playmates and intimate companions. Chums and gang membership may mean more to a child than do the members of his family. This is particularly true in the high delinquency areas. As Warner, Hollingshead, and others have pointed out, our society is stratified on a social class basis. The prestige structure affects the clique and dating relationships of the young, their group affiliations, their jobs, their recreation, and in the end their conduct. What proportion of delinquency is the outgrowth of gang activities is not exactly known. Thrasher found that out of the 1313 gangs studied, only about 52 did not have some demoralizing effects. It is chiefly through the gang that the newly initiated members gain familiarity with the codes and activities of the underworld. The factors underlying ganging are exceedingly complex.

Personality factors, home conditions, and relationships with intimate associates and gang membership are likely to be more important and meaningful to juveniles than the conditions in the community. Any breakdown or failure in these areas of life is likely to produce antisocial behavior. Although the influences coming from these sources may vary in frequency, intensity, and duration, they impinge more directly upon the everyday life of children than the secondary factors in the community and in the larger social world. However, community factors cannot be dismissed as relatively unimportant. They, at times, are the major causes of delinquency, especially if they affect vitally the centers of influence that are closely related to children's behavior.

Community institutions perform vital functions in our society. If any fail to do so, deviant behavior may be the consequence of neglect. Recreation institutions and agencies are of special significance here, partly because they play an important part in a child's life, but chiefly because certain forms of commercial amusements (movies, dance halls, comics, crime stories, radio and television programs, et cetera) have deleterious effects. Notwithstanding the seemingly obvious relationship between the uses of leisure and delinquency, it is difficult to demonstrate the exact correlation between amusements and the behavior of those who frequent them.

That population factors have a bearing on delinquency is evidenced by the statistics of delinquency, which indicate that the peak of law violation is in the adolescent and young adult periods, boys and men have higher rates of delinquency and crime than girls and women, certain racial and nationality groups have unusually high rates of offenses, and lawlessness is especially prevalent in areas of great population heterogeneity and mobility. Possibly the more important aspect to note is that cultural conflicts and differentiation play a conspicuous part in deviant behavior. It is not so much a matter of race or nationality, as segregation, discrimination, and the consequent lower standard of living.

Numerous studies have indicated the influence of economic factors, especially poverty, which is usually regarded as an important cause of delinquency, for a disproportionate number of delinquents come from the lower economic classes, particularly in families that are on relief. Some studies have revealed that the rates of delinquency in the different areas of a city correlate closely with the rates of dependency in these areas. The employment of mothers and certain types of child labor likewise have similar effects. The fact that delinquency rates tend to follow the business cycle, as several studies have shown, does not mean that poverty has no bearing on the problem.

The physical conditions of the community have a relationship to the degree of social disorganization. Slums and blighted areas have the highest criminal rates. The high delinquency areas have not only certain adverse objective realities but subjective elements. Besides high rates of law violation, these regions are characterized by physical deterioration and poor housing, changing and heterogeneous population, low economic status, institutional disorganization, and the spirit of delinquency.

Even though a number of the previously mentioned personal and environmental factors conditioning delinquency may be present in a given situation, and individuals are seriously affected by them, this does not necessarily mean that they will succumb to law violations, provided personal and social controls keep behavior in check. Any breakdown in the system of controls, such as the lack of concern for law observance or inefficient law enforcement, opens the way for deviations from societal norms. In that sense, delinquency is a failure of personal and social controls.

The program of delinquency control requires more than the regulation of behavior. It is necessary to get at the roots of the problem and to eliminate them or at least bring about a readjustment of conditions. The agencies and methods of prevention include social legislation and action, improved services of governmental and private agencies and institutions, community organization, social research to understand the problem, and a greater dissemination of information regarding the basic factors and conditions that lead to delinquency. These aspects will be discussed in the succeeding division of this text.[13]

QUESTIONS AND PROJECTS

For Class Discussion and Research

1. Discuss community attitudes toward law observance and enforcement. Has the public attitude toward law observance improved since World War II?

2. Why is the delinquency tradition such a powerful influence in American communities? What is meant by the "spirit of delinquency?"

3. What social processes are especially involved in the creation of a delinquency situation?

4. Is crime chiefly a matter of chance?

5. Make a list of the most effective methods of work by the best officers on patrol in dealing with deviant children.

6. In what ways may inadequate methods and agencies for dealing with delinquents be considered as causes of delinquency?

7. On the basis of the causes of delinquency discussed in Part Two, which causal or conditioning factors have the most direct effects on children?

8. In what sense is delinquency a failure of personal and social controls?

9. How does the breakdown or failure of law enforcement affect the rate of crime?

SELECTED REFERENCES

BARNES, HARRY ELMER, AND NEGLEY K. TEETER, *New Horizons in Criminology* (New York: Prentice-Hall, Inc., 1943 and 1949).

CANTOR, NATHANIEL F., *Crime and Society: An Introduction to Criminology* (New York: Henry Holt and Co., 1939).

---

13 For summaries of conditioning and related aspects of delinquency, see "A Symposium on Juvenile Delinquency," *Cornell Law Quarterly*, Vol. 35, No. 3 (Spring, 1950). Articles by Ralph S. Banay, Gilbert H. F. Mumford, Martin H. Neumeyer, and Miriam Van Waters.

CAVAN, RUTH SHONLE, *Criminology* (New York: Thomas Y. Crowell Co., 1948).

GILLIN, JOHN L., *Criminology and Penology* (New York: D. Appleton-Century Co., 1945).

MIHANOVICH, CLEMENT S., *Principles of Juvenile Delinquency* (Milwaukee: The Bruce Publishing Co., 1950).

RECKLESS, WALTER L., *The Etiology of Delinquent and Criminal Behavior: A Planning Report for Research* (New York: Social Science Research Council, 1943); and "Juvenile Delinquency," *Encyclopedia of Educational Research,* Walter S. Monroe, Editor (New York: The Macmillan Co., 1950).

SELLIN, THORSTEN, *The Criminality of Youth* (Philadelphia: American Law Institute, 1940).

SUTHERLAND, EDWIN H., *Principles of Criminology* (New York: J. B. Lippincott Co., 1947).

VON HENTIG, HANS, *Crime: Causes and Conditions* (New York: McGraw-Hill Book Co., Inc., 1947).

WOOD, A. E., AND J. B. WAITE, *Crime and Its Treatment* (New York: American Book Co., 1941).

PART THREE

DELINQUENCY CONTROL

The major function of social scientists is the study of the problem of delinquency, analyzing the extent and trends of the problem, the distribution of delinquency cases and types of offenses, the composition of the delinquency population, and the basic factors and conditions that produce delinquent behavior. Etiological research is of special importance, for no system of delinquency control can be effective without a thorough knowledge of the underlying causes of the problem. The study of delinquency causation provides the basis for both treatment procedures and preventive measures. Therefore, social research should be directed mainly toward an increase of our knowledge of why juveniles become delinquent.

This statement does not imply that the study of correctional treatment and preventive programs is unimportant. As was indicated in the preceding chapter, the way deviants are treated often has a bearing on their future conduct. The preventive agencies and methods are even more directly related to the prevalence of the problem of delinquency than are treatment procedures. These will be discussed in the following chapters. Details of applied aspects of correction will not be stressed, for these are of special interest to practitioners rather than scientists. Instructors and students who desire to study in greater detail the practical aspects of treatment and prevention will find references in the bibliographies. The main purpose of Part Three is to provide a broad background for delinquency control.

The control of delinquency involves: (1) an adequate program of apprehension, investigation, detention, protection, juvenile court and probation services, and correctional institutions and agencies; and (2) effective agencies and methods of prevention. Social action, community organization and services, and a systematic study of the causes of delinquency and the available resources to deal with the problem are of special importance in a preventive program. Treatment and prevention are interrelated, for good treatment has preventive effects and an effective preventive program involves the treatment of both the delinquents and predelinquents. However, the two processes are not synonymous and should be dealt with separately.

The treatment process involves numerous stages or phases if carried out in full, beginning with the apprehension or referral of an alleged offender through the necessary steps to bring about a final termination of the process. Carr[1] calls this the correctional cycle and indicates the following steps: (1) apprehension or referral of alleged offender, (2) restraint of custody (detention) pending determination of the desirability of proceeding further, (3) preliminary diagnosis of the difficulty, (4) decision on future action or plan of action, (5) determination concerning need of treatment, (6) prescription of the type of treatment to be given the hearing in court), (7) treatment (probation, foster home placement, institutional care, and the like), (8) gradual attenuation of the treatment, and (9) the final termination of the treatment program. In carrying out this process five agencies are of special importance: (1) the police, (2) the detention home, (3) the juvenile court, (4) the probation department, and (5) the correctional institution. Not all of these are used in every case. The majority of behavior problem cases that come to the attention of law enforcement and correctional agencies are handled without utilizing the full correctional cycle and all the available facilities. The discovery of cases, their diagnosis, the protection of both the alleged delinquents and society, and the application of methods of treatment, using correctional agencies and institutions, constitute the major phases of delinquency control as a treatment process.

The chief objective of treatment is rehabilitation, which may be a simple or complex process, depending upon the degree of complexity of the factors involved. The aim is to restore the delinquent to normal living and to develop his personality, so that he may function usefully in a society that is conducive to this end.

The preventive process includes various types of social action and community services and the organization of agencies and institutions into a coordinated and cooperative enterprise in order to make a united attack upon the problem.

Chapters XII and XIII are devoted chiefly to the correctional cycle, with special consideration being given to the matters of apprehension and discovery of behavior problems, detention and protection services, and case analyses, followed by a description of the

---

[1] Lowell J. Carr, *Delinquency Control* (New York: Harper & Brothers, 1950), 223.

juvenile court, probation services, and correctional institutions and agencies. Chapters XIV and XV will be devoted to preventive programs, chiefly the necessity of getting at the roots of delinquency, group work and recreation, and the functions of government agencies in delinquency, followed by a consideration of community organization and methods of research.

XII

Apprehension, Investigation, Detention, and Protection

The first steps in the treatment process are the apprehension of children with behavior problems and the discovery of conditions that endanger them. The law enforcement agencies in the community must get into action as soon as deviant behavior becomes apparent, and readjustive and preventive forces must be mobilized as soon as deviant pressures endanger children.

An awareness of the multiple causation is a prerequisite to any enlightened control of delinquency. The factors of delinquency, as was pointed out in the preceding chapters, are numerous and complex. To deal effectively with a delinquent, it is necessary to ascertain and understand the motives and conditions that lead to misbehavior.

Apprehension and Discovery of Children in Trouble

The investigation of cases usually begins when juvenile offenses are called to the attention of law enforcement agencies or to school attendance officers. Often the antisocial tendencies are well developed by the time the investigation is begun. This definitely points to the need for the discovery of deviant children while they are still in the "problem" stage of maladjustment.

Finding the Children Who Are in Need. Many community agencies are in a position to detect deviant behavior in the early stages. Police officers on the beat are in a strategic position to observe the conduct of juveniles in the area. Precautions can be taken to prevent trouble. School teachers and officials can discern deviant behavior in classrooms and on the school playgrounds. Recreation and group work leaders have opportunities to observe unusual behavior while children are at play. Health authorities—doctors, nurses, public health officials, school health workers, and medical social workers—come in contact with physical and mental problems. Case workers are frequently confronted with behavior as well as welfare problems. These, and others who contact the juvenile population of the community, represent the chief sources of information regarding the behavior tendencies of children and youth.

Communities are increasingly equipping themselves with workers who can help parents, as well as the boys and girls themselves, to deal with problems of social behavior at any stage where difficulty arises. This is especially true in large communities, but it is also being extended to rural areas. Social hazards of everyday life must be recognized.

Many forms of unusual behavior are discernible. For clinical purposes, it is important to discover the conditions or forms of behavior that indicate inadequate adjustments to situations. Personality factors, such as those pointed out in Chapters IV and V, manifest themselves in the daily conduct of children. Physical handicaps and diseases, mental subnormality and disorders, emotional conflicts and instabilities, and behavior tendencies are frequent sources of trouble. Disobedience, incorrigibility, temper display, fighting, quarrelsomeness, lying, swearing, stealing, truancy from school, running away from home, sex misbehavior, acts of violence, and selfishness are some of the symptoms of maladjustment.

Various instruments and methods have been devised to discover behavior problems. Besides the personality and prediction tests and inventories mentioned in Chapter IV, the Haggerty-Olson-Wickman Behavior Rating Scale and similar techniques have been used to ascertain conditions of personality that may lead to misconduct. Carr states that the six main methods for the discovery of problem behavior are:

(1) direct observation of "symptoms"; (2) ratings by teachers; (3) ratings based on a child's reputation with his playmates—the "guess who" technique; (4) questionnaires; (5) information or conduct tests; and (6) appraisal of correlated conditions.[1]

Except for the various scientific tests, the difficulty with many of these devices is that they involve too much guesswork or personal opinions.

Some communities have set up committees or formed groups to correlate facilities and services.[2] Representatives of law enforcement agencies, schools, case-work agencies, and other agencies and institutions that deal with delinquents and predelinquents can spot children in danger of deviant behavior and refer them to the proper agency best equipped to deal with the cases. Such cases can be cleared through a central registry, if there is such a unit, school records can be obtained, and other pertinent data can be assembled. On the basis of available information, a plan of action can be worked out and the workers can proceed to meet the need.

Systematic methods of discovery can reveal cases of delinquency that are often hidden from public view and would otherwise not be detected. The Cambridge Somerville Youth Study[3] may be cited as an example of an organization that has maintained an intimate contact with a large group of boys through their adolescent years, which practice has afforded a unique opportunity to arrive at some measure of the amount of delinquency in this section of Massachusetts. The value of counseling service is especially stressed, although the results were not entirely satisfactory. For the purpose of the study, two groups of boys were selected: one, in which there were many potential delinquents, to each of whom was assigned a friendly counselor; the other, in which there was an equal proportion of potential delinquents, none of whom received the guidance of a special counselor. In this way the success of preventive techniques can be measured.

When juveniles have already gotten into difficulties and have violated laws, the responsibility for handling such cases rests prima-

---

[1] Lowell J. Carr, *Delinquency Control* (New York: Harper & Brothers, 1950), 265. Used by permission of publisher. See Chapter XII on "The Child and Behavior Problems" for a discussion of technology of discovery and diagnosis.

[2] See Elizabeth Fajen, "Curing Delinquency at the Source," *Survey Midmonthly*, Vol. LXXXII, No. 10 (October, 1946), 260-263, describing the setup in New York City. Another example is the case conference committee, formerly research-adjustment division, of the community coordinating councils of Los Angeles county.

[3] Edwin Powers and Helen Witmer, *Prevention of Delinquency* (New York: Columbia University Press, 1951). For an earlier report of the study, see Murphy and Others, "The Incidence of Hidden Delinquency," *American Journal of Orthopsychiatry*, Vol. XVI, No. 4 (October, 1946), 686-696.

rily with the law enforcing agencies, of which the police or sheriff officers are usually the first to contact these juveniles.

Functions of Police in Apprehending Delinquents and in Processing Cases.[4] Case finding and investigation are central functions of the police. Since police officers are usually the first officials to contact offenders, the program of investigation and discovery of cases is carried on chiefly by them. This is particularly true of first offenders and those who commit minor offenses, which cases are handled directly by the police or sheriff officers. The probation departments and juvenile courts are used for the more serious offenses, especially if decisions are made to "file on" the cases. Besides the law enforcing agencies, school attendance officers and other community leaders may take part in the investigation process. The prosecuting attorney, state attorney, and, in violations of federal laws, the Federal Bureau of Investigation may take part in the process of apprehension and treatment, especially in the more serious cases.

The juvenile bureaus of police, sheriff, and probation departments, if such bureaus exist, have the major responsibility for investigating cases of juvenile offenders, and for handling the cases. In the larger cities the officers on the beat and in substations refer juveniles to the central bureau of the department. These officers usually bring in a large proportion of the cases apprehended. They may make preliminary investigations. If the offenses are serious, the parents are contacted. Many noncourt cases are handled each day. The patrol officers warn children, discuss matters with them, take them to their homes and confer with parents, and in other ways make adjustments without resort to the full process of the law.

Courtesy is the stock in trade of police officers, which consists chiefly of quiet, unassuming behavior based in a sincere consideration for the feelings of the people—children and their parents—with whom they must deal. On duty, whether contacts with the public are made in the community or at the desk in police headquarters,

---

4 For a comprehensive treatment of the work of police in dealing with juveniles, see John P. Kenney and Dan G. Pursuit, *Police Work with Children* (Springfield, Illinois: Charles C. Thomas Co., 1954). The material of this book was derived chiefly from the practical experience in instructing police officers and the research work in the Delinquency Control Institute of the University of Southern California, where Dan G. Pursuit is Director, and John P. Kenney, Associate Professor of Public Administration, is a staff member. Compare *Police and Children: A Study of New York City's Juvenile Aid Bureau* (Citizens' Committee on Children of New York City, Inc., 1951); Alfred J. Kahn, "The Function of Police and Children's Courts," *The Community and the Correctional Process: 1951 Yearbook*, edited by Marjorie Bell (New York: National Probation and Parole Association, 1951), 60-74; and Lt. Bernard Berkowitz, "The Juvenile Police Officer," *Focus*, Vol. 31, No. 5 (September, 1952), 129-234.

personal appearance, tone of voice, and mode of behavior are essential matters in dealing with offenders and those affected by the offenses committed.

Faced with the problem of protective custody, law enforcement agencies must follow more definite procedures. If abandoned or neglected infants are found, they may be taken to the general hospital and special institutions for infant care. Other small children are frequently provided for in children's homes. Juvenile detention homes and hospitals are used for others who are under certain ages. Unfortunately, many older boys, and girls too, are still detained in police jails and lockups.

Taking juveniles into custody is done for various purposes and for different periods of time. The chief reasons are to provide better opportunities for investigation, protection, medical care, and preliminary treatment. After the preliminary investigation or treatment, various steps in the correctional cycle may be decided upon. The disposition of a case by the police depends upon many factors, such as the kind of offense, the record of the offender, the policy of the department, the court calendar, and the availability of facilities for treatment. Modern police departments, with juvenile bureaus manned by competent officers, are in a position to handle many types of cases without referring them to the juvenile court, especially if the children and the parents show a cooperative attitude and their behavior warrants confidence.

The police and other local law enforcement authorities have important responsibilities in the apprehension, investigation, treatment, and prevention of delinquency. Inasmuch as they are often the first to learn about the misconduct of children, they are in a strategic position to deal with such children or to refer them to the appropriate governmental or private agencies. In order to carry out these responsibilities effectively, it is desirable that the local law enforcement agencies include, within their personnel, officers specially trained to take care of children's cases.

The role of the police in the correctional program is not always fully understood. It is not the purpose of the present text to deal with police power and practices. That is a field for special study and consideration. However, it is important to note that police power is invested in duly recognized law enforcement agencies.

The police power is an inherent function of government. This embraces the power to legislate and to carry out the program of law enforcement. The police operate under the police power of the government. While the American attitude toward the police has been notoriously unsympathetic, the officers of the law have the responsibility of setting in motion the machinery of justice. Sheriff, constable, coroner, city police, state police, federal police, and other officers have the responsibility of detecting law violations, the enforcement of penal and other codes, and the protection of society. These are the arresting agencies. Action in criminal cases is initiated in a variety of ways, such as immediate arrest or arrest after the issuance of a warrant, grand jury indictment, accusation by prosecutor, or through action of a coroner's jury. To arrest means to detain or take a person into custody by legal authority. To accomplish the various functions, police departments have established a system of organization, with bureaus and divisions to carry out functions of patrol, traffic control, criminal investigation, records, vice control, management of personnel and property, and treatment and prevention of crime and delinquency.

Police work with minors is confined chiefly to apprehension of juvenile offenders and preliminary investigation of their cases, treatment of minor and special cases, and activities in the preventive field. Juvenile police work is based upon the premise that special techniques are required in the proper handling of children's cases. Prompt and thorough investigations of all cases where delinquency has been committed by or against juveniles, followed by disposition of the cases, which may be direct treatment or referral to juvenile court or to other agencies, are important phases of the work. The average juvenile officer is not equipped to undertake a complete social case analysis and treatment program; and even if he were in a position to do so, he would be duplicating the work of other agencies. Therefore, it is necessary to know the procedure of referral and of cooperation with other agencies in meeting the needs of the individual.

In order to do a good job of handling juveniles, police departments and sheriff offices have established juvenile departments, divisions, or bureaus. The over-all objective is to protect life and property, apprehend offenders and investigate cases, provide treatment and/or referral services, and engage in preventive activities. In these operations officers use the services of the juvenile court and probation department, schools, case-work and group-work agencies, churches, coordinating or community councils, various types of clubs, and other community agencies and sources. The records of some of these agencies are invaluable. If clinical facilities are available, they should be used in certain types of cases. These records and resources do not take the place of the case material assembled by the officers through interviews and from other direct sources, but they are valuable supplements. Community agencies are likewise used to aid in the treatment procedure.

In order to accomplish the best results, the juvenile division not only is an investigating and treating agency, but must cooperate with other units of the police department and other law enforcement agencies in dealing with certain types of cases. In large police departments, various divisions deal with juveniles, such units as traffic, missing juveniles, truancy, dance hall, and narcotics and liquor control. Furthermore, the regional patrol divisions, which are all-services units, are usually the ones to make the first contacts before the juveniles in trouble are referred to the special sections for more thorough investigation, the determination of procedure, and the treatment process. A record system is important in order to have adequate reports of delinquencies, information regarding assignments and/or arrests, and disposition of cases, also for daily reporting.[5]

The role of police women in handling girls' cases is not fully appreciated, but the police departments, especially in large cities, have found women officials indispensable. According to a recent government report,[6] over 1000 women are engaged in police work and about 2000 are in other government law enforcement work, as deputy sheriffs, probation officers, and the like. These officers deal primarily with children and women who are involved either as offenders or as victims of offenses. They are in a position to deal more effectively than men officials with these problems.

Referral of Cases. The more serious cases are "filed on" in the juvenile court, which usually entails a more thorough investigation by the probation department or by the officers of the detention institution. Both court and police authorities may refer cases to other agencies. Referral of cases to the agency best equipped to deal with them is a common practice. Cases may be referred to social agencies, because they are in a position to help individuals and to modify existing environmental conditions, thus aiding in the ultimate prevention of undesirable behavior. Juvenile courts handle both delinquency and welfare cases, and this is true also to some extent of police departments. Delinquency and welfare problems are frequently associated in the same case.

Officers are ready to refer cases to correctional and welfare agen-

---

[5] Consult manual of a local police department for further details regarding functions of the various units and procedural instructions.

[6] *The Outlook for Women in Police Work,* United States Department of Labor (Washington, D. C.: Government Printing Office, 1949).

cies, when they have confidence in the ability of leaders to bring about rehabilitation or prevention programs and when the individuals in difficulty desire to be helped. If they show signs of responding favorably to the treatment, the procedure is usually continued.

No referral can be successful unless the case is properly diagnosed. To do the job well, the officer in charge not only must get the usual case record type of information, but must have a knowledge of human behavior based upon the philosophy of multiple causation, secure the child's own story, and relate the individual and his acts to the total situation. Furthermore, he must have information regarding existing agencies that may be helpful in dealing with the case—their policies, procedures, and practices.

The techniques of referral relate to the individual in difficulty, the parents, and the representatives of correctional and social agencies. A plan of cooperation is needed to bring about an amiable relationship between the law enforcement officers and the various agencies dealing with the child and his family.

The importance of referral of cases can be seen by analyzing the statistics of cases handled by police (including sheriff and similar law enforcement agencies) and by the juvenile courts. As was indicated in Chapter II, the police agencies contacted about a million juveniles during 1951, most of whom had violated laws. Of these, about one fourth were referred to juvenile courts. In addition to the quarter of a million individuals referred to juvenile courts by police authorities, an additional hundred thousand came to the juvenile courts from school authorities, social agencies, other courts, parents, and various other sources.

In view of the great volume of cases handled, case screening and referral are important processes. Police officers must use discretion about arresting, screening, referring, or handling cases directly. Minor offenders are usually given "a second chance." Parents, teachers, club leaders, clergymen, and other interested persons may be in a position to effect adjustment and reform without further action.

PROCESS OF INVESTIGATION AND PRELIMINARY TREATMENT

It is not the purpose here to indicate in detail the process of investigation, the types of data to be included in case records, and the preliminary treatment procedures. The description of comprehensive case studies is beyond the scope of the present analysis. However, a broad outline of the kinds of studies that are made and the accompanying treatment based on the diagnosis and prognosis of the case will serve to indicate the importance of investigation before proceeding to any type of treatment.

Case Analysis and Diagnosis. The social study of a case involves the exploration of many conditions. All factors that have exerted or are exerting any appreciable influence upon the life and experiences of the offender must be explored for adequate treatment purposes. There are few short cuts or easy solutions. Shifting the problem without getting at the sources of trouble is no solution. This does not mean, however, that the case worker must wait with the treatment process until all conditions are known. Treatment and case study can go hand in hand.

To make an adequate study of a case, at least three types of information are essential: (1) the personal elements, including the offender's own story, especially his personal attitudes, feelings, interests, and role in the group; (2) the social and culture world of the person, also the physical setting and economic condition; and (3) the sequence of events that had a bearing on the act or the behavior problem under consideration.

Offenders come to the attention of law enforcement officers in a variety of ways. When an officer is called upon to investigate a case, certain preliminary items of information are necessary in order to determine what to do with the case and how to proceed to meet the situation. What was the offense? The nature of the offense—whether begging, vagrancy, intoxication, incorrigibility, sex immorality, petty larceny, assault, burglary, running away from home, truancy from school, or any of a variety of other acts—is an important consideration. But this is only the beginning of the investigation, and often it is difficult to find out exactly what happened, for witnesses and victims, as well as offenders, often present conflicting reports. Were there associates in the offense? Were weapons used? If goods were taken, what was their disposition and where are they to be found? What were the circumstances of the offense? All data must be verified.

Case records range all the way from brief reports of what happened and a few accompanying data to comprehensive case histories. Sometimes it is not necessary to record more than a few items on an official form. Usually the police record contains information regarding the arrest (if a juvenile is arrested), the division arresting and reporting, the date and time of arrest, the place of the offense, the itemized evidences and where found, aliases, record of witnesses, statement of arrested person, and where the person is confined. Certain personal data are also included, such as the person's full name, address, also the names and address of parents, age (including birth date), sex, grade in school, occupation (if any), race, and certain other items that help to identify the person.

If more information is needed, certain sources are contacted. If there is a central registry, as in Los Angeles County, arresting agencies call the Central Juvenile Index for information regarding previous arrests and juvenile court action (if any)—all items that aid the officers in determining the course of procedure. If the individual is already a ward of the court, he is taken to the appropriate authorities for further action. In this case, the probation department has a record of the individual. Schools usually have information regarding offenders, especially if they are truants or problem cases. Social agencies can supply information regarding the families of delinquents if they have been or are on relief.

There are many problems connected with the interviewing process. To obtain facts about a person and the social situation and to get the child's own story require interviewing; and the interview data must be supplemented by official and other reports. It is difficult to standardize the interviewing procedure, but a few items are important. The child must be treated with consideration and a condition of *rapport* must be maintained throughout. His confidence must be gained before he will reveal much about himself and his activities. Friendliness, coupled with a certain amount of firmness, helps to get the child to tell his story. To discover the child's problems, it is desirable to interview him alone and let him feel that the interviewer is there to help him. The interviewer must identify himself properly at the beginning and be a good listener. This requires patience, careful questioning, and alertness. John P. Kenney and Dan G. Pursuit, previously referred to, list thirty items that are of importance in an interview and that should be observed.

Pauline V. Young[7] describes the phases of comprehensive case studies. The large juvenile courts are increasingly using more detailed case studies, especially of the more serious offenders, such as the recidivists. Hence, probation departments and correctional agencies have trained staff members who know how to make thorough studies of cases. Where clinical facilities are available, more extensive social case work is possible, involving both comprehensive investigations of cases and social treatment.

Besides the face sheet type of information and the legal history

---

[7] *Social Treatment in Probation and Delinquency: Treatise and Casebook for Court Workers, Probation Officers, and Other Child Welfare Workers* (New York: McGraw-Hill Book Co., Inc., 1952), Chapters III-VIII. Note especially the cases of Marilyn Smith and Alex Alexander.

as required by law, the case study includes information regarding the family of the delinquent (parents, marital history and adjustment or maladjustment, sibling relation, economic condition of the home, whether the home is broken or otherwise disorganized, and other pertinent data), the playmates and gang association, the kind of neighborhood, and other information pertaining to the social and physical environment in which a child lives. The child's own history is likewise important, including the early development, physical and mental health, educational experience and school life, moral and religious training, recreation activities, and other personal data. In this connection, the life history of a child should include his (or her) own story, not merely information about the child obtained from other sources.

The Illinois Institute for Juvenile Research has long been known for thorough case studies. The staff includes medical authorities, psychologists, psychiatrists, case workers, sociologists, and other specialists. The published reports by Clifford R. Shaw and collaborators [8] are among the best sociological studies of cases. These investigators not only had the advantage of the findings of the Institute staff, but succeeded in getting the boys' own stories in considerable detail. Treatment procedures were based on the analysis of the case records.

The Delinquent's Own Story. A complete life history of a person necessitates a knowledge of how the individual feels about the situation. The delinquent's own story enables an investigator to ascertain the child's point of view. The personal attitudes, feelings, interests, and reactions play a very important part in a child's conduct. The role a person conceives himself to play in relation to others, the interpretation he places on the social situations in which he lives, and his attitude toward those with whom he has to deal are important factors to consider in the treatment process. The individual, in telling his own story, throws light upon the social world in which he lives and which conditions his own life organization. The life history enables a worker to reconstruct the sequence of events that led to the difficulty. It is especially important to note the early experiences and influences that shape a child's life.

While William Healy attempted to procure the child's own story in interviewing individual delinquents, he never fully applied the technique. It remained for Shaw to demonstrate the value of the boy's own story, written by the subject himself, as a significant proce-

---

8 *The Jack-Roller: A Delinquent Boy's Own Story* (1930); *The Natural History of a Delinquent Career* (1931); and with Henry D. McKay and James F. McDonald, *Brothers in Crime* (1938). These cases were reviewed in Chapter VI.

dure to discover how a boy looks at life and his own situation, to what he responds in the social environment, and how he is affected by the situations in which he finds himself. While it is not possible or necessary to get every child to tell his own story in detail, no effective treatment of a case is possible without knowing something about the motivation of acts and how the individual feels about his behavior.

The life history record is a relatively new device of sociological research in the field of delinquency and crime, although considerable use has been made of such material in other fields. The life history of a delinquent may be obtained in various ways. The boy may write an autobiography, or keep a diary of his experiences, or tell his story to an interviewer. Sometimes a combination of methods is used to get the delinquent's own account of his experiences. Part of the story is obtained by interviews. The subject may be willing to write part of his story, with or without a guide. A diary has the advantage of a day-by-day record of events and inner reactions. Defective memory is a handicap in getting an accurate and complete story.

No matter how incomplete the child's own story may be, such a document is helpful in interpreting the case. Each case record should include a life-history document, together with the usual family history, the medical, psychiatric, and psychological findings, the description of the play group and companionships, the official record of offenses, arrests, and commitments, and other data that may throw light upon the personality, the actual experiences, and the environmental influences of the delinquent in question.

Social case histories, if relatively complete, facilitate social diagnosis. The complexity of conditioning factors and related phenomena must be recognized. Oversimplification is a temptation that must be avoided. However, the techniques of social investigation have been perfected sufficiently to make it possible to ascertain the major factors in the situation to enable the case worker to proceed with the treatment process.

DETENTION AND PROTECTION

Juvenile Detention. Although the first place of detention specifically for children was set up in 1880 in Massachusetts, the detention of juveniles in separate institutions prior to formal hearing is an outgrowth of the philosophy of the juvenile court, emphasizing the protection of the child. The movement grew out of the objection to detaining juveniles in jails and lockups. Detaining children in jail is not advisable. It is not known how many children are still kept in jails; but according to studies made by the Federal Bureau of Investigation and the Bureau of Prisons of the United States Department of Justice, it runs into tens of thousands, with many of them cared for in city and county jails that are poorly equipped and managed, with inadequate facilities for the care of juveniles. Estimates of the number of children who are taken to jails, lockups, and penitentiaries during a given year vary considerably, but the United States Children's Bureau (*Juvenile Court Statistics, 1950-1952*, Statistical Series No. 18, 1954, p. 5) has estimated that 30,000 children are held in jails or police stations annually waiting for a court hearing and another 70,000 are held in jails by police or other law enforcement agencies without referral to a juvenile court. However, some of these may be awaiting hearing in other courts. Throughout the United States all too many children are arrested and thrust into local jails and lockups in which drunks, hardened criminals, and many other types of adult offenders are kept. Some are accused of only trifling offenses, but are held for days or even weeks before they are given court hearings. Kangaroo courts, especially severe methods of such courts, as used in some places are a travesty on justice.

The Bureau of Prisons has inspected and rated city and county jails and workhouses. Of those inspected from July 1, 1930, to June 30, 1947, a total of 2580 of 3111, or 82.9 per cent, were given ratings under 50 per cent. While too many juveniles are still detained in undesirable jails, improvements have been made in detention since the early attempts to segregate juvenile from adult offenders.

The juvenile court laws during the early part of the present century emphasized that the function of the juvenile court is to treat, not to punish, delinquents, and that separate detention both before and after hearing is an essential part of the treatment process. By 1912, 23 states had adopted similar laws, and by 1925, all but two states had juvenile court laws, including separate detention clauses. Now all states have some kind of legal provisions for the hearing and detention of juveniles, but the applications of law vary by states and by localities. No separate detention homes or institutions are available in some counties, and, even where they are available, the facilities may be too limited to take care of all cases.

Sherwood Norman [9] has pointed out that after fifty years of opera-

---

9 "Detention Intake," *Crime Prevention through Treatment: 1952 Yearbook* (New York: National Probation and Parole Association, 1952), 141. Compare Sherwood and Helen Norman, *Detention for the Juvenile Court,* a mimeographed report published by the National Probation and Parole Association, 1946; National Conference on Prevention and Control of Juvenile Delinquency, *Report on Juvenile Detention* (Washing-

tion, juvenile courts in all but a very few states are still using county jails and police lockups for the detention of children. Illinois has only one detention home for the exclusive use of children requiring secure care pending court disposition, and even in this county the jail is used extensively for children of juvenile court age.

In order to present a picture of current conditions and practices of detention, one of the larger states may be used as an example. The California Advisory Committee on Detention Home Problems has recently issued a report of a survey that covered the entire state.[10] In 1945, a total of over 36,000 children under 18 years of age was admitted to detention facilities of various types in 48 of the 58 counties in California. These children received more than 397,000 days of care. Of this number, 13,392 admissions were in Los Angeles County. Only 16 counties used foster or boarding homes to a limited extent to detain children awaiting hearing, involving only 180 children during 1945. But more than 11,000 children were admitted to city and county jails in 45 counties of the state, of whom 6408 were detained in Los Angeles County alone, where older boys are detained in such jails because of inadequate facilities in the county detention home. The total time of care in 26 counties of the state amounted to over 93,000 days. While such care is restricted chiefly to older boys, and to a few girls, it is indicative of the overcrowded conditions of special detention institutions. In 27 jails, accommodating 6918 children (6689 boys and 229 girls), 6151 were 16- and 17-year-old boys. Fortunately, the average length of stay was only 2.5 days for the boys and 2.8 days for the girls.

Twenty-nine of the 32 detention homes in the state accommodated 24,469 cases for a total of 304,047 days, with an average stay of 12 days for all children. The periods of detention ranged from one to 357 days for delinquent girls, from one to 142 for delinquent boys, and from one to 364 for dependent children (both boys and girls). The long periods of detention were due chiefly to difficulties encountered in foster home placement and to congested conditions in state institutions. The ratio between boys and girls of both delinquents and nondelinquents was over 2 to 1, and the ratio of delinquents to nondelinquents was 5 to 1. The range of capacities in these institutions is from 9 to 330. Some institutions are overcrowded most of the time, whereas others have never been filled to capacity.

---

ton, D. C.: United States Government Printing Office, 1947); and Austin H. MacCormick, "Children in Jails," *The Annals of the American Academy of Political and Social Science,* Vol. 261 (January, 1949), 150-157.

[10] Ruth S. Tolman and Ralph G. Wales, *Juvenile Detention in California,* Current Practices and Recommended Principles. A Report to the California Advisory Committee on Detention Home Problems (July, 1946).

The field workers observed that most of the detention homes were clean, but many were cheerless and barren, and some were reminiscent of jails and penal institutions. Approximately half of the buildings were erected before 1920. The facilities, services, discipline, and activities varied considerably in the institutions. On the whole, the professional services (medical, psychological, psychiatric, case work, and nutritional) available for the children were far from adequate, especially in small rural counties, and the staffs were insufficient to do a good job. Hence, the investigators came to the conclusion that the detention homes in the state failed to meet the needs of the children who must be cared for in this manner, especially as measured by the standards indicated in the Welfare and Institutions Code of California and by the advisory group responsible for the study.

The first detention homes in the United States tended to be merely private houses. Later, public detention homes were established, education and recreation facilities were added, and detention was used for purposes of study and of preliminary treatment. Many types of detention facilities are used today, including public detention homes and hospitals, boarding homes, private child care agencies, institutions for dependents, police stations, jails, and prisons of correctional institutions.

Norman [11] says that, in general, there are three types of detention homes: (1) the type found in large cities for mass custodial care, often with twenty or more children under one supervisor; (2) the homes operating with small groups but offering custodial care only; and (3) the larger detention homes that offer more than custodial care. He discusses the types of children who should be detained. These include the serious offenders, the repeaters, and those whose parental relationships are so strained that they would be almost certain to run away or commit other offenses prior to court disposition.

The National Advisory Committee on Social Protection of the Federal Security Agencies [12] gives three reasons for detaining a child: (1) The parents or guardians are definitely unable or unwilling to produce the child in court on the proper notice. (2) There is good reason to believe that pending court hearing the juvenile will be unable to avoid, or the parents or guardians will be unable to pre-

---

[11] Sherwood Norman, *op. cit.,* 142 f.

[12] *Recommendations on Standards for Detention of Juveniles and Adults* (Washington, D. C.: Government Printing Office, 1945), 10. See Matthew Matlin, Editor, *Reappraising Crime Treatment,* 1953 Yearbook (New York: National Probation and Parole Association, 1954), especially reports on "Detention and Shelter Care," pp. 141 220.

vent, repetition of the behavior which is harmful to the child and the community. (3) There is substantial evidence that the child is in immediate need of special services or treatment which can best be given in an institution.

This raises the question regarding the purpose of detention and what it implies. What is juvenile detention? The term "detention" refers to the temporary care of children who are removed from their homes pending investigation and decision by the juvenile court. The reasons for using detention are chiefly those of safekeeping and protecting children, service to them, and case study. The laboratory use of detention is to enable investigators to study and classify cases as early as possible. Some children are held as witnesses or to assure their appearance in court if their parents are not responsible, or they are held until the police decide what to do with them. Neglected and dependent children are held until suitable places are found for them. Occasionally, detention is used as a means of punishment.

The Normans emphasize that detention is not an ordinary child care job, not just another means of shelter or custodial care, not a punitive institution or a dumping ground for other agencies, and not for long-time care, study, and treatment purposes. Detention should provide primarily: (1) "Physical care and custody under safe and healthful conditions, including a sound medical program." (2) A place to meet nonphysical needs, such as orientation and follow-up interviews, supervision of recreational, educational, and religious activities, taking into account the age and developmental levels. (3) "Information to the court based on observation and clinical study of the child's capacities and needs as revealed during detention." [13]

The larger institutions make a distinction between detention for security and for other purposes. Good detention homes separate delinquents from those who are detained for other purposes, and cases are further separated on the age and sex bases; diagnostic and treatment services are provided to fit the needs; trained workers are employed in supervising the activities; homelike atmosphere is provided; and the period of detention is shortened as much as possible.

The complexity of the problem of detention is evidenced by the types of cases cared for, including serious offenders and difficult behavior problem cases, delinquents who have committed minor offenses, children awaiting transfer to correctional institutions, runaways from other institutions, habitual truants from school, mental defectives, uncared for and lost children, material witnesses, and others.

---

[13] *Detention for the Juvenile Court* (National Probation and Parole Association, 1946), 3.

Detention Principles and Practices. The number of children detained should be kept to a minimum, thus reducing the complexity of the problem. This policy is functionally and financially sound and tends to preserve the child's relation to his own home. The length of detention should be shortened as much as is feasible and in accordance with good practice. The needs of those detained should be met, and a homelike atmosphere be provided. The detention facilities need to be adequate, making possible the segregation of types of cases and the provision of adequate physical and medical care, educational and recreational activities, and counseling services. A distinction needs to be made between shelter care and detention care. The former has reference to emergency and temporary out-of-home care of children where physical restraint is not involved, whereas detention care involves security features to insure the children's safekeeping. The difficulty in many states is that the law provides inadequate authority for taking into custody a minor child who has not committed an offense against the law but who requires protective custody for his own welfare.

To accomplish the best results, it is necessary to have not only good building and equipment, but also a well-trained staff, with specialists in the various fields of service. An appropriate agency in each state should inspect detention homes, set up standards, and assist in developing the best service. The activity program should be varied and cover all areas of need—individual and social, physical and mental, moral and spiritual. Adequate records are necessary for both court and treatment purposes. To achieve and maintain adequate detention facilities and services, it is necessary to have public support. Hence, public relations work is an important part of the program.[14]

Protection of Individuals and Society. One of the functions of detention is protection of children with various kinds of problems and the protection of society from the juveniles who constitute a threat to the community. This is more than a protection against physical violence or destruction of property. The preservation of the personality of the child is an important consideration. Detention may have disastrous psychological effects on a child; and thus, instead

---

[14] For discussions of detention home services, see articles by Richard Allaman, "A Detention Home Activities Program"; Sherwood Norman, "The School in the Detention Home"; and Henry Lenz, "Guidance in the Detention Home Program," in *Current Approaches to Delinquency, 1949 Yearbook* (New York: National Probation and Parole Association, 1949), 112-137.

of a protection, the detention period becomes a threat to the very objective of the treatment process, namely, the rehabilitation of the individual to normal living.

Detention has different psychological meaning for each child, depending upon his experiences, the interpretation given for his detention, the reason for being detained, and various other factors. Some children are frightened by the possibility of detention or by a "jail record." They feel uncertain. Time passes slowly and monotonously. A sense of helplessness may overtake the child. The emotional disturbances aroused by detention are often related to and aggravated by past experiences. Parental neglect, mistreatment in the community, and previous experience with law enforcement agencies may be in the background of their reaction to detention. A variety of reactions are observable in disturbed individual cases, including anxiety, bewilderment, remorse, uncertainty, fear or distrust, hostility, defiance, resentment, and outward indifference. However, children often try to cover up their feelings and reactions.

It is necessary to provide a well-rounded program of constructive activities that is not merely time filling. The evils of poor physical conditions, indiscriminate mixing, unintelligent and unkind treatment must be eliminated. The clinical use of case studies to classify the population and aid the court in making its disposition, together with adequate treatment, education, and counseling, aids in the rehabilitation process.

QUESTIONS AND PROJECTS

For Class Discussion and Research

1. What is meant by social control? Indicate the chief functions and means of social control.

2. Describe the process of treatment of an offender, following the steps in the correctional cycle. Use a concrete case to illustrate the process.

3. What community agencies are able to detect deviant behavior? Indicate the devices that may be used to detect deviant behavior.

4. Describe the functions of police in the apprehension of delinquents. What is the rate of the police in the correctional cycle?

5. Prepare a detailed report of an apprehension situation which shows the operation of factors that cause misbehavior.

6. What is the place of referral in the treatment process? List the main problems in making referrals. Draw up an agency face sheet on basic data form.

7. Explain what is meant by juvenile detention. How would you explain "the lag" in the development of proper detention facilities in the United States? What are the criteria for the use of detention facilities?

8. What are the basic principles and practices of detention?

9. Discuss juvenile detention homes.

10. Work out a schedule for a comprehensive social study of a case.

11. Indicate the value of the delinquent's own story as a part of a case study.

12. Diagnosis procedure of children's behavior problems.

13. Clinical treatment of antisocial deviants.

SELECTED REFERENCES

Annals of the American Academy of Political and Social Science, Vol. 261 (January, 1949); articles on "Children and Our Jails," by Austin H. MacCormick; "The Detention Home," by Sherwood Norman; and "Institutions for Juvenile Delinquents," by John B. Costello.

CARR, LOWELL J., *Delinquency Control* (New York: Harper & Brothers, 1950), Part III.

Comparative Survey on Juvenile Delinquency (Division of Social Welfare, Department of Social Affairs, United Nations, Part I. North America, prepared by Paul Tappan, 1952), Chapter IV.

Current Approaches to Juvenile Delinquency, 1949 Yearbook (New York: National Probation and Parole Association, 1949), Part III, "Detention Home Services."

DEUTSCH, ALBERT, *Our Rejected Children* (Boston: Little, Brown and Company, 1950).

ELLINGSTON, JOHN R., *Protecting Our Children from Criminal Careers* (New York: Prentice-Hall, Inc., 1948).

GOLDBERG, HARRIET, *Child Offenders* (New York: Grune and Stratton, 1948).

HARRISON, LEONARD V., AND PRYOR MCNEILL GRANT, *Youth in the Toils* (New York: The Macmillan Co., 1938).

KENNEY, JOHN P., AND DAN G. PURSUIT, *Police Work with Children* (Springfield, Illinois: Charles C. Thomas Co., 1954).

NORMAN, SHERWOOD AND HELEN, *Detention for the Juvenile Court* (New York: National Probation and Parole Association, 1946).

PIGEON, HELEN D., AND OTHERS, *Principles and Methods in Dealing with Offenders* (State College, Pennsylvania: Public Service Institute, 1941).

———, *Probation and Parole in Theory and Practice* (New York: National Probation and Parole Association, 1942).

Police and Children: A Study of New York City's Juvenile Aid Bureau (Citizens' Committee on Children of New York City, Inc., 1945).

Social Work Year Book. 1951 Edition, Editor, Margaret B. Hodges (New York: American Association of Social Workers, 1951), articles on "Juvenile Behavior Problems," by Marian Gennaria Morris, 276-284; "Social Casework," by Florence Sytz, 460-466.

TAPPAN, PAUL W., Editor, *Contemporary Correction* (New York: Mc-Graw-Hill Book Co., Inc., 1951).

YOUNG, PAULINE V., *Social Treatment in Probation and Delinquency* (New York: McGraw-Hill Book Co., Inc., 1952).

XIII

JUVENILE COURT, PROBATION SERVICE, AND CORRECTIONAL INSTITUTIONS

A new era dawned in the history of treatment of offenders when juvenile courts were established, probation services were extended to children, improvements were made in detention and correction institutions, and state programs of delinquency control were instituted. No single event equaled the contribution made by the juvenile court in the treatment of offenders. Roscoe Pound has called it "the greatest advance in judicial history since the Magna Charta."

THE JUVENILE COURT

History of the Juvenile Court. The idea of a specially organized court to deal with juvenile offenders was largely the product of American thinking and the welfare movements of the nineteenth century. Under the old English laws, a diversity of methods was used by which courts could handle juveniles. Under the common law of England, courts were authorized to act as *parens patriae* over all infants. The English Court of Chancery dealt with neglected, dependent, or destitute children. Any child over 9 years of age might be found guilty and punished for a felony, and even younger children were tried and sentenced for less serious offenses. The Juvenile Offenders' Act of 1847 was amended in 1879, with other modifications made later. Switzerland passed a law in 1862 dealing with the official handling of children's cases, and other developments occurred elsewhere in Europe. But the systematic development of the juvenile court has taken place in the United States.[1]

Various steps led to the creation of the court during the nineteenth century. Certain features of a juvenile court, such as separate confinement, separate hearing, and probation, were practiced in some places, prior to the advent of the juvenile court as a separate institution. Since certain aspects of the newer procedures developed both abroad and in some American states other than Illinois, there is a difference of opinion as to the country or state that deserves the credit for having established the first juvenile court. It is, however, a generally accepted fact that the Juvenile Court of Cook County (Chicago Juvenile Court), established in 1899, was the first of its kind, not only in the United States but in the world.[2] The first juvenile court law was state-wide in application, but Cook County was the only jurisdiction in a position to take advantage of the act. It was the result of the combined efforts of social workers, civic lead-

---

[1] For a comprehensive history of the early development of the juvenile court, see Herbert H. Lou, *Juvenile Courts in the United States* (Chapel Hill, North Carolina: University of North Carolina Press, 1927). Cf. *The Child, the Clinic and the Court* (Proceedings of the Twenty-fifth Anniversary of the Cook County Juvenile Court in Chicago, 1925); *Current Approaches to Delinquency. 1949 Yearbook,* edited by Marjorie Bell (New York: National Probation and Parole Association, 1949), Section I. "Juvenile Court at the Half Century Mark," articles by Charles L. Chute, Roscoe Pound, and Gustav L. Schramm; Marjorie Bell, "Juvenile Court at the Half Century Mark," *Focus,* Vol. 28, No. 5 (September, 1949), 129-134; and "Juvenile and Domestic Relations Courts," by Gustav L. Schramm, *Social Work Yearbook* (New York: American Association of Social Workers, 1951), 1269-1276.

[2] *Laws of Illinois,* 1899, 131. See Herbert H. Lou, *ibid.,* 19. During the same year, Judge Ben Lindsey, under the "school law" of Colorado, set up a juvenile court in Denver.

ers and organizations, and a committee of the Chicago Bar Association. The law was called "An Act to regulate the treatment and control of dependent, neglected, and delinquent children," with separate treatment by a specially designated judge. The fundamental idea of this first juvenile court law was that the state must exercise guardianship over a child found under adverse conditions that develop delinquent behavior.

No provision was made for paid probation officers until 1905, although probation work with adults had been in existence for some time. By 1909 the Juvenile Psychopathic Institute was established to aid in the study of cases. William Healy was the director, and Mrs. W. S. Drummer supported it until 1914. The Illinois Institute for Juvenile Research, a successor of the earlier organization, is a publicly supported agency, which has been one of the major organizations for the study of delinquency cases since its inception. Illinois has pioneered in other ways. Cook County was one of the first to have a separate court for girls presided over by a woman judge elected for that purpose. The Juvenile Court has become a tribunal for the entire family, for the new law permits the Court to hear cases against parents who are charged with contributing to the delinquency of minors. Previously, such cases had been divided between juvenile and domestic relations courts.[3] The family court is not new, for a number of states have established various types of such courts; but Chicago undoubtedly is making a contribution in its development.

The movement soon spread to other states and to foreign countries, following the success of the Cook County Court and the court in Denver originally set up by Judge Ben B. Lindsey in 1899 under the "school law," with limited jurisdiction over delinquent children of school age, but in 1903 established as a regular juvenile court. Within five years, juvenile court laws had been enacted in ten states (California, Indiana, Iowa, Maryland, Missouri, New Jersey, New York, Ohio, Pennsylvania, and Wisconsin). Some of these laws resulted in separate juvenile courts in only a few of the large centers, for the court was still in an experimental stage. However, some of the other states or local jurisdictions established separate courts for children's cases. Boston set up such a court in 1906. There was considerable diversity in organization, jurisdiction, and functioning of the various courts. By 1925, the National Probation Association

---

[3] "Chicago Juvenile Court Becomes Family Tribunal," a report in *Federal Probation*, Vol. 13, No. 3 (September, 1949), 79. Compare Judge Paul W. Alexander, "The Family Court of the Future," in *The Community and the Correctional Process: 1951 Yearbook* (New York: National Probation and Parole Association, 1951), 129-148.

(now the National Probation and Parole Association) published the first Standard Juvenile Court Act, which will be analyzed later.

In 1908 Utah established a state-controlled juvenile court system, but it was not until recent years that the movement to establish state-wide systems of special courts for juveniles began to be considered seriously. Connecticut, in 1941, was the second state to establish a state juvenile court, and Rhode Island passed a law in 1944 setting up a similar system. These courts make it possible to have a unified system for a state, to provide service for all children, including those in more remote rural areas, and special full-time judges and probation officers can be assigned to the various districts of the state. Many feel that the juvenile court is a state responsibility and the advantages of such a system have been pointed out.[4]

To date, four general types of specialized courts for children have developed.[5] (1) Independent courts with city, county or state-wide jurisdiction and with probation services supplied by the courts or by city, county, or state agencies. (2) Family courts with jurisdiction over specified offenses and various types of family situations, including jurisdiction over children and with separate or attached services. (Only nineteen of these possess divorce jurisdiction.) (3) Juvenile and domestic relations courts, either independent courts or parts of other courts, with attached or independent services, and seldom with jurisdiction over divorce and separation. These are also found mainly in urban centers. (4) Juvenile courts as parts of courts with more general jurisdiction. In these courts the judges hold juvenile sections, sometimes in rotation, with services attached or separate. These are found chiefly in the nonurban areas.

After more than thirty years of the development of the juvenile court, and nearly all states had passed laws establishing such courts, no program for the separate treatment of children brought before federal courts had been evolved. In 1932 Congress authorized the transfer of juvenile delinquents from federal courts to juvenile courts in home jurisdiction. The Federal Juvenile Court Act of 1938 set up a new system for handling juveniles who commit federal offenses.

Other improvements have been made in the various states, as Sol Rubin has pointed out in his annual digest of legislation and court decisions.[6] New types of courts have been established, such as the

---

4 William N. MacKay, "The Juvenile Court as a State Responsibility," *The Community and The Correctional Process: 1951 Yearbook, ibid.*, 114-128.

5 *Comparative Survey on Juvenile Delinquency* (Division of Social Welfare, Department of Social Affairs, United Nations, Part I. North America, prepared by Paul W Tappan, 1952), 25 f.

6 See the yearbooks of the National Probation and Parole Association.

Wayward Minors' Court of New York City, which handles the adolescent cases. The courts in the large urban areas have become social agencies in the sense that they take care of welfare and neglect cases. Other evidences of development could be noted, but it must be recalled that not all jurisdictions are served by juvenile or other courts that meet the standard of effective correctional procedure.

As Carr [7] has pointed out, of the more than three thousand counties in the United States, only the larger centers have fully established juvenile courts, with probation services and other accompanying facilities for effective work. The majority of the courts are still below par. Few reach the excellence of the Chicago or the Toledo courts. Carr thinks that about two thousand of the small town juvenile courts have no clinics, and many have no detention facilities.

The main objectives of the juvenile court are now fairly clear, even though much needs to be done to improve its efficiency and to expand its use. The juvenile court is a court of equity, with constantly improved administrative facilities and efficiency. It focuses attention in a positive, rather than a negative, manner upon the needs of children, and it tries to personalize justice.

The basic idea behind the juvenile court is guardianship of youth rather than a penal-judicial agency. Instead of a judicial tribunal trying cases for determination of guilt and inflicting punishment according to relatively inflexible rules of law, the juvenile court is an agency in which the relations of a child to society or to his parents are adjusted according to the scientific findings about the child and his environment. Instead of magistrates limited by legal provisions of procedure, the juvenile judges are usually social-minded individuals who treat cases in the best interest of both the child and society. No juries, prosecutors, lawyers, legal battles, and other paraphernalia of the criminal court are needed. The work is done chiefly by probation officers, doctors, psychiatrists, psychologists, and social workers, who investigate, diagnose, make recommendations, and treat the case.

Criminal versus Juvenile Court Procedure. The juvenile court procedure can be more clearly shown by comparing it with criminal court procedure. The comparison refers to the conventional criminal

---

[7] Lowell J. Carr, "Most Courts Have to be Substandard," *Federal Probation*, Vol. 13, No. 3 (September, 1949), 29-33. This is a special issue "Commemorating the Fiftieth Anniversary of the Juvenile Court." Besides the article by Carr, others deal with "The Juvenile Court in Retrospect," by Charles L. Chute; "The Expansion of the Juvenile Court Idea," by John O. Reinemann; "Thoughts about Juvenile Courts," by William Healy; "Juvenile Court Idea," by Judge Gustav L. Schramm; and "The Juvenile Court Today," by Katharine F. Lenroot.

court, without recent reforms, and the more or less ideal juvenile court. In practice, the two procedures overlap considerably, and there are great variations in the several states and territories as to the operation and functions of juvenile courts.

A. Criminal Court Procedure. Criminal law rests upon the theory that for the protection of society the offender must be punished and that the punishment must be in accordance with the seriousness of the offense. Offenders are tried for specific offenses and only in case of actual violation of law. A person must be accused of having committed a crime, and a charge is lodged against him. Crime is defined legally as any overt act of commission or omission (carried out with culpable intent) that is in violation of law. For any act to be a crime it must be so defined by law, and the law usually attaches an appropriate penalty for its violation. Since it is the purpose of the trial to determine the guilt of the person, and, if guilty, to fix the penalty in accordance with the nature and seriousness of the offense, only the evidences pertaining directly to the case are presented. No material except that which pertains to the specific act is permitted. Social environmental conditions and circumstances that may have constituted the background of the offense are usually excluded. Criminal courts are more concerned with specific acts, and with the motives or intentions, than with circumstances. The prosecutor, grand jury, and others authorized to issue a complaint bring the case to court, levying the indictment or charge and initiating the prosecution. The accused person may be held in custody or released on bail before and during the trial, depending upon the nature of the crime.

The criminal court conducts a public trial, characterized by contentiousness, with two partisan groups in conflict. The procedure is based upon penal theories and legal requirements, and only matters of high judicial import are handled. A jury is used unless it is waived by the defendant. The trial deals with the specific criminal act only. The accused may employ an attorney, or he is provided a counsel for his defense. The accused person may be held in custody or released on bail before and during the trial, but he must be present while the trial is in process. Witnesses are sworn in; and the two contending parties, the prosecutor and the attorney for the defense, quiz witnesses, present evidences, and battle for the inclusion or exclusion of evidences. Clerks and attendants make out complaints and other forms, record the proceedings, and take care of other details pertaining to the trial. Audience and publicity, problems of evidences and testimony, and sometimes "fixing the case" are factors to contend with in public trials. The fact that there is no machinery for securing information regarding the character of the accused and background information regarding the person and the total situation is a handicap.

If the defendant is found guilty, the punishment is prescribed by the court; if found not guilty, the case is dismissed and the defendant is released, unless prosecuted on other grounds. The treatment is determined, not by the need of the offender but by law, in advance, which prescribes within limits the type or types of punishment that may be administered. The court does not follow up the case after sentence or fine. No control is exercised by the court over the institutions to which an adjudged criminal may be sentenced, and no preventive work is undertaken.

B. Juvenile Court Procedure. The juvenile court law assumes that official action is necessary when a child is alleged to have committed a violation of law or is in danger of deviant behavior, but the chief object is not to administer punishment in accordance with the nature and seriousness of the offense. Punishment may be administered, but the main considerations are guidance, care, protection, and rehabilitation. Therefore, the determination of guilt, or the degree of guilt, is not so important a matter as it is in a criminal court. The welfare of the child is the chief concern.

A person is brought into juvenile court because of alleged deviant behavior—although many cases do not involve direct offenses—and a petition is filed in his behalf. The purpose of the hearing is to determine the nature of the offense, the circumstances and environmental influences, the condition of the home, and other matters, in order to deal with the child in the most effective manner. The case study usually precedes the hearing, although additional data may be requested or obtained by the court. The case may be brought into the court by police, sheriff, probation officers, public school officials, or other public or private agency workers, or by parents or guardians. The court itself may start proceedings in the case. The child may be held in custody in a detention home or police jail, although the latter is not recommended, or he may remain in his own home or be placed in any suitable home. The hearing is semiprivate, usually in the chamber of the judge, or in the referee's office; and the decision as to procedure in dealing with the case is based on facts assembled prior to the hearing. In the larger courts, the hearing is characterized by scientific methods of investigation carried on by an elaborate machinery for securing information regarding the character of the child and the environment in which he lives. Protection, guardianship, care, training, and change of environment are important considerations.

The treatment of a case is determined by the needs of the individual without reference to other actual or potential delinquents. The case may be dismissed or continued; the child may be placed on probation, institutionalized, placed in a foster home, or otherwise dealt with as seems best to the court. The juvenile judge may change the disposition of the case at any time. The court may investigate the institution or the home in which a child is placed. It is also commonly understood that the juvenile court may initiate or participate in preventive work.

The juvenile court hearing and general procedure vary a great deal in the courts. The juvenile judge is the key person. His personality, training and background, concept of the purpose of the court, and ability have a great deal to do with the way cases are processed. The selection of the judge is very important. It is not easy, however, to indicate the qualifications of a judge. Legal training is important, for he must be able to interpret the law and follow legal procedures, and often must decide controversial cases. He must likewise be well informed on case work and related social services. Above all, he must be a man of character, good judgment, tact, and sympathetic understanding. In the larger courts, commissioners and/or referees assist the judge in handling cases. A woman is especially valuable in handling girls' cases. These, as well as other court assistants, likewise need to be well trained and capable. Probation services, as will be indicated later, are indispensable, for the probation officer is both an investigator and a case supervisor. If there is a clinical agency, either as a part of the detention institution or as a separate unit, the clinical staff is an important part of successful juvenile court work.

Besides the personnel of the court and of the probation and other agencies, the policies and methods of procedure are an integral part of the process of handling cases. The intake controls the case load and directs to the proper agencies those people who have come to the juvenile court for help but who may have misconstrued the court's functions. Since the agencies or individuals of referral are police and other law enforcement departments, parents and relatives or other individuals, court and school officials, welfare agencies, and federal authorities, it is necessary to adopt certain principles and procedures of operation. The screening function of the intake division includes the determination of those cases that require court action, those that do not require court action but can be adjusted under the guidance of probation officers, and the referral service.[8] And, as was pointed out in the preceding chapter, adequate case work is essential for the hearing of cases in the court.[9]

The Standard Juvenile Court Act. Since no uniformity has existed as to the legal provisions for and the practices of the juvenile court, no general statement regarding common practices can be given. However, the National Probation and Parole Association has published "The Standard Juvenile Court Act." [10] Courts have been called "Juvenile Courts," "Juvenile and Domestic Relations Courts," "Family Courts," and the like. Many counties have both juvenile and domestic relations courts. Whatever the designations given the courts and the functions that they perform, most of these are on the county basis, even though authorized by state laws. The states of Utah, Connecticut, and Rhode Island have state juvenile courts. The original provisions of the Standard Act were designed chiefly for local jurisdictions, but the 1949 edition contains provision for a state-wide court established on a district basis.

In the new revision, the standards heretofore considered desirable have been retained. These, as summarized by Rubin, are:

. . . (1) exclusive jurisdiction over children, and jurisdiction over adults in children's cases; (2) private, friendly court hearings and informal, noncriminal procedure; (3) a sufficient staff of professionally trained probation officers; (4) facilities for physical examinations and for psychiatric study of problem children; (5) a well-equipped detention home or selected boarding homes for temporary care of children; (6) an efficient record and statistical system; (7) cooperation with other agencies and community support through interpretation to the public.[11]

The new state system, as proposed, provides that the judges be specially selected, appointed by the governor from an approved list of candidates nominated by a panel of representatives of the courts, the bar, and departments of education, mental hygiene, and public

---

8 Cf. Harry W. Lindeman, "Intake in the Juvenile Court," and Charles S. Antolina, "Principles of Intake Control," in *Crime Prevention through Treatment. 1952 Yearbook* (National Probation and Parole Association, 1952), 126-139.

9 Cf. Harold R. Muntz, "Casework in the Juvenile Court," *The Community and the Correctional Process: 1951 Yearbook, op. cit.,* 89-102.

10 Originally published in 1925; revised editions published in 1927, 1933, 1943, and 1949.

11 Sol Rubin, "State Juvenile Court: a New Standard," *Focus,* Vol. 30, No. 4 (July, 1951), 103. Used by permission of National Probation and Parole Association. Compare Justine Wise Polier, "The Standard Juvenile Court Act, 1949," *Advances in Understanding the Offender: 1950 Yearbook* (New York: National Probation and Parole Association, 1950), 9-23; and Harrison A. Dobbs, "Realism and the Juvenile Court," *Focus,* Vol. 31, No. 4 (July, 1952), 104-108.

welfare. It is hoped that by this means and by paying adequate salaries, highly qualified judges will be attracted to the new type of court and that all areas, rural as well as urban, will receive equal service.

Even though states do not adopt state-wide systems of juvenile courts, the Standard Act provides a pattern for the local courts. In addition to the items mentioned by Rubin, the various editions of the Standard Act have stressed procedures regarding the appointment of judges, referees, and other employees of the court, the initiation of children's cases, detention, the hearing and disposition of cases, and various other provisions.

As Katharine F. Lenroot [12] has pointed out, certain problems require consideration in improving and standardizing the juvenile court. These may be itemized as follows: (1) jurisdiction of the court as to the age group and whether it should be exclusive or concurrent with other courts; (2) geographic area served by the court (local or state); (3) the court as strictly a legal or primarily a social agency; (4) the relationship between the court and administrative social welfare agencies; (5) the relationship between the court and the juvenile bureaus of police departments, sheriffs' offices. and other law enforcement agencies; (6) the qualification of judges, other court officials, and probation officers; and (7) the treatment resources.

The Federal Juvenile Court Act, enacted by the 75th Congress of the United States and approved June 16, 1938, provides another general standard of court procedure. It states that a person 17 years of age or under who commits an offense against the laws of the United States is not punishable by death or life imprisonment. Any juvenile who is charged with the commission of any offense against the laws of the United States, other than an offense punishable by death or life imprisonment, and if he is not surrendered to the authorities of any state, shall be prosecuted as a juvenile delinquent at the discretion of the Attorney General and if the accused consents to such procedure. The district court of the United States has jurisdiction to try such a person. The court may convene at any time and place within the district, and the trial shall be without a jury. If the accused is found guilty, he may be placed on probation or committed to the custody of the Attorney General for a period not exceeding his minority. The Attorney General may designate any public or private agency for the custody, care, subsistence, and training during the period of commitment and pay for such support.

---

12 "Problems Requiring Special Consideration," *Federal Probation*, Vol. 13, No. 3 (September, 1949), 9-15.

Other details of the Act pertain to matters of arrest, notification, and the basis of release.[13]

The standardization of juvenile court laws and the supervision of the work of the court, improved probation service, the addition of psychiatric clinics for the study of children, the extension of the juvenile courts to rural communities, and the gradual evolution of the family court, combining juvenile and domestic relations courts, are some of the trends in this field. The larger courts have expanded their services and have become, in many instances, social agencies serving the needs of youth in the community.

While the chief need is the further extension of the juvenile court movement, especially in rural areas, questions have been raised regarding the desirability of the court becoming a social agency. Many courts are overloaded and unable to give sufficient attention to the more serious cases of delinquency. The problem is especially acute, because many courts are suffering from lack of trained personnel. There is a growing feeling that the unchecked expansion of the court's functions has placed upon it too heavy a load for any one agency to carry. Some courts are trying to limit the intake by discouraging the filing of complaints for minor offenses. It is urged that neglect, dependency, health, and maladjusted cases that do not involve offenses should be referred to social agencies rather than be taken to the court. This would prevent overloading of the court as a case-work agency. The court, of course, must use case-work procedures in handling offenders, but it has functions quite apart from a case-work agency. In fact, case analysis is increasingly being applied in treatment processes.[14]

The juvenile court has an important place in the community. It combines legal and administrative functions. Legal justice and general security or welfare are sometimes in conflict, in which case a balance must be sought. It is more fitted than an administrative social agency to maintain a balance between justice and security.

---

13 See reprint from the *FBI Law Enforcement Bulletin*, November, 1938.

14 See Alice Scott Nutt, "The Future of the Juvenile Court as a Case-work Agency," *The Child*, Vol. 4 (July, 1939), 17-22; "Juvenile Court Function," *Social Defense Against Crime: 1942 Yearbook* (New York: National Probation and Parole Association, 1942); and "The Juvenile Court in Relation to the Community," *Social Service Review*, Vol. 17 (March, 1943), 1-7. The Youth Court Act differs from the Youth Correction Act, referred to later in this chapter, in that it relates to the process of determining whether or not an accused youth has committed a crime and should be subjected to the rehabilitative treatments of the Correction Act. The objectives of the Youth Court are to shorten the time that elapses between the arrest of a youth and the final disposition of his case, and the improvement of conditions to which he is subjected during this period. For a more detailed discussion of the problems of the juvenile court, including the confusion in the court, see Paul W. Tappan, *Juvenile Delinquency* (New York: McGraw-Hill Book Co., Inc., 1949), Part III.

Neither the tendency to revert to criminal court procedures nor its expansion into a social agency will give the juvenile court its proper place.[15] The more nearly it becomes a social work agency, the less it can retain the structure and functions of the court. However, the tendency to combine juvenile and domestic relations courts for the purpose of dealing with the total family situation has considerable merit, for often it is the parent instead of the child who should be before the court. In a family court all problems affecting the family circle can be handled by the one tribunal instead of the various courts of different jurisdictions—the latter often resulting in delays and lost motion.[16]

Paul W. Tappan [17] has made a study of the judicial, administrative, and social processes of the Wayward Minor Court in New York City, which is an experimental tribunal for adolescent girls, known officially as Girl's Term. He considers the legal process in terms of social objectives, the confusion of purposes, the limitations of the statute under which it operates, and the court itself in the process of change. It is suggested that the combined approach of law and sociology (sociolegal) might contribute to a better understanding of the court, its development and functional operation. Courts are social institutions, and the court process is a form of social behavior. Sociologists and psychologists can be of service in the understanding and clarification of the mechanics of the courtroom, and the legal authorities (lawyers) can contribute their skills and special frames of reference.

The development of courts for adolescents is a significant trend because the problems of adolescent offenders are in many ways more difficult to solve than those of younger delinquents. The total number of offenders is high in the adolescent group as compared with the offenses of either younger or older people. It is a period of "storm and stress," during which physiological, mental, and emotional transformations are rapid and character has not yet fully developed. At least, many adolescents are not yet mature in their judgment and behavior, so they need specialized handling. A num-

---

15 Cf. Roscoe Pound, "Juvenile Court and the Law," *Cooperation in Crime Control: 1944 Yearoook* (New York: National Probation and Parole Association, 1944); and "The Juvenile Court in the Service State," *Current Approaches to Delinquency: 1949 Yearbook* (New York: National Probation and Parole Association, 1949).

16 See Walter H. Beckham, "One Court for Family Problems," *Social Defenses Against Crime: 1942 Yearbook* (New York: National Probation and Parole Association, 1942).

17 *Delinquent Girls in Court: A Study of the Wayward Minor Court of New York* (New York: Columbia University Press, 1947); compare *Juvenile Delinquency, op. cit.,* Chapter X.

ber of states, notably New York, Michigan, and Pennsylvania, have made provisions for such courts through legislation. Other states, like Idaho, have made special provisions for the disposition of adolescents or have provided special training schools for the older delinquents.

Legal Aspects of Delinquency Control.[18] Some of the laws pertaining to delinquency, covering types of offenses, age and sex, and related matters were discussed in Part One. A brief summary of the highlights of types of laws that may apply to juveniles will indicate the importance of the legal aspects of delinquency control.

The juvenile court is a part of the judicial system of the state. It operates under the laws of the state, which specify its jurisdiction, procedure and functions, the types of cases handled, and the disposition of cases. Since there is considerable variation in the legal provisions of the several states and territories, and even greater variation in practice, no two juvenile courts are exactly alike. Each state specifies the age group, the types of offenses, and the welfare cases that are subject to official action.

In California, for instance, the laws peculiar to juveniles come under Section 700 of the Welfare and Institutions Code; but other laws, such as the Civil Code, Health and Safety Code, Alcoholic Beverage Control Act, Vehicle Code, Labor Code, Penal Code, and Education Code also pertain to juveniles. In addition, certain federal statutes and city and county ordinances pertain to juveniles. Curfew laws are examples of local ordinances. In a broad sense, cases handled by law enforcement officers may be classified as: (1) offenses committed by juveniles, which breaches of the law by adults would be punishable by fine or imprisonment; (2) behavior problems peculiar to children, such as truancy from school, running away from home, and incorrigibility; and (3) dependency, neglect, health, adoption, and other types of welfare cases.

Stealing, acts of carelessness or mischief, running away from home and truancy from school, being ungovernable, traffic violation, sex offenses, and injury to person are the chief reasons for reference to court in boys' and girls' cases disposed of by the juvenile courts, according to reports submitted to the United States Children's Bureau.

---

18 For concise yet fairly comprehensive summary of laws pertaining to delinquency, consult: Frederick B. Sussmann, *Law of Juvenile Delinquency* (New York: Oceana Publications, 1950). See also a brief summary in *Comparative Survey on Juvenile Delinquency, op. cit.*, Chapters III and IV. For earlier summaries, see: Gilbert Cosulich, *Juvenile Court Laws in the United States* (1939), and F. N. Hiller, *Juvenile Court Laws in the United States* (1933).

Besides the substantive laws applicable to juveniles, legislative provisions contain types of laws that pertain to adults in their conduct with minors, including those in a parental or quasi-parental relationship and certain prohibitive laws, regulating specified activities of persons which have an impact upon minors. The substantive laws applicable to the parent-child relationship are directed primarily toward the protection of minors in their relationship with those in a parental position.

The other legal provisions pertain chiefly to the judicial structure and function, the law of arrest, and the law of evidence. The juvenile court in California, for example, was first created and established by means of the Original Juvenile Court Act of 1903, which was later (especially 1911 and 1915) amended, rewritten, and improved, increasing the age of jurisdiction to 21 years, adding referees and probation officers to the court, and extending the power of the court. Legal provisions regarding institutional commitment of juveniles are further implementations of the court's powers and duties.

Disposition of Cases. In view of the variation in practices, it is difficult to summarize the disposition of boys' and girls' cases disposed of by courts. However, on the basis of reports submitted to the United States Children's Bureau, the following dispositions of cases are common practices: (1) cases are dismissed, adjusted, or held open without further action; (2) children are placed on probation, under the supervision of probation officers, although other persons may be designated for this purpose; (3) children are committed or referred to institutions (state correctional or penal institutions, other public or private institutions) or agencies (public departments or other agencies) or to individuals; (4) cases are referred to other courts; (5) fine and cost are ordered, or restitution of property is required; (6) runaways are returned; and (7) a variety of other dispositions of cases are made. Court cases are disposed of in a variety of ways, depending upon the offenses, circumstances, conditions of homes, and administrative practices.

PROBATION SERVICES

There is a great deal of literature on probation and parole.[19] The investigation and supervision of juveniles on probation or

---

[19] See publications of the National Probation and Parole Association, especially the yearbooks and *Focus,* a monthly publication; and *Federal Probation,* a Quarterly Journal of Correctional Philosophy and Practice, published by the Administrative

parole and the keeping of records are important services in dealing with delinquents. To discuss adequately the history, nature and functions, standards, practices, organization and control, personnel, present status and problems of probation would take us too far afield. However, a brief statement of the main aspects of juvenile probation will give the highlights.

It is generally agreed that the first probation officer was John Augustus, who, as early as 1841, began to reclaim and save persons in the Boston police court by asking the judge to put prisoners under his care. This was a voluntary service. Later, a number of private agencies and then certain public agencies began to perform such services. Probation was first established by statute in Massachusetts in 1878, which was soon followed by similar laws in other states, until it became a common means of handling cases. Although all states have authorized probation, not all of them have paid probation officers.

Probation is a form of disposition made by the court. It is a nonpunitive method of treating offenders, resting on the right of the court to suspend sentence. It is not to be interpreted as leniency or mercy, but as a constructive treatment process. Although it developed as an adult service, it is now generally applied to children's cases under the juvenile court laws.

Juvenile Probation. Probation as applied to juveniles is a chancery procedure. It means a judicial guardianship. Children adjudged delinquent are declared in need of care and guardianship, as well as discipline and guidance. Juvenile probation is a specific form of correctional treatment. It is a treatment outside an institutional setting. The main purpose is to adjust those on probation to normal living.

It is not known how extensively probation is used. Also the standards vary widely. The personnel is still poorly selected in many places, with no basic qualifications and no uniform system of ap-

---

Office of the United States Courts in Cooperation with the Bureau of Prisons of the Department of Justice. See also Belle Boone Beard, *Juvenile Probation* (New York: American Book Co., 1934); *Probation and Related Measures* (New York: Department of Social Affairs, United Nations, 1951) [this publication summarizes the origin, development and spread of probation and related measures; probation in selected countries, and the content of probation]; Jay Rumney and Joseph P. Murphy, *Probation and Social Adjustment* (New Brunswick, New Jersey: Rutgers University Press, 1952); Clyde B. Vedder, Samuel Koenig, and Robert E. Clark, *Criminology: A Book of Readings* (New York: The Dryden Press, 1953), sections XIX and XX on probation and parole; and Pauline V. Young, *Social Treatment in Probation and Delinquency* (New York: McGraw-Hill Book Co., Inc., 1952).

pointment. The percentage of cases adequately investigated and supervised is still relatively low. To be effective, each case should be carefully investigated before being placed on probation, followed by intensive supervision according to sound case work. This requires an adequate staff of qualified case workers, especially trained for children's work, and with a case load not exceeding fifty.

The duties of juvenile probation officers are usually described in the juvenile court law, the chief of which include investigation of cases, presentation of cases to court, custody of children before and after hearing, and supervision on probation. Besides these functions, juvenile officers of probation departments keep records, report violations, collect fines and restore properties, and in some states serve other courts or agencies. To do the work well, it is necessary to cooperate with arresting agencies, especially juvenile bureaus of police departments and sheriffs' offices, schools, and case-work agencies.

Probation is a specific form of correctional treatment, chiefly outside an institutional setting. Since the major objective of probation is to adjust the offender to society and restore him to normal living, which is accomplished by the probationer's own efforts with the help of parents and the guidance of the probation officers, it is necessary to individualize him in terms of the total life situation. Therefore, it is necessary to ascertain the conditions of the individual and his home, his associates, and the neighborhood environment. The social drives behind action, the offender's response to his environment, and the adjustment forces that may be utilized are important factors to consider. The probation officer sometimes has to manipulate or adjust environmental conditions, such as changing the attitude and behavior of parents, finding a foster or boarding home, providing wholesome organized recreation and group affiliation, making school adjustments, obtaining employment, and securing medical care. The probation officer frequently cannot do the job alone, but must seek the cooperation of agencies and their workers in meeting the needs of a child.

In most instances, behavior problems are so complicated that no quick diagnosis is possible. Child guidance clinics have been established to facilitate the matter of investigation. In the larger centers, detention homes have clinical divisions for the study of the physical, mental, and other personality problems. It is obvious that effective probation requires careful study of each case by experts in diagnosis, who have specialized in that work. Although the method of making such studies has not been definitely standardized and the necessity for it has not been generally realized, it is clear that probation work would be greatly improved if it could be based on careful case studies.

Contacts between probation officers and probationers are very important. These are usually in the form of office calls, but home visits are also desirable, because they enable a probation officer to appraise the most important part of the child's environment and to secure the cooperation of parents in the rehabilitation process. Some probation departments and commissions make home visits a requirement. The usual procedure is for probationers to report at regular intervals to the probation officer in charge of the case, either in his office or in some other place selected by him. The procedures in making these reports vary, and opinions regarding their value differ. Possibly the greatest values of reporting are that it enables the officer to keep in touch with the case and it has some disciplinary value, although the latter has been questioned.

The treatment process involves efforts of probation officers to help the probationer. This usually involves the changing of the attitudes and habits of probationers. Since the attitudes of an individual are largely a product of his social contacts, principally in the home, the play group, and the neighborhood, the procedure in modifying attitudes consists essentially in changing the person's group relations. The web of relationships may be altered by the probation officer himself or by a Big Brother or a group worker. The probation officer is limited in his capacity to become an intimate associate and leader, but he can use group workers and citizen groups in assisting with the program of rehabilitation.

The juvenile probation officer should be a person of mature judgment, have high ideals of personal conduct and great personal integrity, and be well trained. He should possess knowledge of the sociological factors of crime causation and of the psychological factors that operate in human motivation. Likewise, it is necessary to have a knowledge of community resources that may be utilized in the treatment process. The skills and techniques of social case work are essential to good probation treatment. In setting up standards of probation work and of the qualifications of officers, the National Probation and Parole Association and other standardization bodies have emphasized the importance of having college-trained personnel with additional training in social work. Experience in case work is now considered an essential qualification. Because of the personal nature of the work, the personality, especially the character, of an officer is very important.

Organization and Function of Probation Departments. Two agencies are officially designated as the proper bodies to control probation work: the court and an independent administrative body, usually known as the probation department. Since probation originated in the suspended sentence, its control is in the hands of the court. However, the work of investigation and supervision is essentially administrative, not judicial. It is, therefore, desirable to have a probation department, preferably organized on the county basis, corresponding to the jurisdiction of the juvenile court. In states where other jurisdictions are used, the court and the probation department should cover the same territories. Cooperation with other local government departments and with social agencies, as well as with state and federal agencies, is essential to good probation work.

Two examples will be given to illustrate the organization and operation of probation departments. The Los Angeles County (California) Probation Department is one of the larger systems of probation service. Organized in 1903, the same year that Juvenile Court and Adult Probation bills were passed by the State of California Legislature, it soon was destined to become one of the leading probation departments in the country.[20] Since 1930 the department has been chiefly responsible for the establishment of the juvenile forestry camps, coordinating councils, toy loan program, a central juvenile index, and various permanent county committees in the interest of child welfare and the control of delinquency. The Department has four main divisions: (1) Adult, which investigates and supervises adult cases; (2) Juvenile, which has sections for boys' and girls' cases, including intake, field units, placement, adoption, and investigation units, and the division operates the probation and senior forestry camps; (3) Staff and Community Services, which include, besides personnel and training, the community organization, group guidance, toy loan units, and county committees for Church and Community Cooperation and Human Relations; and (4) the Business Division. The Probation Research Analyst serves all divisions by keeping records, tabulating and supplying statistical data, and operating the Central Juvenile Index. The Los Angeles County Probation Committee, a separate lay group appointed by the Board of Supervisors, has control of the Juvenile Hall and Hospital, a detention home.

---

[20] For a brief history as well as annual report, see *Forty-Second Annual Report*, Probation Department, County of Los Angeles, California, 1946, especially the statement by John M. Zuck, Probation Officer. The functional organization chart of the 1952 report is used as the basis of the description of the different divisions.

The Essex County Probation Department, as described by Rumney and Murphy,[21] has five main divisions: (1) Adult Supervision, (2) Adult Investigation, (3) Women and Girls, (4) Domestic Relations, and (5) Juvenile. The duties of probation officers and volume of work, records of the department, and the plan of treatment are outlined.

The keeping of records, the analysis of cases, and a central registration center that may be used by all law enforcement officers are important services of a probation department. The Central Juvenile Index of Los Angeles County, which was described in Chapter II, is an example of a confidential central registry of all juveniles (under 18 years) who have been contacted, arrested, or booked for infractions of law or otherwise dealt with by law enforcement departments and agencies in the county. This is a valuable source of information, but it is also helpful in dealing with individual cases. It expedites the process of apprehension and discovery, preliminary case analysis, and the determination of the course of procedure to be followed in handling cases.

National Probation and Parole Association. For nearly a half century the National Probation and Parole Association has been the most outstanding national study and standardization organization for adult and juvenile probation and parole work. It is a voluntary organization to study the conditions of probation and parole, to set up standards of work, to promote legislation, to improve the work of juvenile courts, and to cooperate with local, state, and national agencies to bring about efficient treatment and prevention programs. The original organization was formed in 1907, known as the National Association of Probation Officers, "to offer a broader medium for the exchange of ideas, methods, reports and questions; to secure a working acquaintance between probation officers from different sections of the country; to arrange for informal meetings of probation officers at future national conferences." [22] In 1911 the name was changed to National Probation Association, and in 1947, when the National Parole Association was merged with it, the present title was adopted. A number of pioneers worked to expand the functioning of the Association, but it was not until 1921 when Mr. Charles Lionel Chute set forth on his own to raise funds for the organization that it started on an independent career and undertook an ambitious program of formulating national probation standards. By 1925 Mr.

---

21 *Op. cit.,* Chapter II.
22 Will C. Turnbladh, "Building the NPPA," *Focus,* Vol. 31, No. 6 (November, 1952), 161.

Francis H. Hiller was added to the staff as a field consultant, and later other specialists were added.

The accomplishments of this organization are too numerous to list here. The Standard Juvenile Court Act, first drawn up and published in 1925; the promotion of state and federal legislation to expand and improve the juvenile courts, probation departments, and related agencies; the studies and surveys of probation and parole work, the operation of courts, the detention and correctional institutions; the consultation and advisory services; the annual and regional conferences; and the publications are among the most generally recognized achievements. Its service in correctional work, of which it is a part, represents its greatest field of usefulness.

CORRECTIONAL INSTITUTIONS AND AGENCIES

Special institutions for juveniles have been in existence in the United States for more than a century. The first juvenile reformatory was the House of Refuge on Randall's Island, New York City, which was opened in 1825. The first correctional institution under state control was started in Massachusetts in 1847. The early institutions were reformatories, somewhat similar to penal institutions, except that they were for children and the chief objective was reform. In actual practice, they retained much of the atmosphere and methods of treatment found in prisons. Since there were few separate institutions for children, most of the delinquent children were cared for in jails and prisons, although some of these had children's wards. Some cases were referred to private agencies. The cottage system of care was introduced about the middle of the nineteenth century.

Before describing the types of institutions and agencies that take care of the more serious types of offenders that cannot easily be cared for through probation and similar services, a brief statement of the purposes of institutionalization will indicate the goals toward which the correctional system is aimed and some of the methods that are employed to accomplish these aims.

Objectives and Types of Correctional Institutions and Agencies. Paul W. Tappan [23] states the broad objectives of correction as fol-

_____

23 *Contemporary Correction* (New York: McGraw-Hill Book Co., Inc., 1951), Chapter I. This book, edited by Tappan, deals with the philosophy and methods of correction, administrative organization and classification, programs in the correctional institutions, types of correctional institutions, and extramural treatment. Articles were written by many authorities in the field of correction and the volume as a whole represents a landmark in the study of correctional penology.

lows. (1) The protection of society is one of the alleged objectives of correction. This objective is a popular one but it is too generalized a concept, for social protection is predicated upon more immediate goals. (2) Retribution is still an objective of penology. Historically one of the oldest primitive methods, it is still regarded by many as a desirable objective. (3) The principle of deterrence has come down from the classical school of criminology and is still emphasized in certain quarters. (4) Incapacitation is held to be necessary in some cases of offenders. Official recognition of the need to prevent adult offenders from persistent offenses is displayed in the death penalty and life imprisonment. (5) Rehabilitation is the major objective of the juvenile correctional system. The chief goal is to restore the offender to normal living and to produce a law-abiding citizen. (6) Tappan refers also to the notion that penalties should be employed as a tool of social reconstruction.

The objectives of juvenile correctional institutions can be discerned further in some of the methods that are employed to achieve security and rehabilitation through the treatment of offenders. Juvenile courts are given considerable latitude in disposing of cases. The disposition of cases is preceded by analysis and diagnosis of individual cases, and the classification of offenders with the view of inaugurating the proper procedure. The orientation of the offender in the early stages of the correctional process is important. The placement of offenders in the appropriate institution is essential to rehabilitation. But the process does not end with the institutional program. Upon release, a reorientation to the home and community is necessary.

The programs in correctional institutions that have for their objective the rehabilitation of the juveniles who are in their custody involve medical services, psychiatric and psychological testing and services, careful case work, group therapy, education, recreation, religious and moral education, and vocational training. This, in turn, requires a staff of specialists.

The use of institutional care in the treatment of delinquents varies widely in scope and function. Four types of institution seem to predominate: (1) detention homes; (2) public correctional institutions, formerly called reformatories; (3) private research, welfare, and placement agencies; and (4) foster and boarding homes.

Detention institutions were discussed in the previous chapter and need not be reviewed here. However, it might be pointed out that the main functions of such institutions are temporary custody and protection of children, pending investigation and referral to the juvenile court or to other agencies. This enables authorities to study cases under controlled conditions prior to treatment, although treatment for physical ailments and other conditions may begin during the detention period. Since correctional institutions are overcrowded, detention facilities are sometimes used for the care of children for longer periods.

Public Correctional Institutions. Today, the chief institutions for the treatment of juvenile offenders are the public training schools and forestry camps. Most of these institutions are operated by state, county, and municipal governmental agencies, and some cases are taken care of in national penal and correctional institutions. In 1949 approximately 117 state and national training schools had an average population of nearly 22,000, of whom 15,500 were boys and 6,300 were girls.[24] These figures represent children and youths from around 6 or 7 to 20 years of age who were adjudged delinquents, felons, or misdemeanants, and some truants. Usually some neglected and dependent children are included in the total statistics.

These training schools are special child welfare institutions to re-educate and to prepare delinquents for normal living in the community. To help them to establish wholesome habits and attitudes, to become acceptable members in society, and to give them individualized care in accordance with their needs are basic functions of such institutions. Children who have serious personality and behavior problems, who are subjected to extreme deviant environmental pressures, requiring removal from the community for their own protection and security, or who are emotionally so disturbed that they cannot easily adjust themselves to a family-like setting benefit from institutional care.

To be successful, a training institution must have adequate equipment, well-qualified and adequately trained and paid personnel, a program of activities and classroom curriculum adjusted to fit the individual needs of the children, medical and research facilities that enable proper diagnosis and classification of cases, also efficient treatment, and a follow-up program that will assure greater success in restoring the children to normal living. Case work is an essential phase of the treatment process. The educational program

---

24 *Social Work Year Book,* 1951 Edition (New York, American Association of Social Workers, 1951), 282. The 1947 *Social Work Year Book* (p. 266) states that there were in 1944 approximately 166 training schools under public auspices, of which 115 were state and national schools and 51 county and municipal schools, with a total enrollment of 24,000. Including the quasi-official schools operated under private auspices, the total enrollment was in excess of 30,000. Compare Bertram M. Beck, "Juvenile Delinquency," *Social Work Year Book,* 1954, pp. 296-305.

should be child centered, and at the same time should prepare pupils for vocations, worthy use of leisure, and social living. The recreation program is a vital part of institutional treatment. The administrative problems pertain chiefly to personnel, plant, and program. Group work and case work should be combined. Living arrangements should embody order, discipline, regularity, and consistency, yet be sufficiently flexible to give children choices and to develop initiative and self-control.

Correctional (training) institutions often fail in modifying conduct and in readjusting the clients to normal living. There are many reasons for failure.[25] Most of these institutions have little or no authority to determine the kinds of children that are admitted—the decision usually rests with juvenile courts or state authorities. They get the cases after other attempts at rehabilitation have failed and the child has had a long habituation to antisocial behavior. Because of previous experience and attitude toward authority, many come to institutions with deep-seated feelings of hostility and suspicion. They are afraid and insecure. Besides, many have personality defects, are slow learners and educationally retarded, and possess other defects that handicap the rehabilitation program even under the best of circumstances. Institutional programs are often highly formalized and fail to reach the underlying difficulties of the inmates. The individualization of treatment, based on sound diagnosis and case-work procedure, has made slow progress. At best, institutional programs are somewhat ineffective, because the cases do not remain long enough in the correctional schools to change fundamentally antisocial traits of the inmates. Rehabilitation is a slow process, requiring continuous guidance and supervision, and a constructive program of activities to overcome deep-rooted antisocial habits and attitudes. The inmates themselves usually carry on an informal but none the less powerful counteradjustive process of their own, tending to perpetuate and even to strengthen antisocial tendencies and to offset the constructive effort. The dismissal from institutions is still predicated upon the number of credits earned

---

25 Albert Deutsch, *Our Rejected Children* (Boston: Little, Brown and Co., 1950). Deutsch has presented an extreme and somewhat journalistic picture of how children in trouble are treated in the correctional institutions. Compare Jeremiah P. Shalloo, "The Dilemma of Correctional Procedure," *Focus.* Vol. 32, No. 3 (May, 1953), 83-85. Shalloo maintains that we have progressed from the old idea of punishment to the new concept of correction, but many correctional institutions are still penal agencies and few of them are designed to accomplish the rehabilitation of the delinquents. For a description of a positive program of institutional care, see Frank J. Cohen, *Children in Trouble: An Experiment in Institutional Child Care* (New York: W. W. Norton & Co., 1952). This book stresses the nonpunitive handling of juveniles given to antisocial behavior.

while in the institution, the lapse of a specified time period, or the need for space for new admissions. Release should not be determined merely on the basis of the adjustment a child makes in the institution. The conditions of living, education, and work arrangement after release should also be considered. Institutions have little control over the home and the neighborhood to which the parolees return.

Recent years have also witnessed changes in attitude and emphasis from the protection of the community to the proper care, education, and supervision of the inmates in an institution. Instead of isolating correctional institutions from the welfare field, the administration of training schools is being transferred to child welfare departments or to other agencies. The coordination of all agencies dealing with delinquents is essential for a unified treatment process. The process of treatment should be continuous, and the agencies and methods should be integrated.

Several new systems of group treatment have been started recently. The English Borstal has been widely acclaimed and is perhaps the outstanding example of the principle of rehabilitation and individualized treatment of young offenders.[26] It is a name given to the English method of dealing with youthful offenders, 16 to 23 years of age. This goes back to 1894 and 1895, and the name comes from Borstal village on a hill above Rochester, where the first institution was located. The system is the outgrowth of many years of study and experimentation. The offenders are classified according to their personality qualities, the severity of their offenses, and their educational and vocational needs. The personnel is separated into disciplinary and treatment staffs. Courts cannot commit persons to institutions until prison commissioners have approved the suitability of such treatment. After allocation, the subjects receive care; and they are not released until the after-care program is discussed with them, so they understand the whole process. Institutionalization and parole go together. Improvement of home and community relationships is made by leaders, who are designated to assist those who are released. Parole agents meet parolees on the average of once a fortnight. The highly trained personnel and the intensive preparation for and supervision of parolees are two keys to the success of this system.[27]

---

26 See William Healy and Benedict S. Alper, *Criminal Youth and the Borstal System* (New York: The Commonwealth Fund, 1941).

27 England established Special Training Units during World War II for the study of young delinquent soldiers in wartime, their offenses, their background, and their treatment under an Army experiment. The stories of 200 delinquent soldiers and how

In America, forestry camps have developed as a new type of treatment of juvenile offenders. The juvenile forestry camps, such as those in Los Angeles County under the auspices of the Probation Department and the camps established by the California Youth Authority, have been successful enterprises. In 1931, the Probation Department and Juvenile Court of Los Angeles County, with the approval of the Board of Supervisors, established the first forestry camp for vagrant boys from other states who were in serious trouble. The experiment was so successful that similar camps were established for local boys. The camps are a cooperative enterprise. The Department of Forestry and the Fire Warden, and the county and city schools and health authorities work with the Camp Division of the Probation Department in carrying out the program of education and of work projects. The placement of a boy in camp is instituted by the juvenile court.

The physical layouts and structural requirements of the forestry camps are very simple, consisting of dormitories, mess hall, laundry and storeroom, recreation hall and athletic field, staff headquarters, classroom or workshop, forestry equipment and service buildings, and other facilities. The administrative and operational staff is very important. The camp educational program is usually a project of one of the local schools. Teachers are assigned to camps, usually three or four nights weekly, to conduct classes. The camp entertainment program is vital to the success of the camp. Self-government, camp paper, and the work program under the auspices of the Camp Forestry Administration add much to the morale of the boys. Case diagnosis and treatment by the camp counselor are difficult but important tasks, for individual supervision is essential to the program. Each camp boy has a case file, which is kept up to date by the counselor. As a means of evaluating individual adjustment and effort, to record individual reactions under the program, and as a means of effecting disciplinary control, a merit system is used, which is an important instrument in determining the desirability of release from camp. The group treatment means control by the standards set for the group and group influence on personal conduct. A certificate is issued to certify camp citizenship. Vocational guidance and aptitude tests are helpful means of adjusting individuals to employment after release.

From 75 to 85 per cent of the boys sent to juvenile forestry camps have made good upon release. The success of the camp program depends especially upon the ability and alertness of the administration

---

they were rehabilitated are contained in a book by Joseph Trenaman, *Out of Step* (New York: Philosophical Library, 1952).

and personnel, the principles and practices of control, the budgeting of the boys' time and work, the personal counseling, and the influence exerted by the group itself on individual citizens of the camp.[28]

During the war years, 1941 to 1943, in response to a recognized need, the junior probation camp program came into being.[29] These camps provide wholesome camp environment and program, with regular meals and sleep, no corporal punishment, (the boys are on their honor), but with awards, privileges, and recognition for good conduct. Professionally trained probation officers are camp directors, assisted by staffs of workers, including teachers, medical workers (doctors and nurses are available), and others. The program includes psychotherapeutic treatment, recreation, religious training, and personal services and attention.

In addition to training schools and correctional institutions or forestry camps, the juvenile court may use other public agencies to take care of some of the children for whom the public assumes responsibility. This is particularly true of health, welfare, and dependency cases, but certain types of delinquents may also be provided for in such institutions.

Private Institutions and Foster Homes. Besides the public detention, correctional, and welfare institutions used for treatment purposes, various kinds of private agencies may be used for study, care, and treatment of both delinquents and nondelinquents. Beginning with the George Junior Republic, a colony of boys and girls at Freeville, New York, founded in 1895 by W. R. George, a number of similar institutions have been established in various sections of the country. Mr. George conceived of the idea that youth in their teens have sufficient intelligence and character to assume responsibilities of self-government and self-support, and by giving them such responsibilities they will develop respect for law and order and become respectable citizens. The Junior Republic has served to launch the self-government movement for youth in institutions, schools, and communities in various parts of the world. Many of these institutions are philanthropic and nonsectarian.

---

28 Kenyon J. Scudder, then the Chief Probation Officer of Los Angeles County, was chiefly responsible for starting these forestry camps. He has more recently applied new methods of treatment to adult offenders in the California Institution for Men at Chino. Cf. *Prisoners Are People* (Garden City, New York: Doubleday & Company, Inc., 1952). For an analysis of the camps in Los Angeles County, see Kenneth E. Kirkpatrick, *The Juvenile Forestry Camp and Its Administration* (Master of Science in Public Administration dissertation, University of Southern California, 1946).

29 John M. Zuck, "The Junior Camps of Los Angeles County," in *Current Approaches to Delinquency, op. cit.*, 76-89.

They combine work, usually farm work, with school and recreation activities. They are usually for boys of a particular age, run by the boys themselves, under proper supervision. The Boys Republic at Chino, California, has been in existence since 1907 and has cared for more than 6,400 boys.

Institutions for the care of dependent and neglected children have been in existence for many centuries. They go by various names (children's homes, orphanages, and the like), are established under such auspices as churches and private agencies, and are designed to care for and to protect children who cannot be adequately cared for in their own homes or in foster homes. Institutions for the physically and mentally handicapped are of special importance because handicapped children are often a burden at home, if they have a home. Children born out of wedlock and homeless children likewise often require special care. It is estimated that over a quarter of a million children are provided for in the different kinds of child-care institutions in the United States.

When institutionalization is necessary, the institution should be as homelike as possible. Feeble-minded, blind, deaf and hard-of-hearing, crippled, and other types of handicapped children require special treatment.

Foster care may be provided in institutions, but usually it is thought of as the care in foster family homes. Legally, it refers to the care given in homes that are not related to the child by blood or marriage. Administratively, foster homes are classified as: boarding, free, wage, or adoption. Each classification has an economic component and varying legal components. Foster home care is generally thought of as service to children who are dependent and neglected, but it also refers to those awaiting placement for adoption; those who are delinquent, crippled, convalescent; and to other types of defectives and problem cases.

The use of foster-home care for delinquent children is relatively recent in origin and is more restricted. The trend in this direction is growing, for the results are encouraging. When Healy and others made studies of the success or failure of placements and reports of clinical cases were published, foster-home care for delinquents gained in prominence. While the findings generally are favorable to foster care, the procedure has not worked out successfully in all cases. Cases studied by the Gluecks showed a high rate of recidivism. The difficulties of finding good foster homes, the problems of placement, and administrative costs must be recognized. However, the results usually justify the efforts. There is no type of behavior that cannot be treated in the foster-home environment, provided the homes are carefully selected and the cases are adequately supervised. Foster homes can be used for children released from institutions if natural homes are lacking.

The importance of the child's own family in the treatment process has been stressed by many authorities. It is necessary to maintain or create wholesome relationships between parents and siblings. When parents and children cooperate, especially if parents recognize their responsibility to their offspring, the children have a better chance to become adjusted to normal living.

A close relationship should exist between the juvenile court and the public and private social agencies of the community. The court contributes special resources and services in treating delinquents. Child-care agencies relieve the court of many services that are, after all, outside the central function of the court. Such agencies and other community institutions are especially helpful in meeting the needs of those who have been released from correctional institutions.

STATE YOUTH AUTHORITIES AND COMMISSIONS

Whelan [30] states that during the past decade thirty-five state commissions or committees on youth have been established. These, he thinks, fall into four main categories. (1) The commissions or committees with broad objectives, such as those in New Jersey and New York are concerned with the whole field of youth needs and problems, with emphasis on the prevention of delinquency. (2) The "code commissions," such as those in Alabama, Montana, Oklahoma, and Florida, are concerned chiefly with the review and improvement of laws relating to youth, with emphasis on children's court. (3) The state agencies, which are designed to prevent delinquency and to improve the treatment of young offenders through probation, parole, and correctional institutions. (4) The state youth authorities or commissions, such as those in California and Minnesota, which are patterned after the Youth Authority Act of the American Law Institute.

These state organizations in one way or another, according to Whelan, carry on research into youth and community needs; attempt to guide and advise operating agencies, especially with respect to recreation facilities and programs; conduct programs of public education with respect to youth problems; supervise probation, parole, and institutional care of delinquents; attempt to coordinate

---

[30] Ralph W. Whelan, "Heading Off Delinquency by State Youth Commissions," in *The Community and the Correctional Process, 1951 Yearbook* (New York: National Probation and Parole Association, 1951), 184-194.

and to foster cooperation among state and local agencies, both public and private; and grant financial aid to local agencies for youth work. Some state commissions perform only a few of these functions, whereas others have more comprehensive functions.

The most outstanding youth authorities are those in California, Minnesota, Wisconsin, Massachusetts, Texas, and Illinois.[31] These states have organizations authorized by state law, including the specifications with respect to administrative organization, age jurisdiction, type of commitment, probation, administrative facilities, duration of control, and discharge on parole.[32] A brief review of the model draft and the California Youth Authority will indicate what a youth authority is and what it may accomplish.

In 1940, The American Law Institute prepared a draft of a Youth Correction Authority Act, later called Youth Authority Act. As stated in the introduction,

. . . the purpose of the Act is to protect society more effectively by substituting for retributive punishment methods of training and treatment directed toward correction and rehabilitation of young persons found guilty of violation of law.[33]

The designation "violation of law" is preferred to the term "offense" or "crime" in referring to the acts of children that come under the jurisdiction of the authority. The chief function of the authority is to provide and administer corrective treatment and preventive training of persons committed to its care. It is a state organization, with a board of three members appointed by the governor. The organization, functions, and methods of commitment of cases are indicated. The juvenile court must determine the suitability of a person to be referred to the authority. Certain types of violations of law are recognized as subject to commitment, but the authority is empowered to use discretion in accepting or rejecting commitments from juvenile courts. After once committed, the judges have no power to

---

[31] Only the one in California is designated "Youth Authority." The others are called—Youth Conservation Commission (Minnesota), Division of Child Welfare and Youth Service in the Department of Public Welfare (Wisconsin), Youth Service Board (Massachusetts), and Youth Development Council (Texas), Youth Commission (Illinois).

[32] For a résumé of the Model Act (American Law Institute) and the youth authority provisions of the five states, see Sol Rubin, "Changing Youth Correction Authority Concepts," *Focus,* Vol. 29, No. 3 (May, 1950), 81, and discussion of changes, 77-81. Compare Will C. Turnbladh, "More about Youth Authority Concepts," *Focus,* Vol. 30, No. 1 (January, 1951), 23-26; and George Reed, "Minnesota's YCC Program," *Focus,* Vol. 32, No. 2 (March, 1953), 49-50.

[33] Official Draft, *Youth Correction Authority Act,* The American Law Institute (1940), 1.

suspend commitments. Those committed may appeal from the judgments, and decisions may be reversed.

The authority operates under a budget. It may establish and operate treatment centers, create and administer districts suitable to performance of duties, employ all persons needed for proper execution of duties or discharge them, make use of existing institutions and agencies, establish operative institutions, examine persons committed, place them in institutions, terminate treatment and control, and carry on preventive functions.

California led the way in establishing the California Youth Authority in 1941. Its organization follows the pattern set up by the American Law Institute. The three members of the authority are appointed by the Governor, approved by the State Senate, and serve for four years, subject to reappointment. The two main objectives are: (1) The training and treatment of juvenile offenders under 21 years of age who are referred to the Authority, directed toward the correction and rehabilitation under its care; and (2) the prevention of the occurrence of delinquency. The rehabilitation program includes clinical diagnosis of the cases; classification of youths on the basis of age, mental capacity, emotional maturity, interest and aptitude, and type of treatment needed; the treatment process, which usually is in the correctional institutions and forestry camps operated by the Authority; and parole supervision after release from institutionalization. The preventive work consists of attempts to strengthen existing community facilities for child welfare and to organize community coordinating councils, initiating new services wherever needed through surveys of local conditions and needs, and collecting statistical data. The *California Youth Authority Quarterly* is the main publication.

The California Youth Authority has broad responsibilities: to inquire into the antecedent history of its charges, to determine the causes for commission of crime, and to bring about rehabilitation of the minors under its jurisdiction. To carry out its purpose, it may establish public councils, or cooperate with existing agencies to further the work of prevention or decrease of delinquency in the state, improve recreation and other facilities, enter research fields for the study of delinquency and of the resources for treatment and preventive purposes, compile statistical data, and issue public reports. The Authority exercises supervision and control over state correction institutions, and may establish and approve homes for temporary detention of wards to be examined and for those already committed for confinement or education. It not only commits its charges to institutions, but may parole persons to private homes. It has broad discretionary powers regarding commitments to institutions or permission for charges to remain at liberty under supervision. It has been instrumental in improving and expanding the institutional facilities of the state for the treatment of offenders, in raising the standard of treatment and of law enforcement, and in providing field services to various agencies in local areas.

The Chairman of the three-man board is also the Director of the staff. For administrative purposes the staff is grouped under three major divisions, with subsections: (1) the Division of Diagnosis and Classification; (2) the Division of Training and Treatment, which has charge of the correctional institutions and camps; and (3) the Division of Field Services, which has the parole section and delinquency prevention functions.

There is little new in the program except that the functions of delinquency control in the state are concentrated in one agency; new methods of dealing with offenders, especially in the camps, are used; and a program of delinquency prevention covers the entire state. The delinquency prevention section of the Division of Field Services represents perhaps the most distinctive contribution of the program. Its establishment was made possible when the legislature added a section to the Welfare and Institutions Code providing that the Youth Authority

. . . may establish or assist in the establishment of any public council or committee, and may assist and cooperate with any existing agency, having as its object the prevention or decrease of delinquency among youths; and the Authority may cooperate with or participate in the work of any such councils, or any existing councils, including the improving of recreational, health, and other conditions in the community affecting youth.[34]

During the period of its existence, the staff of this division has made numerous surveys of youth agencies, including existing facilities and the conditions of delinquency. The surveys have led in many instances to recommendations for the reorganization of old agencies or the creation of new agencies. Community coordinating councils, teen-age centers, and various conferences have been stimulated or organized as a result of the efforts of the organization. Workshops for leaders in delinquency prevention fields have been conducted throughout the state.

By establishing camps and augmenting the correctional schools, a larger number of delinquents can now be provided for and given better training. The parole service makes it possible to give closer

---

[34] Section 1752.5 of the Welfare and Institutions Code.

supervision of parolees. Thus, after a few years, The California Youth Authority has become an important state agency with its own clinics, correctional schools, camps, parole programs, and community services. As Karl Holton has put it, the great need is more effective community service for children.

> From our work with boys and girls who come to correctional schools we are more than ever impressed with the need for strengthening community service for children. Remedial work can be done with the boy or girl after he (or she) is removed from the community and sent to a correctional school. Nothing we can do, however, can ever completely erase the harm which has been done by years of neglect, bad association and unwholesome experiences. The end is not in sight when juvenile delinquency can be abolished, but with study and understanding work over a period of years and with the cooperation of those who really wish to see conditions improved, we can hope to see a gradual decrease in the delinquency rate among our boys and girls.[35]

The Minnesota Youth Conservation Commission, established in 1947, consists of six members appointed by the governor for six-year terms, of whom three are public officials serving ex officio; and the governor designates the chairman. The Wisconsin Youth Service Division of the Department of Public Welfare (1947), renamed Division of Child Welfare and Youth Service in 1949, is modeled after the American Law Institute draft and the California act, but it is a part of a major department of the state government. The Youth Service Board of Massachusetts (1948), a three-man board, has many of the provisions of the other acts, but its jurisdiction is limited to children within the juvenile court age; whereas the model draft provided primarily for commitments from 16 to 21. The Youth Development Act of Texas (1949) has a six-man board appointed by the governor and eight state officials serve as ex-officio officers. Illinois established a Youth Commission in 1954, with a three-man board, which now has administrative control over state training schools, the parole program, and the youth and community services activities.

These state youth authorities and the various types of citizens' groups have rendered an important service to improve the treatment of juvenile offenders and to promote preventive programs. They differ in basic concept, organization, and functions. It is recognized

---

[35] Karl Holton, "The California Youth Authority," *Society's Stake in the Offender, 1946 Yearbook* (New York: National Probation and Parole Association, 1947), 126. Karl Holton was the first Director, succeeded by Heman Stark. For a summary statement of the functions, organization, and operation of the Authority, see mimeographed report prepared by Vandyce Hamren, Assistant to the Director (February 1, 1951); and report of California Youth Authority, *Program and Progress*, 1943-1948.

that no one system fits the needs of all states. Hence, the movement to establish state youth provisions has followed several directions.[36]

QUESTIONS AND PROJECTS

For Class Discussion and Research

1. Trace the history of the juvenile court, giving background, trends and changes, and present status.

2. What constitutes the chief differences between the juvenile court and criminal court procedures?

3. What modifications of the juvenile court would you suggest?

4. Do you agree that the juvenile court should be limited in its functions and not assume case-work functions?

5. How could criminal courts be socialized, by adopting some of the procedures of the juvenile court? What is meant by the socialization of juvenile court procedure?

6. How can juvenile courts be more closely related to the community?

7. What are the essential legal aspects of delinquency control?

8. Define probation, parole, indeterminate sentence, and correctional institution.

9. How does juvenile probation differ from adult probation?

10. State the main qualifications of: (1) a juvenile court judge, (2) a juvenile probation officer.

11. How would you differentiate between voluntary probation (by law enforcement officers) and official probation? Trace trends in probation work.

12. State the values and the weaknesses of correctional institutions? In what ways can forestry camps overcome weaknesses of institutional treatment?

13. What standards would you recommend for the operation of training schools for delinquents?

14. State the advantages and the disadvantages of using foster homes for certain types of delinquents.

15. Secure case records of children who have received institutional treatment or foster home care, or who are on probation in their own homes.

16. What are the best case-work and treatment procedures in training schools for delinquents?

17. Follow-up studies of discharged offenders.

18. Discuss predicting the success or failure of those released from correctional institutions.

---

36 For a more detailed analysis of correction at the state level and services to all youth at the community level, including a description of youth authorities, see John R. Ellingston, *Protecting Our Children from Criminal Careers* (New York: Prentice-Hall, Inc., 1948).

19. Discuss group work approach to the treatment of juvenile offenders.
20. Discuss psychiatric clinics in the treatment of conduct disorders
21. Discuss educational programs for problem children.

SELECTED REFERENCES

Annals of the Academy of Political and Social Science, Vol. 261 (January, 1948), sections on "The Court and the Juvenile Delinquent," and "Detention and Institutional Treatment."

BEARD, BELLE BOONE, *Juvenile Probation* (New York: American Book Co., 1934).

COHEN, FRANK J., *Children in Trouble: An Experiment in Institutional Child Care* (New York: W. W. Norton & Co., Inc., 1952).

Comparative Survey on Juvenile Delinquency, Part I. North America, prepared by Paul W. Tappan (New York: Division of Social Affairs, Department of Social Affairs, 1952), sections on "Courts and Agencies with Jurisdiction Over Children," and "Treatment of Juvenile Delinquents."

ELLINGSTON, JOHN R., *Protecting Our Children from Criminal Careers* (New York: Prentice-Hall, Inc., 1948). (This book contains detail descriptions of correction at the state and community levels. It was published too late to use in this chapter.)

Federal Probation, quarterly published by the Administrative Office of the United States Court.

NATIONAL PROBATION AND PAROLE ASSOCIATION, The Yearbooks and *Focus* (recent issues).

RUMNEY, JAY, AND JOSEPH P. MURPHY, *Probation and Social Adjustment* (New Brunswick, New Jersey: Rutgers University Press, 1952). Published for the Essex County Probation Department.

SUSSMANN, FREDERICK B., *Law of Juvenile Delinquency: The Laws of the Forty-Eight States* (New York: Oceana Publications, 1950).

TAPPAN, PAUL W., *Contemporary Correction* (New York: McGraw-Hill Book Co., Inc., 1951).

YOUNG, PAULINE V., *Social Treatment in Probation and Delinquency* (New York: McGraw-Hill Book Co., Inc., 1952).

XIV

Social Action and Community Services

Recent research has demonstrated the importance of the social factors in delinquency, as the studies reported in Part Two have amply shown. Delinquents cannot be viewed simply as individuals. They can be understood only by fully recognizing the influences of their families, their group associations, and their community.

Individuals can do much to help themselves, and much can be done for them, but most of the social problems are so complex that no solution is possible without the concerted efforts of the group. The preponderance of thinking in delinquency prevention is in agreement that the most effective way to attack the problem of delinquency is through concerted social action, such as through social legislation, various forms of institutional and community services, and community organization. More specifically, this means personal services, the strengthening of home life, group work and community recreation, effective work of the school and the church, and the control of community conditions. Government departments have important functions to perform. Broad and progressive social legislation is necessary for effective control by government agencies, giving them the responsibility and the authority to act in critical situations and to carry on preventive work. However, unless community institutions, agencies, and groups are coordinated and integrated, little effective work can be done on the local level.

The traditional approaches to delinquency control have been questioned. Lukas [1] questions the effectiveness of certain control, rescuing, and character-building measures. They dominate, he thinks, the guidance services (that is, the provisions of social and psychiatric services for strengthening the individual and the family). Concerted action is needed to measure the quantum of predelinquent behavior, to promote understanding of the nature of the problem and the manner in which it may be handled, and to be able to act promptly to correct those conditions that contribute to delinquency.

The main outline of social action and community services will be presented in the present chapter, which will be followed, in the next chapter, by a consideration of community organization and social research.

Getting at the Roots of Delinquency

Prevention of delinquency means fundamentally getting at the roots of delinquency. In developing crime prevention it is important to point out that no program can have any hope of success without striking at the causes of crime. We cannot cure a disease merely by attacking its symptoms.

The problem of juvenile crime is so complicated that we must not fall into the fallacy of attributing it to any one cause. To understand the problem thoroughly, a complete analysis of the individual delinquent is essential, together with an understanding of the environmental conditions under which misconduct takes place. To prevent delinquency, it is necessary to deal with both the personality factors and the environmental influences, especially those emanating from the home, the intimate associates, and the community. Since personality is molded by the individual's contact with the environment, in research and in preventive programs it is necessary to find out what influences and stimuli in the environment tend toward

---

1 Edwin J. Lukas, "Limitations in the Traditional Approach to Delinquency," *The Community and the Correctional Process: 1951 Yearbook* (New York: National Probation and Parole Association, 1951), 149-167.

wholesome development of the individual and what contribute to delinquency. Creating a wholesome environment and eliminating undesirable influences are two important phases of a constructive preventive program.

Personal Services. The role of the individual in the program of treatment and prevention must not be overlooked. No matter how strong the environmental pressures may be, it is the individual who decides what to do in a given situation. A child may be endowed with a strong body and a good mind, but he cannot be compelled to use them wisely. He may be taught to know the difference between right and wrong, but he cannot always be forced to obey the rules of behavior. Merely building fine homes, schools, churches, and playgrounds will not prevent some youngsters from going wrong. Each individual has a certain range of free choice, and back of conduct is the element of volition.

The measure of success in local or national efforts to prevent delinquency lies in part in the ability to teach acceptable norms of behavior, to create in children the desire to do right, and to heighten the personal satisfaction found in socially acceptable conduct. Individuals must learn to choose for themselves. This requires character and a sensitive conscience.

While it is true that the social drives behind conduct are lodged within the person, yet no person is immune from social pressures. The dynamic motives of human action include wishes, attitudes, interests, and habits. These are chiefly acquired through experience in group living. Reforms that are based on the notion of treating the child as an individual apart from society are doomed to failure. Nearly all human behavior is a product of group life. Studies by Thrasher, Shaw, and many others have demonstrated this fact. Delinquency is a learned behavior; it is communicated in the gang and is transmitted through the criminal traditions that are prevalent in certain neighborhoods, many of which are slum and blighted areas segregated from the life of the larger community. Hence, it is useless to view the individual and his behavior apart from the social world in which he lives.

This being the case, preventive efforts must be directed chiefly toward the creation of a wholesome environment in which children may grow up to maturity, equipped to meet life's challenges and to overcome temptations. This provides not only the atmosphere for successful living, but also the stimuli that build personality and character. Personality is dynamic, not static. It is subject to social influences. Some hereditary elements or biological conditions are relative, even absolute, determinants of conduct, yet others are largely or wholly the product of social pressures. Temperamental predisposition, biological make-up, mental level, and similar factors are rooted in heredity, constituting the basis for responding to social stimuli. Still other conditions of motivation are almost wholly acquired.

It is imperative, therefore, that children be provided with the personal services that help to strengthen character and to enrich personality. Individual treatment has already been discussed. The importance of proper treatment can hardly be overemphasized. The services rendered in the home, in the club, and in the social institutions of the community are extremely important from the point of view of individual as well as societal welfare.

The work with individuals and the improvement of the kind of services that should be given by the agencies that have a major responsibility for working with delinquent children, together with discussions of some of the ways of preventing juvenile delinquency, have been emphasized by the Children's Bureau.[2] It is suggested that, in view of the increase of delinquency, too little help is available for the boys and girls on charges of delinquency. The police, juvenile court and probation department, the detention homes and training schools, and the state agencies can be assisted by citizen groups, provided they secure the facts, plan and conduct surveys of needs and services, and find ways of effective work with children and families.

Citizens can do much with individual children who are in need. The Big Brother Movement has demonstrated the usefulness of personal contacts, interest, and brotherly helpfulness. Applegate[3] presents a concise description of his experience as a layman in boy guidance and service. His method is that of being a "big brother" to the boy in trouble. During the first interview he points out that the relationship with the boy is to be a friendly and helpful one and that the boy is at liberty to tell him if he does not want his help. If the boy accepts the relationship which has been explained to him, they discuss a program of recreation activities, including athletics, field trips to interesting places, and various other types of leisure pur-

---

[2] Consult the following bulletins: "Helping Delinquent Children," publication No. 341, and "What's Happening to Delinquent Children in Your Town?" publication No. 342 (Children's Bureau, United States Department of Health, Education, and Welfare, 1953). Compare "Children Who Never Had a Chance," Public Affairs Pamphlet No. 183, published in 1952.

[3] Melbourne S. Applegate, *Helping Boys in Trouble: The Layman in Boy Guidance* (New York: Association Press, 1950). Compare Harry E. Burroughs, *Boys in Men's Shoes* (New York: The Macmillan Co., 1944).

suits. On these trips and by mutual participation in various recreational activities, he tries to understand the boy's problems, interests and attitudes, physical condition and mentality, family relationships, school experience, and other outside influences and conditions. After he has some understanding of the boy's difficulties and weaknesses, he encourages him in his activities and in trying to solve his problems. The services of schools, social agencies, and other individuals are used if needed, and cooperation with his family is sought. Vocational training, securing a job, and assisting the boy in improving while on the job are a part of the process.

Although this type of personal service is helpful to boys and girls in trouble, the analysis of the difficulty is not sufficiently comprehensive and scientific to serve as the basis of effective case work with juveniles who have serious behavior problems. The type of comprehensive case analysis referred to in Chapter XII provides the basic information for good diagnosis and prognosis of the case and furnishes the foundation for the treatment process. The value of the combination of case analysis and treatment has been amply demonstrated in the cases described by such writers as Shaw and McKay, Healy and Bronner, Davidoff and Noetzel, and others previously referred to. Clinical treatment affords opportunities for more intensive work with the serious offenders. Some form of clinical treatment should be made available for children with minor behavior problems.

Child guidance clinics have been used in connection with juvenile courts ever since William Healy established the Juvenile Psychopathic Institute in Chicago in 1909. Similar clinics have been started in other metropolitan areas, but few are found in outlying areas. The Passaic (New Jersey) Children's Bureau, as described by Kvaraceus,[4] is an example of a community clinic under the auspices of the school system, but used by all law enforcement agencies. Casework and group-work agencies likewise have facilities for the study and treatment of problem cases. Since the end of World War II there has been a significant increase in the number of child guidance clinics supported by public and private funds. They go by different names, are under various types of auspices, and range from full-time

---

4 William C. Kvaraceus, *Juvenile Delinquency and the School* (New York: World Book Co., 1945). For material on child guidance clinics, see Albert Deutsch, *The Mentally Ill in the United States* (New York: Columbia University Press, 1946); *Encyclopedia of Educational Research,* edited by Walter Monroe (New York: The Macmillan Co., 1950); and *Social Work Year Book,* edited by Russell H. Kurtz (New York: American Association of Social Workers, 1954).

and well staffed clinics or traveling clinic staffs to small concerns, often with inadequately trained staff members.

Strengthening the Home. Character and behavior traits are formed early in childhood, and the family plays a very important part in this process of education and training, as was indicated in Chapter VI. If children develop antisocial tendencies, parents are in a strategic position to curb or correct them, and to stimulate the more desirable tendencies. Children need encouragement and guidance. The home is responsible for much of the early training. Any treatment or preventive program must deal directly with the family. Other institutions may modify and help in the rehabilitation program, but the family is the key institution. Any solution to the problem of delinquency must concern itself with the child's family, for the drives, thwartings, likes and dislikes, preferences, and many other subtle and intangible elements of family relationships constitute the background for the difficulties of the young delinquent. On the positive side, the home provides the most vital influence in the growth of the child, providing guidance, protection, security, and affection.

The importance of the home in influencing a child's behavior was discussed at length as one of the conditioning factors. Any preventive program must include the strengthening of the home and the correction or alleviation of conditions that put undue strain on the developing child. Structural completeness is highly desirable, for broken homes are common factors in delinquency. Functional adequacy of families that are intact is likewise desirable. Parental education, family counseling, family assistance to assure economic security, better housing and sanitation, improvement in the physical care of children, and the assumption by parents of greater responsibility for the rearing and supervising of their children are ways of strengthening the home.

The program of education for marriage, parental training, and family counseling has received wide recognition among educators and family experts. An important function of the education of parents is to train them to recognize symptoms of maladjustment, to be able to supervise the activities of children, and to direct their energies into wholesome channels. The continual process of adjustment to changing circumstances is too much for some families. They need counseling or case-work service.

Financial aid to families that are in need has long been recognized as a public responsibility. Aid to needy children, unemployment compensation, old-age assistance, and old-age and survivors benefits are the important phases of social security, all of which, as well as the health services, are designed especially to provide greater economic security for families. Better housing and sanitation, and improvements in the immediate physical surroundings of children, should improve family functioning. Overcrowding, physical delapidation, and unsanitary slum conditions are recognizable conditions of delinquency areas, which conditions must be removed or improved if adequate family life is to be achieved.

Neglect, unwise discipline, conflicting and emotionally disturbing incidents, and the lack of proper guidance and moral training in the home have serious consequences. Parents must assume primary responsibility for the training of their children. Negligent and lawless parents, and those who otherwise contribute to the delinquency of their children, may be prosecuted.

Domestic relations or family courts are of a compulsory nature and, therefore, have limitations in rehabilitating family life; yet they are important in dealing with the disorganized home and with neglectful parents. Experiments have been conducted with compulsory parental education in cases where such a procedure has been considered advisable.[5]

Group Work and Youth-Serving Agencies. Delinquencies are seldom committed by individuals alone. Gangs and street corner groups, informal play groups and chums have a fascination for children and exert a powerful influence. The types of recreation activities that an individual engages in affect his personality and conduct in a variety of ways.[6]

The promotion of character building and citizenship training through group work and recreation has long been recognized as a preventive program, although group-work agencies have stressed that it is not the primary function of their program to prevent delinquency or to treat those already delinquent. It is rather a positive program of providing opportunities for boys and girls to have fun, to make friends, to acquire skills in various forms of recreation, and, as a step toward the development of social responsibility, to experience the democratic process in small self-motivated groups.

Group work calls for voluntary participation on the part of group members under the supervision of adult leadership. Youth-serving agencies, such as Boy Scouts, Girl Scouts, Camp Fire Girls, Wood-

---

[5] For discussion of the need of preserving the family to combat delinquency, see *Current Approaches to Delinquency: 1949 Yearbook,* edited by Marjorie Bell (New York: National Probation and Parole Association, 1949), Section IV.

[6] See Chapters VII and VIII.

craft Rangers, Boys' Division of the Young Men's Christian Association, Y-Teens (formerly Girl Reserves) of the Young Women's
Christian Association, 4-H Clubs, playground departments, and
many others, are chiefly responsible for group work in most communities. The group-work process is a way of meeting the needs of
youth. Although groups differ in terms of age, sex, experience, capacity for growth, desires, and leadership, the group-work process
has a tremendous socializing effect on individuals. The face-to-face
group is particularly important in the matter of group experience,
for it is the matrix within which individuals react to one another in
intimate ways. Group leaders have unusual opportunities to develop
new interests in the participants, broaden knowledge and skills, develop social attitudes, make adjustments to others in mutually en-
riching ways, and provide experience and training in social living.

Most people think that group work is an effective way of reducing the incidences of misconduct, for when boys and girls are kept
busy with constructive activities they have little time or inclination
to engage in deviant behavior. It is difficult to measure the exact
effects of the group-work process. The findings of the more scientific studies are not in full agreement as to the exact effects of the
program. The influence exerted by club groups depends largely
upon the type of leadership provided, the kinds of activities undertaken, the extent of participation by the membership, and the attitudes and interests of the participants. Youth-serving agencies have
been criticized in that they fail to reach the underprivileged and the
potentially delinquent. Few delinquents belong to organized clubs.

One club agency in a community, even though it may be able
to reach many delinquent and underprivileged children, may not be
able to reduce delinquency by itself, although it renders important
services to the youth of the area. This is what Thrasher discovered
in his study of a Boys' Club, which was established in a crime-breed-
ing area of New York City.[7] Using descriptive, ecological, statistical,
and case-study methods, the study showed that this particular club
during its first four years was not an important factor in delinquency
prevention. The Boys' Club reached approximately 4000 boys, with
a net monthly average of about 63 per cent of the total, which was
far short of the goal. Although the program did not reach all of the
boys it was designed to serve, it did succeed in reaching many underprivileged boys, probably including more potential delinquents
than were represented among the nonmembers of the same age
groups. Because of the large number of such boys enrolled, the

---

[7] Frederic M. Thrasher, "The Boys' Club and Juvenile Delinquency," *The American Journal of Sociology*, XLII, No. 1 (July, 1936), 66-80.

Boys' Club delinquency rates were higher than those of the community in general. However, many joined the Club for one year
only, and some were not very active. Thrasher concludes that crime
prevention is not the function of a single preventive agency, but
requires the concerted attack of a coordinated community program,
in which the services of many preventive and remedial agencies are
integrated in the achievement of a common goal. The Boys' Club is
one of a number of factors in any crime prevention program, and it
performs many other essential services to underprivileged children.

The All Nations Foundation in Los Angeles, especially through
its Boys' Club, has been an important institution in serving the
needs of the underprivileged youth of the area, and it has been
credited with a substantial reduction of delinquency in that section
of the city over a period of years. A survey of boy life in Los
Angeles [8] revealed that the area adjacent to this center was the heart
of delinquency in the city. After the establishment of the Boys'
Club and the addition of other facilities and programs, delinquency
in the area began to decline, although the neighborhood still had the
conditions commonly found in delinquency areas. During the early
part of the 1930's, a five-year program of child guidance was financed
by an anonymous donor. The Child Welfare Clinic was set up in
the Foundation to provide guidance and various kinds of other services to the youth of the area. As a part of these services, an intensive
clinical study was made of 500 (270 boys and 230 girls) underprivileged children.[9] The records included a complete family history of
each child, with special data derived by means of a home rating
scale, a health examination report, behavior and educational achievement records from the school teachers, data from club leaders regarding recreation and social interests and activities, the results of
a recreation interview technique, psychological tests, and various
kinds of behavior rating and adjustment inventories.

The findings of this study revealed that the children studied
lived in an undesirable environment, including sub-standard conditions in their homes, disorganized family life, low economic and
social status, culture conflicts, and harmful neighborhood influences.
The interstitial area in which the study was made can be classified
as a slum district. Of the five primary group situations in which the

---

[8] Survey sponsored and financed by the Rotary Club of Los Angeles. See Emory S.
Bogardus, Social Research Director, *The City Boy and His Problems* (1926).

[9] For a summary of this study see: Everett W. DuVall, *Relative Influence of Primary
Groups on Underprivileged Children* (Los Angeles: University of Southern California
Press, 1938), containing approved portions of a dissertation in partial fulfillment of the
requirements for the degree of Doctor of Philosophy, June, 1936, University of Southern
California.

children were studied (neighborhood, family, school, church, and play groups), the organized play groups had the greatest influence on their personality development and on social adjustment. The family, ordinarily considered as the most important primary group, had less influence on the children than the play groups, as indicated by the child-parent social distance, the close correlation between home rating and behavior rating scores, and by the attitudes expressed by the children. Everett W. DuVall, the director of the Child Welfare Clinic, concluded that,

. . . aside from the limitations imposed by the type of neighborhood in which they live and their inadequate play equipment, the recreation life of the underprivileged children in this study appears to be fairly normal. The importance of the influence of the organized play group is evidenced by the low delinquency rate for the group studied, as compared with the rate established for the other children in the area but not participating in the organized recreational program provided by the agency. The delinquency rate for the underprivileged children included in this study compares favorably with the rate for the normal or average children in the city despite the high incidence in the underprivileged environment of those factors usually associated with delinquency. It is from their experiences in the recreation situation that these children learn to accommodate and become assimilated in the culture of the country. They accept socially desirable values and acquire the more important attitudes in the organized play group in which their fundamental wishes are satisfied. The findings of this study indicate that the experiences in the play group are more important factors than the experiences in the family, school, church, or neighborhood groups in the determination of socialized attitudes and in the personality development and social adjustment of the five hundred underprivileged children.[10]

It should be added that apart from the program of recreation and group work provided by the Foundation, this area has few community recreation facilities.

To serve the least privileged area of Los Angeles, the Youth Project of the Welfare Council of Metropolitan Los Angeles (now the Welfare Planning Council) was set up in 1943. The area served by this organized group-work program is coincidental with the regions of greatest social needs as defined by a comprehensive survey of recreation and youth service of the city.[11]

One of the main purposes of the Youth Project was to serve the minority groups in the mid-city congested sections. Group studies

---

10 *Ibid.*, 30-31. Used by permission of University of Southern California Press.

11 See Roy Sorenson, Director of Survey, *Recreation for Everybody* (1946), a report of a survey conducted by the Community Survey Associated, under the auspices of Community Chests and Councils, Inc., for the Welfare Council of Metropolitan Los Angeles.

conducted in 1945-1946 revealed that of the 1075 groups with definite enrollment, only 35 per cent served Caucasian groups, 15 per cent served Negroes exclusively, 14 per cent served Latin American groups exclusively, and the remaining 36 per cent served mixed groups. As compared with the better residential areas of the city, a larger proportion of youth of minority groups are enrolled in clubs since the project was inaugurated. No statistics can be cited to show the results of the program in terms of youth behavior, but it is believed that the reduction of delinquency in certain areas is attributable in part to the work of the organized groups of underprivileged children.

During recent years, various kinds of youth centers, commonly called "teen centers" or "teen-age clubs," have sprung up in response to felt need. Many of these clubs are self-motivated groups, allowing active participation by the young people in their management and control. Some lack planning, whereas others are well planned, with adequate programs of activities, and usually with some adult leadership. Their success has impressed community leaders with the need for such centers, the capacity of young people to assume responsibilities, and the value of letting youth organizations manage their own affairs.

The teen-age centers are chiefly for the age group from about 14 to 18 years. The activities include music, dramatics, dancing, art, craft work, hobby groups, outdoor athletics and sports, swimming, bowling, discussion groups, and snack bar. From the point of view of youth, these centers provide opportunities to have fun, to make friends, and to participate actively in programs.[12]

Community Recreation. There is a growing demand for governmental and nongovernmental community recreation. From the point of view of organization, recreation may be broadly classified as: (1) the spontaneous and semiorganized kinds that are carried on in the home and in small informal groups, (2) the commercially promoted and provided, and (3) the communally organized. Of the latter, the public, tax-supported, and government controlled provisions for recreation are most important. Increasingly, the public is recognizing a responsibility for the recreation of the people. Parks, play-

---

12 For books on group-work and youth-serving agencies, and what recreation does for individuals, see Bernice Baxter and Rosalind Cassidy, *Group Experience: The Democratic Way* (New York: Harper & Brothers, 1943); M. M. Chambers, *Youth-Serving Organizations* (Washington, D. C.: American Council on Education, 1948); S. R. Slavson, *Recreation and the Total Personality* (New York. Association Press, 1946); and Harleigh B. Trecker, *Social Group Work: Principles and Practices* (New York: Association Press, 1948).

grounds, neighborhood centers, public beaches, camps, and other types of facilities have grown in importance during recent years.

It is not the purpose here to review the progress in recreation legislation, the provisions for space and facilities, the problem of financing, the administration of community recreation, the program of activities, and the problem of leadership.[13] One must recognize the influence of community recreation in combating juvenile crime. Wholesome activities offer children a channel for constructive and enjoyable experience and give opportunity for direction of interest that might otherwise seek satisfaction in misbehavior.

The program of activities should be suitable for youth. The range of activities should meet the physical, psychological, and social needs of youth, offer opportunities for personality enrichment, and prepare individuals for useful citizenship. The leisure activities should be interesting and appealing, give individuals a chance to participate actively in them, and yet have a degree of supervision that assures constructive results.

On the basis of a comprehensive study of recreation in relation to delinquency, the Chicago Recreation Commission recommended, among other things, that (1) more supervised recreation be provided in all areas, particularly in those regions where delinquency rates are high, (2) special provisions be made for the recreation of girls, (3) special efforts be made to reach the older boys, (4) recreation agencies adapt their programs to appeal to delinquents and high-spirited adolescents, (5) more outdoor recreation be provided, and (6) the total program of recreation be integrated through community organization in which the home, the school, the church, and other community agencies cooperate.[14]

In addition to a comprehensive community program of recreation in the localities of high delinquency rates, organized camping programs have been used to provide wholesome outdoor life and recreation for underprivileged children. Camping is regarded as an

---

[13] For a brief description of community recreation, both public and semipublic, or private, see Martin H. and Esther S. Neumeyer, *Leisure and Recreation* (New York: A. S. Barnes and Co., 1949), Chapters XIII and XIV. Compare George D. Butler, *Introduction to Community Recreation* (New York: McGraw-Hill Book Co., 1949); George Hjelte, *The Administration of Public Recreation* (New York: The Macmillan Co., 1940); John L. Hutchison, *Principles of Recreation* (New York: A. S. Barnes and Co., 1949); Harold D. Meyer and Charles K. Brightbill, *Community Recreation: A Guide to Its Organization and Administration* (Boston: D. C. Heath and Co., 1948); Elmer D. Mitchell and Bernard S. Mason, *The Theory of Play* (New York: A. S. Barnes and Co., 1948); and issues of *Recreation,* published monthly by the National Recreation Association.

[14] Ethel Shanas, Director, with the collaboration of Catherine E. Dunning, *Recreation and Delinquency* (Chicago: University of Chicago Press, 1942), especially pp. 245-248.

important phase of group work agency and community recreation programs. Today, many kinds of camps are operated by public recreation departments, youth-serving agencies, churches, schools, and by private groups. The American Camping Association has done much to set up standards of camping, dissemination of information about camping through conferences and publications, and in cooperation with local agencies has promoted camping for youth. One of the major trends in American camping movement is the extension of camping opportunities to all people regardless of race or economic status. Camps have increased in number, the camping periods have been extended, democratic participation is encouraged, and camp leaders are provided better training for their work.

During recent years some police departments, especially through the juvenile bureaus, have attempted to administer or sponsor various types of delinquency prevention programs, with special emphasis on recreation activities. They not only have worked closely in cooperation with community agencies, but have endeavored to fill the gap by sponsoring programs for underprivileged children not touched by other agencies. The activities include the administration and sponsorship of recreation programs, summer camps, the organization of community and neighborhood councils, case-work and counseling services, community education projects, working with gangs, guarding street crossings near schools and recreation centers, using volunteer counselors and juvenile leaders for patrol and other functions, and a variety of other projects. No police department does all of these things, but some have extensive programs. For example, the Los Angeles Police Department has carried on an extensive deputy auxiliary police program, known as DAP, with more than 3000 boys and girls enrolled in the various units and with over 40 police officers and civilian employees directing the activities. But the critics of such programs have questioned the desirability of police departments and sheriff offices undertaking such preventive efforts. Experienced officers do not dispute the need for preventive programs, but some of them doubt the wisdom of using police personnel to administer recreation and welfare projects that should be administered by other agencies. The proponents of such undertakings maintain that if communities fail to provide adequate recreation and welfare activities for the underprivileged children the police department cannot ignore the need, for they must eventually deal with some of the consequences of neglect. Furthermore, by sponsoring preventive work in a community, crime prevention bureaus help to secure more adequate treatment of offenders, provide counseling services for maladjusted adolescents, build up constructive forces for the prevention of law violation, and develop a more wholesome attitude upon the part of youth toward law and toward police officers.[15]

The School and Delinquency Prevention. The problems of unsatisfactory school experience, truants, and out-of-school youth were discussed in Chapter VIII. The development of new methods for dealing with maladjusted pupils and various types of school programs are so extensive that even a brief outline would take us too far afield. The literature on new methods of education is voluminous. Authentic material on the role of the school in delinquency prevention is more limited, however.[16]

The school, because of its constant and intimate contact with children, occupies a strategic position in the prevention of juvenile delinquency. Of the social institutions in the community, the school is the most favorably located and is in the best position to serve children. The opportunity of the school in preventing delinquency is great, because it reaches practically all children at a relatively early period of growth, has the pupils several hours a day, and teachers are able to observe them closely. On the other hand, schools may be handicapped in that they lack adequate equipment and financial support, have poorly trained teachers, and have a program insufficiently adjusted to the varied needs of pupils. However, modern schools stress, in addition to the acquisition of practical knowledge, the development of personality and the preparation of pupils for life situations, especially vocational, leisure, and social living. Special educational facilities have been established for exceptional or handicapped children, the socially maladjusted, and other types requiring specialized treatment.

---

15 Cf. William H. Parker, "The Police Challenge in Our Great Cities," and Jane E. Rinck, "Supervising the Juvenile Delinquent," *The Annals of the American Academy of Political and Social Science,* Vol. 291 (January, 1954), 5-13 and 78-86. The entire issue deals with "New Goals in Police Management."

16 For examples of studies and discussions of the relation of the school to delinquency and its role in the preventive program, consult Nelson B. Henry, Editor, *Juvenile Delinquency and the School: The Forty-Seventh Yearbook of the National Society for the Study of Education* (Chicago: University of Chicago Press, 1948), a series of papers by noted authorities; William C. Kvaraceus, *Juvenile Delinquency and the School* (New York: World Book Co., 1945); Pauline V. Young, *Social Treatment in Probation and Delinquency* (New York: McGraw-Hill Book Co., Inc., 1952), Chapter XXIV, selected bibliography, pp. 479-481; and *Preventing Crime: A Symposium,* edited by Sheldon and Eleanor Glueck (New York: McGraw-Hill Book Co., Inc., 1936), Part II. For an example of material prepared for guidance of school officials in dealing with the problem of delinquency, see Arthur S. Hill, Leonard M. Miller, and Hazel F. Gabbard, "Schools Face the Delinquency Problem," *The Bulletin,* Vol. 37, No. 198 (December, 1953), a publication of the National Association of Secondary-School Principals.

One approach of the school to the problem of delinquency (the negative way) is to avoid student frustrations, maladjustments, and failures. Delinquency may result if the atmosphere in the classroom is austere and antagonistic, the assignments are made arbitrarily without regard to the interests and abilities of children, teachers do not understand the needs and personality weaknesses of their pupils, inadequate testing devices are used to ascertain the accomplishments and deficiencies of pupils, counseling and adjustment techniques are applied too late or not at all, and the school experience as a whole is not satisfactory. The positive approach to the problem of delinquency avoids an overemphasis of the negative aspects, stresses socially acceptable behavior, and creates a wholesome school environment.

Teachers must be prepared to deal with behavior problem cases and delinquents in the classroom. Much can be done to make the experience in the classroom interesting as well as educational, to create a cooperative relationship between teachers and pupils and among pupils, to provide a good emotional climate, to maintain an objective attitude and to avoid resentment, to increase the understanding of pupils' attitudes and behavior, and to enable the teacher to recognize the early symptoms of maladjustment. Differential teaching methods should be employed if pupils have difficulties because of dual language background, reading or other difficulties, and personality handicaps. Many specialized devices are used in schools to provide preventive and corrective adjustments of pupils, such as modifying the curriculum to meet individual differences; assigning work within their capacity to perform and encouraging them to work up to capacity rather than criticizing them because of poor work, thereby reducing the number of failures; establishing permissive rather than austere conditions and using democratic practices in the classroom; capitalizing on students' assets and minimizing their liabilities; providing satisfying school situations and experiences to offset inadequate home life and living quarters; treating maladjusted children with respect and kindness; and understanding the problems of children, especially the adolescents.[17] To accomplish these results, it is obvious that teachers need special training, especially in recognizing early symptoms of children in difficulty and in meeting the situation.

Special classes or schools for maladjusted children and for those with physical or mental handicaps are so common now that it is not necessary to emphasize their importance. However, many of the

---

17 Cf. Esther Grace Nolan, *School Factors Related to Delinquency,* Doctor of Education dissertation, University of Southern California, 1950.

smaller school districts do not as yet have any provisions for the atypical groups. Experimental schools, such as the Montefore School for Problem Children in Chicago, and the Orthogenic School of the University of Chicago, have demonstrated their value in many ways. The physically handicapped, the mentally retarded, and the emotionally unstable children are of special concern.

Counseling and guidance programs are now well established in the larger school systems. Administrators, special counselors, psychologists and psychiatrists, doctors and nurses, and other specialists have considerable counseling responsibility and have opportunities to guide maladjusted children. This includes both personal and group guidance. Trained counselors can identify and diagnose behavior difficulties and provide a program of adjustment, things which are usually outside the capabilities or time of the classroom teachers. The guidance program, especially for groups, can be partially achieved through clubs, out-of-school groups, and community agencies. Parents are an important part of the guidance programs planned for their own children. Visiting teachers, case workers, and home nurses have considerable responsibility in working with parents and the adjustment and service procedures. School authorities need to work with all parents to accomplish the best results in schools, and to prevent maladjustments of children; but the work with the parents of children who are already in difficulty is of special importance. Child-guidance clinics or departments make clinical treatment possible. Cumulative records of all cases that have been dealt with by any group of specialists are valuable for treatment procedure over a period of time.

Kvaraceus [18] points out that national surveys of attempts to cope with the problem of delinquency through the school reveal four general modes of attack: (1) individual guidance bureaus, as provided in Newark, New Jersey, and in New York City; (2) group guidance programs, as illustrated by the Providence, Rhode Island, schools; (3) special experimental schools, such as the Montefore School for Problem Children in Chicago; and (4) community plans, best typified by the public schools of New York City.

The Passaic Children's Bureau, which Kvaraceus describes, is operated by the Board of Education under the direction of Assistant Superintendent of Schools in charge of Guidance, Research, and Curriculum. It unites special school services (attendance, social work, psychological, medical, guidance, and curriculum planning) with the Juvenile Aid Unit of the Passaic City Police Department. It is a

18 William C. Kvaraceus, *op. cit.,* 204.

center for the diagnosis, investigation, treatment, and referral of cases.

The division of child welfare and attendance has responsibilities in keeping children in school, in dealing with the truants, and in handling many other kinds of problems.[19] The problems of truancy and of the out-of-school youth were stressed in Chapter VIII and need not be reviewed here except to indicate that the degree of efficiency of the welfare and attendance workers had an important hearing on the adjustment of children with behavior problems. The supervisors of child welfare and attendance are in key positions, not only to help individual cases and to work with their families, but as public relations officials to work with community agencies and groups. The education of the public regarding the problems of attendance and welfare is a part of the task. The supervisors are in effect social welfare workers in positions of authority and responsibility, for they deal with the welfare of children in their school, home, and community circles. Therefore, they must understand children in all of these and other relationships. While the modern trend is away from detention, suspension, and expulsion in order to secure proper school behavior, the supervisors must be prepared to deal with the difficult cases and understand thoroughly the procedures to be followed in enforcing school attendance laws, especially in referring cases to juvenile courts and other law enforcement agencies.

The superintendents and principals have great responsibilities with respect to the problem of delinquency control and prevention. On the school level, they can improve the effectiveness of the educational institution as it deals with children by giving special attention to problem cases. On the community level, they can stimulate and coordinate group action through planning on the part of all youth-serving agencies. Some administrative actions have a direct bearing on the development of either acceptable or unacceptable forms of behavior on the part of school pupils.

Of the various types of organizations that work with schools or are associated with schools, none has a wider participation than the

---

19 Cf. *Child Welfare and School Attendance Accounting,* a pamphlet prepared by the Division of Child Welfare and Attendance, Office of the Los Angeles County Superintendent of Schools, September, 1953. "This manual deals with matters concerning child welfare and attendance problems for use by school administrators and supervisors of child welfare attendance in Los Angeles County schools." The practical suggestions and concrete material pertain to attendance work and compulsory educational provisions, attendance accounting, truancy and related problems, work permits and employment of minors, relation of school districts to other agencies, central attendance record keeping, missing children, and a summary of the laws and ordinances affecting youth.

Parent-Teacher Association, commonly known as the PTA. The National Congress of Parents and Teachers has a record of over 34,000 local parent-teacher organizations with a total membership exceeding 6,000,000 and with an extensive program of activities in the interest of schools and child welfare.

The New York State Youth Commission [20] has endeavored to spot the warning signals of future maladjustment and possible delinquency in children at an early age. They used ten measures in the multiple-criteria survey of the Capital District. The adjustment measures included two teachers' check lists (withdrawn and aggressive), two classmates' guess who games (withdrawn and aggressive), and the study of the "social isolate" and truants. The teachers used Schedule A of the Haggerty-Olson-Wickman Behavior Rating Schedule (1930) to study aggressive behavior, and for the withdrawn scale they used items of the form developed by Carl R. Rogers. Similar behavior evidence was secured from pupils' classmates by means of Rogers' modification of the Guess Who Technique, which had been developed by Hartshorne and May.[21] After three years (from 1946 to 1949), 5299 cases were checked with the four children's courts that served the areas of the ten school systems in the Capital Area. It was found that 114, or 2 per cent, of the 5299 had appeared on delinquency petitions. It was also found that 77 per cent of the 114 delinquents had been selected by the adjustment and school situation scales, singly or in combination, as possible future delinquents. The adjustment measures selected more than the school situation measures. The delinquents showed up more frequently on the aggressive scales than on the withdrawn scales. The single measure that selected the largest percentage of delinquents was the Guess Who Aggressive Scale.

If it is possible by such devices to pick potential delinquents, then a broad program of personal services, group activities, and other measures in school and in the community may prevent the occurrence of some of their delinquent activities. At any rate, this is one device that is aimed at getting at the sources of difficulties before children become delinquent.

The Role of the Church and Service Agencies in Delinquency Prevention. Statistics were presented in Chapter VIII to indicate

---

20 *Reducing Juvenile Delinquency* (Albany, New York: New York State Youth Commission, 1952).

21 See Carl R. Rogers, "Measuring Personality Adjustment in Children Nine to Thirteen Years of Age" (New York Teachers' College, Columbia University Bureau of Publications, 1931).

the extent of church membership and enrollment in church schools, as well as of studies that dealt directly with the extent of church attendance by delinquents and nondelinquents. The fact that there are over 92,000,000 church members in 251 religious bodies, or 59 per cent of the population, and that 231 religious bodies reported 257,318 church schools with an enrollment of nearly 33,000,000, not counting parochial and other week-day church schools, indicates the extent of the influence of the church. That the churches reach the delinquents is indicated by the proportion of the deviants who claim having church connections. That they have failed in some instances in preventing delinquent behavior is also evident from the extent of church attendance by delinquent groups.

There are at least four basic functions of churches: (1) to conduct worship services, including ritual, prayer, sacred music, and other devotional activities; (2) to carry on a religious educational program; (3) to engage in various types of social services; and (4) to provide wholesome leisure time and recreational activities. These are interrelated, and there are many other specialized activities.

Opinions differ in regard to the influence of religion and the church as means of preventing deliquency. It is generally believed that an effective church program is a powerful force in community life and plays a dynamic part in the prevention of delinquency. The ethical ideals that provide contemporary American society with moral standards are largely those that religious groups—Christian and Jewish—have promulgated throughout the centuries. Character development is one of the main objectives of religious education.

The special provisions for religious instruction in church schools, release time from public school for religious instruction during the week, vacation schools, group work programs for boys and girls, camps for summer activities, discussion groups, recreation programs, community center activities, social welfare projects, church supported institutions for the care of children, juvenile protective agencies, big brother and big sister programs, and similar services represent the major efforts of churches to help boys and girls, as well as older people, to achieve a more abundant life. While these programs are not especially set up for delinquency prevention, they have preventive effects.

Churches, through spiritual guidance, can help children to gain a proper perspective of life and develop character that enables them to overcome temptations and face difficulties with confidence. They likewise can provide spiritual guidance by private counseling and through worship and instruction. In its role as a community institution, the church provides opportunities for young people to form wholesome associations.

Philip M. Smith,[22] in appraising the functions of the church in delinquency prevention, calls attention to the changing conception of religion and of the church; and he indicates that the consensus of ecclesiastical opinion, empirical research, and testimonies of numerous individuals suggest that the church can be a powerful instrumentality for human betterment. But he raises the question, "Precisely what steps are the churches taking for the purpose of curbing juvenile delinquency?" As is true of youth-serving agencies, it is not the main function of the church to prevent delinquency or other forms of deviant behavior. Yet churches have carried on many types of activities and institutional work that have in part been designed to prevent misconduct.

By means of a questionnaire sent to denominational executives in all parts of the country, Smith found that there is a strong conviction of the need for positive action. Only one of the major Protestant bodies had an official agency specifically designed for combating delinquency. On the basis of the kinds of activities reported by the denominational executives, he classifies the various types of institutional work as follows:

. . . (1) denominationally sponsored institutions, such as settlement houses or Christian centers, offering a social-recreational program in areas of high delinquency risk; (2) denominational agencies, staffed by specialists, set up purposely to promote and administer programs of delinquency control; (3) youth organizations operated under religious auspices with delinquency prevention as a major objective; (4) nonsectarian neighborhood houses, now beneficiaries of community funds, which have some religious as well as social features; (5) youth organizations sponsored by nonsectarian religious groups whose attack on delinquency is indirect through their character-building program; (6) institutional socioreligious work among Negroes and other minority groups supported by missionary funds; (7) city missions, financed by churches and individuals, which maintain social services for youth of limited scope; (8) Gospel missions conducted by independent fundamentalist groups, whose constituency consists largely of homeless men but which make some helpful contacts with youth; (9) agencies having a strong evangelistic emphasis in their program for disorganized urban areas but which do considerable social work and receive nonsectarian financial support from the community; (10) institutional youth-serving projects supported by financially strong urban churches as a form of social service; (11) city mission and church extension agencies of major denominations which place trained case workers, group workers, and specialists in community organization in disadvantaged areas needing their services; (12) church federations spon-

---

22 "Role of the Church in Delinquency Prevention," *Sociology and Social Research*, Vol. 35, No. 3 (January-February, 1951), 183-190.

soring city-wide services to youth in cooperation with other community agencies, while enlisting leadership from among their member bodies in addition to financial aid.[23]

Some of the large youth-serving agencies are under denominational sponsorship. In the Protestant denominations are such organizations as the International Society of Christian Endeavor with approximately a million and a half members in eighty thousand local societies affiliated with eighty-seven Christian denominations, and the Methodist Youth Fellowship with a membership of over a million, to mention only a few of the largest church-centered youth organizations. Nearly all Protestant denominations have similar organizations emphasizing Christian education and character development, recreation, social service, and a variety of special functions. The Catholic churches have local units of such organizations as Catholic Students' Mission Crusade and Sodality of Our Lady, Knights of Columbus (Boy Life Bureau), National Catholic Welfare Council, and the National Catholic Youth Council. The Jewish have B'nai B'rith Hillel Foundation, B'nai B'rith Youth Organization, Council of Jewish Federations and Welfare Funds, and the organizations associated with the national Jewish Welfare Board.

In addition to the church organizations for youth, churches make use of the Boy Scouts, Girl Scouts, Y.M.C.A., Y.W.C.A., Boys Clubs, and other youth-serving agencies described earlier in this chapter. Besides, many of the private welfare organizations are church operated or sponsored agencies, although many derive part of their funds from Community Chest and other fund-raising organizations.[24]

The social welfare agencies, both public and private, serve the people of the community in many ways. The most important of these are those groups that deal more directly with the children or with families in need. The *Social Work Year Book*, published by the American Association of Social Workers (formerly published by the Russell Sage Foundation) has descriptions of organized activities in social work and related fields, a directory of agencies, both national and international, and bibliographies. Articles dealing with such subjects as child welfare, the crippled, the deaf and hard of hearing, family life education, family social work, foster care for children, guidance and counseling, juvenile and domestic relations

---

23 *Ibid.*, 185. Used by permission of University of Southern California Press. Smith likewise summarizes the various types of denominational youth programs.

24 For further discussions of the role of the church in delinquency prevention, consult Lowell J. Carr, *Delinquency Control* (New York: Harper & Brothers, 1950), Chapter XXIV; and Pauline V. Young, *Social Treatment in Probation and Delinquency, op. cit.*, Chapter XXIII.

courts, juvenile behavior problems, maternal and child health, mental hygiene, psychiatric social work, public health service and nursing, recreation, school health and social services, social centers, social case work and group work, and youthful offenders have concise materials on welfare programs that touch the lives of many people.

Besides these and other types of welfare services for children and young people, service clubs, women's organizations, lodges, the American Legion, businessmen's organizations, labor unions, and many others have interested themselves in underprivileged people and have sponsored, either directly or through other established agencies, projects designed to serve specific groups. The extent of service programs throughout the country cannot be measured, for many organizations do this type of work on the local level.

Although the youth-serving, recreation, school, church, social service, and other agencies reach many of the underprivileged people, it is generally recognized that some of the predelinquents as well as the delinquents are not reached in an effective manner. The belief that it is necessary to deal with the problem of delinquency on the area basis, using local leaders and resources, led to the organization of the Chicago Area Project in 1932 by Clifford R. Shaw with the support of Chicago businessmen and civil leaders, who were convinced that a more effective program of treatment and prevention was needed in low-income areas of the city. The studies by the Illinois Institute for Juvenile Research pointed to the need for organization of the natural leaders and citizens of the neighborhood.[25] The basic assumption was that the local residents should organize constructive programs in their communities to deal more effectively with local problems. Outside assistance may be needed, but the organization should be from within rather than from without.

Five basic principles govern the work. (1) The local community or neighborhood is the unit of operation. (2) A committee of local citizens is responsible for the planning and management of the project. (3) In so far as possible, the staff is recruited from the locality. (4) All community resources are utilized and coordinated. (5) All publicity is controlled by the local committee, and credit is given to the local residents for their efforts.

In view of the fact that delinquency among children in the high delinquency areas exists in the form of a social tradition, and is transmitted from group to group within the community, it is desira-

---

25 See Edward Haydon, "Community Organization and Crime Prevention," *Social Defense Against Crime* (New York: National Probation and Parole Association, 1942); *Report of the (Illinois) Coordination Committee* (1943), with recommendation for a plan of treatment and prevention.

ble to control the conditions that produce and support these traditions. Youth groups, especially gangs, must be directed into
constructive channels, and the most effective direction is from
within.

Control of Community Conditions. Control over harmful or
potentially harmful influences is a public responsibility for the protection of young people, especially over those factors in the community that can be controlled by direct social action.

The control of commercial amusements is peculiarly the
responsibility of the community. Movies, radio broadcasts, dance
halls, poolrooms, bowling alleys, skating rinks, roadhouses, beer
parlors, salacious literature, and many other forms of commercial
amusements have attracted youth. While the activities involved in
these types of amusements may or may not be harmful in themselves,
the manner in which they are conducted, the associations that may
occur, and the surrounding influences may make them detrimental
for children.

The legal regulation of dance halls, the enforcement of liquor
laws, and the enforcement of laws regarding other places of recreation are essential to good control of delinquency. Dance halls require constant supervision as to restrictions against minors, health
requirements, conduct in the dance hall, closing hours, and other
items included in dance-hall ordinances. The sale of liquor to
minors is punishable by law; yet liquor regulations are difficult to
enforce. Besides dance halls and bars, various other commercialized
leisure pursuits are potentially harmful.

The control of movies and radio programs must be at the source.
Both are affected by three forms of control: (1) administration from
within, (2) legislative control, and (3) influence of public opinion
and patronage. The effectiveness of public control depends somewhat upon an aroused public and the machinery of law enforcement.
Community organizations can serve as agents of information regarding undesirable amusements.

It is not enough to have effective control over undesirable amusements. This is the negative approach to the problem. Substitutes
for them must be found. Teen-age centers, organized clubs, supervised recreation, and other opportunities must be provided, and
these must be made more attractive than the undesirable places.
Municipal dances controlled by interested citizens' organizations
seem to be able to provide more wholesome recreation than commercial concerns can.

The control of population factors is exceedingly difficult. This is particularly true with regard to minority groups, excessive migration, and the changing composition of the population. Immigration has always created problems of adjustment, whether this be immigration from foreign countries or internal mobility. The influx of large numbers of immigrants and migrants, the overcrowded conditions and anonymity in cities, and the lack of cultural assimilation tend to facilitate crime and delinquency. The industrial demand for labor has brought thousands of wage earners into cities. The housing and living conditions of low-wage earners are unusually acute. The second generation of immigrants is subjected to many disintegrating influences. The adoption of controls to harmonize and adjust cultures, the Americanization projects through education and group work, and slum clearance have aided in bringing about accommodation and control.

Economic conditions and physical environment are hard to control. An effective control would necessitate regulation of the major aspects of production, marketing, financing, and distribution of goods. Raising the standard of living for the masses, providing employment opportunities, and raising the level of vocational education are examples of helpful reforms. Social insurance in case of illness and unemployment, and in old age, as provided for many through the social security program, is a constructive way of meeting the financial needs of many groups.

We have not as yet adequately housed the poor. Slum clearance has touched only a few areas in large cities. No city has as yet been able to stop the spread of blight.

Ecological studies of delinquency have pointed to the concentration of cases in what is commonly designated a "delinquency area," in which physical dilapidation, poverty, family disorganization, institutional deterioration, population heterogeneity and mobility, and excessive adult crime are present. These areas tend to remain deteriorated, with a high delinquency rate prevailing as long as slum conditions exist. People come and go, but delinquency remains on a high level. No city can hope to cope with its delinquency problem unless it eliminates its slums and blighted areas. Improved housing alone does not solve the problem. Slum people tend to acquire slum patterns, which must be changed through education and by other means before complete reconstruction of such areas is possible.

No matter how difficult it is to get at the roots of delinquency, no solution of the problem is possible until the conditioning factors are controlled. Besides the methods of approach indicated thus far, the respective roles of the government and community organization are important elements in the preventive program.

THE ROLE OF THE GOVERNMENT IN DELINQUENCY PREVENTION

The attitude of the public toward law observance, the effectiveness of law enforcement, and the methods of dealing with offenders have a bearing on the extent of delinquency. As was pointed out in Chapter XI, any breakdown in either law observance or enforcement opens the way for increased anti-social behavior. The way offenders are treated has a great deal to do with their attitude toward law and their subsequent behavior. This point has been stressed in previous chapters, and it need not be repeated here.

The government's role in delinquency prevention is not as yet fully appreciated, but great progress has been made in this direction. For centuries the function of government with reference to deviant behavior was mainly repressive and punitive. This still is largely true with regard to the treatment of adult offenders, although protective measures have been devised. The humanitarian movements of the last century or so have greatly modified and improved the treatment of juvenile offenders, as evidenced by progressive social legislation and the establishment of the juvenile courts, probation services, and correctional institutions.

Besides improvements in the methods of treating offenders, government functions have been expanded in many other fields. Federal, state and local institutions for the care of neglected and handicapped children, mothers' pensions, and aid to needy children, the expansion of public schools and compulsory attendance laws, state supervision of private welfare institutions, and many other protective and service measures have been established by government agencies in the interest of children.

Social Legislation and Social Action. The term "social legislation" applies to all laws and ordinances designed to protect classes of people or unfortunate individuals, to safeguard human rights, and to set in motion the machinery for the administration of those measures that are enacted. Laws pertaining to the poor and the dependent classes, child welfare, housing, health and sanitation, public education and recreation, control of labor conditions, social insurance, regulation of public morals, and various kinds of humane measures come under its designation.

Social action has reference to a concerted effort or movement in the field of social welfare designed to bring about the solution of a problem. Formerly such actions were regarded as reforms. When social workers turn to the forces of government or community to achieve certain objectives, they usually think of this as social action.

This procedure represents a mass attack on a problem; a concerted movement by an organized group to achieve socially desirable objectives. The promotion of social legislation is a typical example of social action. However, social action is broader and more inclusive than social legislation itself, for it involves the application of law to various situations, and in recent years it has been regarded as one of the processes of social work. The methods of social action include social research, planning, social organization, and law enforcement procedures.

Social agencies occupy a strategic position in dealing with delinquency. They are particularly important in safeguarding children. The full utilization of the social services in the community would go a long way toward meeting the needs of special classes of needy children. Social agencies are in a position to initiate new legislation and to bring about social reforms. Many times social workers are the first to sense new social problems that may arise in the community.

The law enforcement agencies are at the forefront of the application of law to specific situations. The community can have no better investment in maintaining law and order than an alert, well-trained personnel in law enforcement organizations. The attitude of officers toward offenders and the public affects the attitude of the people toward law, also law observance and enforcement. The police and the juvenile court, together with probation, sheriff, and other law enforcement agencies, represent the chief authoritative sources of control. The officers of these agencies can do much not only to detect and deal with offenders, but to prevent delinquency. Besides maintaining law and order, the police now sponsor, and in many cases administer, recreation programs and other services.

Juvenile and Crime Prevention Bureaus. The larger police departments, sheriff's offices, and probation departments have special bureaus or divisions to control and prevent delinquency, as well as to deal with delinquents. These are variously designated as "juvenile bureau," "crime prevention bureau," "delinquency control bureau," and "youth guidance bureau." The chief purposes of such bureaus (departments or divisions) are: to centralize and improve the treatment of juvenile offenders, to find and remove community conditions that hinder law enforcement and tend to contribute to misconduct, to build up constructive forces that tend to keep youngsters out of mischief, and to develop a more cooperative attitude upon the part of youth and the community toward all law enforcement activities.

While there is a lack of uniformity in the services offered by such bureaus, the following characteristics seem to be common to most of them: (1) the approach to the juvenile is non-judgmental, (2) the legal authority for dealing with juveniles is conceived to be broad enough to include dependent and neglected children in need of police services, (3) greater discretion is used in the disposition of cases even to the extent of releasing those who are technically guilty of offenses, (4) cases are sometimes referred to social agencies for treatment and for other services, (5) traditional police procedures are dispensed with so far as possible, (6) special case work, recreational, and educational services are sometimes provided delinquents or potential delinquents, (7) the personnel selected for such an agency is chosen on the basis of personality or training or both, and (8) administrators of such bureaus participate in community planning with administrators of other social agencies.[26]

The authority, responsibilities, and duties of juvenile or crime prevention bureaus or divisions vary by departments. In the larger police departments such bureaus are major divisions, each with an executive head and subordinate officers, all of whom have special assignments. The procedures are outlined regarding arrests, treatment, detention, referral, and preventive measures.

Many reasons may be given for police participation in crime prevention.[27] In the United States, the law enforcement agencies have a clearinghouse (the F.B.I.) of statistical and other information, especially data regarding the extent, fluctuation, and trends of crime, including juvenile arrests, of which summaries are published in *The Uniform Crime Reports*. Local police are best acquainted with focal points of difficulties, know the methods employed by criminals, have the manpower to patrol the community on a twenty-four hour basis, receive reports of law violations and make the first contacts with lawbreakers, as well as juveniles in the predelinquent status. The police usually have the most clearly defined legal power and authority to take action, to apprehend adults who are responsible for the exploitation of youth, to observe and patrol places where youngsters congregate, and to get information regarding law violators and the conditions contributing to delinquency.

The difficulties must not be overlooked. Police departments almost invariably have inadequate funds and insufficient personnel to carry on an extensive program of prevention. A substantial portion of the police personnel has no special training in dealing with juve-

---

26 Robert W. Bowling and Wayne R. Davidson, *Administrative Aspects of Delinquency Control* (1946), used as a teaching syllabus in the Delinquency Control Institute of the University of Southern California.

27 See Report of the International Association of Chiefs of Police, Committee on Juvenile Delinquency and Prevention, presented at the Annual Conference at Mexico City, Mexico, September 1946. Report issued by the Federal Bureau of Investigation.

niles and in participating in community programs outside the scope of normal police functions. Often there are no statutory or other legal requirements for police participation in rehabilitation and preventive programs; and, if officers do it on their own, they may be subjected to criticism for engaging in activities for which they have no legal responsibility. The unavailability in some communities of facilities for constructive or preventive work is a handicap.

The establishment of junior police not only augments the work of protection and control, but creates a different attitude in the community toward law enforcement. Those who participate develop leadership ability and a sense of responsibility. They must, of course, adhere to a rigid code of rules and regulations. The junior police can be very helpful in handling traffic more efficiently in school areas.

State and Federal Programs. Since the need for coordinated efforts of all law enforcement agencies in a systematic crime prevention program among juveniles has long been recognized, efforts have been made to organize state-wide systems of control. The California Youth Authority, previously referred to, is a good example of a state organization that has authority to move into situations requiring special attention and that can provide leadership in unifying methods of procedures. Other state departments or bureaus perform educational, recreational, and welfare functions that aid in preventive measures, as was indicated in the previous chapter. Peace officers' association and the national, state, and local probation officers' associations have taken a lead in furthering more uniform methods of procedure. A uniform crime prevention system throughout a state would enable all law enforcement and related agencies to act as a unit.

To accomplish the best results, it is necessary to coordinate federal, state, county, and municipal law enforcement agencies, each major unit with juvenile bureau or division, manned by especially trained personnel. Uniform crime reporting by all units, the establishment of central registration organizations, and systematic record keeping are essential phases of adequate crime control. The new system established by the United States Children's Bureau, which leaves to the states the assembling of data, should produce good results. State and local registration centers are needed to keep accurate records and to facilitate the matter of handling cases.

The State of Illinois has pioneered in state-wide research and delinquency prevention programs, as exemplified by the work of the

Illinois Institute for Juvenile Research and several other delinquency prevention divisions of the Department of Public Welfare.

The federal agencies that render the most important services in matters of law enforcement, statistical reporting, and preventive measures are the Federal Bureau of Investigation of the Department of Justice and the Children's Bureau of the Department of Health, Education, and Welfare. Federal agencies in the social work field have as their primary function the serving of basic human needs. Welfare functions are carried on by several departments. It is difficult to determine how extensively their services tend to prevent delinquency, but the ramifications of their welfare programs are indications of the extension of government services.

On the national level, one of the basic needs is field consultant service for the states. The work in law enforcement agencies, and in the detention and correction institutions, needs to be put on a professional basis, with adequate and well-trained personnel in government agencies that deal with juveniles. This requires national assistance in standardizing the work and in providing consultation services.

On the state level, one of the great needs is a re-examination of juvenile court laws, especially with reference to the organization and functions of the court, and the detention and probation services, in the light of the standards set up by the National Probation and Parole Association. From the point of view of treatment, the juvenile court is the most important agency to deal effectively with the more difficult problem cases. In most states, the jurisdiction of the court needs to be broadened to permit it to deal adequately with children's problems, and with adults contributing to them, including jurisdiction in nonsupport and other welfare cases. In order to accomplish the best results, the judge of a juvenile court should have special qualifications, including personality and character, legal training, knowledge of juvenile problems and community resources, understanding of children, and an ability to deal successfully with them, and with their parents. The court should have the services of social workers who are qualified by personality, training, and experience to deal with children, selected through civil service examination, and provided either as a part of the court's own staff or probation department or through cooperative arrangement with another agency. The court, of course, needs adequate physical facilities and equipment, the procedure should be that of equity and not criminal in nature, and the policies with regard to the intake and the detention of children should be clearly understood by all agencies concerned. The detention facilities must be adequate for the care and study of cases prior to a court hearing, the hearing must be prompt and private, and the disposition of cases must be on the basis of the child's needs and the social situation in which he has lived. The coordination of all agencies in the state that deal with youth is an important forward step. Local agencies need the guidance and supervision of state standardizing departments.

The Governor's Conference on Youth Welfare, in California, recommended the adequate staffing and training of all law enforcement agencies, the organization of police juvenile bureaus, and more careful supervision of juvenile offenders. Detention and protective care of children are important. Shelter care should be differentiated from detention care, and the responsibilities for the care of all types of cases should be clearly understood and designated. Institutional treatment for juvenile delinquents requires institutions that are adequately equipped with facilities, personnel, and clinical service to make the program effective in rehabilitating cases. The administration of juvenile justice requires prompt court hearing and efficient handling of cases; uniform minimum standards of qualifications of judges, commissioners, referees, probation officers, and all personnel administering juvenile justice; and adequate facilities in all departments dealing with the problem.

Special attention needs to be given to transient youth, the employment of youth, and those suffering from physical and mental health problems. California, in particular, is the mecca of many transients, including youth under 18 years of age. Adequate vocational training and guidance of all youth, and vocational adjustments of youth, are requisites to meeting their employment problems. The health problems of youth must be met by a coordinated effort of all agencies that can render effective services.

It is evident that a strengthening of the services on the national and state levels is needed in order to coordinate properly and activate the work of the many agencies engaged in delinquency control. Many local areas are inadequately provided with facilities, personnel, and programs to take care of the basic needs of youth and to administer justice properly. Standardization of police, probation, and court work is needed in most states. While centralization of control and services is needed, it should be remembered that the local agencies are in the best position to get at the roots of delinquency. The central movement to strengthen community agencies is that of community organization, which will be discussed in the following chapter.

Thus, on the local level, the strengthening and integration of all services in the interest of youth, the improvement of facilities and personnel in dealing with delinquents, and the correlation of local efforts with state and national agencies constitute the chief needs.

QUESTIONS AND PROJECTS

For Class Discussion and Research

1. In view of the complexity of causal factors, which programs of social action and community service seem to have the greatest promise for delinquency control?

2. Can delinquency be controlled by saving individuals from difficulty?

3. Why is the strengthening of the home so important?

4. What agencies in the community are making the greatest contributions to the strengthening of the home?

5. Compare the functions of the youth-serving agencies and public recreation departments. Describe the functions of youth-serving agencies.

6. Make a survey of all agencies in your community that do group or recreation work?

7. Prepare a suggested program of recreation to meet the needs of all persons and groups within the community.

8. Describe the commercial recreation enterprises that the police department must keep under close observation. What concrete efforts have been made in your community to gain the cooperation of these enterprises to provide more wholesome amusements?

9. What problems are created in the community by the rapid influx of population groups, especially those classed as minority groups?

10. What are the main organizations in your community to improve economic and living conditions?

11. Indicate what the police department can do to create public interest in law observance and enforcement.

12. What school programs are especially designed to reduce or prevent juvenile delinquency? Outline the intramural and extramural guidance programs.

13. Describe the work of churches in delinquency prevention.

14. Analyze crime prevention bureaus of police departments and sheriffs' offices as to organization, functions, and relation to the community.

15. Map out a program for the integration and coordination of all agencies dealing with delinquency prevention in the state.

SELECTED REFERENCES

CHALMERS, M. M., *Youth-Serving Organizations* (Washington, D. C.: American Council on Education, 1948).

GLUECK, SHELDON AND ELEANOR, *Preventing Crime: A Symposium* (New York: McGraw-Hill Book Co., Inc., 1936).

HENRY, NELSON B., Editor, *Juvenile Delinquency and the School: The Forty-Seventh Yearbook of the National Society for the Study of Education* (Chicago: University of Chicago Press, 1948).

KVARACEUS, WILLIAM C., *Juvenile Delinquency and the School* (New York: World Book Co., 1945).

NEUMEYER, MARTIN H. AND ESTHER S., *Leisure and Recreation* (New York: A. S. Barnes and Co., 1949), Chapters XI-XIV.

Reducing Juvenile Delinquency (Albany, New York: New York State Youth Commission, 1952), a pamphlet.

SHANAS, ETHEL, *Recreation and Delinquency* (Chicago: University of Chicago Press, 1942).

Social Work Year Book (New York: American Association of Social Workers, 1954).

TAPPAN, PAUL W., *Contemporary Correction* (New York: McGraw-Hill Book Co., Inc., 1951).

YOUNG, PAULINE V., *Social Treatment in Probation and Delinquency* (New York: McGraw-Hill Book Co., Inc., 1952).

XV

Community Organization, Social Planning, and Methods of Research

Community organization, social planning, and studies are increasingly being relied upon as means of understanding and controlling delinquency as a social problem. The present chapter is confined to some of the more recent developments in community organization, a brief description of social planning, and the methods of research that are most commonly used in the study of delinquency.

The community contains to a remarkable extent the essentials of life, for it includes families, social institutions, various primary groups, and social classes, and carries on the basic activities of society. The community process is dynamic. The American way of life is chiefly the common denominator of the ways of life found in the communities of the nation. The progressive disappearance of the small community from the American scene is regarded by many as one of the most disturbing elements in modern society.

The community is usually thought of as an aggregation of peo-ple living in a contiguous geographic area, functioning together in the chief concerns of life, with common centers of interests and activities. As a primary group, it refers chiefly to the locality group-ing of people, with limited range of face-to-face contacts. As a sec-ondary group, it means more impersonal relations, with subgroups within the area. Communities differ widely in organization, unity, and size.[1]

COMMUNITY ACTION IN DELINQUENCY CONTROL

A good community helps to build good citizens. Although community conditions have always been important in the lives of growing boys and girls, they are especially deserving of attention at present. Making the community a wholesome place in which to live requires the combined efforts of the constructive forces of the area.

Mobilizing the Community for Action. Communities do not act unless they are stimulated and mobilized to act. This requires lead-ership, the creation of a favorable public opinion, and the organi-zation of community agencies for social action.

Although rural communities sometimes are apathetic, the most disorganized conditions are found in urban areas. The modern city is known for its size, heterogeneity and mobility of its people, com-plexity of life, diversity of cultures, the multiplicity of groups and institutions, and the prevalence of social disorganization. In many areas of the city, institutions and social agencies function more or less independently of one another. They are not sufficiently inte-

---

[1] For books on the community, its organization and functions, see Jesse Bernard, *American Community Behavior* (New York: The Dryden Press, Inc., 1949); Wayland J. Hayes, *The Small Community Looks Ahead* (New York: Harcourt, Brace & Co., 1947); Arthur Hillman, *Community Organization and Planning* (New York: The Macmillan Co., 1951); Ray Johns and David F. De Marche, *Community Organization and Agency Responsibility* (New York: Association Press, 1951); John A. Kinneman, *The Community in American Society* (New York: F. S. Crofts & Co., 1947); Wayne McMillen, *Commu-nity Organization for Social Welfare* (Chicago: University of Chicago Press, 1945); Arthur E. Morgan, *The Small Community: Foundation of Democratic Life* (New York: Harper & Brothers, 1942); Jean and Jess Ogden, *Small Communities in Action* (New York: Harper & Brothers, 1947); Herbert H. Stroup, *Community Welfare Organization* (New York: Harper & Brothers, 1952); and Carle C. Zimmerman, *The Changing Com-munity* (New York: Harper & Brothers, 1937).

grated to meet the pressing needs and problems. A condition of cultural lag exists. Sometimes deep fissures are created within the social structure of society. The resistance to social change complicates matters.

Social disorganization implies a decrease in the existing rules of behavior, a disintegration of communal life, and a breakdown of the organizational structure of society. The presence of cliques and factions, diversity of interest groups, conflicting social classes, excessive competition, and a lack of coordination of the constructive forces tend to disintegrate community solidarity.

Control of delinquency requires concerted action. Democratic and effective action must be secured in meeting local needs through existing agencies and institutions. There is, of course, no gain in putting forth great efforts, only to find later that the community has moved in the wrong direction. A sense of direction is needed. Planning must precede the mobilization of social resources in order to meet the needs of youth. Basic community services must not be abandoned in the interest of a new program. On the other hand, it may be found that some of the older forms of agency activities are not really important and can be discontinued without serious loss. The tasks of community leaders in this regard are to discover essential needs, to eliminate unnecessary functions, to strengthen and vitalize basic community services, and to give direction to all communal efforts. Mere organization is not sufficient. Effective delinquency control includes the utilization of existing agencies and institutions, the creation of new services if needed, and the coordination of all efforts to make the community a better place in which to live.

No program of delinquency control can be successful without effective community leadership. Carr [2] points out seven functions of community leaders: (1) define the difficulty, (2) propose solutions, (3) enlist cooperation, (4) allocate functions, (5) develop *esprit de corp* and maintain *morale,* (6) release and direct action, and (7) appraise results. The first steps in a program of delinquency control are to find out what the causes are, what community resources may be used to combat them, and how to go about setting up the program, after which solutions may be proposed. Cooperation of organizations and interested people is essential to success of any program. This should be a democratic cooperation. However, even in a democracy it is necessary to assign functions, to create good will and determination, and to direct action.

---

[2] Lowell J. Carr, *Delinquency Control* (New York: Harper & Brothers, 1950). Chapter XVI.

Leadership may come from many sources. Besides law enforcement agencies, the churches, schools, recreation and group work agencies, civic organizations, newspapers, radio broadcasting concerns, welfare groups, and many others can provide leaders in the various endeavors to meet community needs. All need to be brought together into a cooperative enterprise to secure the best results.

Experiments in Delinquency Prevention Programs. Sheldon and Eleanor Glueck [3] have presented a symposium of experiments in crime prevention. These are classified, largely on the administrative basis, as (1) coordinated community programs, predicated upon the recognition of the community or neighborhood or area as a natural cultural and social entity, necessitating the integration of all forces in an over-all program; (2) school programs, ranging from coordinated community efforts initiated by schools to specialized schools for delinquent children; (3) police programs, as crime prevention bureaus and the collaboration with other constructive agencies; (4) intramural guidance programs, exemplified in the George Junior Republic, Longview Farm, Boys' Town, and various summer camps for delinquent boys; (5) extramural programs, including child guidance clinics, big brother and big sister services, and parent schools of domestic relations courts; and (6) various kinds of boys' clubs and special recreation programs of group-work agencies. These types overlap and can be variously classified, but they indicate the range of efforts made to prevent crime and delinquency, each with varying degrees of success. They are evidence of an awakening of the citizenry in various communities regarding their responsibility in this matter and a desire to participate intelligently in the amelioration of crime-producing conditions.

Some of these programs have already been referred to, and community organization will be discussed later in this chapter; but their importance can be understood only as one analyzes the details of the various programs. No one type of program is a cure-all, nor are the various experiments as a whole sufficient to meet all situations. However, they represent concerted efforts to apply the best-known methods to the treatment of delinquents or to predelinquents and to control the sources of antisocial behavior. The specialized programs of delinquency prevention change from time to time as experience in handling cases and preventive activities increases.

3 *Preventing Crime* (New York: McGraw-Hill Book Co., Inc., 1936). Compare *An Outline of a Community Program for the Prevention of Juvenile Delinquency,* California Youth Authority, 1953.

Some of the basic principles that govern experiments in crime prevention include the recognition that criminal tendencies show up early in childhood; that in most instances it is better to keep children away from police stations, courts, and correctional institutions until other community agencies have failed; that existing agencies and institutions, of which the public schools play an especially significant role, should be used to the fullest; that mass treatment is undersirable, for it is necessary to take into consideration the behavior traits and conditions of individuals; and that in this intensive work with problem and delinquent children, the parents and the whole familial configuration must be taken into consideration. This requires adequately trained personnel and the cooperation of various agencies. No one system is necessarily superior to others, and in all instances the experimental attitude should be maintained. In crime prevention programs it is necessary to provide a wide range of activities, giving ample outlets for the energies and interests of children.

Community Organization as a Means of Delinquency Prevention. One of the significant movements in modern society is the trend toward community organization. The changes in rural life, the rapid growth of cities, accompanied by widespread social disorganization, the breakdown of many former social controls, and the shifting of responsibility from the local community to state and national agencies and the larger units of government have created a need for the unification and coordination of local groups to increase their efficiency and to adjust the community to the larger units of which it comprises an integral part. While it is an attempt to foster local responsibility to offset the trend toward centralization and to compensate in some measure for the breakdown of formal controls, it is primarily a trend toward group responsibility in fields of activity that formerly were considered matters chiefly of individual and family concern. The modern attitude that such matters as illness, unemployment, and juvenile delinquency, as well as education, religion, recreation, and social work, are community concerns does not mean that the individual has no responsibility for his own actions and conditions. Rather, it means that we are beginning to realize the tremendous effects of environmental conditions in shaping the welfare and destiny of the individual. The very complexity of social relationships and the increasing interdependence of people make the welfare of individuals a matter of group concern. Thus, community organization contributes to both individual and national welfare.

In a broad sociological sense, community organization is a process whereby people in a given area build up common centers of interests and activities and tend to function together in the chief concerns of life. In a more technical sense, as used by social workers, it is fundamentally a method of coordinating institutions, agencies, groups, and individuals to make collective adjustments and to cooperate in meeting common needs.[4]

The forms of community organization vary considerably. The most common characteristic is that it is a cooperative and coordinated body of member organizations or individuals, not merely another organization. In the broad sense, it is a process, not merely a framework of organization.

The movement to plan and organize on the local or regional basis is not new. It has several roots in more or less independent movements. Prior to World War I efforts to integrate community organizations came from many different kinds of sources. When the war came, the Council of National Defense promoted state and local community councils in the interest of national defense. While joint fund raising for social welfare work dates back to the latter part of the nineteenth century, community and war chests received an impetus during the war. Campaigns for Community War Service and other war efforts were conducted throughout the country. Following the war, community chests were developed rapidly. Councils of social agencies were formed in the larger communities to integrate functional agencies.

The organization of functional agencies in the community or in the larger area is needed to avoid confusion, duplication, and working at cross purposes, but also to make sure that the needs of all groups and regions are adequately met. While there are many kinds of community organizations, the two most common systems are the councils or federations of social agencies and the community or neighborhood coordinating types of local organizations.

Councils of social agencies, or welfare councils as they are sometimes called, are built upon representation of organized groups performing services and meeting certain criteria for membership. Both locally and nationally, these councils have had great influence in developing interest in and techniques for community organization. The purpose of these councils is chiefly social work planning through representatives (both professional and volunteer leaders) for operating social service units, together with representatives of other important community interests. Private agencies have played a conspicuous part in such councils, for community chests are closely

---

4 See *Dictionary of Sociology* (New York: Philosophical Library, 1944).

identified with them. During World War II, war chests were combined with local chests. Public departments have representation in the councils, and in the various committees of both the councils and the chest organizations, for such organizations provide vehicles for the coordination and planning of all functions in the field of social work. Councils of social agencies tend to limit their administrative functions to agencies or activities on behalf of the total health and welfare program. Special studies are made to provide a basis for securing action and for improving the quality of service. Regardless of the plan of operation, a functional unity usually exists between the planning and financing bodies. In the larger cities and metropolitan areas, councils frequently establish divisions within their structure, such as health, family welfare, child welfare, group work and recreation, and research.

The community, neighborhood, coordinating, and youth types of councils, as they are variously called, attempt to get participation of all community forces, organized or not, that are at work in the area. An increasing number of councils of social agencies are looking upon these local councils as valuable adjuncts from the standpoint of interpretation of needs and in securing social action, and are devoting funds and personnel for their supervision and promotion.

COMMUNITY COORDINATING COUNCILS

One of the outstanding developments in local community or area organization is the community coordinating council program as this has evolved in California. The Berkeley (California) Coordinating Council was originally formed in 1919. This provided the pattern for the community coordinating councils in Los Angeles where nearly a hundred local councils are in operation. The first one was organized in 1931, in the community of Whittier, under the leadership of Kenyon J. Scudder, then Chief Probation Officer of the county. Following the democratic principles of the old New England Town Meeting and the various efforts to bring together the forces of the community to meet common problems, the community coordinating councils attempt to form a united front among agencies and institutions of a locality to make the community a better place in which to live, focusing attention upon the problem of juvenile delinquency. The Los Angeles Juvenile Research Council, which was formed a year previous to the formation of the first local council, acted as a research and advisory group. In 1934, this council was reorganized and expanded into the policy-forming group, known as the Executive Board and later changed to the Assembly of the Federation of Community Coordinating Councils. The local councils and the over-all coordinating of the program are under the general sponsorship of the Community Service Division of the Los Angeles County Probation Department. Such sponsorship is by authority of the California Welfare and Institutions Code and of the Penal Code, which give juvenile courts and probation departments or committees the right to expend public funds for councils and committees having for their purpose the prevention of delinquency.

Meaning, Functions, and Activities. While community or coordinating councils vary considerably in name, purpose, and activities, the following definition gives the basic elements. The coordinating council is

. . . an organization composed of representatives of governmental departments, private social agencies, civic organizations, religious and educational institutions, and other groups and services, as well as interested citizens, to promote cooperation among them, to integrate their efforts and functions, to study conditions and resources to inform the public regarding conditions, and to secure democratic action in meeting local needs. As a community or neighborhood council, with activities built around geographic and area problems and interests, it has a degree of formal organization, composed of representatives of a wide range of groups, yet it functions informally, being a coordinating rather than a functional agency.

In basic purposes and organization coordinating councils differ widely, centering attention of the community on plans designed to prevent or reduce delinquency; to promote protection of children and youth and to meet their physical, recreational, cultural, and social requirements; to develop citizenship and to provide civilian protection; to improve family life; and to plan all welfare services of the community through coordinated effort designed to make the region a better place in which to live. By M.H.N.[5]

An analysis of the development and decline of cooperative enterprises reveals many factors that play a part in furthering or frustrating efforts of coordination. The successful community organizations are those that: (1) have able and devoted leaders who have clearly in mind what they wish to accomplish; (2) have the support of the leading people of the community who are conscious of the need for cooperative effort; (3) enlist the interest of lay persons as well as professional leaders; (4) bring both public and private agencies together in agreeable and working relationship; (5) do important work and use effective methods of getting things done; (6) have a regional sponsoring agency to guide and stimulate local

---

[5] *Dictionary of Sociology, ibid.,* 69.

councils, to relate local activities to a larger regional program, and to act as a clearing center of information and counseling service; (7) establish a central executive board or regional committee, composed of representatives of local councils and major groups of the area, to serve as an advisory group; (8) employ a permanent staff of trained field workers to represent the sponsoring agency and executive board, rendering continuous service and guidance to local councils; (9) have a fact-finding group to study conditions and resources; and (10) carry on a program of education to keep the public informed as to conditions and what is being done about them. Although these points overlap, they represent essential elements in a permanent program of community organization.

While the chief functions of community coordinating councils are to bring about cooperation among the various institutions, agencies, and groups interested in child welfare, to integrate their efforts, to study conditions and resources, to educate the public regarding conditions and programs of improvement, and to secure democratic social action to meet local needs, the organization is particularly suited to deal with the problem of juvenile delinquency. The National Conference on Prevention and Control of Juvenile Delinquency emphasized that delinquency is a problem for the whole community. It is a composite problem, rooted in the basic strains within our culture involving the values, customs, and structure of the entire community. Many organized efforts to prevent delinquency already exist in communities, but they must be integrated and coordinated. Existing services that develop without careful planning are inadequate. Conditions keep changing and programs must be changed to fit new needs. All citizens benefit by effective control and suffer if such control fails. Specialized skills and agencies are needed. Community organization makes it possible to get the facts and to study the complete picture of the community needs and resources, to promote public understanding of them, to achieve a balanced growth of services, to relate the problem of delinquency to other social problems, and to take action jointly to control conditions that contribute to delinquency. Social service exchange, central registration of cases, case-work conferences, joint allocation and referral of cases, and the integration of the special services of schools, police and health departments, and related agencies for the early discovery of problems are some of the cooperative activities that can be conducted by community organization.

Coordinating organizations should be "grass roots" agencies with the broadest possible membership of both professional and lay citizens. The organizational structure should be kept simple and flexible, autonomous, and on the area level, yet with professional guidance and assistance by a larger sponsoring agency. The program should cover the field of child welfare and not be confined to one interest. Participation in community organization should be broad and democratic, including citizens who recognize civic and social responsibilities, and youth should have ample representation in at least a part of the program. Research is needed as the basis of democratic social action. The emphasis should be on positive programs for positive gains. Both urban and rural communities need professional guidance, but this service is especially needed in outlying communities. State and local cooperation is needed, especially in state-wide programs of social legislation and action. On the other hand, both state and local organizations must keep in mind that the family is a basic unit in any program designed to enrich living in the community.

Community organization as it is currently operating in some places has failed and is lacking in vitality, especially where such organizations are not representative of the people of the area or are lacking in natural leadership. Segmented thinking hinders attempts to coordinate efforts.

Merely increasing the number of organizations does not necessarily mean better community organization. Machinery is no automatic guarantee of coordination. Not all citizens' groups are representative groups. Little can be expected of a coordinating group made up of people who have little, if any, operating responsibility or who have little planning experience. Community councils or committees must choose between coordinating and operating functions. "Patterns" of community organization are to be avoided, for no one pattern fits all communities. The role of the government in coordination is a varying rather than a standard one. Local coordination and planning need to be integrated with national programs.

Schools, churches, public recreation agencies, and social welfare agencies, both public and private, are especially important in getting at the roots of difficulties and in getting things done for youth. If these fail to give youth the training, guidance, and services that are needed, the community fails to provide adequately for youth. Community environment planning for better housing and health service is essential also for better living.

August Vollmer, after years of experience as a police chief and as Professor of Police Administration at the University of California, stated that

. . . the most powerful deterrent to delinquency and crime is found in the coordinated efforts of all constructive forces in the community, as exemplified in coordinating councils. No other method has as great a chance of actually attacking this problem with success as that employed by this movement. These councils can discover the maladjusted children in the early grades and can see that they receive the special consideration they require. Coordinating councils are daily demonstrating their ability to improve the physical environment in some of the worst sections of our cities and towns. The coordinating council is the only agency attacking this problem through the process of community coordination. Such cooperation is entirely lacking in most communities and this lack constitutes the greatest weakness in the American form of government.

These councils can influence public opinion, can raise cultural standards and can gradually bring about the changes that will promote good citizenship and will decrease delinquency and crime.

I have spent my life in enforcing laws. It is a stupid procedure and has not, nor will it ever, solve the problem unless it is supplemented by preventive measures. Law enforcement is necessary in the present state of our civilization, but we must place much greater emphasis on preventive measures, such as I have outlined.[6]

Many community programs may be inspired or sponsored by community coordinating councils, including recreation facilities, health and safety programs, organizations for boys and girls, teenage centers, educational opportunities for special groups, improvement of community conditions, elimination of community hazards, raising the standard of home life, and various types of community events.

Organization and Federation of Community Coordinating Councils. The local councils are organized in various ways, depending upon the purposes, composition, and activities. Usually, however, a council has a chairman, vice-chairman, secretary, and treasurer. The chairman presides at all council meetings, appoints committees, prepares the agenda, sees to it that the program is put into action, and endeavors to stimulate interest and to integrate the member agencies. The vice-chairman acts in the absence of the chairman, and has charge of special functions, such as a program committee chairmanship. The other officers have the usual responsibilities, except that, since many councils do not have special funds, the treasurer has a limited function.

The membership consists of representatives of local institutions and agencies, also various groups and interested individuals who have a special contribution to make. Government departments as well as private agencies, civic organizations, and religious institutions have representation.

When a local council decides upon a course of action, it usually

---

[6] *Community Coordination* (March-April), 1939.

functions through committees composed of those members representing organizations and groups that are in a position to do the job, for councils usually function through member agencies. Committees may be formed for a variety of purposes, depending upon the projects undertaken. Some of the better organized councils have committees or divisions for such purposes as community study, case conferences, education, health and safety, recreation, toy loan centers, literature, legislation, housing, summer camping, and public relations.

In Los Angeles County it was found desirable to establish a Federation of Community Coordinating Councils, the general purposes of which are to facilitate cooperation between local councils and the federal, state, and county agencies interested in child welfare and youth services, to foster coordination of such organizations to provide a more effective program of delinquency prevention, to serve as a medium for the exchange of information and experiences in community coordination, to provide guidance and assistance to local councils so that they may function more effectively, and to give support to constructive programs on the local and regional levels. Studies of conditions and resources are made with the view of keeping the public informed regarding them and to provide a basis for effective social action. All community coordinating councils that are organized for the purpose of giving support, coordination, and cooperation to programs looking to the improvement of the general welfare of the community, particularly those whose primary interest is in the welfare of youth, may affiliate with the Federation. The membership in the Federation is voluntary, and there are no dues or other obligations attached to membership except participation in its program of activities. In addition to the representatives of the autonomous local councils, the membership consists of representatives of the leading governmental, social welfare, and civic agencies of the county (as ex officio members), a selected group of members-at-large, and such members of the cabinet as are not members under the first three categories. The chief officers of the Federation are a president, three unranked vice presidents, the immediate past president, a treasurer, and a historian. The Federation, like local councils, functions through standing and special committees in the performance of many of its functions. The members of the professional staff of the Community Organization Section of the Community Services Division of the County Probation Department act as consultants to the Federation, especially to its major committees, as well as to local councils, and the Director of the Division is the Executive Secretary of the Federation.

Los Angeles County has established a number of agencies to deal with specific problems and services. In addition to the work in connection with the community coordinating councils, the Community Services Division of the Probation Department has under its jurisdiction the Central Juvenile Index, the Toy Loan Unit, the Group Guidance Unit, and the Human Relations Committee. The Central Juvenile Index, as previously indicated, is a central registry where identifying data of juveniles who are handled by law enforcement agencies and school authorities (attendance divisions) are indexed. Through this registry, confidential information is readily available to participating agencies. The Toy Loan Unit includes over forty toy lending centers in low-income neighborhoods. The Group Guidance Unit combines both group- and case-work techniques in meeting the needs of special youth groups, primarily minority groups, that are not otherwise reached by the youth-serving agencies. The Human Relations Committee was organized to analyze the causes of race tensions and to attempt to eliminate these causes. Representatives of the various minority groups, as well as county officials and leaders, confer with the view of preventing race conflicts. These divisions and their activities are nonmandatory functions of the Probation Department, established by county ordinances and supported by county funds.

In 1944, the County Board of Supervisors, upon recommendation of the County Grand Jury, established the County Youth Committee as a department of government to effect coordination of effort of the county departments concerned, directly or indirectly, with promoting the welfare of youth. Certain departments of the Los Angeles City government are also members, as well as the Executive Secretary and President of the Assembly of the Federation of Coordinating Councils, the Executive Secretary of the Welfare Planning Council, Los Angeles Region, and the Judge of the Juvenile Court. The county ordinance creating this committee provides that it shall: (1) make continuing studies of county-wide problems related to the welfare of youth, (2) devise ways and means of dealing with such problems, (3) make recommendations to the Board of Supervisors and to the member executives of the Youth Committee respecting the solution of such problems, and (4) endeavor to effect the voluntary coordination of the work of the member executives and their respective departments and agencies. It does not function on the local level, is not a functional or operational department of government, and does not overlap the functions of the Community Services Division of the Probation Department, whose director works in close cooperation with the Committee. This Committee was created mainly to bring together the chief executives of the departments of government that are in a position to do something about the problems that face youth in the county, for they are in charge of the major services of government in the county.

The Welfare Planning Council has a membership of over two hundred agencies and organizations, including all those which share in funds raised by the Community Chest, but likewise includes most of the other approved voluntary, nonprofit organizations, and many departments of government (city, county, and state). The Youth Services Division is one of the four functional divisions of the Council, which was established to make studies, promote extension of existing services, encourage cooperation among agencies, stimulate effective standards of work, encourage the recruiting and training of volunteer workers, and present information to the public concerning the services of youth agencies. This Division includes within its framework the Youth Project, launched in 1943, to provide intensified recreational and group work opportunities for the youth of the underprivileged areas. The Special Services for Groups, which had been operating as a special unit of the Youth Project, was incorporated in 1952 as an agency to deal especially with "gang groups" and with individuals whose social and personal maladjustment has caused them to become problems in the community.

The Youth Services Section of the Los Angeles City Board of Education provides special recreation and group work activities for various groups in the schools, especially in areas where such services are lacking. The activities come under the concept of recreation in its broadest sense, including playground activities, group and club interests, hobby activities, dramatics, teen-age centers, and the like. The program is geared to the different age and grade levels and supplements the work of the physical education departments of the schools.

In order to have a central fact-finding organization in recreation, the Metropolitan Recreation and Youth Services Council was formed in 1949, supported by the Board of Supervisors of Los Angeles County, the City of Los Angeles through the Recreation and Park Commission, the Los Angeles Board of Education, and the Welfare Federation of Metropolitan Los Angeles. It studies the problems of recreation and the resources for youth work, and provides a representative channel for the cooperation of both public and private agencies in the planning and development of a program of recreation and youth services of the area.

The various organizations and agencies have been developed in response to needs that have arisen during the past two or more decades. The overlapping of functions and services has been avoided by wide representations in the planning units, a division of the spheres of activities, and a coordination of the different types of functions. Many new problems arise in a rapidly growing metropolitan region. Unless new ways of meeting problem situations are found, social disorganization is likely to be the ultimate outcome.

By and large most agencies to combat delinquency and gang activities have their limitations. Most of them have limited resources and insufficient personnel for the widespread program. Consequently, they must limit their facilities and programs to meet the needs of specific groups. Furthermore, no matter how effective the preventive efforts may be, juveniles who come from broken or inadequate homes and are otherwise handicapped often are led to delinquent behavior in spite of the constructive work that is being done by youth-serving and community agencies.

SOCIAL PLANNING

One of the most outstanding developments during recent times that is designed to improve physical, economic, and social conditions is known as the planning movement, which started as an effort to improve the physical conditions of urban areas but which soon expanded in other directions. A brief outline of the various aspects of planning will indicate the importance of the movement for delinquency prevention.[7]

Nature and Objectives of Planning. The word "planning" has been widely and loosely used. Planning varies in objectives, in areas and fields of operation, and in other ways. In a broad sense it means the projection of objectives and arrangement of means for their fulfillment. It is the opposite of improvising or proceeding without goals or knowledge of what is to be accomplished. Plans may be designed to ameliorate or adjust conditions, and they may be formulated to prevent the occurrence of problems. The goals may be clearly defined or vaguely formulated. Sometimes planning has specific interests, such as housing, health, recreation, and delinquency prevention. These objectives may be interpreted in terms of physical improvements rather than the broader objective of social reconstruction. Sometimes planning is partial and limited;

---

[7] Compare the writer's text on *Social Problems and the Changing Society* (New York: D. Van Nostrand Co., 1953), 448-458, section on social planning, which is summarized here.

then, again, it may be relatively inclusive, as a master plan of a city or a region. But even such master plans, as mapped out by city or regional planning commissions, usually cover only certain aspects, such as the transportation system, zoning and subdividing, and the locations and development of public utilities.

Conceived of as a process, planning embraces a series of steps or stages. (1) The determination of objectives to be achieved is the first stage, which involves policy formulation, choice of alternate possibilities, and the changing of goals as conditions change. (2) Having decided the broad objectives of the planning, a careful study must be made of the existing conditions before any plan of action can be formulated. Usually, an investigation of conditions is necessary before the specific objectives can be arrived at and stated. Research is an integral part of every stage and phase of planning. (3) The plan of action involves an evaluation of possible plans or programs, the selection of means to achieve objectives, the securing of public support for the plan, and the mapping out of the administrative and operational procedures (known as the layout or design in physical planning).

From the standpoint of social problems, especially the solution of difficulties, modern planning involves a variety of factors. The underlying conditions of the problems must be ascertained before any effective plan of operation can be achieved. The major objective is the control of those factors that cause the difficulty. Thus, planning and prevention are integral parts of a process to control the factors of social and personal disorganization.

Areas and Fields of Planning. Much of physical or social planning is on the area basis, usually involving a political unit, such as a city, a county, a state, or a nation. Since much of present-day planning is sponsored chiefly by governmental agencies, the planning commissions are government departments, sometimes assisted by citizen groups.

American communities (both primary and secondary) have been inadequately planned, but considerable progress has been made in planning cities and metropolitan areas, especially from the standpoint of their physical development. The greatest strides have been made in planning the means of transportation, especially the layout of streets, the development of superhighways (freeways and other arteries of automobile and bus transportation), rapid transit systems, streetcar and bus routes, the development of railways and waterways, and other means of facilitating the movements of the people and in transporting commodities. Efficiency and economy of transportation, and to a lesser extent the beautification of highways and terminals, have been emphasized. The locations of different types of buildings, the acquisition of areas for parks and playgrounds, the construction of public buildings and civic centers, the placement and expansion of schools, and the location of private institutions have likewise received considerable attention. Less attention has been given to local areas, except in connection with new subdivisions. Although considerable progress has been made in zoning legislation, it is still legally possible in most of the states to subdivide a territory without providing adequate space for both public and private institutions.

Area planning has progressed considerably during recent years and has been expanded in many ways. Most of the urban areas now have planning groups, and urban planning has been extended into the hinterlands of cities. One of the most significant phases of the planning movement is the extension of city planning into regional planning, covering not only the major cities of a metropolitan area but the hinterland as well.

Although states have planned on the basis of functional units (field of operation and by departments of government) and have cooperated with national, regional, and local planning organizations, state-wide master planning is not very common. The functions of existing state planning boards or commissions usually consist in planning and directing state programs, in conducting studies on the state level, and in cooperating with other planning agencies to achieve desired objectives. National planning pertains chiefly to investigations of conditions, the formulation of policies, and the implementation of special programs, rather than comprehensive master planning. A number of national agencies now formulate plans for various fields, such as housing, natural resources, public works, social security, and the like. Military planning and programs for national defense are the most expensive and comprehensive undertakings of the national government.

The fields of planning include the physical aspects, economic developments, and what may be designated as social planning. The last, as distinguished from physical planning, is concerned with the physical and mental health of the population, better housing for low-income groups and the elimination of slums, better educational and recreational facilities and programs, the reduction of antisocial activities (crime, delinquency, vice), and the provision of cultural opportunities, such as a wider dissemination of information and scientific knowledge, the development of the arts and music, and other educational values. Accordingly, social planning is concerned chiefly with people, the conditions affecting them, and their welfare, whether in terms of groups or of individual persons. It takes into consideration the dynamic and cultural changes in society, the social resources, and the basic social problems.

The social effects of planning have not been fully measured. In a democratic society, the process of planning must be democratically conceived and carried out, and can be sufficiently effective to influence individuals, families, communities, and even the entire nation in a profound way. Perhaps the ultimate objective of planning is not so much the achievements of beautiful surroundings and well-balanced physical growth of areas or the raising of a standard of living, important as these things are, as it is harmonious human relationships. To be beautiful, a community, city, or nation must have harmony, symmetry, balance, and attractiveness in its physical structure and economic or technical life. But there cannot be a truly beautiful society without harmonious relationships among the people, gracious and unselfish living, and the joyousness and happiness that come from such a life. Well-adjusted families are more important than attractive houses. Likewise, well-adjusted relations in industry, government, and all social institutions, and the efficient functioning of each, are of more enduring value than the material aspects.

It is evident from the foregoing that social problems such as delinquency and crime, and social planning in a democratic society, are complex. Progress has been made to meet the challenge occasioned by the presence of innumerable difficulties. One of the greatest needs is the development of competent leaders to guide and direct social plans and programs. The possibility of progress may be discerned in the fact that human beings can be educated and societal self-direction is possible. Advancement in any field is a slow process, often beset with many difficulties. Genuine social progress cannot easily be achieved until individuals, groups, and the entire social process are effectively controlled and intelligently directed toward desirable goals. This requires a thorough knowledge and understanding of all conditions and factors that play a part in human programs. Thus, social research is basic for the control of social processes and social problems.

THE STUDY OF JUVENILE DELINQUENCY

Throughout this book, references have been made to the various kinds of studies of delinquencies, regarding extent, distribution, causes, treatment, and prevention. Some of the deficiencies of past studies have been pointed out. Although there has been a lag in research in this field, the methods of research have been sufficiently developed to provide answers for some of the questions regarding delinquency if they were fully applied. Scientists and practical technicians could make a substantial contribution to the control of delinquency if their knowledge and skills were fully applied.

Some progress was made in research during the nineteenth century, but the chief advances in the studies of delinquency have been made during the present century. Medical researchers have analyzed the physical conditions of delinquents. Their studies have revealed the influence of physical weaknesses, diseases, handicaps, malnutrition, glandular imbalances, and inherited as well as acquired defects. Psychologists have measured mental traits and appraised personality differences. Their mental testing and personality studies have been especially valuable in revealing mental deficiencies, as was noted in Chapter IV. Psychiatrists have probed into the intricacies of mental disorders and diseases, emotional disturbances, and other mental conditions that are more pronounced among adults than among children, but studies of which have thrown light upon certain behavior tendencies of youth. Sociologists have been most active during recent decades in making studies of the ecological factors involved in the spread of delinquency, the relation of home conditions and gangs to delinquent behavior, and the varied and intricate aspects of environmental influences. Social workers have developed techniques of case studies and have devised methods of treatment. Juvenile court judges and attendants, police and probation officers, and other law enforcement officers have had a great deal of experience in dealing with delinquents, and some of them have recorded their observations and findings. Clinicians, teachers, recreation workers, ministers, and other institutional and community workers have contributed their knowledge to the understanding of the problem. All of this is to the good; and yet it must be admitted that our knowledge of delinquents and their treatment is not adequate. Social action lags even more than the understanding of the problem. Legal authorities have done much to clarify and improve social legislation and to set up the machinery of justice. Yet state laws and local ordinances regarding the age groups that come under the jurisdiction of juvenile courts, the types of misconduct that may be officially dealt with, the methods of treatment that may be used, the machinery of law enforcement, and similar matters of legal import are still woefully confused and inadequate.

Statistical Studies. Statistical material is valuable in that it shows the extent of a problem, the trends in development, the ecological distribution of a condition, and gives some indication of causes.[8] The Federal Bureau of Investigation gathers data and presents reports of information regarding the extent and trend of crime in the United States, based on fingerprints sent to Washington, D. C.[9] Data regarding adult crime are more accurate and complete than is information regarding juvenile offenses. The United States Children's Bureau reports cover only the cases officially disposed of by juvenile courts.[10] The reports carefully state what the statistics do not show, as well as what they include. These are the only overall sources of information that reveal the extent of delinquency, the types of offenses, and trends of development.

As stated in Part One, the population has doubled since 1900, laws have been increased at a rapid rate, and law enforcement agencies have been expanded and have improved their efficiency. All of which would normally result in more offenses year by year and an improvement in the apprehension of law violators; yet it must be recognized that law enforcement agencies are not reporting all offenses by juveniles. Juvenile courts play different roles in the several states, the jurisdictions vary considerably as to the age of children referred to courts and the areas of coverage in the various communities, the types of behavior brought to the attention of courts vary widely, communities differ in their provision of alternate methods of care, and the difference in the mores of the several localities affect the matter of referral to courts. The statistics do not give a true ratio of boys and girls taken into court, for boys are taken to court more readily than girls, except in cases of sex offenses.

The inadequacies of present statistics make it clear that a great deal of work needs to be done in this field. Locally, by means of a central index or registry, it is possible to secure more accurate data.

Statistical reports based on case studies, ranging from fairly complete case studies to information derived from questionnaires, give certain clues as to possible conditioning factors; but, as has been repeatedly emphasized, the results are somewhat predetermined by the methods of research used, the types of cases studied, and the interpretation of the data. It is not amiss to point out that any bias of an investigator preconditions his findings, and few research people are free from bias. As the instruments of study improve,

---

[8] See Chapters II and III, and some of the material presented in Part Two.

[9] *The Uniform Crime Reports.*

[10] Publications, such as *Children, Social Statistics,* and various special news bulletins.

the results will change. The review of the findings derived from mental tests of delinquents, from the earlier studies to the more recent ones made by more refined methods, has revealed clearly what improved methods of research can do to make the results more accurate.

Case Studies. Great improvements have been made in case studies of delinquents, also of behavior problems, as the studies of Healy and Bronner, the Gluecks, Shaw and McKay, and Young show. William Healy was one of the first to apply intensive case diagnosis and prognosis procedures. The case studies of the Judge Baker Foundation clearly show the progress made in this direction. The Gluecks likewise improved their techniques as they traced the histories of the delinquents studied over a long period of time and analyzed thousands of cases. Clifford R. Shaw and Henry D. McKay made wide use of the boys' own stories as part of case studies. The Illinois Institute for Juvenile Research has made perhaps the most extensive case studies. Pauline V. Young has shown how comprehensive explorations of cases can be made, including the steps to be taken prior to the contact with the clients, a study of the offenses, detail analyses of offenders, especially in relation to their social world, the significance of studying the underlying and contributing factors, the delinquents' own stories, studies of families, community conditions, and other sources of information. The organization of data pertaining to social studies is essential for a differential social diagnosis. The major hope of ascertaining more accurately the causes of delinquency lies in the extent to which comprehensive case studies of delinquents and their background are made, especially if these are contrasted with case studies of nondelinquents.

Case studies are most widely used in connection with the treatment of individual cases. Police departments, sheriff offices, and probation departments keep records of the cases handled, which range all the way from meager identification data to more comprehensive case records. The juvenile face sheet of a probation record usually contains identification data, including name, address, telephone, case number, and the like; court data, including petition, detention, companions, court history; birth data, and description of the individual; family data, including parents, stepparents, brothers and sisters, number in household, housing, economic status, relatives and references; health, intelligence, school record, employment, organization memberships and activities; financial data, such as father's earnings, mother's earnings, minor's earnings, total family earnings, and other income or assets; the agencies that have dealt with the case and the disposition of the case. A record of the progress of the treatment process is included. These more or less objective and factual data do not throw a great deal of light upon the causes of the difficulties.

Case analysis is an indispensable method for the study of causation. Yet even the most comprehensive case records do not always reveal the underlying causes. If certain factors stand out as important conditions, it is not always possible to appraise them correctly in terms of their relative significance. One of the best devices used to investigate the causes of delinquency is to study a series of delinquents and then use a control group matched with the delinquents as to age, sex, race, and similar factors. Comparative studies have yielded the most accurate results, making it possible to discern conditions affecting delinquents in comparison with those of the nondelinquents.

Investigators should leave a "map of the road" that was followed in gathering and analyzing data. This would enable others to use the same devices and compare the findings with the original study. Furthermore, a description should be given of the controls, especially as to the method used in making the selection, the matching items employed in making the selection, and other details. This enables the investigator to indicate more objectively why delinquents behave as they do and how they differ from their nondelinquent neighbors.

Clinical tools for measuring various aspects of behavior are as yet inadequate; but by using various research methods, it is possible to piece together considerable items of information that may throw light upon causative factors.

Surveys of Community Conditions and Resources. Studies of the social backgrounds of maladjusted children have opened the way for new approaches to the analysis of delinquency. The studies of gangs by Thrasher, or street-corner societies by Whyte; analyses of urban delinquency areas by Shaw and McKay, and of cultural conflicts by Young, Sutherland, Sellin, and others have demonstrated the possibilities of ascertaining the social conditioning factors.

Broadly, the studies of communities can be classified as the surveys of community conditions affecting delinquent behavior and those dealing with the institutional, agency, and other social resources of the area. One type of study is designed to get at the causes of delinquency, whereas the other type has for its purpose finding out what institutional and other constructive forces are available.

These types overlap considerably. Surveys range in comprehensive-ness all the way from superficial gathering of information that can easily be assembled to comprehensive and interlocking types of studies.

The Chicago study of the relation between recreation and de-linquency [11] covered five selected Chicago communities, four of which are high-delinquency areas, and one, Hyde Park, a middle-class residential area, serving as a control group. While the focus of attention was upon the determination of the extent of delinquent children in recreation, as contrasted with nondelinquents, the sur-vey included a description of each of the five areas in terms of the physical setting, composition of the child population, types of par-ticipating agencies, number of children in the study, recreation activities of the boys and girls, and related data.

Comprehensive community surveys, as outlined by Colcord,[12] cover a wide range of items, including community setting; local government; provisions for dealing with crime; provisions for public safety, workers, wages, and conditions of employment; housing, plan-ning, and zoning; provisions for health care and their distribution; provisions for the handicapped; educational resources; opportuni-ties for recreation; religious agencies; public assistance; special pro-visions for family welfare and child care; foreign-born and racial groups; clubs and associations; and the agencies of community plan-ning and coordination.

In surveying the provisions for the control of crime and delin-quency, it is necessary to know something about the lawbreakers—complaints, arrests, and convictions, also types of offenses, disposi-tion of cases, and the facilities for dealing with delinquents. The conditions that contribute to delinquency and crime need to be dealt with. But no study of a selected problem like delinquency is complete without making studies of related problems.

Administrative Research and Studies of Methods of Treatment. Considerable attention has been given during recent years to the study of public administration, the organization of police depart-ments and sheriff's offices, probation departments and juvenile courts, the staffing of these agencies and personnel problems and training, planning, coordinating, and public relations. A consid-erable number of books, pamphlets, and articles have been pub-

---

[11] Ethel Shanas, *Recreation and Delinquency* (Chicago: University of Chicago Press, 1942).

[12] Joanna C. Colcord, *Your Community: Its Provisions for Health, Education, Safety, and Welfare* (New York: Russell Sage Foundation, 1939 and 1947).

lished on administrative aspects of delinquency control and related problems. The supervision of public service has a variety of meanings and may be exercised through a number of levels of management. The direction of police units, the keeping of records, the mechanical devices of supervision, as well as the organizational setup of a police department, are important aspects of management and control. The functions of a juvenile unit involve the matters of discovery, investigation, treatment or referral, and protection, each of which requires special supervision. Its place in the departmental structure and its relation to other divisions or details are important items to consider.

The problems of personnel have been given increasing attention. The selection, recruitment, qualifications, training, and placement of staff members require the greatest of care. Personnel management now is considered one of the most important aspects of management and administration.

The chief purpose of administrative research is the more effective functioning of a department or agency. Although it is usually limited to projects that do not require a great deal of money and that yield immediate information, in some of the larger counties and cities such research is more comprehensive. In such events, a variety of specialists may be employed, and different methods may be used. Sampling methods are commonly used if the personnel of the research staff is limited. Administrative research has not been extensively applied to law enforcement agencies, except in the larger departments. With the installation of the uniform crime reporting system and other requirements of statistical information, the utilization of the automobile and the radio in police service, and the multiplication of units within the structure of police and probation departments, as well as the increase in size of staff, it becomes apparent that careful checking of the various operations is necessary for the efficient administration of a department or agency. Budgeting and financial planning necessitate some kind of research to know how much money is needed and for what purposes. No budget can be adequately prepared without a knowledge of the functions, operating units, personnel requirements, and administrative processes of a department.

Research in methods of improved treatment is very important. This requires a careful checking of case analysis methods, record keeping, and techniques of treatment. Improvements have been made in treatment, chiefly because of the progress made in the diagnosis and prognosis of cases and in the training of staff members to make the case studies and to administer the treatment. By raising the qualifications of police or probation work, using college-trained people, with special training in police practice or in social work, it has been possible to produce a higher quality of work. In-service training programs are valuable to furthering the work.

Research in the field of delinquency control has not received the attention that it deserves. In fact, there are few research reports on this subject, which condition is indicative of the belated character of this type of research. The opportunities in research are limitless. In this brief statement, only a few of the highlights have been touched upon. Perhaps the most important need in delinquency control is the emphasis on research, looking forward to more objective studies in all aspects of the problem.

Although it is the major function of social scientists to study the problem of delinquency and to present the findings in an accurate manner, delinquency control is a problem that concerns everybody. Delinquency is a national as well as a local and personal problem. This accounts for the interest that national agencies have taken in furthering its prevention.

The two most effective approaches to the problem of delinquency are the treatment procedures for those who have already gotten into difficulty and the prevention of the incidences of law violation. The treatment process includes the procedures of apprehension, investigation, detention, protection, institutional treatment, probation service, and related efforts. The law enforcement agencies (police, sheriff, probation, juvenile courts, detention and correction institutions) have the major responsibility of the treatment of offenders, although citizen groups and private institutions can be helpful in dealing with many types of cases. The functions of law enforcement agencies do not end with mere treatment of the delinquents, for preventive programs have been sponsored and carried out by them. In fact, in many areas the personnel of law enforcement agencies have taken the lead in preventive undertakings and have cooperated with other institutions and agencies in making communities better places in which to live, with a view of reducing the problems that confront them.

In the treatment program, it is essential to find the children who are in need, to reach the potential delinquents and the problem cases, and to deal effectively with the first offenders and those who have committed minor offenses, with the view of preventing recidivism. If deviants are properly handled early in the process, the antisocial tendencies can be changed to law-abiding attitudes and behavior. The police and other law enforcement agencies have a great responsibility in dealing with delinquents, but the problem is of vital concern to the entire community.

Careful case analysis and diagnosis, including the delinquent's own story, and the facilities for such studies, are indispensable phases of the treatment process. If detention of delinquents is necessary, the time spent in a detention institution by juvenile offenders should afford ample opportunities for careful study of their needs and problems and preliminary treatment, as well as for the purposes of custody and protection.

The emergence of the juvenile court heralded a new era in the treatment of juvenile offenders, for no other institution has equaled it in changing the attitudes toward, and the methods of dealing with, law violators. However, the juvenile court procedure has not as yet been fully applied in all areas. On the other hand, some courts, especially those in the metropolitan areas, have become case-work agencies as well as courts, for they handle many welfare, health, adoption, and other types of cases. The growth of state juvenile court systems, the establishment of family courts, and specialized courts for the different age levels as well as for the various types of cases handled (delinquency and welfare) are forward steps in the direction of wider coverage and better services. Juvenile probation services and the work of the juvenile bureaus of police departments and sheriff's offices are developments that are comparable to the emergence of the juvenile court. The close cooperation of all of these agencies is essential for effective work.

Correctional institutions have been improved, but much work needs to be done before their objectives and methods of treatment measure up to the best standards. Such developments as the Borstal system in England and the forestry camps in America are indicative of what can be accomplished by new methods of treatment. State youth authorities and commissions have amply demonstrated their value in unifying and coordinating the systems of treatment of offenders and in promoting preventive work.

Preventive programs cannot be fully successful unless they get at the roots of the problem of delinquency and remove or control the underlying causes. This is so obvious that no elaboration of this point is necessary. Preventive work of this kind includes a variety of personal services to solve the problems of the individuals concerned, the strengthening of the home and the readjustment of family life, an extension of group work and recreation to reach the underprivileged and the predelinquents, improvements in institutional services for youth, especially in schools and churches, and the control of community conditions.

Much can be done on the national, state, county, and municipal levels to control delinquency, but the most strategic groups through which to work are the community and the family. Although the local (primary) type of community is rapidly changing and to some extent diminishing in relative importance, it still contains to a remarkable extent the essential institutions, agencies, and activities of human life. In communities people live together in families, the making of a living is one of the dominant activities, and the educational, religious, and recreational institutions, also many of the welfare and governmental departments, function on the local or regional basis. The community is between the families and the larger society, although the secondary community today encompasses a wide area. In order that the community institutions and agencies may function efficiently, it is necessary to coordinate them into some kind of community organization, such as the community coordinating council.

Social planning, being concerned chiefly with people and their welfare, has considerable possibilities, but its implications are not fully realized. It points the way to a positive approach to social problems, in that it aims to make communities (primary and secondary) better places in which to live and to rear children.

From the standpoint of the social and psychological sciences, also related fields of endeavor, the most important need is a better understanding of the problem of delinquency. More extensive and objective basic research is needed before it is possible to have a comprehensive knowledge of delinquent behavior and its control.

QUESTIONS AND PROJECTS

For Class Discussion and Research

1. What is community organization? Distinguish between community organization and community disorganization.

2. What can community leaders accomplish in the promotion of delinquency control?

3. Describe the different kinds of community organizations, such as the coordinating councils, and point out how such a program of cooperation and coordination can help in delinquency prevention.

4. What studies in the field of delinquency are most needed today? In what ways is our knowledge of delinquency most defective?

5. Work out a schedule for the study of a community from the point of view of delinquency control.

6. What methods may be devised for the evaluation of community programs of delinquency control?

7. Indicate the role of the social sciences in the study of delinquency.

8. Indicate the role of social planning in improving community conditions.

9. How may research and planning be combined in a program of delinquency prevention?

10. State the most important aspects of the problem of delinquency and indicate the main trends in the extent of law violation.

11. Discuss changes in the conditioning factors (causes) of delinquency during the last three decades.

12. What are the most effective programs of delinquency control? Why are they successful?

SELECTED REFERENCES

BRANHAM, VERNON C., AND SAMUEL B. KUTASH, *Encyclopedia of Criminology* (New York: Philosophical Library, 1948). Contains short articles and bibliographies on various phases of crime and delinquency.

CABOT, P. S. DEQ., *Juvenile Delinquency: A Critical Annotated Bibliography* (New York: H. W. Wilson Co., 1946). Contains annotations on important selected books up to 1946.

Comparative Survey on Juvenile Delinquency, Part I. North America, prepared by Paul W. Tappan (New York: Division of Social Welfare, Department of Social Affairs, United Nations, 1952). The first volume of a world-wide study of juvenile delinquency. The other regional reports deal with Asia and the Far East, Europe, Latin America, and the Middle East.

International Review of Criminal Policy (New York: Department of Social Affairs, United Nations, beginning with No. I, January, 1952). A semi-annual publication, containing descriptions and annotated bibliographies of periodical literature on crime and delinquency published throughout the world.

KURTZ, RUSSELL H., Editor, *Social Work Year Book* (New York: American Association of Social Workers, 1954). Contains articles and brief bibliographies on various types of welfare programs, including the treatment and prevention of delinquency.

INDEX

Date Due